John Nix
Farm Management
Pocketbook

FORTY FIRST EDITION (2011)
Published September 2010

Copies of this book may be obtained from:
The Pocketbook, 2 Nottingham Street,
Melton Mowbray, Leicestershire LE13 1NW.
(Tel: 01664 564 508 Fax: 01664 503 201)
www.thepocketbook.co.uk

PRICE £20.00 + £1.50 p&p
5 to 19 copies: £19.00
20 to 100 copies: £17.50
Over 100 copies: *p.o.a*
Postage & Packaging free for 5 or more copies
in single deliveries

ISBN 978-0-9514588-7-7

The John Nix Farm Management Pocketbook
published by Agro Business Consultants Ltd

FOREWORD TO THE FIRST EDITION

This booklet is intended for farmers, advisers, students and everyone else who, frequently or infrequently, find themselves hunting for data relating to farm management - whether it is for blunt pencil calculations on the back of an envelope or for feeding into a computer. The material contained is based upon the sort of information which the author finds himself frequently having to look up in his twin roles as adviser and teacher in farm management. There are several excellent handbooks already in existence, but this pocketbook endeavours to cover a wider field and thus to be substantially more comprehensive. It is intended that most of the data herein contained will have a national application, although there is inevitably some bias towards conditions in the south-eastern half of the country.

The development of farm planning techniques in recent years has outstripped the quality and quantity of data available. It is hoped that this booklet will go a little further in supplying the type of information required. It cannot, however, claim to be the ultimate in this respect. For example, there are many variations in labour requirements according to farm conditions and sizes and types of machine used and there are many more variations in sheep and beef systems than are dealt with here. More detailed data on these lines are gradually becoming available from various sources. It is hoped further to refine the material in this booklet and to keep it up to date in subsequent editions, as the information becomes available. As a help towards this end, any comments or criticisms will be gratefully received.

The author wishes to thank his many friends and colleagues who have given him so much time and help in compiling this information.

John Nix
October, 1966

First published October 1966

Forty-first Edition   September 2010

FOREWORD TO THE FORTY FIRST EDITION

For the last forty five years the Pocketbook has provided information to help those making decisions about their businesses and others interested, for whatever reason, in UK agriculture. This has not changed, although the content has altered as the industry has required different information throughout the years. This reflects the detail of management in modern agriculture. Farmers are becoming increasingly specialist, and new mainstream enterprises are being developed. This is pioneering the advance of skills and performance on a global basis and the Pocketbook continues to play an important role in this developing industry.

As another sign of the changing era, the time has come to freshen the book with a new design on the front cover. It is an image that reflects both the traditional and the progressive aspects of our fine industry. The book retains the rigour within the covers that users have grown to expect. To create an image that captured all aspects of UK farming or all areas that the book covers would be impossible as the industry is so diverse and far reaching.

Most figures in this book are estimated forward one year, i.e. to 2011. Thus the crops data relate to the 2011 harvest. The livestock data relate either to the 2011 calendar year (e.g. for milk production) or to 2011/2012 (e.g. for winter finished beef), as appropriate. In a few cases current (i.e. mid-2010) figures are given, where it is particularly difficult to forecast ahead and have been highlighted as such. The yields and prices assume a 'normal' or average season, based on trends, e.g. for potatoes, looking 18-24 months ahead to 2011/2012, no one can predict what the actual average yield and price for that particular year will be. The data in this book should always be used with caution. *The figures should be adjusted as appropriate according to circumstances and price and cost differences.* Assumptions are set out to enable this to be done.

As ever, all the enterprises have been reviewed and revised for this Edition. I thank The Andersons Centre's Business Research team who have led the production of this edition.

John Nix
August 2010

CONTENTS

I.   GENERAL

1.   THE USE OF GROSS MARGINS

DEFINITION

The data on the crop and livestock enterprises in the Pocketbook is based on gross margins. The gross margin of an enterprise is its output less its variable costs. Enterprise output includes the market value of production retained on the farm. The variable costs must (a) be specific to the enterprise and (b) vary in proportion to the size of the enterprise, i.e. number of hectares or head of stock. The main items of variable costs are: Crops: fertiliser, seed, sprays, casual labour and contract work specific to the crop. Non-Grazing Livestock: concentrate feed, vet. and med., marketing expenses. Grazing Livestock is as for non-grazing livestock, plus forage crop variable costs.

POINTS TO NOTE

1. The gross margin is in no sense a profit figure. The so-called 'fixed costs' (rent, labour, machinery, general overheads), have to be covered by the total farm gross margin before arriving at a profit.

2. The gross margin of an enterprise will differ from season to season, partly because of yield and price differences affecting output and partly because variable costs may vary, e.g. the number and type of sprays required. Different soils and other natural factors, as well as level of management, will also cause differences between farms.

3. Items of variable cost may vary from farm to farm, e.g. some farmers use casual labour (a variable cost) to plant and pick their potatoes, others use only regular labour (a fixed cost); some farmers employ a contractor to combine their cereals (a variable cost), others employ their own equipment (a fixed cost); some employ a contractor to cart their sugar beet to the factory (a variable cost), others have their own lorry (a fixed cost). These differences must be borne in mind in making inter-farm comparisons.

4. Provided points 2 and 3 are borne in mind, comparison of gross margins (particularly averages over several seasons) with standards can be a useful check on technical efficiency.

5. The other main usefulness of gross margins lies in farm planning. This is not simply a matter of substituting high gross margin enterprises for low gross margin enterprises. The gross margin is only one relevant feature of an enterprise, although an important one. It says nothing about the call the enterprise makes on the basic farm resources - labour at different times of the year, machinery, buildings, working capital requirements, etc. All these factors and more have to be taken into account in the planning process.

6. This is not to argue that these other costs should be allocated. Complete allocation of many farm expenses is only possible on an arbitrary basis, since they are shared by two or more, possibly all farm enterprises. Allocation can therefore be completely misleading when making planning decisions. The same is true even when regular labour and machinery are employed specifically on certain enterprises, if such costs are calculated on a per hectare or per head basis. This is because when enterprises are substituted, expanded, contracted or deleted the variable costs for each enterprise will vary roughly in proportion to the size of that enterprise, but other costs will not, except possibly for fuel and some repair costs. Most 'fixed' costs may stay the same, others will change - but not smoothly in small amounts at a time. Either the same regular labour force will cope with a revised plan or a smaller or larger number of men will be

needed. The same is true of tractors, other machines and buildings. Such cost changes must of course be taken into account, but allocating these costs on a per hectare or per head basis will not aid, and may positively confuse, planning decisions. The only point of making such calculations is for efficiency comparisons, e.g. labour costs per cow.

7. Allocating fixed costs at a flat rate (e.g. per hectare) for all enterprises, deducting this from the gross margin and hence calculating a 'net profit' from each enterprise can also be misleading. It ignores the whole problem of enterprise inter-relationships, differences between enterprises in total and seasonal requirements for labour, machinery and capital, and other factors such as different quality land on the same farm.

8. Changes in the scale of an enterprise may well affect its gross margin per unit, e.g. increasing the area of winter wheat from 30% to 55% on a farm will mean more second and third crop wheats being grown and a smaller proportion of the crop being drilled under the best conditions; hence yields will in all probability fall. Even if yields remain the same, variable costs (e.g. fertiliser use) will probably increase.

9. Gross margins used for planning future changes should also take account of possible changes in price, and the effect of changes in production techniques.

LOW, AVERAGE AND HIGH LEVELS

The three performance and production levels given for most crop and livestock enterprises are meant for the most part to indicate differences in natural factors, soil productivity, and/or managerial skill, given the level of variable cost inputs. They refer, at each level, to an average over several years taking trends into account. The evidence on the effect of significantly higher or lower levels of variable inputs on gross margins is conflicting and highly uncertain, depending on many factors, including soil type, and will vary from season to season.

2. COMPLETE ENTERPRISE COSTINGS

Requests are occasionally made for this book to include 'complete' enterprise costings, by which is meant the allocation of all costs to each individual enterprise, not only the variable costs as in the calculation of gross margins.

In the early days of farm business management teaching and research this was the preoccupation of most of those specialising in the subject. The system was, however, abandoned by nearly all practising farm economists in the 1950s. The main reasons are given in item 6 of the previous section explaining gross margins. Much meaningless and arbitrary allocation of 'joint costs' is required, (attempting 'to allocate the unallocatable'), and the results are often misleading in making farm decisions. Furthermore, it requires a considerable amount of record-keeping - in allocating labour on a mixed farm, tractor and machinery costs, telephone bills and so on. Few farmers are prepared to spend the required time and money to do this, nor do they need to.

Another problem in 'complete enterprise costing' is where to stop. Should interest on capital be included, whether borrowed or not? Further problems of asset valuation and allocation are involved if so. What of management and marketing supplied by the farmer? Should these be for free, as is usually assumed in such cases?

Variations between farms in their financial situations are considerable as, for instance, between the farmer who owns all his land without any mortgage and has no other borrowings and the one with both a rent to pay for all his land and heavy borrowings in addition.

In some situations, e.g. in some company-owned farms, farm managers are obliged to supply such data to their employers, whether they want to or not. Also, if enterprise costs are used for price fixing purposes governments, or price negotiators, usually require some such attempt to be made, whatever the difficulties and shortcomings of the methodology employed.

The above problems arise when 'costs per tonne' or 'costs per litre' are calculated. Wheat can be calculated to cost anything between £80 and £160 a tonne according to just what costs are included, how they are calculated (allocated) and the yield level assumed.

This is not to decry the efforts that are sometimes made in this direction. Particularly when product prices are falling it seems a natural thing to want to do - to calculate 'unit costs' to compare with prices received. Sometimes they do make clearer particular costs that need investigating and by that means economies that might be made, and they always attract interest. For these reasons costs per litre of milk are included, although the calculation of some of the 'fixed cost' items is difficult. If a farm has only one enterprise such calculations on that farm are obviously straightforward. However, even on solely dairy farms followers are usually reared, which is a second enterprise to milk production.

If required, a cost per tonne of combinable crops can be calculated by adding the fixed costs per hectare of mainly cereals farms (according to size range, given on page 204) to the variable costs per hectare given in the enterprise gross margin data and dividing by the selected yield. Such calculations need to be interpreted with caution because the allocation of fixed costs per hectare is inevitably fairly crude.

The allocation of specific labour (e.g. a full-time cowman), machinery (e.g. a potato harvester) and buildings (e.g. a grain store) is relatively simple and can provide useful information both for purposes of efficiency comparisons and partial budgeting. For some enterprises on many mixed farms, however, there are few, if any, such specific items and the question of the other so-called fixed cost items remains if a full costing is attempted.

3.   TOTAL FARM GROSS MARGINS

No attempt is made in this book to compile total gross margins for the whole farm, based on the forecasts made for individual enterprises for 2011. Nor has it ever been the intention in The Pocketbook to include 'historical data', except for some of the material in the Agristats section. Hence total farm survey results, which are inevitably a year or two old by the time they are collated, analysed and published, are not included. Their usefulness for any particular farm is bound to be limited. Furthermore, such data is readily available from surveys of farm businesses.

4.   FARM BUSINESS SURVEY DATA

ENGLAND

The Farm Business Survey (FBS) is the main source of business-level data in England. It is carried out on behalf of DEFRA by a consortium of Universities and Colleges. The data is collected regionally, and then fed into a national database. This can be found at - www.farmbusinesssurvey.co.uk. This site gives access to a number of sets of FBS data:

- By Government Office Region, customised by farm type etc.

- Farm Business Benchmarking, allows comparison of farm results with the average and top performing farms of the same type.

- Data Builder, a specialist interactive system for researchers.

The following institutions are involved in the FBS, and in the list below the specialist enterprise reports that they have produced for 2008/09 for England are identified. Most of the reports are available on-line;

- Askham Bryan College, York– www.askham-bryan.ac.uk (Pig Production)
- University of Cambridge – www.landecon.cam.ac.uk (Crop Production)
- Duchy College - www.cornwall.ac.uk/rbs (Lowland Grazing Livestock)
- Imperial College, London – www.imperial.ac.uk
- University of Newcastle – www.ncl.ac.uk (Hill Farming)
- University of Nottingham – www.nottingham.ac.uk (Dairy Farming)
- University of Reading – www.apd.rdg.ac.uk (Horticulture, Poultry Production)

WALES

The Farm Business Survey in Wales is undertaken on behalf of the Welsh Assembly Government by the University of Aberystwyth.   The results are published at - www.aber.ac.uk/en/ibers/enterprise-kt/fbs/

SCOTLAND

In Scotland the data for the Farm Accounts Survey is collected by the Scottish Agricultural College. It is available in the publication 'Farm Incomes in Scotland'. See www.scotland.gov.uk/Topics/Statistics/15631/8884

NORTHERN IRELAND

The Department of Agriculture and Rural Development for Northern Ireland undertakes the Farm Business Survey in the province. Results can be found at www.dardni.gov.uk/index/dard-statistics/statistical-reports/agricultural-statistics-farm-business-survey.htm

5.   MAIN ASSUMPTIONS

Budgeting future prices, by necessity requires making several assumptions about how they are likely to move in the future from current levels (August 2010). This 41st Edition of the Pocketbook uses the following key assumptions:

- The pound: euro exchange rate throughout the book is 85p/ , equivalent to 1.176 per pound.

- Fertiliser prices for nitrogen (N), phosphate (P) and potash (K) are the same throughout. A full schedule of fertiliser valuations can be found on page 255. For calculating the gross margins, the following are used:

  - ○ N: 62 p/kg   (£215/t 34.5% N)   (UK Ammonium Nitrate)
  - ○ P_2O_5:   68 p/kg   (£315/t 46% P_2O_5) (Triple Super Phosphate)
  - ○ K_2O: 54 p/kg   (£325/t 60% K_2O)   (Muriate of Potash)

- Some fertiliser costs have changed in the gross margins not only because of unit costs, but also the new RB209 (2010) fertiliser manual has changed its recommendations.

- Farm machinery fuel price (red diesel) is taken to be 52ppl.

- Feed wheat price (from which many other commodity prices are benchmarked), is £120/tonne. This is an ex-farm price for November /December 2011 delivery.

II.   ENTERPRISE DATA

1.   CROPS

WINTER WHEAT

Feed Wheat

Production level	Low	Average	High
Yield: tonnes per ha (tons per acre)	6.75 (2.7)	8.35 (3.4)	9.75 (3.9)
	£	£	£
Output	810 (328)	1002 (406)	1170 (474)
Variable Costs:			
Seed...		46 (19)	
Fertiliser....................................		188 (76)	
Sprays..		153 (62)	
Total Variable Costs		387 (157)	
Gross Margin per ha (acre)	**423** (171)	**615** (249)	**783** (317)

Milling Wheat

Production level	Low	Average	High
Yield: tonnes per ha (tons per acre)	6.15 (2.5)	7.70 (3.1)	9.00 (3.6)
	£	£	£
Output	824.1 (334)	1032 (418)	1206 (488)
Variable Costs:			
Seed...		49 (20)	
Fertiliser....................................		220 (89)	
Sprays..		157 (64)	
Total Variable Costs		426 (173)	
Gross Margin per ha (acre)	**398.1** (161)	**606** (245)	**780** (316)

1. Prices. The average feed wheat price for the 2011 harvest crop (i.e. 2011/12 marketing year) is taken to be £120 tonne. The average milling price is taken to be £134/tonne. This is based on a 'full specification' premium of £25 over feed wheat, a 'biscuit' grade milling specification of £10 and a 20% failure rate of achieving the specification. The average premium achieved varies widely according to quality and season: see further comments below (note 3). Full Specification is defined as NABIM Group 1 wheat with Hagberg of 250 or more, 13% Protein or more and a bushel weight of at least 76Kg/hl.

2. *Yields.* The average yield for all winter wheat, i.e. all varieties, is calculated as 8.1 tonnes per hectare, the trend yield (3.3 tons (66 cwt.)/acre) based on the above yields and their proportional weighting by area.

3. *Milling v. Feed.* The yield of bread and biscuit wheat (generically known as milling) averages about 8% below that of feed wheat (greater on high-yielding land and less on moderate quality land and also tends to be greater on second than on first wheats). Slightly higher seed, fertiliser and spray costs are normally expected for milling wheats. The price premium varies each season according to quality and scarcity. The average premium for full specification breadmaking quality exceeds the £14/tonne (11%) used. However, that for other (biscuit) milling wheat is generally lower. Also, not all deliveries achieve full specification. Grade 2 varieties normally achieve a

premium of a few pounds a tonne (£10 used here) but their average yields are higher than Grade 1 varieties. Full specification breadmaking premium averaged £17.40/tonne from 2005 to 2009 and £30 for the last three years, with a range of nothing to £62.00 per tonne. The 2009/2010 bread-wheat premium averaged £22/tonne. NABIM wheat group 1 varieties account for about 15% of wheat area. The proportion of Group 4 wheats has been rising steadily to c52% in 2010 from 18% in 2005 at the expense of Group 3 varieties.

4. *First v. Second (Feed) Wheat.* The effect of different types and lengths of rotational breaks on subsequent cereal yields varies given the differences between seasons (weather), soils, varieties etc. The table below (for feed wheat) assumes a yield reduction of approximately 10% for second wheats compared with first and higher input costs as shown; (the later the sowing date the less the yield gap tends to be). Only average and high levels are shown. Third wheats could yield 10-15% below second wheats; variable costs are likely to be similar. This varies according to management, soil type and varietal choice. Heavy, well-structured, well-drained clay soils appear to be best suited to second wheats; lighter, silty soils usually have a greater risk of Take-all; a firm seedbed is needed.

Comparison between First and Second Wheat Crops

Production level	Average		High	
Year (after break)	First	Second	First	Second
Yield: tonnes per ha (tons/acre)	8.75 (3.5)	7.9 (3.15)	10.0 (4.0)	9.0 (3.6)
	£	**£**	**£**	**£**
Output	1050 (425)	948 (384)	1,200 (446)	1080 (401)
Variable Costs	387 (157)	403 (163)	386 (156)	402 (163)
Gross Margin per ha (acre) ...	663 (269)	545 (221)	813 (329)	677 (274)

5. *Straw* is costed as being incorporated. Average yield is approx. 3·5 tonnes per hectare (range 2½ to 5); value £40 to £50 per tonne (£5 less in big bales); variable costs (string) approx. £2.90 per tonne. Unbaled straw (sold for baling): anything from no value to £150/ha (£60/acre), national average around £30/ha (£12/acre).

6. *Seed.* rates vary according to soil, season, variety, drilling date etc. Seed: main range £280-400 per tonne (C2) with a single purpose dressing (£300 and £308 used for feed and milling respectively); 175kg/ha in good conditions; Farm-saved included at 35% (feed) 25% (milling) including grain value, cleaning, dressing, testing and BSPB levy of £36.10/tonne (£5.88 per hectare) for autumn 2010.

7. *Fertiliser* costs are based on P and K replacement cost for an average yield crop, with straw incorporated. RB209 suggests Phosphate and Potash is replaced at 7.8kg/t and 5.6kg/t of grain weight harvested respectively (65 and 47kg/ha respectively in this gross margin). Nitrogen is 190kg/ha for feed wheat and 250kg/ha for milling.

8. *Sprays.* Amounts vary according to season, variety, etc. Typical breakdown: herbicides 43%, fungicides 45%, insecticides 5%, growth regulators 5%, slug pellets 2%.

9. If a *Contractor* is employed, extra variable costs will be approximately as follows:

Spraying:	£10/ha (LV-HV; material included above)
Drilling:	£31/ha
Combining:	£77/ha (excluding carting)
	£108/ha (including carting)
Drying:	£14.90 for 6% moisture per tonne.
Baling Straw:	£32-53/ha (including string) depending on bale type.

10. *Fuel and Repairs* (per hectare). Grain £120, straw £42.

11. *Specialised Equipment Prices.* see p.179.

12. *Labour:* see p. 162.

SPRING WHEAT

Production level	Low	Average	High
Yield: tonnes per ha (tons per acre)	4.75 (1.9)	5.75 (2.3)	6.75 (2.7)
	£	£	£
Output	626.5 (254)	758.43 (307)	890.3 (361)
Variable Costs:			
Seed..		66 (27)	
Fertiliser.....................................		142 (58)	
Sprays...		96 (39)	
Total Variable Costs		304 (123)	
Gross Margin per ha (acre)	**322.5** (131)	**454** (184)	**586.3** (237)

1. *Price:* In general, see Winter Wheat (previous pages). A far higher proportion of spring wheat is sold for milling compared with winter wheat. Here we assume 85% making the average price £131.90/tonne for the 2011 harvest.

2. *Straw:* See Winter Wheat but yields are considerably lower.

3. *Seed:* £350/tonne at 200kg/ha used. Home saved included at 15% including grain value, cleaning, dressing, testing and BSPB levy of £36.10/tonne (£5.88 per hectare) for spring 2011

4. *Fertiliser:* 150kg/ha N used, and P and K replacing off-take at 45kg/ha and 32kg/ha respectively.

4. If a *contractor* is employed, extra variable costs (£/ha) will be shown as for Winter Wheat above.

5. *Fuel and repairs* (per hectare): grain £118, straw £42.

6. *Specialised Equipment Prices:* see page. 179.

7. *Labour:* see p. 162.

Normally, only about 1% of the UK wheat area is spring sown although survey data is hard to come by. It is popular after root crops. The percentage is naturally higher after a particularly wet autumn such as 2008/09. The percentage is even lower in Scotland (1% or less) than in England or Wales. The area is currently rising because of new very hard 'Red Wheat' varieties.

WINTER BARLEY

Feed Barley

Production level	Low	Average	High
Yield: tonnes per ha (tons per acre)	5.5 (2.2)	6.9 (2.8)	7.9 (3.2)
	£	**£**	**£**
Output	632.5 (256)	794 (322)	908.5 (368)
Variable Costs:			
Seed..		47 (19)	
Fertiliser......................................		151 (61)	
Sprays..		110 (45)	
Total Variable Costs		308 (125)	
Gross Margin per ha (acre)	**325** (131)	**486** (197)	**601** (243)

Malting Barley

Production level	Low	Average	High
Yield: tonnes per ha (tons per acre)	4.8 (1.9)	5.85 (2.4)	6.9 (2.8)
	£	**£**	**£**
Output	624 (253)	761 (308)	897 (363)
Variable Costs:			
Seed..		51 (21)	
Fertiliser......................................		111 (45)	
Sprays..		121 (49)	
Total Variable Costs		283 (115)	
Gross Margin per ha (acre)	**341** (138)	**478** (193)	**614** (249)

1. *Prices.* The feed barley price for 2011 harvest (i.e. 2011/12 marketing year) is taken to be £115/tonne, a £5 discount to feed wheat (the average over 5 and 20 years is about £4.60). The winter malting price (£130/tonne) assumes an average premium over feed of £15/tonne. This accounts for some that don't meet malting standards. For the best malting barleys the premium in the past has often been £25 and in some years higher.

2. *Straw* is costed as being incorporated. Average yield is approx. 2·75 tonnes per hectare, value £50 to £60 per tonne, rising to £95 per tonne in the West, baled ex-field (£5 less in big bales); variable cost (string) approximately £2.90 per tonne. Prices rise in years of forage shortage so prices in 2011 could be high.

3. *Seed.* Winter barley seed averages £300 and £325/tonne for feed and winter malting respectively at 175kg/ha. Seed includes 25% farm-saved including seed, dressing, testing and BSPB levy of £35.06/tonne (£5.82 per hectare) for autumn 2010.

4. Fertiliser costs are based on N at 160kg/ha for feed, 100kg/ha for malting crops. P and K replacement cost, with straw incorporated making 53:38kg/ha for feed and 45:32kg/ha for malting crops.

5. *Sprays.* Amounts variable according to season, variety, policy, etc. Typical breakdown: herbicides 47%, fungicides 44%, growth regulators 6%, other 3%.

6. If *Contractor* employed, extra variable costs as shown for Winter Wheat (note 9).

7. *Fuel and Repairs* (per hectare): grain £118, straw £42.

8. *Specialised Equipment Prices*: see p. 179.

9. *Labour*: see p. 162.

SPRING (MALTING) BARLEY

Production level	Low	Average	High
Yield: tonnes per ha (tons per acre)	4.6 (1.9)	5.45 (2.2)	6.3 (2.6)
	£	£	£
Output	621 (252)	736 (298)	850.5 (344)
Variable Costs:			
Seed..		50 (20)	
Fertiliser....................................		95 (38)	
Sprays..		87 (35)	
Total Variable Costs		232 (94)	
Gross Margin per ha (acre)	**389** (158)	**504** (204)	**619** (250)

1. *Prices.* Virtually all spring barley grown is malting varieties, grown for a premium. Spring malting premiums usually exceed those for winter varieties. Here the premium over feed barley is £20/tonne. Again, this allows for failed samples making £135/t.

2. *Seed.* Spring barley seed used is £325/tonne at a seed rate of 175Kg/ha. 35% is home saved with BSPB royalty rates of £40.20/tonne (£7.24 per hectare) for spring 2011.

3. *Fertiliser* costs are based on N at 80kg/ha. P and K replacement cost, with straw incorporated making 41:29kg/ha.

3. *Sprays* consist typically of: herbicides 54%, fungicides 41%, other 5%.

4. *Areas and Use of Winter and Spring Barley.* Since 2001, spring barley has commanded the majority of the UK barley area (around 60% of total UK barley area). In the 1970's, spring barely accounted for over 90% of the combined crop. This fell to around 40% in the 1990's.

5. Approaching 50% of the 2009 barley crop was used for animal feed in the UK and 25% for domestic malting (50% and 29% respectively in 2008).

OATS

Winter Oats

Production level	Low	Average	High
Yield: tonnes per ha (tons per acre)	5.3 (2.1)	6.4 (2.6)	7.7 (3.1)
	£	£	£
Output	577.5 (234)	704 (285)	841.5 (341)
Variable Costs:			
Seed...		49 (20)	
Fertiliser..................................		110 (45)	
Sprays......................................		77 (31)	
Total Variable Costs		236 (96)	
Gross Margin per ha (acre)	**342** (138)	**468** (190)	**606** (245)

Spring Oats

Production level	Low	Average	High
Yield: tonnes per ha (tons per acre)	4.5 (1.8)	5.5 (2.2)	6.5 (2.6)
	£	£	£
Output Feed	495 (200)	605 (245)	715 (290)
Variable Costs:			
Seed...		52 (21)	
Fertiliser..................................		90 (36)	
Sprays......................................		65 (26)	
Total Variable Costs		207 (84)	
Gross Margin per ha (acre)	**288** (117)	**398** (161)	**508** (206)

1. Price used is £110/tonne for the 2011 harvest crop, i.e. the 2011/12 marketing year for milling oats. Milling specification requires a minimum bushel weight of 50Kg/Hl. Conservation grade milling oats may obtain a premium of £10/tonne.

2. Seed: Winter margin uses 175kg/ha seed at £350/tonne, spring margin uses 185kg/ha seed at £350/tonne, both with 40% home saved including the BSPB levy of £32.42/tonne (£4.80 per hectare) for autumn 2010/Spring 2011.

3. *Fertiliser;* winter costs are based on N at 90kg/ha winter and 70kg/ha spring. P and K replacement cost, with straw incorporated making 50:36kg/ha for winter and 43:31kg/ha for spring.

4. Straw is not included above. Average yield is 3.5 tonnes per hectare; value £45 to £60 per tonne according to region and season; variable costs (string) £2.90 per tonne. Prices could be higher in winter 2010-11 because of a possible forage shortage.

5. If a contractor is employed, extra variable costs will be as shown for Winter Wheat (note 9).

6. For Naked Oats refer to page 21

7. *Fuel and Repairs* (per hectare): grain £118, straw £42.

8. *Specialised Equipment Prices*: see p. 179.

9. *Labour:* see p 162.

10. The high majority of GB oats are winter crops; the proportion increases from north to south; (over 90% in England/Wales but less in Scotland). Oats account for about 4% of the UK cereal area.

OILSEED RAPE

Winter Rape

Production level	Low	Average	High
Yield: tonnes per ha (tons per acre)	2.40 (1.0)	3.40 (1.4)	4.40 (1.8)
	£	£	£
Output	624 (253)	884 (358)	1144 (463)
Variable Costs:			
Seed...		38 (15)	
Fertiliser......................................		171 (69)	
Sprays...		130 (53)	
Total Variable Costs		339 (137)	
Gross Margin per ha (acre)	**285** (115)	**545** (221)	**805** (326)

Spring Rape

Production level	Low	Average	High
Yield: tonnes per ha (tons per acre)	1.5 (0.6)	2.00 (0.8)	2.75 (1.1)
	£	£	£
Output	390 (158)	520 (211)	715 (290)
Variable Costs:			
Seed...		41 (17)	
Fertiliser......................................		81 (33)	
Sprays...		79 (32)	
Total Variable Costs		201 (81)	
Gross Margin per ha (acre)	**189** (77)	**319** (129)	**514** (208)

1. *Prices.* The price assumed for the 2011 crop is £260/tonne, including oil bonuses.

2. *Varieties.* Inputs are lower with spring-sown crops, pigeons are less trouble and the late summer/autumn workload is eased. Spring yields average only 60% of those of winter rape; hence normally less than 5% of the total oilseed rape crop is spring-sown. The proportion of the total area sown with hybrid winter rape is about a quarter.

3. *Seed* price is a blend of 42% conventional merchant's seed (£9,000/tonne at 5kg/ha), (£8000/t spring) 25% hybrid (£15,000/tonne at 4kg/ha) and 33% home saved conventional. £20/ha or so can be saved from the gross margin by home saving although other costs appear elsewhere. BSPB levy of £1965.40/tonne (£9.63 per hectare) for autumn 2010 and spring 2011.

4. *Fertiliser* costs are based on N at 190kg/ha for winter, 80kg/ha for spring. P and K replacement cost, with straw incorporated making 45:35kg/ha for winter and 28:22kg/ha for spring crops.

5. *Sprays.* Typically: herbicides 65%, fungicides 25%, insecticides 10%.

6. *Labour:* see p162.

LINSEED

Spring Linseed

Production level	Low	Average	High
Yield: tonnes per ha (tons per acre)	1.25 (0.5)	1.75 (0.7)	2.75 (1.1)
	£	£	£
Output	373.8 (151)	523 (212)	822.3 (333)
Variable Costs:			
Seed...		80 (32)	
Fertiliser......................................		77 (31)	
Sprays..		53 (21)	
Total Variable Costs		210 (85)	
Gross Margin per ha (acre)	**164** (66)	**313** (127)	**612** (248)

Winter Linseed

Production level	Low	Average	High
Yield: tonnes per ha (tons per acre)	1.50 (0.6)	2.50 (1.0)	3.00 (1.2)
	£	£	£
Output	448.5 (182)	748 (303)	897 (363)
Variable Costs:			
Seed...		150 (61)	
Fertiliser......................................		137 (55)	
Sprays..		65 (26)	
Total Variable Costs		352 (143)	
Gross Margin per ha (acre)	**97** (39)	**396** (160)	**545** (221)

1. The price for the 2011 crop is £299/tonne (OSR price plus 15%). Contract prices are normally tied to a standard 38% oil and 9% moisture. Some specialist contracts for specific varieties such as Yellow Linseed can be worth more.

2. Most linseed is spring-sown (about 27,000 of 32,000ha total), drilling mid-March to mid-April (best mid-March to end March). It should not be grown more than 1 year in 5. Too much nitrogen (over 130 kg/ha) can cause lodging, delayed maturity and excessive weed growth and hence difficult harvesting, poor quality and lower yields; it should be applied early. Harvesting: spring normally end Aug-early Sept. Moisture content most likely 12-16%: must be dried to 9% for storage.

4. Inputs: seed, 50kg/ha (sold in hectare bags) minimal home saved, Fertiliser N/P/K of spring 80/24/19 and winter 90:75:50.

Winter Linseed area has been rising with approximately 5,000ha grown in the UK because of easier establishment and earlier harvest (late July). Yield is affected by frost heave, disease and thrips (thunder-bugs), most varieties susceptible to lodging; pigeons and rabbits can also be troublesome. Early sowing (early to mid-September) is best.

Linola is also known by the *misnomer;* 'edible linseed' (all linseed is edible). The oil contains more linolaeic and less linolenic acid than conventional linseed, like sunflower oil so does not dry like linseed oil. It is difficult to see much future for the crop, because its gross margin is very low. It is grown on contract, with the price based on the oilseed rape price. Spring-sown: agronomy and yield similar to conventional linseed; good weed control is essential.

FIELD BEANS

Winter Beans

Production level	Low	Average	High
Yield: tonnes per ha (tons per acre)	3.0 (1.2)	4.0 (1.6)	5.0 (2.0)
	£	£	£
Output	524 (212)	686 (278)	848 (343)
Variable Costs:			
Seed..		56 (23)	
Fertiliser......................................		46 (19)	
Sprays..		112 (45)	
Total Variable Costs		214 (87)	
Gross Margin per ha (acre)	**310** (126)	**472** (191)	**634** (257)

Spring Beans

Production level	Low	Average	High
Yield: tonnes per ha (tons per acre)	2.8 (1.1)	3.7 (1.5)	4.6 (1.9)
	£	£	£
Output	525.2 (213)	682 (276)	838.4 (340)
Variable Costs:			
Seed..		64 (26)	
Fertiliser......................................		43 (17)	
Sprays..		83 (34)	
Total Variable Costs		190 (77)	
Gross Margin per ha (acre)	**335.2** (136)	**492** (199)	**648.4** (263)

Winter Bean Notes

1. *Price.* The 2011 harvest price for winter feed beans is budgeted at £150 per tonne, a premium over feed wheat of £30/tonne. White Hylum varieties carry a premium of another £20/tonne with no yield penalty, thus these are almost exclusively grown. The gross margin builds this into the calculation (60% hitting specification) making the average price £162/tonne. The higher price is achievable subject to meeting minimum quality criteria.

2. *EU Protein Supplement.* Under the Single Payment there is a supplement of €55.57/ha for beans, peas and lupins harvested dry. The output figure above includes the value of this supplement, worth around £38/ha (€1 = 85p) after deducting modulation (19%). This assumes a stipulated maximum EU-wide guaranteed area of 1.648 million hectares is not exceeded. It hasn't been yet. This policy will be removed for 2012.

3. *Seed:* 185-220 kg per hectare (200kg used here) @ £330-400/tonne (£360). About 60% is farm-saved as here and includes BSPB levy of £9.64/ha or £47.71/tonne (winter and spring).

4. *Fertiliser:* 9kg phosphate and 10kg potash/t bean harvested/ha. No nitrogen is applied making 0:36:40kg/ha.

5. *Labour:* see p 162.

Spring Bean Notes

6. *Price*. Spring beans are all grown for the human consumption market. It is only the poor quality beans (predominantly Bruchid beetle damaged) that are rejected and redirected to feed compounders. Damaged samples can be cleaned if the premium justifies it. A large proportion of the crop is exported (to North Africa). Spring bean price is budgeted here at £174/tonne. In a 'normal' year, about 30-40% of spring beans will not make the export (human consumption) grade. This is accounted for in the price.

7. *Seed:* 185-220 kg per hectare (200kg/ha here) at £375/tonne. About 40% is farm-saved. Sprays: as for winter beans.

8. *Fertiliser:* 9kg phosphate and 10kg potash/t bean harvested/ha. No nitrogen is applied making 0:33:37kg/ha.

9. *Winter versus Spring Beans*. The key determinant between which to crop is soil type. Winter beans are more suited to heavy soils and springs on lighter land. As the schedules illustrate, there is little real difference between the gross margins.

FIELD PEAS

Blue Peas

Production level	Low	Average	High
Yield: tonnes per ha (tons per acre)	3.0 (1.2)	3.75 (1.5)	5.0 (2.0)
	£	£	£
Output	548 (222)	676 (274)	888 (360)
Variable Costs:			
Seed...		78 (32)	
Fertiliser.......................................		43 (17)	
Sprays...		134 (54)	
Total Variable Costs		255 (103)	
Gross Margin per ha (acre)	**293** (119)	**421** (170)	**633** (256)

Marofats

Production level	Low	Average	High
Yield: tonnes per ha (tons per acre)	2.7 (1.1)	3.40 (1.4)	4.5 (1.8)
	£	£	£
Output	551 (223)	684 (277)	893 (362)
Variable Costs:			
Seed...		103 (42)	
Fertiliser.......................................		39 (16)	
Sprays...		155 (63)	
Total Variable Costs		297 (120)	
Gross Margin per ha (acre)	**254** (103)	**387** (157)	**596** (241)

1. *Price*. All peas are now grown for a premium market. Only a small proportion (5-10%) are compounded as second grade peas or go for pet food. The high premium for food consumption justifies pea cleaning to remove discoloured and damaged peas. Feed value is therefore not relevant as a base price but a discount. The price forecast for the

Blue Peas here is £170/tonne, taking account of some very high premiums (achieving up to £320/tonne) and a failure rate. Most peas are Blues, used for micronising and exports.

Marofats, the other main group of peas (second half of the table), can achieve even higher prices. They are no longer priced with a premium over wheat, as the markets bear little relationship. They are used for canning, packets and export trade. About a third is grown on a forward contract. They command a higher price than blues but yield about 10% less. The average price in this gross margin is £190/tonne accounting for all samples including those that miss the premium grade and those that have to be cleaned. Sometimes the crop is desiccated before direct combining.

2. EU Protein Supplement. (See Winter Beans Note 2) is included in the above.

3. *Seed:* Blues, £300/tonne planted at 210 to 250kg/ha (230kg here), Marofats £500/tonne at 230kg/ha. About 50% farm-saved including BSPB levy of £9.64/ha or £47.71/tonne.

4. *Fertiliser:* based on 9kg phosphate and 10kg potash per tonne of pea harvested per hectare. No nitrogen is applied making 0:34:38kg/ha Blues and 0:30:34 Marofats.

4. *Labour:* see p. 162.

Peas or Beans?

In 2009 the area of peas was less than 20% of the UK pulse area. It is usually slightly higher than this but pulses, particularly peas are crops for specialist growers. High quality and good yields can return high gross margins and offer wider benefits to the farming system although they can be difficult to grow.

LUPINS

The following table refers to spring sown *white lupins*. Differences in yield and price for yellow and blue lupins are given in the accompanying notes:

Production level	Low	Average	High
Yield: tonnes per ha (tons per acre)	2.25 (0.9)	3.00 (1.2)	3.75 (1.5)
	£	£	£
Output	533 (216)	698 (283)	863 (350)
Variable Costs:			
Seed		130 (52)	
Fertiliser..................................		62 (25)	
Sprays		105 (43)	
Total Variable Costs	296 (120)	296 (120)	296 (120)
Gross Margin per ha (acre)	**237** (96)	**402** (163)	**567** (230)

1. The price used here is £220 per tonne plus £38/ha protein supplement (see Field Bean Note 2.). Very little of the crop is traded as grain, but the price for this tends to be between soya meal and feed bean price.

A leguminous crop traditionally associated with light land. Their protein content is about 40 to 50% higher than peas and beans, making lupins a good substitute for soya bean meal in livestock feed compounds. They are a non-GM source of high quality digestible protein. The crop can be cut whole for silage, crimped or milled and fed directly to stock or the grain traded as a cash crop.

The area grown in the UK has increased from about 2,500 hectares in 2001 to approximately 5,000 hectares. The area is now relatively static. They are virtually all spring lupins. Around 75% of the total area is likely to be whole-cropped. Determinate varieties (single stem, uniform ripening) can be harvested easily; non determinate varieties (with multiple heads at various stages of ripening) are more difficult.

Lupins can be grown on all but the heaviest land but are not tolerant of alkaline soils. They need a good cereal seedbed and pre-emergence weed control. Sowing is from mid-March to early April and harvest from mid-August onwards (and can be late September). If the crop is for silage, sowing can be as late as mid-May using an appropriate variety. No nitrogen fertiliser is necessary although 15-25kg/ha is often used to accelerate early stage growth. Replacement P and K at 30-50kg/ha is assumed. There are no serious crop pests. Anthracnose is a potentially serious threat but plant health measures have so far kept it under control. Other diseases are not a problem. Determinant varieties don't generally need pre-harvest desiccants if weed-free, indeterminant ones do.

Appropriate species and variety choice is important depending on area of the country, soil pH, intended end use and growth habit required. There are three distinct species of spring lupins, white (lupinus albus), blue (lupinus angustifolus) and yellow (lupinus luteus). All are suitable for grain or livestock feed. White lupins have higher protein and potentially greater yield than blue lupins but require a longer growing season. Yellow lupins fall between blue and white on both counts.

About 60% of the national lupin area is white, 20% yellow and 20% blue. In the South-East and East Anglia 90%+ of lupins are white. In Scotland 50% are blue 25% white and 25% yellow, with the blue grown for combining or crimping and white & yellows being used for whole crop.

Lupin characteristics

	White *Lupinus Albus*	**Yellow** *Lupinus Luteus*	**Blue** *Lupinus Angustifolius*
Flower Colour	white or blue	yellow	white or blue
Growth habit	semi-determinate	semi-determinate	fully or semi-determinate
pH tolerance	5 to 7.6	4.6 to 6.8	5 to 6.8
Protein	36-40%	38-42%	31-35%
Oil content	10%	5%	6%
Main use	Combining in Southern England on acidic land. Forage in all areas	Mainly used for forage in the North.	Combining in the North (determinate) Forage in the very North (semi-determinate)
Yield	3.0-3.5 t/ha	2.5-3.0 t/ha	3.0-3.5 t/ha

Acknowledgement: Thanks to - Soya UK, Tel: 02380 696922. Premium Crops, Tel: 02392 632 883.

HERBAGE SEEDS

	Italian Ryegrass		Early Perennial Ryegrass	
	Average	High	Average	High
	£	£	£	£
Yield (tonnes per ha)	1.3	1.7	1.25	1.60
Price per 50 kg (£)	35		35	
Output	910	1190	875	1120
Variable Costs:				
Seed		95		85
Fertiliser		213		213
Sprays		95		95
Cleaning / Certification.............	221	281	213.5	266
Total Variable Costs	624	684	607	659
Gross Margin per ha	**286**	**506**	**268**	**461**
Gross Margin per acre	116	205	109	186

	Intermediate Perennial Ryegrass		Late Perennial Ryegrass	
	Average	High	Average	High
	£	£	£	£
Yield (tonnes per ha)	1.3	1.6	1.25	1.60
Price per 50 kg (£)	40		45	
Output	1000	1280	1125	1440
Variable Costs:				
Seed		95		85
Fertiliser		213		213
Sprays		100		100
Cleaning / Certification.............	214	266	213.5	266
Total Variable Costs	622	674	612	664
Gross Margin per ha	**378**	**606**	**513**	**776**
Gross Margin per acre	153	245	208	314

	Hybrid Ryegrass		Kent Wild White Clover & Kent Indig. Peren. R'grass	
	Average	High	Average	High
	£	£	£	£
Yield (tonnes per ha)	1.2	1.6	0.09 (Clover)	0.11 (C)
			0.6 (R'grass)	0.8 (R)
Price per 50 kg (£)	40		300 (C)	45 (C)
Output	960	1240	1080	1380
Variable Costs:				
Seed		95		65
Fertiliser		203		85
Sprays		100		95
Cleaning / Certification.............	206	259	143	179
Total Variable Costs	604	656	388	424
Gross Margin per ha	**356**	**584**	**692**	**956**
Gross Margin per acre	144	236	280	387

1. The following were the number of hectares entered for certified seed production for the main grasses and clovers in the UK for the 2009 harvest;

Italian / Westerwold Ryegrass	176	Cocksfoot	279
Early Perennial Ryegrass............	70	Timothy..................................	49
Inter. Perennial Ryegrass............	1,157	Red Fescue	349
Late Perennial Ryegrass	1,677	White Clover	9
Amenity Perennial Ryegrass.......	992	Red Clover..............................	80
Hybrid Ryegrass	456	Common Vetch.......................	116

   The ryegrasses total 4,528 ha (11,189 acres).

   All herbage seeds total 5,410 ha (13,368 acres).

2. The *yields* shown are averages for cleaned certified seed. The crop is risky, i.e. yields are highly variable, depending especially on the weather at, and precise timeliness of, harvesting. However, the use of growth regulators and stripper headers has reduced the risk. A considerable amount of skill is necessary to average the 'high' levels over a number of years. Most grasses give their highest yield in their first harvest year, assuming good establishment. Yields can be increased by up to 30% with a combination of higher Nitrogen applications along with a growth regulator (e.g. Moddus). The cost of the growth regulator is likely to add £25/ha (£10/acre) to the chemical figure in the margins above, with a similar cost increase for the extra Nitrogen.

3. Prices in the table are estimated prices for certified seed for the 2011 year. The figures relate to Diploid varieties. Very little early Diploid is now grown. Tetraploid prices are slightly lower, but yields should be higher (intermediate and late varieties achieving 1,500-2,500 kg/ha). High sugar varieties should command a small premium over the values seen in the tables. Amenity ryegrasses and fescues also command a premium for high quality sports use, and some yield nearly as much as agricultural varieties.

4. No allowance has been made above for by-products. Some crops produce 4 to 5 tonnes of threshed hay, which is, however, of low feeding value. This could be worth £200 or more per hectare. Some grasses, especially spring-sown ryegrass, also provide substantial quantities of autumn and winter grazing. Clovers can be either grazed or cut for hay or silage and do not have to be 'shut up' until mid or late May, or, in some cases and seasons, even early June. More grazing (until end of May) and better quality threshed hay is provided with a combination of ryegrass and white clover than with the specialist herbage seed grasses.

5. The seed rate is around 10kg/ha for autumn sowing, less for spring. If the seed crop is to be undersown, specialist growers often reduce the seed rate for the cover crop by up to half and restrict nitrogen dressing: the cereal yield may thus be reduced by up to 0.6 t/ha. If this is not done the grass seed yield is usually lower in the first year compared with direct drilling, except for ryegrass.

6. Chemical costs will vary depending on the prevalence of grass weeds. Autumn sown crops will have higher costs than spring sown ones, although yields for autumn crops should be higher in the first year. The margin assumes an autumn-sown crop.

7. Labour: see page 162.

Acknowledgement: Thanks to - British Seed Houses, Tel: 01522 868 714; Herbage Seed Services, Tel: 01962 774 432; NIAB, Tel: 01223 342 238.

RYE

Production level	Low	Average	High
Yield: tonnes per ha (tons per acre)	4.90 (2.0)	6.20 (2.5)	7.50 (3.0)
	£	£	£
Output	588 (238)	744 (301)	900 (365)
Variable Costs:			
Seed		80 (32)	
Fertiliser..		163 (66)	
Sprays		95 (38)	
Total Variable Costs	338 (137)	338 (137)	338 (137)
Gross Margin per ha (acre)	**250** (101)	**406** (165)	**562** (228)

1. The price assumed is £120/tonne for 2011 harvest. The contract is made up of two parts; half of the tonnage is at a fixed £110/t, the other half at a £10.50/t premium to the prevailing feed wheat price at the point of movement, based on Oct-Dec delivery. The price assumes the milling specification is achieved. Deductions are made for low quality, and if it is feed grade, price then falls between feed wheat and feed barley. Only a small percentage of the crop is grown for the free market.

Largely grown on light, low fertility, sandy or stony soils, not suited to other cereals. Yields would clearly be higher on better soils, but then rye has difficulty in competing with wheat and barley; it could never do so on good wheat land. The average yield in the UK in the five years 2005 to 2009 was 6.24 tonnes/ha.

The area grown in the UK has ranged between 5,000-6,000 ha for several years. Rye crispbread is the major outlet. It is also milled into flour, used in mixed-grain bread and muesli. About two-thirds of UK requirements are imported, mainly from Canada (which produces the highest quality), Denmark, Germany and Spain. Demand for UK-grown rye has been falling in recent years, owing to increased competition in the crispbread market.

Rye, which is autumn-sown, is drought tolerant and very hardy, can withstand low temperatures and starts growing early in the spring. It has all-round resistance to wheat and barley diseases, e.g. eyespot, and suffers less from take-all than wheat – hence it is a possible replacement for third or fourth wheat. Its vigour keeps weeds down. Its herbicide, fungicide and fertiliser requirements are lower than for other cereals, except for growth regulators. Rye is harvested earlier than winter wheat (useful for following with oilseed rape).

Drawbacks: it sprouts in a wet harvest: must therefore harvest early, at relatively high moisture content. It grows very tall and lodges easily: hence high levels of nitrogen are not possible; but growth regulators help. Its heavy straw crop means very slow combining (takes about twice as long per hectare as wheat and barley), and difficult straw incorporation. New hybrid varieties, with shorter, stiffer straw, are being developed; these would improve the comparative profitability of rye on better soils.

Drilling: 2nd and 3rd weeks September. Harvesting: by mid-August at relatively high moisture content, then dry to 14-15% (no drying costs included in margin).

TRITICALE

Production level	Low	Average	High
Yield: tonnes per ha (tons per acre)	4.00 (1.6)	5.00 (2.0)	7.20 (2.9)
	£	£	£
Output	460 (186)	575 (233)	828 (335)
Variable Costs:			
Seed		51 (21)	
Fertiliser...............................		149 (60)	
Sprays		65 (26)	
Total Variable Costs	264 (107)	264 (107)	264 (107)
Gross Margin per ha (acre)	**196** (79)	**311** (126)	**564** (228)

A 'man-made' cross between rye and hard wheat. It combines the hardiness of rye and the marketability of feed wheat. It is used in livestock feed, particularly pig and poultry rations, having high levels of lysine. However it is not widely used by feed compounders. The area grown in the UK has risen over recent years to over 18,000ha. A large proportion of this rise is likely to be in the newer spring varieties (see below).

The price is usually £4 or £6 per tonne below the price for feed wheat, but this tends to vary from season to season; £115 per tonne is assumed above for the 2011 harvest crop.

The average yield in the UK in the five years 2005 to 2009 was only 4.18 tonnes/ha,. But in the five years 1996-2000 the average had been over 5.90 tonnes per ha – showing that the potential of the crop is not always fully realised. The low yields are a result of it mainly being grown on light land, especially thin, drought-prone, poorish, marginal cereal-growing soils. In these circumstances, it can frequently out-yield wheat or barley, especially the former, and it has lower input requirements. Its yields tend to be more consistent on such soil than those of barley. Triticale tends to do well compared with second and subsequent wheats owing to its resistance to drought and fungal diseases.

Lower levels of fungicide are needed because of its good disease resistance, except for ergot, but including take-all (making it a possible replacement for a third or fourth wheat, as indicated above). It is a tall crop, which helps to suppress weeds, but it is susceptible to lodging; growth regulators are beneficial. New semi-dwarf varieties are being developed, to overcome straw strength weakness and susceptibility to rust infections.

The crop is best drilled early (September) on very light, drought-prone soils; otherwise October is satisfactory. Harvesting is at approximately the same time as wheat. There is more straw, which slows combining, and incorporation is difficult; this is less of a problem on poor soils as there is less straw.

Spring Triticale

New spring varieties of this crop have been introduced in the last few years. These have been taken up strongly in livestock areas – the north and west of England, as well as western Scotland, Wales and N. Ireland. Being a spring crop means that winter water logging is not an issue, and it can be grown on a wider range of soils. In total over 5,000 ha of spring triticale may well now be grown in the UK: either on its own or as part of a mixture.

It has lower yields than winter triticale if it is harvested for grain in the conventional way. However, most is whole-cropped to produce an 'arable forage'. Often it is grown in a mixture with a proteins crop – peas or lupins for example. Inputs for spring triticale will be lower than those for winter varieties.

NAKED OATS

Production level	Low	Average	High
Yield: tonnes per ha (tons per acre)	4.50 (1.8)	5.50 (2.2)	6.50 (2.6)
	£	£	£
Output	720 (292)	880 (356)	1040 (421)
Variable Costs:			
Seed ………………………………....		65 (26)	
Fertiliser…………………………..…		124 (50)	
Sprays ………………………….….		95 (38)	
Total Variable Costs	284 (115)	284 (115)	284 (115)
Gross Margin per ha (acre)	**436** (177)	**596** (242)	**756** (306)

Naked oats have a higher protein, energy and oil content than 'traditional' oats, but the fibre content is lower – as the husk is removed during harvesting. Contracts require a maximum moisture content of 14%, which is also recommended for long-term storage.

The area being grown continues to increase steadily. Naked oats now account for in excess of 10% of the traded tonnage of UK oats (i.e. excluding those grown for on-farm use). The traditional markets such as racehorse feed, dog food, and bird feed markets are all increasing. Over recent years the human consumption market has developed so that at least half the crop is now sold for health foods, fancy breads and breakfast cereals. In future, a further growth area is likely to be from demand for inclusion of the crop in monogastric animal feeds. The poultry industry in particular is setting up supply chains.

The 2011 harvest crop price assumed is £160 per tonne, based on contracts offering premiums 35% above the average feed wheat price. The premium can be reduced according to husk content.

In a normal cropping year, over 90% of the crop is winter sown, although the proportion of spring cropping rises after a wet autumn. The margin above assumes winter cropping. NIAB survey results have suggested that yields average 20%-25% less than conventional oats. New spring varieties have become available that offer yields much closer to winter crops. The actual difference in yield will depend on the particular season, but are likely to be in the range 15%-20%.

The agronomy of naked oats is similar to that of husked oat varieties. Variable inputs are lower than for wheat or barley. Traditionally, high nitrogen use has not been possible due to the risk of lodging, however, new semi-dwarf varieties with stiff straw have been introduced. As well as increasing the scope for higher fertiliser applications, this means the crop is also suited to more fertile soils, and growth regulators may be avoided. Oats provide a break in the take-all cycle.

Harvest is early (coming just after winter barley). New varieties are less susceptible to shedding than in the past, however care needs to be taken with both the timing of harvest, and the set-up of the combine, to ensure a clean, saleable, sample.

Naked Barley

Naked barley, suitable for roasting, flaking or milling as pearl barley, is now rarely heard of. It is grown like normal barley, but yields are reckoned to be some 15% lower. It could be either autumn or spring sown.

DURUM WHEAT

Production level	Low	Average	High
Yield: tonnes per ha (tons per acre)	5.20 (2.1)	6.20 (2.5)	7.50 (3.0)
	£	£	£
Output	884 (358)	1054 (427)	1275 (516)
Variable Costs:			
Seed ………………………………....		90 (36)	
Fertiliser……………………….….		161 (65)	
Sprays …………………………….		115 (47)	
Total Variable Costs	366 (148)	366 (148)	366 (148)
Gross Margin per ha (acre)	**518** (210)	**688** (279)	**909** (368)

Extra drying costs estimated at £10 per tonne not shown in the margin.

A Mediterranean crop. As well as pasta, it is used to produce ethnic foods, semolina, biscuits, etc. Must be grown under contract as there is a very limited number of end users. Domestic demand is relatively small, but expanding; UK consumption per head is approx. 4% that of Italy and 10% that of France but total UK use nevertheless amounts to about 60,000 tonnes a year.

The crop started to be grown in England in the late 1970s and built up to 11,000 ha (27,000 acres) in 1984. A series of years of poor yields reduced this to a few hundred hectares by the mid-1990s. It had recovered to a couple of thousand hectares, but lower milling premiums has seen the area restricted to less than 500 hectares (1,200 acres) in recent seasons.

On average the crop should yield 75%-80% of conventional feed wheat in the same situation. These levels are assumed in the margins above.

Contracts are based on a premium over the feed wheat price. For the 2011 harvest this is assumed to be £60 per tonne delivered, resulting in an assumed ex-farm premium for 'Grade A' durum of £50 per tonne. This gives an estimated price of £170 per tonne. The price will be reduced if the crop does not fully meet quality specifications.

As with milling wheat, there is a risk of rejection if contaminated with excess foreign seeds, especially self-set cereals from previous crop; thus safer as a first cereal crop. A poor price is obtained if quality is too poor for pasta and thus has to go for feed.

The crop is likely to be grown only in the driest parts of the east/south east, where it can best compete with second and third wheats. It may be either autumn or spring sown; around two-thirds is currently autumn sown and this is assumed in the table above. The crop is very sensitive to stress and frost-kill in severe winters; the spring-sown crop is more reliable, and cheaper to grow, but the yield is usually 15-20% lower. Spring crops also allow more opportunities for black grass control. The crop has a higher disease resistance than other wheats, except for eyespot and ergot.

Harvesting is a critical operation; it needs to be done as soon as the crop reaches 20% moisture content, or at most 18%: it is very prone to sprouting and the quality for semolina is reduced if harvest is delayed. Durum must be dried (slowly) to 15%. It is easier and quicker to dry than normal wheat. The straw is of poorer quality and lesser quantity than conventional wheat straw and is therefore rarely baled.

MINORITY CROPS

Borage

Borage is indigenous to Britain (or at least here since Roman times); it has both grown in the wild, and been cultivated for centuries. It is produced principally for use as a dietary supplement, but it may also be used in cosmetics and pharmaceuticals. The oil has a high gamma linolenic acid (GLA) content. It was first grown as a field crop in the UK in the early 1980's. The last few years have usually seen around 5,000 hectares planted per year. However, due to a world-wide surplus of GLA, few, if any, contracts were offered for 2009 or 2010 crops. At the time of writing it seems likely that no contracts will be offered in spring 2011 either. As the market tends to be volatile, it is essential for a grower to have a buy-back contract with a reputable company. The crop should not be grown speculatively.

The crop is spring sown (March-April) into a good seedbed. Its aggressive growth gives good weed control with a high plant density. There are no significant pests and diseases, except for powdery mildew. Low rainfall areas are preferred owing to harvesting difficulties in wet conditions. It is combined in late July/early August, after swathing and drying, which takes a minimum of two weeks. Harvesting can be difficult and seed shedding at maturity is a problem. Seed should be promptly dried to 10% for safe storage. Cleaning may be necessary.

Borage should only be considered by those prepared to invest sufficient time in the crop's husbandry, harvest and storage. Borage is a low yield / high risk crop – yields are from virtually nothing to 0.75 tonnes/ha (6 cwt/acre); average 0.4 (3.2).

Contract prices in the past have been around £2,500/tonne. Growing costs are likely to be in the range £250-£300/ha.

Camelina Sativa

Camelina, Gold of Pleasure, or False Flax is a fast growing spring (or occasionally winter) sown crop. It is easily grown and harvested and is drought tolerant. The oil contains a range of essential fatty acids. It can be used as a food supplement or in industry as a drying oil. There is currently no commercial scale production in the UK that the authors are aware of. It is thought that current domestic usage requirements could support around 1,000 ha of the crop in the UK. Yields are in the 2.5tonne/ha range. Price is uncertain due to the absence of a domestic market but an indicative price is likely to be around £250/tonne.

Crambe - Abyssinian Mustard

Crambe is an industrial oilseed that contains high levels of erucic acid. Converted into erucamide it is used as a slip agent in plastics and is a constituent of heat sensitive dyes. The area of crambe in the UK had grown to around 5,000 ha. However, the major promoter/buyer of the crop went into receivership and little is being currently grown.

Crambe is a cruciferous spring crop managed in a similar way to spring oilseed rape. It has a short growing season, requiring only 100-120 days to reach maturity after emergence. As with oilseed rape, timely harvesting is important. Crambe can be combined direct, desiccated and combined or swathed. The crop should be stored and marketed at a moisture content of 9% or less. Yields are in the 2.5tonne/ha range. Contract prices offered in the past were £180/tonne. Growing costs are likely to be around £250/t.

Echium

Echium is a relatively new commercial plant to the UK. It has been cultivated on contract for less than a decade. It is a member of the Boraginacea family and is rich in stearidonic acid, which is used in cosmetic creams to reduce skin wrinkling and the effects of sunburn.

In past years there has been somewhat less than 1,000 ha or so grown in the UK. Similar to borage, a glut of the active ingredient led to no contracts being offered in 2009 or 2010. The same situation is likely to persist into 2011. It is essential for a grower to have a buy-back contract with a reputable company, and the crop should not be grown speculatively. In the past prices have collapsed to almost nothing due to over-supply in the market.

The crop can be grown as far north as Yorkshire. It has a husbandry programme similar to that of borage but does not shed its seed as readily as borage. The seed is relatively small in size. Echium is suitable for light to medium land whereas borage performs better on a wider range of soil types.

The crop is sown in April and should come to harvest in July/August. There appear to be no significant pests of the crop. Harvesting is carried out with the use of a swather. Yields are approximately 250kg/ha (100kg/acre). Contract prices in the past have been around £3,500/tonne of clean seed.

Evening Primrose

This crop is an important source of gamma linolenic acid (GLA), but it is no longer grown in the UK and very little is cultivated elsewhere in Western Europe – it has been largely superseded by borage, which is easier to grow. The crop is still widely grown in China where the climate is more suitable, and labour costs are lower. Previous editions have given details of the crop and possible gross margin data.

Flax (cut flax for industrial fibre)

Flax was re-introduced into the UK during the 1990s, not as the traditional, pulled, long fibre variety used for linen textiles but as a cut, combinable crop producing shorter fibres for industrial uses – 'short-fibre flax'. As a natural, biodegradable fibre and a renewable resource it was promoted as a 'green' alternative to synthetic fibres and plastics. New markets were developed and several processing plants set up - the area of flax expanded to 20,200 ha in 1996. Following low prices and reform of the subsidy regime, the area fell to less than 2,000 ha by 2003, and the one remaining processing facility in Wales was closed. Little, if any, is currently grown.

The agronomy of flax is similar to that of linseed but it is harvested earlier. It is spring sown, suitable for most soil types although lighter soil is preferred. It is a low input crop but weed control is essential. It grows best in areas of high rainfall such as Wales and the South-west. There are several harvesting options (described in earlier editions). Currently the preferred option is desiccation followed by combining. The straw is left to rett in the field and then baled. Retting takes 10-21 days, depending on weather conditions. The price paid for straw will reflect quality. The fibre content of a reasonable crop is 20-30%.

Hemp

The traditional use for hemp was in canvas and rope manufacture. New markets have recently been opened up, with the main uses of the fibre from the crop being in building insulation, and producing internal panels for the automotive industry. The core or pith of the plant is used for horse or poultry bedding. Although there is still a strong and growing demand from this market, it is also now being mixed with lime and used as a thermally efficient, environmentally friendly material in the construction industry.

The severe downturn in the automotive sector sharply reduced demand for hemp fibre. This resulted in the UK's main processor, Hemcore of Essex, to enter into administration. The company had opened a new factory in Suffolk for the 2008 crop. This has the capacity to process the crop from 4,000 ha. The factory has been purchased by one of its customers as a going-concern and is now called Hemp Technology Ltd. Contracts for 1,200 ha were placed in 2010, with a larger area planned for 2011.

Hemp is drilled in late April/May and the fibre crop grows 3 to 3.5m (10-12 feet) tall. Hemp Technology suggests a minimum area of 10 ha. A well-grown crop should have no weed or pest problems. Improved technology in the new factory means fibres do not have to be left to rett in the field for as long. Instead of a retting period of 4-6 weeks, the crop is mowed, and then baled when it is dry, bleached, and partially retted after 2-3 weeks. This increases saleable yields as the crop is allowed to grow for longer (cutting mid to late August), and there is less field-losses from the rows. Average yields should be around 7.5 tonnes/ha (3.0t/acre), with target yields at 9.5t/ha (3.8t/acre). The margin below assumes that the grower will undertake the cutting and baling operations. If contractors are used then the variable costs will obviously be higher.

The crop must be stored under cover, and is delivered to the factory throughout the year. Due to the bulkiness of the crop, the majority of hemp is grown in the eastern counties, near to the processing facility. An average delivered price of £130/tonne is assumed in the table below. The 2010 contract operated on a base price of £125/tonne delivered to the factory in October, with £1.50/tonne monthly increments. The 2011 contract is likely to offer similar terms. Transport costs need to taken into consideration. A figure of £15/tonne is used in the table below. This should be applicable up to 50 miles from the factory (less if closer).

Hemp Gross Margin Schedule

Yield 7.5t/ha (3.0t/acre), Price £130/t delivered	£/ha	(£/ac)
Output	975	(395)
Variable Costs:		
Seed	135	(55)
Fertiliser	175	(71)
Sprays	0	(0)
Haulage to factory (£15/tonne)	113	(46)
Total Variable Costs	422	(171)
Gross Margin per ha (acre).................................	**553**	(224)

Dual Hemp

Hemp may also be grown as a dual-purpose crop. In recent years, up to 10-15% of the national hemp crop was of this type. The crop is left to mature longer, and then the top can be combined for the seed before the straw is mown and retted. A yield of 1.0-1.2 tonne/ha (0.4-0.5 tonne/ac) of seed is possible, with a contract price estimated to be £480/tonne. However, the yield of straw is lower at 5-6 tonnes/ha (2.0-2.4 t/ac), with the price being the same as 'conventional' hemp. The seed is cold-pressed to produce high-value cooking oil, and is also used for bird feed, fishing bait and in nutritional supplements and cosmetics. Agronomy and costs are likely to be similar to a fibre crop. Because of the time needed to let the seed heads mature, an earlier-maturing variety is used. The later harvest also means that this crop is more suitable for early land in the East and South.

Grain Maize

Maize is one of the major global grains – with world output being higher than that for wheat. However, the climate of the UK has made it difficult to ripen the crop and most maize is grown for forage rather than grain. A combination of earlier varieties, the development of machinery that copes with wet conditions, and even possibly the effects of warmer summers has improved the prospects of this crop.

There is market potential, as well over a million tonnes of grain maize are imported annually. It is used in animal rations, human foods, and in industrial processes. Marketing the UK crop is a problem at present as consignments are generally not big enough to interest the major buyers. The animal feed market is the likeliest outlet for domestic production - a specialised or local market can be developed, for example feed for pigeons or corn-fed chickens. The basis of pricing in the margin is a £20-£30/tonne premium over feed wheat.

There is no fundamental difference between forage and grain maize – the same varieties are simply left in the field for 3-6 weeks longer to let the cobs mature. It is difficult to know how much of the total UK maize area is taken for grain but it could be around 3,000 ha. The crop can be grown south of a line from Bristol to East Anglia, excluding the far south-west. Fields should be below 500ft in elevation and south-facing. To maximise heat units, the crop should be drilled as soon as soil temperatures are above 8°c – usually late April/May. Harvest by conventional combine with an adapted header in October/November. In UK conditions grain maize seldom drops below 30% moisture. The crop needs to be dried to 15% for storage which can be expensive and time-consuming. On good land the crop can yield 8-10 t/ha but the average is not likely to be so high.

Grain Maize Gross Margin Schedule

	£/ha	(£/ac)
Yield 7.5t/ha (3.0t/acre), Price £145/t ex-farm		
Output	1088	(440)
Variable Costs:		
Seed	110	(45)
Fertiliser	181	(73)
Sprays	60	(24)
Total Variable Costs	351	(142)
Gross Margin per ha (acre).................................	**737**	(298)
But note high drying costs:		
£12-18/t on-farm; £15-25/t off-farm	90-188	(36-76)

The majority of grain maize is currently stored as a crimped product. This sees the crop cut at 30-35% moisture from mid October to early November with the 'wet' grain being processed, and an additive added (usually an organic acid). The overall cost of crimping and preservative is around £12/tonne. The grain is clamped or put into large bales or bags. It provides a very digestible dairy feed of high nutrition content. Yields can be 11-13t/ha and it sells of £100-£125/tonne ex-farm.

Acknowledgement: Thanks to - Maize Growers Association, Tel: 01363 775040.

Millet

Millet describes a range of small-seeded grain plants covering a number of different species. The most commonly grown type in the UK is proso (also called white or common) millet. Millet has been cultivated since prehistoric times. It is a major food source in arid and semi-arid parts of the world; predominantly India, China, and parts of Africa. The crop has been grown in the UK for game cover for many years, but it has recently been commercialised to supply grain to the bird seed market.

Millet Gross Margin Schedule

Yield 3.0t/ha (1.2t/acre), Price £230/t ex-farm	£/ha	(£/ac)
Output	690	(279)
Variable Costs:		
Seed	100	(41)
Fertiliser	102	(41)
Sprays	45	(18)
Total Variable Costs	247	(100)
Gross Margin per ha (acre)...............................	**443**	(179)

The UK currently imports approximately 25,000 tonnes of millet for bird and pet feed each year. Domestic plantings in 2009 were in the region of 2,000-2,500 ha. There is the potential to raise this to around 6,000 ha. Full import substitution is unlikely to be possible as UK seed cannot match the quality of the best imported millet.

The crop can be grown on a range of soil types, but as it is drought tolerant, it is often planted on lighter land. It does not grow well in heavy or very chalky soils. The crop requires warm temperatures to ripen and is therefore best suited to the South of England.

The crop is late drilled, usually in May once the soil has warmed up sufficiently. It can be planted as late as June. It requires a fine seedbed. The crop grows to about a metre high and is ready to harvest after 4½ months in mid to late September. The crop is usually desiccated before harvesting with a conventional combine harvester.

Yields are in the range 2.5-4.0 t/ha. The contract price for 2011 is not known at the time of writing, although values of £200-£250/t have been seen in the past couple of seasons.

Acknowledgement: Thanks to - Premium Crops, Tel: 02392 632 883. Soya UK, Tel: 02380 696922.

Navy Beans

Navy beans are the basis for the familiar canned 'baked beans'. Over 100,000t of these are consumed annually in the UK – with the vast majority of these being imported from North America. A few years ago there was some interest in the crop, as varieties adapted to the soil types and climate of the UK were introduced. However, disappointing prices, variable yields, and the lack of area aid discouraged growers. Even following the change to the Single Payment, the economics of navy bean production in the UK looks marginal. Few, if any, contracts are currently available.

The crop requires good fertile land and some care in growing. Sowing is in mid-May when there is no further frost risk. Harvesting is late August/early September. The target yield is 3.0t/ha but the average is likely to be substantially less. When budgeting, an average of around 2.0t/ha (0.8t/acre) could be assumed. There is very little market information available on price, but it is likely to be in the region of £250-£300/tonne. Variable costs are likely to be in the range £300-£350/ha.

Poppies

The growing of this crop in the UK is a relatively recent development. The poppy heads are processed to produce morphine for pharmaceutical purposes. The seeds are sold into the culinary market. A bit less than 3,000 ha of the crop are currently grown – all on contract to the sole UK processor.

The crop needs free-draining alkaline soils; it is planted in the second half of March, and is harvested in early to mid August. The processor undertakes the harvesting operation with a specialised machine. Seed is included as part of the contract, as is agronomy advice (the processor specifies the pesticides to be used). The grower needs to be able to offer on-floor drying facilities.

Growing costs (excluding seed) will be in the range £250-£300/ha. The contract for the 2011 harvest has not yet been finalised. In previous years a basic fee of £200/ha was paid by the processor, which was then topped-up by a bonus based on the yield of the alkaloid from the crop. Total returns were in the range £700-£900/ha. Returns may be different under the 2011 contract – contact the processor for more details.

Acknowledgement: Thanks to – Macfarlan Smith, Tel: 01225 793 679.

Soya Beans

Soya is a sub-tropical crop in origin, grown mainly in North and South America, but also to a small extent in southern Europe. The UK imports three quarters of a million tonnes each year as beans and almost a further 2 million tonnes as meal, all for animal feed, so there would appear to be a ready market for the home grown product.

Various attempts have been made to commercialise the crop in the UK. In the late 1990's new varieties were introduced and by the early 2000's the area expanded to 1,700 ha. But after several difficult years the planted area declined. In recent years, less than 100 ha were being grown. However, the plant breeding process has continued and further varietal improvements yield and earliness have been made. Importantly, the soya price has also improved making the economics more attractive. An expansion in area is expected with contracts being offered for the 2011 harvest.

Soya Bean Gross Margin Schedule

Yield 2.5t/ha (1.0t/acre), Price £325/t ex-farm	£/ha	(£/ac)
Output	813	(329)
Variable Costs:		
Seed	140	(57)
Fertiliser	55	(22)
Sprays	70	(28)
Total Variable Costs	265	(107)
Gross Margin per ha (acre)................................	**547**	**(222)**

The crop is sown in late April or early May, depending on soil temperature, into a fine moist seedbed. The crop has a requirement for high temperatures and cumulative day-degrees of heat (similar to maize). This effectively restricts the crop to the southern half of England. The crop is combine harvested in September, usually after desiccation. The crop should be cleaned and dried to 14% moisture and 2% admixture.

As a legume, soya is a good alternative break crop, largely fixing its own nitrogen. Maintenance P and K is required plus 10-20kg of N to get the crop started. Spray costs also tend to be low.

Target yield is 3.0t/ha but the average is likely to be less; an average of 2.5t/ha (1.0t/acre) can be assumed. The price is largely determined by the price of imported crop. The UK crop is GM free, for which a premium is paid. A further premium may be paid for Identity Preserved UK crop which goes into human consumption or for organically grown soya. For 2011 the price is estimated to be £325/tonne.

Sunflower

The UK imports the equivalent of about 400,000 tonnes of sunflower seed each year, mainly as sunflower oil. Currently none is commercially crushed in the UK. There has been continued interest in sunflower, but late harvests and low yields have restricted the development of the crop. Currently only about 500 ha are grown, producing some 1,000 tonnes of seed. Almost all UK production goes into the pet-food or bird seed market; with good demand, but only in localised areas. Producers should satisfy themselves of the end-market before planting the crop. The birdseed market takes 20,000 tonnes of sunflower seed annually, so there is scope for import substitution. Some attempts have been made to cold-press sunflowers to produce a UK-sunflower oil, but this market is still in its infancy.

Extra-early maturing semi-dwarf hybrid varieties are the most suitable to conditions in the UK. The crop needs a relatively mild climate and is best grown south-east of a line from the Wash to east Dorset.

Sowing is from April to early May when the soil temperature is 7-8°C. Although sunflower will grow on a broad range of soil types its capacity to do well in dry and sandy soils and areas of low rainfall is a recommendation. Pre-emergence weed control may be necessary; at the right plant density weeds should not subsequently be a problem. As it is a broad row crop, chemical or mechanical weed control is possible. Sclerotina and botrytis, in a wet season, may affect the crop; on areas of less than 6 ha bird damage can be serious. Sunflower has a low nitrogen requirement.

Harvesting is from mid-September by combine harvester. Yields of up to 2.5t/ha with oil content of 44% are possible. The crop is dried to 8-9% for safe storage, which can be expensive. The price is usually based on a premium over the price of oilseed rape (around £50/t), but other pricing mechanisms may be used in specialist markets. Growing costs will be in the region of £250-£300/ha.

Others

Other crops that have been in the news in recent years as possible new crops for the future (or present crops capable of substantial development) include the following: chickpeas and lentils, fenugreek, meadowfoam, cuphea, peppermint, quinoa, buckwheat, honesty and herbs for their essential oils. At present there are no reliable data for these crops on average yield expectations and little on prices or variable costs, when grown on a commercial scale in this country. A number of them are either for the health food market or are sources of oil for industry as replacements for whale oil and light mineral oil. Research continues on many of them. More details may be available from the contact listed below;

Contact: National Non-Food Crops Centre (NNFCC): www.nnfcc.co.uk

VINING PEAS

Production level	Low	Average	High
	£	£	£
Output	1000 (405)	1200 (486)	1500 (608)
Variable Costs:			
Seed...		205 (83)	
Fertiliser......................................		93 (38)	
Sprays...		114 (46)	
Total Variable Costs		412 (167)	
Gross Margin per ha (acre)	**588** (238)	**788** (319)	**1088** (441)

1. The table above relates to vining peas grown on contract where harvesting (approx. £65/tonne) and haulage (approx. £38/tonne) are paid for separately; the average price in this situation ranges from £250 to £320/tonne depending primarily on quality. The average yield is taken as 4.75 tonnes/ha; the national average (fresh weight) for the last five years has ranged between 3.8 and 4.9 although growers are paid on frozen weight. Top quality ('150 minute') peas have to be grown within 40 miles of the factory. More distant 'long haul' peas will be in the lower price range. A pea viner costs £300,000 - £350,000.

   The average yield of petit pois is lower but the price averages 12 to 15% more.

2. *Fertiliser.* many growers use no fertiliser; but RB209 suggests P&K. Here $P_2O_5:K_2O$ = 85:65kg/ha respectively.

3. *Sprays.* both herbicide and aphicide are commonly used with fungicides being used dependant on seasonal requirements.

4. *Labour:* see p.162.

5. *Total Area:* Around 34,000 ha are grown in the UK annually with a view to vining a 150,000-tonne crop.

MAINCROP POTATOES

Production level	Low	Average	High
Yield: tonnes per ha (tons per acre)	37.0 (15)	45.0 (18.2)	53.0 (21.5)
	£	**£**	**£**
Output	5180 (2098)	6300 (2552)	7420 (3005)
Variable Costs:			
Seed...		678 (275)	
Fertiliser.....................................		388 (157)	
Sprays..		553 (224)	
Casual lab. (harvest & grading)............	648 (262)	788 (319)	928 (376)
Sundries (levy, sacks, etc.)...............	380 (154)	432 (175)	489 (198)
Total Variable Costs	2647 (1072)	2839 (1150)	3036 (1230)
Gross Margin per ha (acre)	**2533** (1026)	**3461** (1402)	**4384** (1776)

1. *Prices.* The price assumed above is £150 per tonne for ware and £10 for stock feed (assumed to be 7½ per cent), which is £140 per tonne for the whole crop. The actual price in any one season depends largely on the national average yield but also increasingly international trade. Variations according to quality and market (as well as season) are now considerable. The seven-year average GB price for wares between 2002 and 2009 was £120/tonne.

2. *Physical Inputs.* Seed: 60% planted with certified seed: 2.8 tonnes per hectare at £220-280 per tonne (the price varies widely from season to season); 40% with once-grown seed: 2.6 tonnes per hectare at £180 per tonne. Sprays: herbicide, blight control, and haulm destruction.

3. *Casual Labour.* The figure in the table above is for assistance during (machine) harvesting and for grading/riddling (approx. £17.50/tonne); it is assumed that most of the labour for the latter is supplied by casuals.

4. *Contract* mechanical harvesting: approximately £580/hectare (excl. pickers, carting, etc.), £970 inc. carting. Other contract work see page 185.

5. *British Potato Council (AHDB) levy*: £40.17/ha (£16.27/acre) for growers in 2010, £45.32/ha for late payers; exempt from levy if less than 3ha grown. 2011 rates as yet unpublished.

6. *Potato Land Rentals* range depending on the year, location, soil and water from over £750/ha (£300/acre) to around £500/ha (£200/acre).

7. *Sacks.* Approx. £7.90 per tonne.

8. *Fuel and Repairs* (per hectare): £270.

9. *Specialised Equipment Prices*: see page 179.

10. *Potato Store Costs*: see page 212.

11. *Labour:* see p. 162.

EARLY POTATOES

Production level	Low	Average	High
Yield: tonnes per ha (tons per acre)	18.0 (7)	23.0 (9.3)	28.0 (11.3)
	£	**£**	**£**
Output	3420 (1385)	4370 (1770)	5320 (2155)
Variable Costs:			
Seed..		805 (326)	
Fertiliser.....................................		276 (112)	
Sprays...		278 (113)	
Casual labour...............................		360 (146)	
Sundries (levy, sacks, etc.)...............		275 (111)	
Total Variable Costs		1994 (808)	
Gross Margin per ha (acre)	**1426** (578)	**2376** (962)	**3326** (1347)

1. *Prices and Yields.* The price assumed above is an average of £190 per tonne for a 23 tonne/ha yield. However, yields increase and prices fall as the season progresses. Thus both depend on the date of lifting, e.g. late May to early June, 7 to 12 tonnes per hectare; July, 20 to 30 tonnes per hectare. Prices in late May to mid June are typically three times those in July; the very earliest crops (early May) can even fetch more than £1,000 per tonne, but the price could be down to £500 by mid May and to £250 or even £200 by the end of May (although in 2010 they remained far higher). Thus the average output of £4,370 given above could be obtained from 10 tonnes at £437 per tonne, 15 at £291, 20 at £218 or 30 at £145.

2. *Casual labour for planting*: £130 per hectare, plus help with harvesting/grading (£10/tonne).

3. *British Potato Council (AHDB) levy*: £40.17/ha (£16.27/acre) for growers in 2010, £45.32/ha for late payers; exempt from levy if less than 3ha grown. 2011 rates as yet unpublished.

4. *Fuel and Repairs* (£ per hectare): £245.

5. *Labour:* see p. 162.

    The percentages of the total potato area in Great Britain planted in early, second early and main crop, respectively are approximately 5, 31 and 63 in England, 20, 52 and 28 in Wales, 3, 38 and 59 in Scotland and 5, 33 and 62 of the total GB potato area.

SUGAR BEET

Production level	Low	Average	High
Yield: tonnes per ha (tons per acre)*	52.0 (21)	66.0 (26.7)	75.0 (30.4)
	£	**£**	**£**
Output	1445 (585)	1833.6 (743)	2084 (844)
Variable Costs:			
Seed……………………………….....		163 (66)	
Fertiliser………………………….…..		172 (70)	
Sprays…………………………….…..		180 (73)	
Transport (Contract)…………….........	237 (96)	300 (122)	341 (138)
Total Variable Costs	752 (304)	815 (330)	856 (347)
Gross Margin per ha (acre)	**693** (281)	**1018** (412)	**1227** (497)

* 'Adjusted tonnes' at standard 16% sugar content

1. *Prices*. The 'all-in' delivered price for the 2011 crop is expected to be £27.78 per adjusted tonne. This is based on 95% sold 'in contract' and 5% over contract tonnage. The 'in-contract' beet price is 23.60 plus average transport allowance of £4.75/tonne and the rest is forecast at £17/tonne.

   Late delivery bonus. 26December - 7 January: 0.8% of price; thereafter, the rate rises by 0.2% per day.

   As of the 2011 campaign, a new sugar beet pricing formula will be run in May/June, to arrive at the following year's price. It will take into account four elements:

   a) the direct costs of producing beet

   b) a fixed uplift over this figure to cover overheads and a margin

   c) a profit related adjustment linked to changes in currency

   d) a wheat price related bonus linked to the LIFFE wheat futures price.

2. *Effect of Harvesting Date*. As the season progresses, changes occur in the crop before lifting, approximately as follows:

	from early Sept to early Oct.	from early Oct to early Nov.	from early Nov to early Dec.	from early Dec to early Jan.
Yield (tons of washed beet /ha)	up 3.75	up 1.9	up 1.25	up 1.25
Sugar Content (%)	up 1%	up ¼%	down ¼%	down ¾%
Yield of Sugar (kg / ha)	up 1000	up 375	up 190	down 60

3. *Sprays*. Herbicides normally comprise 85% to 92.5% of the total spray cost.

4. *Contract*. Contract mechanical harvesting costs £220-£230 per hectare excluding carting or £255-£265 per hectare including carting.

5. *Transport*. Contract haulage charges vary according to distance to factory. The figure assumed above is approximately £4.75 per (unadjusted) tonne of unwashed beet including loading and cleaning (dirt and top tare assumed at 14% in total).

6. *Fuel and Repairs* (per hectare): £265

7. *Specialised Equipment Prices*: see page 179

8. *Labour*: see page 162

TOP FRUIT

The figures indicate a range within which the performance of most orchards is likely to fall. The gross margin is calculated as lower yields less lower costs/higher yields less higher costs. In practice, of course, higher yields are not necessarily linked to higher costs, and vice versa. Figures here are for established crops.

	Dessert Apples	Culinary Apples	Pears
Yield: tonnes/ha	15–55	25-50	15-30
Price (£/tonne)	500-850	250-500	450-650
	£	£	£
Output	7500-46750	6250-25000	6750-19500
Variable Costs*			
Orchard Depreciation	250-1600	150-1200	100-300
Fertilisers/Sprays	900-1350	700-1200	700-1050
Crop Sundries	50-200	50-100	50-100
Harvesting	825-3025	1125-2250	825-1650
Grading/Packing	1950-7150	3250-6500	1950-3900
Packaging	600-8250	400-3000	525-3000
Transport	850-4500	400-3000	600-1800
Commission/Levies	500-5000	300-2500	300-1950
Total Variable Costs*	5925-31075	6375-19750	5050-13750
Gross Margin	1575-15675	(125)-5250	1700-5750

* Excludes Storage

1. *Price:* Average of all grades. Price is not only influenced by grade-out, but also by variety, customer and pack format (which in turn may affect packing, packaging costs).

2. *Orchard Depreciation:* Establishment costs written off over lifetime of orchard. Establishment includes trees and stakes and, in newer plantings, support structures and irrigation. Total establishment costs of £4000 - £30,000 per hectare at planting densities of 750 – 4000 trees per hectare.

3. *Orchard Duration:* Traditional dessert apples around 20 years, with culinary and pears frequently 30 years plus. More recently planted denser apple systems likely to be nearer 15 years, with full cropping in years 3-5 (6-9 for traditional systems).

4. *Crop Sundries:* Including tree ties, stake replacement, bee hire, picking hods, etc.

5. *Harvesting:* Based on £55 per tonne average (to include supervision, Employer's NI & holiday allowance) for dessert apples and pears and £45 per tonne for bramley. In practice can vary significantly with variety, yield, fruit size and quality, etc.

6. *Grading and Packing:* Based on £130 per tonne. Can vary considerably, particularly with crop quality.

7. *Packaging:* Typical average of between £40 and £150 per tonne, although may be higher with specialist formats (e.g. overwrapped packs). Considerable variations arise from both crop quality (i.e. grade-out), customer and pack format.

8. *Transport:* Includes allowance for farm to packer cost, as well as delivery to final customer.

9. *Commission/Levies:* Including both marketeer's and retailer's commission, as well as levies (e.g. English Apples and Pears, HDC).

SOFT FRUIT

The figures indicate a range within which the performance of many, but not all crops is likely to fall. The gross margin is calculated as lower yields less lower costs/higher yields less higher costs. In practice, of course, higher yields are not necessarily linked to higher costs, and vice versa.

	Strawberries Raised Bed June bearers	*Strawberries Ever bearers*	*Raspberries*
Yield: tonnes/ha	18-23	20-30	8-15
Price (£/tonne)	2400-3000	2500-3300	5000-6750
	£	£	£
Output	43200-69000	50000-99000	40000-101250
Variable Costs			
Plants/planting/Sterilisation/Wirework	2850-3650	9500-15000	1400-1700
Structures (average annual cost)	5000-8000	5000-8000	5000-8000
Fertilisers/Sprays/Predators	950-1350	1000-1550	800-1150
Fieldwork	1500-3000	1800-3500	3000-4750
Harvesting	13000-17000	11000-19500	14000-26250
Grading/Packing	5850-7475	6500-9750	7600-14250
Packaging	6300-8050	7000-10500	3040-5700
Transport/Commission	5200-7800	6300-9500	4800-11250
Total Variable Costs	40650-56325	48100-77300	39640-73050
Gross Margin	3200-13550	2600-22650	360-28200

1. *Strawberries – June bearers:* Plants – assumes 35,000 per hectare with 60 day cropping in year 1 followed by 2 further years. Plants/planting/sterilisation written off over crop life of 3 years. Bed making not included as a variable cost.

    Structures – annual cost of poly-tunnels including both metalwork (w/o 10 years) and plastic (w/o 3 years). Costs also included for erection, dismantling and venting.

    Fieldwork – weeding, runner removal, leaf thinning etc.

    Harvesting- including supervision, Employer's NI & holiday allowance.

    Grading/Packing at £325 per tonne. Packaging at £350 per tonne.

2. *Strawberries – Ever bearers:* Plants – assumes 25,000 per hectare. Plants/planting written off over crop life of one year. Sterilisation cost w/o over 3 years. Bed making not included as a variable cost.

    Structures/ Fieldwork/ Harvesting / Grading, Packing / Packaging - as for June bearers.

3. *Raspberries:* Plants – 8000/ha at 40p per plant. Planting at 12p per plant.

    - Structures – as for strawberries.

    - Wirework – to include material and labour.

    - Plants/planting/wirework written off over crop life of 5 say years (crop life typically 4 to 7 years).

    - Harvesting (including supervision, employer's NI & holiday allowance) – at £1750 per tonne (£1.75 per kilo).

    - Grading/Packing – at £950 per tonne (95 pence per kilo).

    - Packaging – at £380 per tonne (38 pence per kilo).

Blackcurrants

Although a soft fruit, this crop is much more of a field crop grown on arable farms with machine harvesting. The majority of the UK blackcurrant crop is grown for processing into cordial drink. Typical output is 6-7 tonnes/ha sold at £650-£700 per tonne = £3,900-£4,900/ha, with annual variable costs of say £1,400/ ha (principally share of crop establishment, fertilisers and sprays) leaving a gross margin of £2,400-£3,500/ha. Establishment costs approximately £7,000/ha for bushes with full production in year 2 followed by up to 10 years cropping.

Acknowledgements (Top & Soft Fruit): Andersons Midlands and Farm Advisory Services Team Ltd.

FIELD-SCALE VEGETABLES

The enterprises shown are grown by 'non specialist' farmers with suitable land, and the figures shown are on the basis that these output levels and variable costs represent 'typical' levels for the farmer with other major costs such as harvesting, packing and marketing expenses born by the produce company taking the crop.

Per Hectare (acre)	Dry Bulb Onions	Cauliflower	Calabrese
Yield: tonnes/ha (tons/acre).	41 (16.6)		
Net Price (£/tonne)	100		
	£	£	£
Output	4,100 (1659)	2,150 (871)	1,950 (790)
Variable Costs:			
Seed	600 (235)	860 (348)	754 (305)
Fertiliser	319 (129)	376 (152)	339 (137)
Sprays	530 (215)	180 (73)	208 (84)
Total Variable Costs	1,449 (587)	1,416 (573)	1,301 (527)
Gross Margin	2,651 (1074)	734 (297)	649 (263)

Most of the fresh produce crops included in past Editions such as carrots, parsnips, leeks, lettuce, rhubarb, and many of the brassicas, are now grown predominantly by a few highly specialised growers or produce companies. These growers supply the multiple retailers with high volumes and work to high specification. The other key market for fresh produce is the local market with growers usually on a small scale and often tied into a local food chain such as a farm shop. These crops have a high entry cost relative to other cropping alternatives, and bear significant risk. It is therefore necessary to research carefully the potential end market in terms of its expectations and cost structure.

HOPS

Output Data

Yield: 2009; 26.73 zentners per ha (1 zentner = 50 kg), 2008, 26.31 z/ha 2004-2008 average: 27.25 zentners; range 26.0 (2006) to 31.6 (2004).

Average Price (£ per zentner)	Contract	Spot	Overall
2002	177	114	142
2003	160	104	155
2004	164	67	134
2005	191	136	186
2006	199	-	198
2007	241	419	254
2008	241	394	265
2009	284	356	305

Main Varieties	2009		prices (£ per zentner) 2009			2008		
	Ha	(z./ha)	contract	spot	overall	contract	spot	overall
Target	111	32.5	136	157	183	126	340	151
Challenger	81	30.0	250	320	259	230	-	230
Goldings	199	26.8	250	370	297	250	450	288
Fuggles	103	33.2	285	345	300	260	450	307
First Gold	162	15.2	300	300	300	178	450	185
Phoenix	9	35.5	195	-	195	170	350	200
Admiral	46	39.7	230	357	238	150	324	165
Others	352	26.4	260	350	325			300
Organic	19	13.0	650	-	650	560	-	560

Total area of hops (ha): 2009; 1080.7, 2008: 1,071ha, 1997: 3,067; 1984: 5,091.

Variable Costs per mature hectare (acre) (materials only)	£/ha	(£/ac)
Fertilisers and Manure	225	(91)
Insecticide / Fungicide	618	(250)
Herbicide	133	(54)
String	198	(80)
Pockets / Bales	63	(26)
Drying Fuel	475	(192)
Total	1,713	(694)

Average Direct Labour Costs per mature hectare (acre)	£/ha	(£/ac)
Growing	1,162	(471)
Picking	2,083	(844)
Drying	489	(198)
Total	3,734	(1,512)

A new hop garden (erecting the poles, wiring and planting) could cost in the order of £20,000 per hectare (£8,000 per acre).

Acknowledgement: Thanks to - Chris Daws, English Hops and Herbs.

VINEYARDS

As at August 2009 the total area under vines in England and Wales was 1,215 hectares, although the actual area in production was 946 ha. This was the highest recorded area since the 'revival' of English wine industry in the 1980's. Total plantings have increased markedly in the last few years, after hitting a low point of 773 ha in 2004. Industry observers estimate that these official figures underestimate the area planted and that today (2010) the area under vines is nearer 1,400 ha.

There were 381 registered vineyards as at August 2009; any vineyard over 0.1 ha must be registered with the Wine Standards Branch of the Food Standards Agency (FSA), though many of the smaller vineyards are run purely as a hobby. Although the average size of vineyards in the UK is only 3.2 ha, there are several vineyards of over 100 ha and around 60 vineyards account for 70% of the planted area.

In 2009 2,383,500 litres (2,520 litres per productive hectare) were produced in the UK. This was a particularly good year after poor average yields in both 2007 and 2008. The five-year average yield is 2,078 litres per ha. The low level of these average figures is down to there being many young vineyards included, together with vineyards that are under-performing and poorly managed. Yields in well run, favourably sited vineyards would be many times these levels. Around 80% of production is white wine and 20% red or rosé. Since the very warm year of 2003, the plantings of Champagne varieties (Chardonnay, Pinot Noir and Meunier) have increased significantly, and almost all plantings in the last few years (2004-2010) have been for the production of sparkling wine. Pinot Noir is now the most widely planted variety (300 ha), followed by Chardonnay (250 ha). Although these varieties now account for around 50% of the total vine area, the amount of sparkling wine on the market is still small as bottle-fermented sparkling wines take between 2 and 5 years to mature after bottling.

There is no EU ban on planting vines in the UK, and in 2008 it was confirmed that there will not be one in the future, whatever level production reaches. Changes to the vine variety legislation also mean that from August 2009, almost any variety may be legally planted in the UK. From 2009, to conform with EU legislation, English table wine is now called United Kingdom wine and may bear the vintage and name of the grape varieties.

A Quality Wine Scheme for England and Wales was introduced in 1991 and a Regional Wine Scheme in 1997. Hybrid varieties may be planted in the UK but may not currently be made into Quality Wine. They may be used for Quality Sparkling Wine and Regional Wine. From the 2003 vintage, regional wines have been allowed to carry details of vintage, vineyard and varieties on their labels. Since then there has been a marked increase in successful applications for Quality and Regional wine labelling and overall, quality levels have risen. Sparkling wines are not currently covered by the Quality or Regional Wine Schemes but will be from December 2010. A new system of Protected Designation of Origin and Protected Geographical Indications will come into place which will be available for still wines as well as sparkling wines.

Domestically-produced wine supplies only 0.3% of the home market. The UK Vineyards Association (UKVA) has set up a marketing arm, English Wine Producers, to promote all English wine. All wines sold in the UK bear the same VAT and duty, irrespective of origin (although the duty on sparkling wines is higher than that for still wines). A significant proportion of home-produced wine is sold at the farm gate but supermarkets and off-licences are increasingly stocking it

The quality of any wine is dependent on the quality of the site, and vineyards ideally need south facing, well-drained and sheltered land, less than 100 metres (330 ft.) above sea level, in the southern half of England or Wales. A high level of management and marketing is essential, as is expert advice. There is no minimum area for profitable production. A small enterprise selling wine at the farm gate and to local hotels and restaurants may be more profitable than one with 10 hectares selling only grapes. Some vineyards have associated gift shops and restaurants and are involved with corporate entertaining, which provide extra income. It is now possible to grow grapes under contract for several successful vineyard-wineries that have run out of suitable land of their own. Contracts vary, but prices can be up to £1,000/tonne for grapes for still wine and £1,500/tonne for sparkling.

The main growing system used in modern UK vineyards is the intensive Double Guyot; also the most commonly found in France and Germany. Other systems such as the extensive Geneva Double Curtain (GDC) and the divided canopy Scott Henry system are occasionally found, but are not the first choice of today's growers. The Double Guyot system will yield little until year 3 and with good management should be in full production in year 4. Geneva Double Curtain will not have a full yield until year 5 or 6 but crops more heavily. The Scott-Henry system crops fully in year 4 or 5.

Investment capital (to include materials and labour for planting and the first two years establishment but not the cost of the land) of £18,000 to £24,000/ha is typically required for the vineyard. Equipment for a winery costs a minimum of £50,000-£60,000 and a suitable building is needed. Contract winemaking is, however, generally considered better for smaller vineyards of less than 4 ha as it gives them access to state-of-the-art equipment and techniques. Growers who produce their own wine will also have to budget for the picking, processing and bottling of at least two vintages (still wine) or three to five vintages (sparkling wine) before income from selling their wines starts making a meaningful contribution to the enterprise.

Yields and quality are very variable, according to the variety of grape, the year and the quality of management - in particular the quality of pest and disease control. In a reasonable year a well-sited, well-managed vineyard should yield 7.5-10.0 tonnes/ha (3-4 tonnes/acre), but higher annual yields are possible. An average yield over ten years could be around 8.65 tonnes/ha (3.5 tonnes/acre). For still wine production, around 950 75cl bottles will be produced from 1 tonne of grapes; for sparkling wine the production will be nearer 750-800 75cl bottles per tonne.

The following costs refer to a commercial enterprise on a suitable site with a broad variety range. Establishment costs could be double if the site has to be drained and provided with windbreaks and rabbit and deer fencing. Annual growing costs can also be significantly greater, depending on planting density, variety, yield and management.

	Double Guyot	
	per ha	per acre
Number of Vines	2,600 - 5,000	(1,050 - 2,020)
	£ per ha	£ per acre
Establishment Costs:	over two years	
Materials	14,800	5,990
Labour	12,350	4,998
Total Establishment Costs	**27,150**	**10,988**
Subsequent Annual Costs:		
Materials	975	395
Labour (growing)	3,850	1,558
Harvesting*	450	182
Total Variable Costs	**5,275**	**2,135**

*   Harvesting costs are very yield dependent. Growers without wineries will also have transport costs.

Prices: Grape prices will vary according to the variety and the vintage. They range from £600 to £1,000 /tonne delivered to a winery. Pinot Noir or Chardonnay for sparkling wine may be £1,200 to £1,500 /tonne. Wine prices vary widely but are likely to be in the range £5 to £6.50 per bottle for typical still white wines, and up to £10 for red wine at retail. English sparkling wine may retail at £15 to £20 a bottle but is more costly to produce. A retail price for still wine of at least £6.00 /bottle is necessary to break even for most enterprises.

e.g.   £6.00 less 20% VAT and £1.69① duty = £3.31②

Less own winery costs (materials and labour) £1.75 per bottle③ = £1.56.

At 8.65 tonnes per ha and 950 bottles per tonne = £12,819 /ha (£5,190/acre).

①   Sparkling wine of 8.5% or more has a duty rate of £2.16 per 75cl bottle; still wines £1.69 per 75cl bottle

②   If wines are sold via a wholesaler and/or retailer, gross profit margin of at least 10% (wholesaler) and 30% (retailer) on duty-paid prices must be allowed for.

③   Having still wine made under contract costs about £2.50 a bottle. Sparkling wine will be £5.00 per bottle.

Acknowledgements: Thanks to - Stephen Skelton MW, Viticultural Consultant, 1B Lettice Street, London, SW6 4EH. Tel: 07768 583 700. www.englishwine.com United Kingdom Vineyards Association, Mrs Sian Liwicki, General Secretary, PO Box 534, Abingdon, OX14 9BZ. Tel: 01865 390 188.

2. GRAZING LIVESTOCK

DAIRY COWS

Holstein Friesians (per cow per year)

Yield Group (1)	Low	Average	High	Very High
Milk Yield per Cow (litres) (2)	5,500	7,000	8,000	9,000
	£	£	£	£
Milk Value per Cow (3)	1347.5	1715	1960	2205
Plus Value of Calves (4)	119	126	125	124
Plus Value of Cull Cows (5)	112.5	112.5	112.5	112.5
Less Cost or Market Value of Replacements (6, 7)	£350	350	350	350
Output	1229	1603.5	1847.5	2091.5
Concentrate Costs (8)	248	330	429	536
Miscellaneous Variable Costs (10)	205	211	219	230
Gross Margin before deducting Forage Variable Costs (inc. Bought Fodder)	777	1063	1200	1325
Margin of Milk over Concentrates (MOC) (9)	1100	1385	1531	1669

Gross Margins per Cow and per Hectare (acre) at 4 different stocking rates (11)

Performance Level	Low	Average	High	Very High
1. **At 1·75 cows per forage hectare (low):**				
(0·57 forage hectares (1·4 acres) per cow)				
Forage Var. Costs & Bulk Feeds per Cow (11)	110	110	110	110
Gross Margin per Cow	667	953	1090	1216
Gross Margin per Forage Hectare	1167	1667	1907	2127
Gross Margin per Forage Acre	472	674	771	860
2. **At 2 cows per forage hectare (average):**				
(0·5 forage hectares (1·25 acres) per cow)				
Forage Var. Costs & Bulk Feeds per Cow (11)	**138**	**138**	**138**	**138**
Gross Margin per Cow	**638**	**924**	**1061**	**1187**
Gross Margin per Forage Hectare	**1277**	**1849**	**2123**	**2374**
Gross Margin per Forage Acre	**516**	**748**	**858**	**960**
3. **At 2·25 cows per forage hectare (high):**				
(0·45 forage hectares (1·1 acres) per cow)				
Forage Var. Costs & Bulk Feeds per Cow (11)	154	154	154	154
Gross Margin per Cow	622	908	1045	1171
Gross Margin per Forage Hectare	1400	2044	2352	2635
Gross Margin per Forage Acre	566	826	951	1065
4. **At 2·5 cows per forage hectare (very high):**				
(0·4 forage hectares (1 acre) per cow)				
Forage Var. Costs & Bulk Feeds per Cow (11)	181	181	181	181
Gross Margin per Cow	595	881	1018	1144
Gross Margin per Forage Hectare	1489	2204	2546	2860
Gross Margin per Forage Acre	602	891	1030	1157

1. *Yield group per cow:* Increases in this are usually (though not necessarily) associated with more intensive farming operations. Intensification focuses on higher gross

margins per hectare, whilst extensification on higher gross margins of other resources. Increase in concentrate feeding (kg/litre) and other inputs have been assumed as yields rise: see note 8.

2. *Yield.* The yield is annual herd production divided by the average number of cows and calved heifers in the herd. The average yield given (7,000 litres) is an estimated national figure for sizeable herds of black and white cows in 2011. The average yield for organic milk producers is around 6,500 litres.

3. *Milk Price:* This is assumed (as an average for the 2011 calendar year) to be 24.5p per standard litre, after deducting transport costs. It incorporates adjustments for milk composition and seasonality assuming an average-sized herd. Smaller herds achieve a lower price. The average price received by individual producers depends on seasonality of production and compositional quality.

Output and Gross Margin Change from a 0.25p/l price change per Cow

Low	Average	High	Very High
±£13.75	±£17.50	±£20.00	±£22.50

Seasonality Price Adjustments. These are diverse between the various dairy companies. An increasing number of companies no longer operate conventional seasonal adjustments but instead have payment systems that encourage a level monthly production, with a range of deductions and bonuses related to the individual producer's spring and autumn deliveries. The average adjustments for a selection of companies operating conventional adjustments are as follows in 2010/11:

April	May	June	July	Aug	Sept	Oct	Nov	Dec	Jan– Mar
–2	–3	–2	0	+1.5	+2	+2	+1.5	+0	0.00

Some companies also offer a premium for a level delivery option if supplies in a calendar month are within 10% of an agreed daily volume; the premium is typically 0·2 ppl. The trend towards new production profile payments is continuing, with more and more co-ops and companies introducing them, along with more individual pricing mechanisms.

Compositional Quality Payments:

Constituent values vary widely between buyers and months. As an example, the average values for the major dairies, in July 2010 were:

Butterfat: between 1.1p and 2.5p per litre per 1 per cent; average 2.0p.

Protein: between 1.9p and 4.6p per litre per 1 per cent; average 3.5p.

The *standard litre* is 4·15% butterfat and 3·35% protein.

Proportional Split of Dairy Breeds and milk Compositions

	Cows %	Butterfat %	Protein %
Holstein Friesian........................	96	3·93	3·20
Ayrshire.................................	1·4	4·1	3·33
Jersey....................................	1·3	5·39	3·87
Guernsey.................................	1·0	4·66	3·57
Dairy Shorthorn........................	0·3	3·86	3·29
All Breeds...............................		3·94	3·23

Data from Dairy Co data from Defra.

Within Breed Quality Variation. For Holstein Friesians without going to extremes the range can easily be: 3.5% to 4.1% butterfat and 3.1% to 3.4% protein. The difference in value between these two levels combined is about 2.25p per litre depending on milk contract. This is being achieved by both breeding and feeding for different milk quality to meet varying contractual requirements.

Hygiene Price Adjustments. These vary widely between the different dairy companies. A mid-2010 example is as follows:

A. *Bactoscan (bacteria measure)*

Bactoscan Reading	Price Adjustment (ppl)
0- 50,000	+0.5
51-100,000	nil
101-200,000	− 1
Over 200,000*	− 6
Over 250,000**	−10

*1st month. **2nd and any subsequent months.

B. *Somatic Cell Count (Mastitis)*

Count	Price Adjustment (ppl)
0-200,000	+ 0.5
201-250,000	nil
251-300,000	− 0.5
301-400,000	− 2
Over 400,000*	− 6
Over 400,000**	−10

*1st month. **2nd and any subsequent months.

Several milk buyers have no bonus for top hygiene bands, they expect suppliers to deliver top quality milk in order to receive the standard litre price.

C. *Antibiotics.* The price of all milk in a consignment that fails an antibiotics test ranges from 1-5p/litre.

Organic milk. Organic milk price fluctuates over a large range depending on supply and demand. Farmgate organic milk price currently about 6ppl more than conventional farmgate price. Organic milk price for 2011 is forecast at 30.5ppl, 6ppl above conventional. Organic dairy feed is £280/tonne for 2011; this is 3.3ppl more expensive than conventional feed.

4. *Value of Calves.* Average annual value per cow at 10-20 days old, allowing for 5% mortality and an average calving index of 385 days.

Average value comprised as follows:

Dairy bull calf	(dairy x dairy)	£ 45
Dairy heifer calf	(dairy x dairy)	£160 (non-freemartin)
Cross bred bull	(beef x dairy)	£160
Cross bred heifer	(beef x dairy)	£130
Average		£126 after mortality

High yield herds normally have less beef genetics so dairy bull calves are less valuable than from lower yielding herds.

5. *Value of Cull Cows.* £450 allowing for casualties and a 25% per year replacement rate.

6. *Cost of Replacements* (N.B. average in 2010). £350 is £1,400 per down-calving heifer (purchase price or market value (mainly home-reared)) and a 25% per year replacement rate.

7. *Herd Depreciation* thus averages £238 per cow per year, i.e., 25 per cent of £1,050 (i.e., £1,400-£450).

Net Replacement Cost = £112 to £119 per cow per year, i.e., herd depreciation (£238) less value of calves (£119 to £126).

Bull. AI is assumed in the tables; bull depreciation would be approx. £150 a year (£1,500 purchase price less £750 cull value, 5-year herd life); tight calving pattern: 60 cows per bull, well spread calving pattern: 100; 10 to 20 tonnes silage, 0·75 tonnes concentrates a year. Very high yield herds may use more expensive (dairy) bulls reaching £2,000 purchase price).

8. *Concentrate Costs.*

Amounts:	*Yield Group*	*Low*	*Average*	*High*	*Very High*
	kg/litre (approx.)	0.273	0.286	0.325	0.361
	tonnes/cow	1.50	2.00	2.60	3.25
	pence / litre (ppl)	4.50	4.71	5.36	5.96
	pence/ marginal litre*		5.50	9.90	10.73

* *This is the additional cost of feed between yield groups, and the cost of the additional feed divided by the additional litres production.*

Concentrate Price: taken (for 2011) as £165 per tonne, which is an average of home-mixed rations and purchased compounds of varying nutritive value, averaged throughout the year. Use of blends and straights are currently about 5-6% cheaper at £155/tonne average and compounds £175/tonne.

A difference of £5 per tonne has approximately the following effect on margin over concentrates and gross margin per cow, on the assumptions made regarding the quantity fed at each performance level:

Low	Average	High	Very High
±£7.50	±£10.00	±£13.00	±£16.25

Seasonality: Typically, specialist spring calving herds (60% or more calvings between January and May) use 0.09 kg per litre / 630 kg (£104) per cow per year less concentrates compared with autumn calving herds (60% or more calvings between August and December). See further note 12 below.

Typical Monthly Variation in Concentrate Feeding (kg per litre, 7,000 litre herd)

Winter			Summer	
October	0.30		April	0.27
November	0.33		May	0.16
December	0.33		June	0.16
January	0.33		July	0.22
February	0.33		August	0.24
March	0.30		September	0.27
Average winter: 0.32			Average summer: 0.22	
Weighted average whole year: 0.28				

The distribution on farm varies according to factors such as seasonality of calving, milk yield, summer grazing productivity, the quantity and quality of winter bulk feeds, and turnout and housing dates. The March figure in particular will be affected by type of soil and seasonal rainfall.

Yield with no concentrates and good quality silage: approximately 4000 litres for spring calvers.

9. Margin over Concentrates and Concentrates per litre

The emphasis in the initial tables should be laid on the differences between the margin of milk value over concentrates per cow; the same large variation can occur with widely differing combinations of milk yield and quantity of concentrates fed.

In the following table, at each yield level figures are given for *(a) margin of milk value over concentrates* per cow (£) and (b) *concentrates per litre* (kg) at seven levels of concentrate feeding.

Margin Over Concentrates (£) and Concentrates per Litre (kg)

Yield Level	Low		Average		High		Very High	
Milk yield per cow (litres)	5,500		7,000		8,000		9,000	
	(a)	(b)	(a)	(b)	(a)	(b)	(a)	(b)
Concentrates per cow	£	kg	£	kg	£	kg	£	kg
1.0 tonne (£165)	1,183	0.18	1,550	0.14	-	-	-	-
1.5 tonne (£248)	1,100	0.27	1,467	0.21	1,712	0.19	-	-
2.0 tonne (£330)	1,018	0.36	1,385	0.29	1,630	0.25	1,875	0.22
2.5 tonne (£413)	-	-	1,302	0.36	1,547	0.31	1,792	0.28
3.0 tonne (£495)	-	-	-	-	1,465	0.38	1,710	0.33
3.5 tonne (£578)	-	-	-	-	-	-	1,627	0.39
4.0 tonne (£660)	-	-	-	-	-	-	1,545	0.44

At £165/tonne, 1kg feed costs 16.5p. This means that using 0.44kg feed per litre would cost 7.26p for every litre of milk.

10. *Miscellaneous Variable Costs (average)*

	£
Bedding*	60
Vet. and Med**	64
A.I. and Bull Hire**	30
Recording, Consultancy, Consumables, Dairy Stores	57
Total	211

* Straw can vary from 0.4 to 1.5 tonne per cow and from £45 to £65 per tonne (or even more in some areas in exceptional years).

** Both Vet and Med and A.I. and Bull Hire tend to increase with higher milk yield. This explains the higher variable costs in the higher milk yield data.

11. *Stocking Rate and Forage Costs.* The stocking rates given assume that nearly all requirements of bulk foods – both winter and summer – are obtained from the forage area, i.e. little is bought in. On average about 55 per cent of the forage area (or production) is grazed and 45 per cent conserved. Note that as the stocking density increases, gross margin per cow falls, but gross margin per hectare rises.

The levels of nitrogen on forage area are assumed to be as follows:

Stocking rate Cows per Ha (acre)	Kg N/Ha	units/acre
1.75 (0.7)	180	143
2.00 (0.8)	220	175
2.25 (0.9)	275	220
2.50 (1.0)	360	287

An increase in potash application is also assumed. Seed costs clearly depend on the percentage of permanent pasture, if any, the length of leys, etc. The following total variable costs per hectare (fertiliser, seed and sprays) have been assumed for grassland:

Inputs per hectare of forage area depending on stocking rate

Stocking rate Cows per Ha (acre)	£/Ha	£/acre
1.75 (0.7)	148	60
2.00 (0.8)	212	86
2.25 (0.9)	259	105
2.50 (1.0)	338	137
Forage Maize	325	132

Refer to the Forage Variable Cost section for more information on this. A small amount of purchased bulk fodder is normal, and is included in these costings increasing with the stocking rate as follows (per cow): low £25, average £32, high £39, very high £46, raised for 2011 based on expected short supply in some regions.

An increase in stocking density can be obtained not only by intensifying grassland production, as above, but also by buying in winter bulk fodder (assuming the same level of concentrate feeding in both cases). Theoretically, a zero-grazed farm buying in forage needs no land. In this situation, the gross margin per hectare could be extreme.

Overheads such as labour and depreciation on buildings are likely to increase per hectare and fall per cow as stocking density rises. Management challenges occur with higher stocking rates such as poaching which can be alleviated with good cow tracks. In addition the Nitrate Vulnerable Zone regulations must still be met.

12 *Seasonality.* Price and concentrate feeding differences according to the seasonality of production have already been outlined in notes 3 and 8.

Under similar levels of management mainly autumn calving herds average up to 1,000 litres more milk/cow/year than mainly spring calving herds but feed around a tonne more concentrates per cow/year; spring calving herds should normally only be feeding about 0.15 kg/litre. The average milk price would be expected to be higher for autumn calving herds, but the difference is less than might be supposed and has been steadily reduced with better prices being paid for summer milk.

13. *Quota.* The milk quota policy will end on 31 March 2015. To make gentle transition to this date, more quota is being allocated to all producers (see chapter III Section 1 for details). UK milk production is now so far below total quota restrictions, the regime is irrelevant.

14. *Labour:* see page 174.

15. *Building Costs:* see page 212.

Costs of Milk Production per Litre (Holstein Friesians)

	Average (pence)		Premium (pence)	
Concentrates	4.71		4.01	
Forage and Bought Bulk Feed	1.97		2.21	
Vet. & Med.	0.91		0.61	
Other Variable Costs	2.10		1.47	
Total Variable Costs		9.70		8.30
Labour: direct (milking etc.)	3.86		3.32	
: field/farm work	1.13		0.77	
Power and Machinery	3.96		3.11	
Rent/Rental Value	1.50		1.15	
General Overheads	1.25		1.07	
Total Fixed Costs		11.69		9.42
Net Replacement Cost *(Herd Dep'n)*		3.39		2.65
Total		**24.78**		**20.37**

1. *The average variable costs* per litre are derived from the data (and therefore the assumptions made) in the main per cow cost table using the 7,000l per cow data. The labour cost is linked to page 174. The average fixed costs are as for the medium-sized farm data on page 202, with adjustments made to allow for the greater use of resources by dairy cows compared with followers (and possibly cereals). The 'Premium' figures are as estimated for the average of the most profitable 10% of herds, with lower than average costs per cow (except forage costs).

2. *Labour* includes farmer and any unpaid family labour.

3. *Power and machinery* cover all machinery and equipment costs, including the use of farm vehicles, etc.

4. *General overheads* similarly relate to the whole farm, including property repairs.

5. Neither interest on capital nor any management charge have been included.

Channel Island Breeds

Performance level (yield)	Low	Average	High	Very High
Milk Yield per Cow (litres) (1)	4,150	5,000	5,550	6,250
	£	£	£	£
Milk Value per Cow (2)	1162	1400	1554	1750
Concentrate Costs (3)	149	231	289	396
Margin of Milk over Concentrates (MOC)	1014	1169	1265	1354
Herd Depreciation less calf value (4)	170	170	170	170
Miscellaneous Variable Costs (5)	205	211	219	230
Gross Margin per cow before deducting Forage Variable Costs	639	788	876	954
Forage Variable Costs (inc. Bought Fodder)	113	120	127	134
Gross Margin per Cow	525	668	749	820
Gross Margin per Forage Hectare (6) (2.4 cows per ha: 0.42ha/cow)	1260	1602	1797	1967
Gross Margin per Forage Acre (1.05 cows per acre: 0.97acre/cow)	510	649	728	797

1. *Yield.* Average of Jerseys and Guernseys. See Note 2 for Holstein Friesians (page 42). Guernsey yield averages slightly higher than Jerseys and Jerseys achieve a higher butterfat and protein (see page 42).

2. *Milk Price.* This is 28.50p per litre (average of Jerseys and Guernseys), i.e. 4.0p above Holstein Friesian milk; (30p Jersey milk, 27.5p Guernsey). In addition to the higher price obtained through the higher compositional quality for Channel Island milk some companies pay a premium for Channel Island milk.

3. *Concentrate Costs.* The price taken (for 2011) is £165 per tonne.

Amounts:	Yield Group	Low	Average	High	Very High
	kg/litre	0.27	0.33	0.39	0.44
	tonnes/cow	1.33	1.80	2.28	2.81
	pence / litre (ppl)	4.52	5.54	6.42	7.30
	pence/ marginal litre*		15.35	15.84	17.66

    * *This is the additional cost of feed between yield groups, and the cost of the additional feed divided by the additional litres production.*

4. *Net Annual Replacement Value*: (i.e. Value of Calves less Herd Depreciation) were calculated as follows:

	£ per cow in herd
Cost of replacements: 25% of herd per year @ £1,000	250
Less Value of culls: 25% of herd per year @ £200 (allowing for casualties)*	50
Herd Depreciation	200
Annual Value of Calves**	30
Net Annual Replacement Cost	170

    * Cull cow prices for Guernseys are about £40 higher than for Jerseys.

    ** Allowing for calving index of 390 days and calf mortality; mixture of pure bred calves and beef crosses. Guernsey calves, especially crosses, fetch more than Jersey calves, averaging perhaps £10 more per head and substantially more for some Guernsey beef crosses.

5. *Miscellaneous Variable Costs.* See Note 10 for Holstein Friesians (page 45).

6. *Stocking Rate.* See, in general, Note 11 for Holstein Friesians (page 45). The effect of varying the stocking rate on gross margin per forage hectare is as follows:

Gross Margin per Cow before deducting Forage V.C.s

Cows per Forage Hectare	Forage Hectares (acres) per cow	Low £639	Average £788	High £876	Very High £954	Forage V.C. £ per cow*
		Gross Margin £ per Forage Ha (acre)				
2.1	0.48 (1.18)	1183 (479)	1497 (606)	1683 (681)	1846 (748)	75
2.4	**0.42 (1.03)**	**1260 (510)**	**1619 (656)**	**1831 (741)**	**2017 (817)**	**113**
2.7	0.37 (0.91)	1393 (564)	1797 (728)	2035 (824)	2245 (909)	122
3.0	0.33 (0.82)	1509 (611)	1958 (793)	2222 (900)	2456 (994)	135

* A small amount of purchased bulk fodder is assumed, increasing with the stocking rate as follows (per cow): low £25, average £32, high £39 very high £46.

At the average stocking rate given above for combined Channel Island breeds (2.4 cows per forage hectare) the average figure for Jerseys would be approximately 2.55 and that for Guernseys 2.25 cows per forage hectare.

Ayrshires

Performance level (yield)	Low	Average	High	Very High
Milk Yield per Cow (litres) (1)	5,300	6,000	6,700	7,400
	£	£	£	£
Milk Value per Cow (2)	1405	1590	1776	1961
Concentrate Costs (3)	202	260	324	395
Margin of Milk over Concentrates (MOC)	1202	1330	1451	1566
Herd Depreciation less calf value (4)	170	170	170	170
Miscellaneous Variable Costs (5)	205	211	219	230
Gross Margin per cow before deducting Forage Variable Costs	827	949	1062	1166
Forage Variable Costs (inc. Bought Fodder)	113	120	127	134
Gross Margin per Cow	714	829	935	1031
Gross Margin per Forage Hectare (6) (2.4cows per ha: 0.42ha/cow)	1713	1989	2243	2474
Gross Margin per Forage Acre (1.05cows per acre: 0.97acre/cow)	694	805	909	1002

1. *Yield.* See Note 2 for Holstein Friesians (page 42).

2. *Milk Price.* See in general, note 3 for Holstein Friesians (page 42). The price assumed in the above table is 26.5p per litre. The compositional quality of milk from Ayrshires is higher than for the black and white breeds.

3. *Concentrate Costs.* See notes 8 and 9 for Holstein Friesians. In the above table, the levels of feeding kg/litre (and tonnes per cow) are as follows: low 0.25kg/l (1.225 tonne/cow), average 0.275kg (1.575t), high 0.30kg (1.965t), very high 0.325 (2.397t); price £165 per tonne.

4. *Net Annual Replacement Value*: i.e. Value of Calves less Herd Depreciation is calculated as follows:

	£ per cow in herd
Cost of replacements: 25 per cent of herd per year @ £1,000	250
Less Value of culls: 25 per cent of herd per year @ £200 (allowing for casualties)............	50
Herd Depreciation..…......	200
Annual Value of Calves*....................................…...	30
Net Annual Replacement Cost	170

*Allowing for calving index of 385 days and calf mortality; mixture of pure bred calves and beef crosses.

5. *Miscellaneous Variable Costs*. See Note 10 for Holstein Friesians (page 45).

6. *Stocking Rate*. See, in general, Note 11 for Holstein Friesians (page 45).

Shorthorns. The above data could be used for Shorthorns, although one would expect their average yield to be about 5% lower, their cull and calf prices to be higher and their stocking rate to be slightly lower – similar to Holstein Friesians.

DAIRY FOLLOWERS

(per Heifer reared)

A. Holstein Fresians

Performance Level	Low	Average	High
	£	£	£
Value of heifer (allowing for culls) (1)	1260	1260	1260
Less Value of calf (2)	200	200	200
Output	1060	1060	1060
Variable Costs:			
Concentrate Costs (3)	215	196	176
Miscellaneous Variable Costs (4)	138	125	113
Total Variable Costs			
(excluding Forage)	353	321	289
Gross Margin per Heifer, before			
deducting Forage Variable Costs	707	739	771
Forage Variable Costs (5)	100	100	102
Gross Margin per Heifer	608	640	670
Forage Hectares (Acres) per Heifer			
reared (6)	0.95 (2.3)	0.73 (1.8)	0.58 (1.4)
Gross Margin per Forage Hectare (7)	640	882	1165
Gross Margin per Forage Acre	259	357	472

B. Channel Island Breeds

Performance Level	Low	Average	High
	£	£	£
Value of heifer (allowing for culls) (1)	900	900	900
Less Value of calf (2)	30	30	30
Output	870	870	870
Variable Costs:			
Concentrate Costs (3)	183	166	150
Miscellaneous Variable Costs (4)	124	113	101
Total Variable Costs			
(excluding Forage)	307	279	251
Gross Margin per Heifer, before			
deducting Forage Variable Costs	563	591	619
Forage Variable Costs (5)	90	90	91
Gross Margin per Heifer	474	501	528
Forage Hectares (Acres) per Heifer			
reared (6)	0.68 (1.7)	0.58 (1.4)	0.50 (1.2)
Gross Margin per Forage Hectare (7)	702	872	1055
Gross Margin per Forage Acre	284	353	427

N.B. on average Channel Island heifers calve about three months younger than Holstein Fresian Heifers

C. Ayrshires

Performance Level	Low	Average	High
	£	£	£
Value of heifer (allowing for culls) (1)	800	800	800
Less Value of calf (2)	30	30	30
Output	770	770	770
Variable Costs:			
Concentrate Costs (3)	194	176	158
Miscellaneous Variable Costs (4)	127	115	104
Total Variable Costs			
(excluding Forage)	320	291	262
Gross Margin per Heifer, before			
deducting Forage Variable Costs	450	479	508
Forage Variable Costs (5)	72	72	73
Gross Margin per Heifer	378	407	435
Forage Hectares (Acres) per Heifer			
reared (6)	0.68 (1.7)	0.58 (1.4)	0.50 (1.2)
Gross Margin per Forage Hectare (7)	560	708	870
Gross Margin per Forage Acre	227	287	352

1. *Heifer values* are based on the purchase price of down-calving heifers, allowing for culls. Most heifers are home-reared. If heifers are reared for sale, the price of whole batches is likely to be lower than the values given in the tables, by 10 or 15 per cent. On the other hand the purchaser will often take the batch a few months before the average expected calving date, thus reducing feed and area requirements for the rearer.

2. *Calf Value;* is based on the cost of a heifer dairy calf (hence worth considerably more than the average calf sold from the dairy enterprise) and known not to be a freemartin. It accounts for mortality of 5%.

3. *Lower levels of concentrate* costs are the combined result of more economical feeding and a lower average calving age. (Other things being equal, including the overall level of management, a lower calving age requires higher levels of feeding.) Average (Holstein Friesians) = £55 to 3 months (see Calf Rearing on page 55) plus 290 kg calf concentrates @ £195/tonne and 500 kg @ £165/tonne = £194 per calf.

4. *Miscellaneous* variable costs include bedding (£45): straw requirements average approx. 1 tonne per heifer reared, but are variable, depending on time of year and age when calved, as well as system of housing and extent of out-wintering. Vet. and med. approximately £44 per heifer reared.

5. *A "replacement unit"* (i.e. calf + yearling + heifer) equals about 1·25 livestock units with an average calving age of 2 years 4 months. The three stocking rates used above are equivalent to approximately 1.2, 0·9 and 0·7 forage hectares (0.48, 0.37, 0.31 acres) respectively per Holstein Friesian cow (Livestock Unit).

6. *Forage variable costs.* Grass for both grazing and conservation, at £100 to £102/ha including a small amount of bought and bulk food (£8, £13, £18 a head).

7. *Much higher gross margin figures* per hectare can be combined by intensive grazing methods, particularly if combined with winter feeding systems which involve little dependence on home-produced hay or silage (cf. Note 11, last three paragraphs, page 45).

8. *Contract Rearing*: see page 70.

9. *Labour*: see page 174.

SELF-CONTAINED DAIRY HERD: COWS AND FOLLOWERS

At average annual replacement rates (25 per cent of the milking herd), nearly one-third of a replacement unit is required for each cow in the herd, i.e. roughly one calf, yearling and heifer for every three cows (including calved heifers), allowing for mortality and culling. At average stocking rates for both, this means more than 1 hectare devoted to followers for every 3 hectares for cows. Since surplus youngstock are often reared and frequently the stocking rate is less intensive the ratio often exceeds 1:2 in practice. 1: 2·75 is about the minimum where all replacement heifers are reared, unless their winter feeding is based largely on straw and purchased supplements, or unless there is a combination of long average herd life and early calving, i.e. at 2 years old or just over.

The table below shows the combined gross margin per forage hectare (acre) for the whole herd (i.e., Cows and Followers Combined); (at four levels of performance, including four commensurate levels of stocking rate, for the dairy cows; and three levels of performance, including different stocking rates, for the followers) are as follows, assuming a 2:1 land use ratio (dairy cow area: followers area); (Holstein Friesians only). It is linked to the schedules on pages 41 and 51:

Gross Margin per Forage Hectare for Cows and Followers Combined

			G.M per Forage Hectare (acre) Dairy Cows			
			Low	Average	High	Very High
			£	£	£	£
G.M. per			1167 (473)	1849 (749)	2352 (953)	2860 (1158)
Forage	Low	640 (259)	991 (401)	1446 (585)	1781 (721)	2120 (859)
Hectare	Ave.	882 (357)	1072 (434)	**1526** (618)	1862 (754)	2201 (891)
(acre)	High	1165 (472)	1166 (472)	1621 (656)	1956 (792)	2295 (930)

As an example, the above table indicates that at the average level of performance and stocking rate for both cows and followers, the whole dairy gross margin per hectare (acre) figure falls to £1,561 (632) compared with £1,849 (749) for the dairy cows alone, a reduction of 15 per cent.

If more than the assumed (minimum) number of dairy followers are kept and the ratio is 1·5:1 (i.e. 40% of the dairy herd forage area is devoted to followers rather than a third) the gross margin for the whole forage area figure (on the assumption again of average performance) falls to £1,253 (507), which is a reduction of 32 per cent compared with cows.

BEEF

Outlook for 2011

The GB deadweight cattle price saw a steady decline throughout the first half of 2010. It is likely that this was as a result of an increased number of cattle being presented for slaughter, an increase in beef imports and a subdued consumer demand for beef products. Cynics have also suggested that the major companies operating within the beef supply chain have overreacted to these factors in order to put pressure on farm gate prices.

It is widely anticipated within the beef producing sector that the depressed finished beef price of mid-2010 will be short lived and an increase in prices will materialise in late 2010 and into 2011. Beef exports still also remain strong with about 13% of the national production being exported mainly to EU countries. The extent of this activity of course greatly depends on the sterling to euro exchange rate. World demand for beef products is still prevalent and global production will remain under pressure which suggests that some of the optimism for price increases may be well founded. However, whilst it is important to monitor the beef commodity markets, producers should continue to focus on the elements of their beef enterprises that they are in complete control of; essentially the type of system implemented and the associated cost of production.

Those systems that require store cattle to be purchased for further rearing and or finishing face some difficult decisions going into 2011. A significant risk is posed where store buyers purchase in a buoyant store market and sell the same cattle into a depressed finished market at a later point in time; many businesses are likely to suffer from this situation in 2010-11 which may dampen the store cattle price over the next 18 months through nervousness and subdued demand.

Forage costs in 2011 are likely to be marginally higher than 2010 as a result of the forecast increase in fertilisers and the continued inflationary factors affecting other forage miscellaneous costs (bale wrap and netting, seed and spray costs etc). Those systems that have a high reliance on concentrate or cereal usage will suffer from the upturn in cereal and protein crop prices. Feed costs are therefore likely to increase in early 2011 on the back of these improved crop prices. Although extremely regional, the general increase in the straw price is likely to have a significant effect on the total variable costs of most beef systems in 2010-11.

Finished Cattle Prices

Deadweight prices for R4L classified finished steers in January 2010 were between £2.72 to £2.85 per kg. By early August 2010, prices for the same type of animal had dropped to lows of £2.55 per kg in some parts of the country. The deadweight price of finished heifers typically trails the steer price by 2 to 4p per kg. The liveweight finished price of cattle followed a similar trend to that of the deadweight trade throughout the first half of 2010, starting the year at about 153p per kg and reaching about 144p per kg in early August 2010.

Conversely, the store cattle trade remained buoyant in autumn 2009 and spring 2010. Store cattle prices typically reflect the trends of the finished market, albeit with a time lag. It is likely that store prices will be lower in autumn 2010 and spring 2011 than seen in previous years unless the finished cattle price has a significant rally in the second half of 2010 (see comments above).

Cull cow beef prices remained more stable than the prime animal finished prices in the first half of 2010. Strong beef cows were achieving 110p/kg liveweight in mid-2010 with well fleshed dairy types averaging around 90p/kg liveweight.

Calf Prices

Calf prices remain reasonably strong. This continues to be driven by the apparent shortage of animals at a national level with rearers therefore willing to offer higher prices in order to secure their supply. Live calf export activity all-but ceased in 2009, in part due to the concerns of British calf importers about TB prevalence in British cattle but also because of the strength of the domestic calf trade. Black and white bull calves have gone from being worthless in many cases to achieving in excess of £60 per head. The welfare concerns of foreign calf rearing units also continue to dissuade both the public and farmers from supporting calf export activity. As ever with calf prices, there can be significant regional and seasonal variations.

The values in the table below are for 2011 and relate to Black and White bulls or beef cross calves of average quality, less than three weeks old. These values have been used in the budgets for the various beef systems.

Calf Values of various Beef Cattle

	Bulls	Heifers
Holstein Friesians	50	*(Home Market)*
Hereford Cross	160	120
Continental Cross	210	170

Calf Rearing

	3 months	6 months
	£	£
Value of Calf	320	450
Less Calf Purchase (1)	198	198
Output	**122**	**252**
Variable Costs:		
Milk Substitute (2)..	32	32
Concentrates (2)...	31	88
Hay (3)..	1	11
Miscellaneous Variable Costs (4)...................	22	34
Total Variable Costs	**86**	**165**
Gross Margin per Calf Reared	**36**	**87**

1. *Calf Purchase:* Assumes equal number of male and female calves (Holstein Friesian/Continental beef cross, 1-2 weeks old). £190 average price, plus 4% mortality assumed, mainly in first 3 weeks. Value of pure Holstein Friesian bull calf £135 less; sale value at 3 or 6 months old correspondingly less).

2. *Milk substitute*: 20 kg @ £1,600/tonne = £32.00. Calf concentrates: to 3 months, 160 kg @ £195/tonne = £31.00; to 6 months, additional 290kg @ £195/tonne = £88.00. Calves fed on machine or lib milk systems will use more milk powder.

3. *Hay:* 10kg to 3 months, 190kg to 6 months. Variable costs assume made on farm; double the cost if purchased.

4. *Misc.* Variable Costs include vet. and med.: 12 (3 months), 15 (6 months); bedding: 6 (3 months), 10 (6 months); plus ear tags etc.

5. *Weights:* at start, 45 to 50 kg; at 3 months, 115 kg; at 6 months, 210 kg. Contract rearing charge (both 0 to 3 months and 0 to 6 months): £11 per week. Direct labour cost: approximately £23 per head to 3 months, £38 per head to 6 months.

6. *Labour requirements* (all beef systems): see page 174.

Suckler Cows

Single Suckling (per Cow): Lowland

System	Spring Calving		Autumn Calving	
Performance Level	Average	High	Average	High
	£	£	£	£
Value of Calf (2)	403	448	497	578
Calf Sales / Valuation per Cow (3)	363	413	447	531
Less Cow and Bull Depreciation and				
Calf Purchases (4)	85	85	95	95
Output	**278**	**328**	**352**	**437**
Variable Costs:				
Concentrate Costs (Cow and Calf).......	37	29	72	62
Misc Variable Costs (5)	65	60	83	78
Total Variable Costs (excl. forage)	**102**	**89**	**155**	**140**
Gross Margin per Cow, before				
deducting Forage Variable Costs	176	239	197	297
Forage Variable Costs	105	130	115	145
Purchased Bulk Feeds	20	15	20	15
Gross Margin per Cow	**51**	**94**	**62**	**137**
Cows per Hectare	1.80	2.20	1.65	2.00
Forage Hectares (Acres) per Cow	0.56	0.45	0.61	0.50
	(1.37)	(1.12)	(1.50)	(1.24)
Gross Margin per Forage Hectare	**92**	**206**	**103**	**274**
	(37)	(84)	(42)	(111)

1. *Performance level* relates to variations in two factors: weaned calf weight and stocking rate. 'High' refers to the average levels likely to be achieved by the better fifty per cent of producers. It is clearly possible to set still higher 'targets'.

2. *Value of Calves:* Weight of calves (kg) at sale/transfer: spring calving: average 280 (at 7.25 months), high 295 (slightly older); autumn calving: average 345 (at 10.25 months), high 380 (11 months old). Price (per live kg): spring calving: average 144p, high 152p; autumn calving: 144p, 152p. These prices are averages for steers and heifers.

3. *Calves reared* per 100 cows mated: average 90, high 92.

4. *Assumptions.* Herd life: spring calving, 8 years; autumn calving, 7 years. Purchase price £900, average cull value £450. Calves purchased: average per 100 cows mated: spring calving 2, autumn calving 3; at £190. Bull: purchase price £4,000, cull value £550; (one bull per 35 cows on average; 4-year herd life). Dairy cross beef cows have better fertility performance than continental pure bred cows, but lower cull sale prices.

5. *Vet. and med.:* spring calving £20, autumn £25; bedding: spring calving £30, autumn £40; miscellaneous: spring calving £15, autumn £18. *Straw:* where yarded in winter, straw requirements average 0.5-0.8 tonne per cow for spring calvers and > 0.75 tonnes for autumn calvers.

6. *The Forage Area* includes both grazing and conserved grass (silage and hay) plus any other forage crops, such as kale. The higher stocking density implies better use of

grassland. Higher stocking rates can also be achieved by buying in more of the winter bulk fodder requirements, or by winter feeding largely on arable by-products, including straw. Purchased bulk fodder and/or straw balancer concentrates will reduce gross margin per cow but increase gross margin per hectare.

7. Single Payment: A payment is made in Scotland on three-quarter breed beef calves from Suckler Cows. Payments under the Scottish Beef Calf Scheme in 2010 were £57/head (£114/head for the first 10 calves claimed).

8. In lowland conditions rearing two or more calves per cow is an option, but needs substantially greater labour input. Output is raised by fostering a second purchased calf onto a cow soon after calving, with little impact on costs of keeping the cow. The cow breed needs to be of a quiet temperament and have enough milk to rear two calves.

Single Suckling (per Cow): Upland/Hill

System	Spring Calving		Autumn Calving	
Performance Level	Average	High	Average	High
	£	£	£	£
Value of Calf (2)	382	426	482	555
Calf Sales / Valuation per Cow (3)	347	396	439	516
Less Cow and Bull Depreciation and				
Calf Purchases (4)	86	84	94	92
Output	**261**	**311**	**345**	**424**
Variable Costs:				
Concentrate Costs (Cow and Calf).......	39	33	75	65
Misc Variable Costs (5)......................	65	60	83	78
Total Variable Costs (excl. forage)	**104**	**93**	**158**	**143**
Gross Margin per Cow, before				
deducting Forage Variable Costs	157	218	187	281
Forage Variable Costs	85	105	95	120
Purchased Bulk Feeds	20	15	20	15
Gross Margin per Cow	**52**	**98**	**72**	**146**
Cows per Hectare	1.60	1.90	1.25	1.50
Forage Hectares (Acres) per Cow	0.63	0.53	0.80	0.67
	(1.54)	(1.30)	(1.98)	(1.65)
Gross Margin per Forage Hectare	**83**	**187**	**90**	**218**
	(34)	(76)	(36)	(88)

1. *Performance level* relates to variations in two factors: weaned calf weight and stocking rate. 'High' refers to the average levels likely to be achieved by the better fifty per cent of producers. It is clearly possible to set still higher 'targets'.

2. *Weight of calves* (kg) at sale/transfer: upland spring calving: average 265 (at 7 months), high 280 (7.25 months); upland autumn calving: average 335 (at 10.25 months), high 365 (11 months); Price (per live kg); upland spring calving: average 144p, high 152p; upland autumn calving: average 144p, high 152p. These prices are averages for bull and heifer calves.

3. *Calves* reared per 100 cows mated: upland average 91, high 93.

4. *Assumptions.* Herd life: spring calving, 8 years; autumn calving and hill, 7 years. Purchase price £900, average cull value £450. Calves purchased: upland average, 3 per 100 cows mated, premium 2, at £175. Bull: purchase price £4,000, cull value £550.

5. *Vet and Med.* Spring calving £20, autumn £25; bedding: spring calving £30, autumn £40; miscellaneous: spring calving £15, autumn £18. *Straw:* when yarded in winter, requirements average 0.5-0.8 tonne per cow for spring calvers and >0.75 tonne for autumn calvers.

6. *The forage area* includes both grazing and conserved grass (silage and hay) plus any other forage crops, such as kale. The higher stocking density implies better use of grassland. Higher stocking rates can also be achieved by buying in more of the winter bulk fodder requirements, or by winter feeding largely on arable by-products, including straw. Purchased bulk fodder and/or straw balancer concentrates reduce gross margin per cow but increase gross margin per hectare.

Support: all headage payments have been decoupled under the Single Payment, apart from the Scottish Beef Calf Scheme (see above margin notes). Hill payments: Hill Farm Allowance in England was replaced in 2010 by the Uplands Entry Level Stewardship scheme (UELS) and is available on farmland with Severely Disadvantaged Areas (SDA's). Tir Mynydd payments are available in Wales and LFASS in Scotland – these are not included in the gross margins. LFASS payments are available in disadvantaged and severely disadvantaged areas and are paid on an area basis (but have a minimum stocking density). See Page 152. Additional payments for keeping native beef suckler cows are available from environmental schemes such as ELS in England and Tir Gofal in Wales.

Rearing / Finishing Stores

Traditional Finishing of Strong Store Cattle (per head) (1)

	Summer Finishing	Winter Finishing
	£	£
Finished Sales	803 (2)	838 (3)
Less Purchased Store (incl. mortality)	605 (4)	627 (5)
Output	**198**	**211**
Variable Costs:		
Concentrates...	6	73 (6)
Miscellaneous Variable Costs.........................	26	65 (7)
Total Variable Costs (excluding Forage)	**32**	**138**
Gross Margin per Head, before		
deducting Forage Variable Costs	166	74
Forage Variable Costs	82	44
Gross Margin per Head	**84**	**30**
Animals per Hectare (Acre)	4 (1.6)	9 (3.6)
Forage Hectares (Acres) per Head	0.25 (0.62)	0.11 (0.3)
Gross Margin per Forage Hectare	**336**	**266**
Gross Margin per Forage Acre	*136*	*108*

1. *The financial results* of this enterprise are highly dependent on the market margin, i.e. the difference between the price per kg paid for the store and the price per kg obtained for the finished animal. Other important factors are the stocking rate and the degree of dependence on cash-crop by-products and the quality of conserved grass (and hence

the quantity of concentrates required in relation to the liveweight gain) in the case of winter finishing.

There is a large price range for store cattle based on quality, which will be reflected in carcase classification results. Heifers tend to finish better off grass with less concentrate requirements and therefore are more appropriate than steers for summer finishing at grass.

2. 550 kg @ 146p.

3. 570 kg @ 147p.

4. 410 kg @ 146p. Includes mortality at 1%.

5. 425 kg @ 146p. Includes mortality at 1%.

6. 415 kg @ £175/tonne.

7. *Including straw*: average 0.75 tonnes per head

BEEF

Finishing Suckler-Bred Stores
(per head):

Performance Level	Winter Finishing Average	Winter Finishing High	Grass Finishing Average	Grass Finishing High	Overwintering & Grass Finishing Average	Overwintering & Grass Finishing High	Grazing & Yard Finishing Average	Grazing & Yard Finishing High
Weight at Start (kg)	325	320	335	330	310	315	285	270
Weight at Sale (kg)	585	595	540	575	520	560	520	560
Purchase Price (p per kg liveweight)	144	152	145	153	144	152	145	153
Sale Price (p per kg liveweight)	144	146	147	149	147	149	144	146
Concentrates per Head (kg)	575	545	50	40	375	335	460	340
Silage per Head (tonnes)	3.25	3.25	-	-	3.40	3.30	2.10	2.30
	£	£	£	£	£	£	£	£
Finished Sales	842	869	794	857	764	834	749	818
Less Store Purchase (1)	473	491	491	510	451	484	417	417
Output	**370**	**377**	**303**	**347**	**314**	**351**	**331**	**400**
Variable Costs:								
Concentrates (2)	101	95	9	7	66	59	81	60
Misc Variable Costs (3)	57	51	24	22	49	45	45	40
Total Variable Costs (excl. Forage)	**158**	**146**	**33**	**29**	**115**	**104**	**126**	**100**
Gross Margin per Head, before Forage	212	231	270	318	199	247	206	301
Forage Variable Costs	78	72	49	51	96	99	73	77
Purchased Bulk Feeds	6	5	0	0	8	6	7	4
Gross Margin per Head	**128**	**155**	**221**	**267**	**95**	**143**	**126**	**220**
No. per Hectare (Acre)	8.0 (3.2)	9.0 (3.6)	4.0 (1.6)	5.0 (2.0)	3.8 (1.5)	4.5 (1.8)	4.0 (1.6)	5.0 (2.0)
Gross Margin per Forage Hectare	**1,025**	**1,391**	**886**	**1,334**	**357**	**642**	**502**	**1,101**
Gross Margin per Forage Acre	*415*	*563*	*358*	*540*	*145*	*260*	*203*	*446*

All-System Assumptions:

(1) Allowing for mortality at 1%. (2) Concentrate costs all assumed to be £175 per tonne. (3) Including vet.& med. and bedding.

Additional Note: The gross margin per ha figures must be treated with considerable caution, especially with regard to winter fattening/rearing systems: small variations in land requirements and margins per head cause wide variations in the per ha figures, and capital requirements are considerable. Differences in buying and selling prices per kg can be critical. Very little recent survey data is available on several of these systems.

BEEF

Finishing Dairy-Bred Stores
(per head):

Performance Level	Winter Finishing		Grass Finishing		Overwintering & Grass Finishing		Grazing & Yard Finishing	
	Average	High	Average	High	Average	High	Average	High
Weight at Start (kg)	385	385	350	350	325	315	230	240
Weight at Sale (kg)	560	580	485	525	490	525	500	550
Purchase Price (p per kg liveweight)	140	142	143	145	140	142	143	145
Sale Price (p per kg liveweight)	144	146	146	148	146	148	144	146
Concentrates per Head (kg)	500	480	55	45	395	370	550	475
Silage per Head (tonnes)	3.40	3.50	-	-	3.50	3.40	3.50	4.00
	£	£	£	£	£	£	£	£
Finished Sales	806	847	708	777	715	777	720	803
Less Store Purchase (1)	544	552	506	513	460	452	332	351
Output	**262**	**295**	**203**	**264**	**256**	**325**	**388**	**452**
Variable Costs:								
Concentrates (2)	88	82	10	8	69	65	96	83
Misc Variable Costs (3)	55	42	24	22	49	45	45	40
Total Variable Costs (excl. Forage)	**143**	**124**	**34**	**30**	**118**	**110**	**141**	**123**
Gross Margin per Head, before Forage	120	171	169	235	138	215	247	328
Forage Variable Costs	82	70	48	50	108	94	107	106
Purchased Bulk Feeds	5	3	0	0	7	5	7	4
Gross Margin per Head	**33**	**98**	**121**	**185**	**23**	**116**	**133**	**218**
No. per Hectare (Acre)	6.0 (2.4)	8.0 (3.2)	4.0 (1.6)	5.0 (2.0)	3.5 (1.4)	4.2 (1.7)	3.5 (1.4)	4.5 (1.8)
Gross Margin per Forage Hectare	**197**	**784**	**484**	**923**	**80**	**493**	**464**	**983**
Gross Margin per Forage Acre	*80*	*317*	*196*	*373*	*32*	*199*	*188*	*398*

All-System Assumptions:
(1) Allowing for mortality at 1%. (2) Concentrate costs all assumed to be £175 per tonne. (3) Including vet.& med. and bedding.
Additional Note: The gross margin per ha figures must be treated with considerable caution, especially with regard to winter fattening/rearing systems: small variations in land requirements and margins per head cause wide variations in the per ha figures, and capital requirements are considerable. Differences in buying and selling prices per kg can be critical. Very little recent survey data is available on several of these systems.

Intensive Beef

Cereal Bull Beef (per Head)

System	Continental Cross Holstein/Friesian Bulls		Holstein Friesian Bulls	
Performance Level	Average	High	Average	High
	£	£	£	£
Finished Sales (1)	665	722	595	667
Less Calf Purchase (2)	215	213	51	51
Output	**450**	**509**	**544**	**616**
Variable Costs:				
Concentrates (3)	390	378	390	378
Other Feed	5	5	5	5
Misc Variable Costs (4)......................	74	69	74	69
Total Variable Costs	**469**	**452**	**469**	**452**
Gross Margin per Head	**-19**	**57**	**75**	**164**

1. *Weight at slaughter (kg):* Cont cross bulls, average 500kg, high 535kg; Dairy bulls, average 465kg, high 505kg. Prices: Cont cross bulls, average 133p/kg lw, high 135p/kg lw; Dairy bulls, average 128p/kg, high 132p/kg. All year round production is assumed. Average slaughter age is 14 months, with killing out percentages ranging from 54% to 59%, with the better conformation continental cross bulls achieving higher percentages.

2. *Calf prices* of £210 for continental cross male calves at 3 weeks of age including mortality; £50 for dairy bulls including mortality. Mortality, average 2.5%, high 1.5%.

3. *Concentrates:* £86 calf rearing (to 12 weeks: see page 55) + finishing ration. Finishing ration: 17 parts barley @ £110 per tonne, 3 parts concentrate supplement @ £220 per tonne; plus £10 per tonne milling and mixing cost. Total, £137 per tonne.

   Feed quantity (kg from 12 weeks (115 kg) liveweight to slaughter; FCR average 5·0, high 4·6): average 2,225kg, high 2,140kg.

   Margins are very sensitive to calf price and feed price movements. A £10 per tonne feed price movement equates to a margin change of £22 per head.

4. Vet. and med. £18, bedding £30, misc. £26.

   Interest on Capital Note: Beef systems require large capital outlay on livestock and variable costs alone. For cereal beef with an interest rate @ 6% on the calf price, and half the variable costs, interest charges amount to £27.00 per head.

18 Month Beef and Silage Beef (per Head Produced*)

System	18 Month Beef		Silage Beef	
Performance Level	Average	High	Average	High
	£	£	£	£
Finished Sales	803	844	788	829
Less Calf Purchase	177	173	177	173
Output	**626**	**670**	**612**	**655**
Variable Costs:				
Concentrates (incl. milk substitute)......	243	227	295	269
Other Feed..	5	5	6	6
Misc Variable Costs............................	84	81	81	75
Total Variable Costs (excl. forage)	**332**	**313**	**382**	**350**
Gross Margin per Head, before				
deducting Forage Variable Costs	294	358	230	306
Forage Variable Costs	136	136	132	132
Gross Margin per Head, before	**158**	**222**	**98**	**174**
Animals per Hectare	3.4	3.8	8.0	10.0
Forage Hectares (Acres) per Cow	0.29	0.26	0.13	0.10
	(0.73)	(0.65)	(0.31)	(0.25)
Gross Margin per Forage Hectare	**538**	**842**	**781**	**1,737**
	(218)	(341)	(316)	(703)

18 Month Beef Notes:

1. * *The variable costs*, including feed and forage, the forage area and gross margin per head all relate to the full production period - 18 months or less for silage beef. Nevertheless, the gross margins per forage ha or acre are per year. During the winter there will be both the 0-6 month old calves and 12-18 month old cattle on the farm.

2. *General:* Autumn-born dairy-bred calves, beef crosses.

3. *Slaughter weights* (kg): average 550, high 570. Sale price per live kg: average 146p, high 148p.

4. *Calf price/value:* £170 (2 week old beef cross male calves, e.g. Limousin cross); mortality: average 4%, high 2%.

5. *Feed:* Concentrates (kg; average with high performance in brackets): Calf rearing to 12 weeks £85 incl. milk substitute. Other: first winter 220kg @ £175 (200kg), at grass 90kg @ £175 (80kg), second winter 560kg @ £185 (500kg). Silage: 4.5 tonnes/head total, 0.75 tonne first winter, 3.75 tonnes second. Intensive grazing of fresh leys and good quality silage are needed - especially to achieve the high performance levels.

6. *Other Costs:* Miscellaneous (average): vet. and med. £23, bedding £35, other £26.

Silage Beef Notes

1. General: Dairy-bred calves (beef crosses) fed indoors on grass silage and concentrates, for slaughter at 14 to 17 months old. Good quality silage is the key to high performance per head (otherwise concentrates per head rise and/or daily liveweight gain falls). High yields of silage per ha raise gross margins per ha.

2. *Slaughter weights (kg):* average 540, high 560. Sale price per live kg: average 146p, high 148p.

3. *Calf price/value:* £170 (2 week old beef cross male calves, e.g. Limousin cross); mortality: average 4%, high 2%.

4. *Concentrates per head*: (kg) (from 3 months (£85 to rear including milk powder)): average 1,200kg @ £175, high 1050kg @ £175. Silage required: approximately 5.5 tonnes per head.

5. *Other Costs:* Miscellaneous (average): vet. and med. £18, bedding £38, other £25.

Note that the gross margin per hectare figures must be interpreted with considerable caution: small differences in silage yields can have a large effect and, more important, the working capital and building requirements per ha are extremely high: well above even the high needs of 18 month beef.

Veal

General points: Veal consumption is very low in the UK; only a small fraction of the per capita consumption in France for example. Continental demand is mainly for white veal, produced in individual veal crates, a system that is illegal in the UK. Until recently, there was still live calf export activity from the UK to the continent for veal production, but this now all but ceased.

There is some activity in UK 'welfare friendly' domestic veal production where calves are kept in groups in straw yards producing heavier calves with 'pink' meat a.k.a. 'Rose Veal'. This is a premium product and is considerably more expensive than imported 'white veal'. As very little veal is produced in the UK, validated economic data is rarely seen. For this reason the provision of gross margin data has been discontinued.

SHEEP

Outlook for 2011

The significant and continued downward trend in the size of the UK sheep breeding flock may be starting to slow. There is even a small possibility that the number of lowland ewes could very marginally rise in 2011 as the strength of the lamb price continues. Many hill and upland producers still face financial challenges in achieving a sustainable living from sheep production alone and so the number and size of these flocks may continue to reduce. This is likely to affect the workings of the 'stratified' structure of the UK sheep industry in the future meaning lowland producers may seek alternative ways of securing replacement ewes, for example, from lowland areas or by breeding their own ewe lambs.

Around one third of the GB lamb output is exported annually with most this being sent to EU markets. The importance of the export trade to UK lamb production should not therefore be underestimated. As has been widely reported before, this trade is greatly influenced by the sterling to euro exchange rate. The weak sterling of recent times has undoubtedly acted as a mainstay to the (sometimes marginal) profitability of UK lamb production. The weak sterling is set to continue, but even if it does strengthen in 2011, important overseas markets have been opened up and reduced supply from other sheep producing countries provides some confidence that a dramatic price fall will be avoided.

The many years of marginal profitability in the sheep sector along with the sometimes laborious aspects of sheep production has resulted in a severe shortage of skilled management and labour. This is restricting entrepreneurial spirit and the long term strategy that many businesses in the sector require. Scale is also required to make most sheep enterprises financially viable. Despite these challenges, sustainable profits can be made from sheep production where high level management expertise and useful technology are invested in a system suitable for the business in question.

Lowland Spring Lambing per Ewe (selling lambs off grass)

Performance Level	Low	Average	High
Lambs Reared per Ewe put to Ram (1)	1.3	1.45	1.6
Finished Lamb Liveweight (kg)		39.0	
Finished Lamb Liveweight Price (£/kg)		1.52	
Store Lamb Price (£/head)		48.0	
Average Price per Lamb (£) (2)	55.5	57.6	59.6
Sales:	£	£	£
Lamb sales...	72.2	83.5	95.4
Wool (3)...	1.7	1.7	1.7
Cull Ewes and Rams (4)..................	11.0	11.0	11.0
Sub Total	84.9	96.2	108.1
Less Ewe and Ram Replacements (4)	27.6	27.6	27.6
Output per Ewe	**57.3**	**68.6**	**80.5**
Variable Costs:			
Concentrates (58kg ewes, 8kg lambs) (5)		11.2	
Vet and Med.....................................		5.8	
Miscellaneous and transport (6)......		10.2	
Total Variable Costs (excluding Forage)		**27.1**	
Gross Margin per Ewe, before			
deducting Forage Variable Costs	**30.2**	**41.5**	**53.4**
Forage Variable Costs (inc bought-in			
Forage and Keep)	10.9	11.2	12.4
Gross Margin per Ewe	**19.3**	**30.3**	**41.0**
Stocking Rate (Ewes with Lambs per forage			
Hectare (acre)) (7)	8 (3.2)	10 (4.0)	14 (5.7)
Gross Margin per Forage Hectare	154	303	574
Gross Margin per Forage Acre	62	122	232

1. *Target Rearing Performance.* Lambs reared per ewe put to ram are based on: -
    Ewes lambing: 92% (2.5% deaths, 5.5% barren)
    Lambs born: per 100 ewes lambing = 168
    Live lambs: born per ewe lambing = 156
    Lamb mortality: 14% (7% at birth, 7% post birth)
    Lambs reared: per 100 ewes put to ram = 145

    These performance figures are assumed for flocks of mature ewes, i.e. shearlings and older. Where ewe lambs are included in flock performance adjustment needs to be made. The *Breed* will obviously have a large effect on lambing percentage, liveweight gains and carcase grades.

2. *Lamb Prices.* Prices for lambs sold for slaughter are based on the forecast for the 2011 season and assumes a continuation of the robust EU export market without restrictions (and therefore a continuation of the autumn 2010 Euro to sterling exchange rate).

    An average market price of 152p/kg liveweight (equivalent to 330p/kg deadweight) has been assumed giving £59.28 per finished lamb at an average liveweight of 39kg.

The average budget price in the table above allows for 15% sold as stores. Store price is assumed at £48 per head. Low performance is £2.05 a lamb less, high £2.05 per lamb more for variations caused by differences in weights, time of marketing and proportion sold finished or retained as stores.

3. *Wool*. The wool price recovered significantly in 2010; reasonable, clean wool yields now mean that a small margin can be made over the cost of shearing. Budget price assumed for lowland flocks is £1.71 per ewe, based on a price of 95p/kg at 1.8kg/ewe. Variations between flocks will occur due to ewe breed affecting wool quality and ewe size affecting weight of wool produced.

4. *Flock Depreciation*. (i.e. Market price of replacements less value of culls). It is assumed that 19% of the ewe flock is culled each year @ £56 each and that, allowing for 4% mortality, 22% are purchased or home-reared at £106 each. Rams: 1 per 40 ewes, 3.5 year life, purchased @ £450, sold @ £45. The net cost (flock depreciation) is £16.60 per ewe per year. N.B. Cull ewe prices vary considerably depending on the weight and 'fleshiness' of the ewes. Cull values tend to be highly variable but remain high, partly at least through a strong, consistent demand from the UK ethnic sector. No other changes in flock valuation are assumed.

5. *Concentrate Feeding*. Feed costs may increase slightly in 2011 as a result of the more optimistic cereal and protein crop prices. Concentrate finishing of late season lambs has been common, but there has been a swing to sell as stores (for finishing on winter forage crops) rather than finish on high cost concentrates. Late season grass availability will influence the store trade.

6. *Miscellaneous Costs* include contract shearing @ 120p/ewe, scanning 60p/ewe and lamb and replacement ewe tags 105p/ewe (assuming non-EID slaughter tags are used), carcase disposal £1.00/ewe, straw £1.15/ewe, minerals and licks etc 140p/ewe, marketing, levy and transport £3.75/ewe.

7. *Stocking Density*. The stocking rates assumed are based on land requirements for the main grazing season (April to October) including land for conservation of winter forage.

Land quality and location will also have an effect on potential stocking density. However higher stocking rates can be achieved by catch crop roots for autumn/winter grazing or away wintering on grass keep which carry higher costs on a per ewe basis. Away grazing costs can range from 40p to 60p/ewe per week depending upon location.

On farms with grazing livestock other than sheep, the ewe flock is able to utilize land in the winter utilized by cattle in the normal grazing season. Alternatively ewes can be winter housed pre lambing to rest the land, but this does carry additional costs e.g. £6/ewe per year for building depreciation and interest over 10 years, plus straw and hay costs.

Ensuring good lamb growth rates and early finishing off grass also eases stocking pressures late in the season. Late lamb finishing into autumn and winter in most cases necessitates additional land available for lamb finishing lambs on catch crops or away grazing for ewes.

8. *Other Costs*

    a.   *Prices of Specialised Equipment*

Troughs (2.75 m)	£45 to £60
Racks (2 to 3 m)......................	£200 to £225
Foot Baths (3 m)	£100 to £150
Shearing machines	£450 to £1,050
Lamb Creep Feeders	£350 to £650

b. *Fencing:* Approximately £5.50 per metre *for posts, sheep netting, 2 strands of barbed wired and labour inclusive.*

c. *Labour:* see page 162.

Home-reared tegs (shearlings)

Output: value £103 (allowing for culling and mortality) less £70 for the lamb, plus wool at £1.50, gives an output of £34.50/head. Variable costs (including forage) = £28/head. Gross margin per head = £6.50, per forage hectare £82 (£33 per acre).

Rearing replacements can be treated as a separate enterprise and margins compared on a per hectare basis. Where ewe lamb replacements are lambed in their first year they can be combined with the breeding flock which will reduce lambing percentage and output (£) per ewe, but benefit from a reduction of replacement cost.

Other Sheep Systems (average performance level only)

	Early Lambing	Winter Finishing of Stores	Upland Flocks	Hill Flocks
	per ewe	per head	per ewe	per ewe
Lambs Sold per Ewe (put to ram)	1.375	-	1.325	0.75
Finished Lamb Liveweight (kg)	37.0	41.0	35.0	32.0
Finished Liveweight Price (p/kg)	195	150	142	142
Average Price per Lamb Sold (£)	72.2	61.5	49.7	45.4
	£	£	£	£
Lamb Sales..	99.2	60.3	65.9	34.1
Wool...	1.7	-	1.1	0.9
Sub Total	100.9	60.3	67.0	35.0
Less Purchases (net of Culls)	15.4	48.0	14.8	(5.6)
Output	**85.5**	**12.3**	**52.2**	**40.6**
Variable Costs:				
Concentrates....................................	38.5	4.4	12.1	6.6
	(175kg)	(20kg)	(55kg)	(30kg)
Vet and Med....................................	6.8	1.8	5.7	4.1
Miscellaneous.................................	9.8	2.4	7.7	3.8
Total Variable Costs (excl. Forage)	**55.1**	**8.6**	**25.5**	**14.5**
Gross Margin per Ewe/Head, before Forage Variable Costs	**30.4**	**3.7**	**26.7**	**26.1**
Forage Variable Costs (inc bought-in Forage and Keep	13.2	2.8	14.8	7.0
Gross Margin per Ewe/Head	**17.2**	**0.9**	**11.9**	**19.1**
Stocking Rate (Animals per forage Hectare (acre))	13 (5.3)	30 (12.1)	9 (3.6)	-
Gross Margin per Forage Hectare	224	26	107	-
Gross Margin per Forage Acre	91	11	43	-

1. *Early Lambing.* This system assumes January/early February lambing with all lambs sold by the end of August. Recent years have seen lamb prices peak later in the

season, i.e. mid-May rather than the traditional Easter market peak. This has been due to the large retailers contracting to New Zealand lamb in the first part of the year and switching to UK new season lamb when large enough supplies are available from May. Hence early marketing of substantial numbers in April has not been beneficial.

This system is also very dependant upon concentrate feed inputs to ewe and lambs which will reduce margins per ewe to a level where they are now below the margins for Spring Lambing Flocks.

2. *Winter Finishing of Store Lambs.* The gross margin per head is particularly variable, being very dependant on the difference between purchase and sale price of the lambs. Some of the forage variable costs consist of bulk feed and grass keep. It is risky to assume any great uplift in prices per kg from purchase to sale. Marketing and transport costs are a significant part of total costs so longer keep lambs gaining 8 to 10kg liveweight on low cost forage are the most likely to be worthwhile. Margin assumes 2% mortality from purchase to sale.

3. *Upland Sheep.* Due to the breeds used, the finished lamb weights from these flocks are likely to be lower than for lowland ewes. The margins assumes that all progeny are sold finished, but in practice many of these flocks will be selling breeding stock to lowland producers. Male lambs are often sold as stores in the autumn.

4. *Hill Sheep.* These flocks are self-maintained and a high proportion of the ewes bred pure. The overall lambing percentage is likely to be around 110%, but 0.35 lambs per ewe will be as flock replacements. Only rams are purchased to maintain the flock. Wool income includes yearling ewes carried on the farm. Results vary according to the quality of the hill grazing and stocking density.

    Many flocks have historically away wintered ewes for up to six months to maximise ewe premium claims and latterly to be eligible for environmental schemes. Where ewes are away for 6 months, £12 per ewe needs to be added to the forage costs set out in the table above.

5. *Support:* Upland Entry Level Stewardship (UELS) in England, Tir Mynydd in Wales and LFASS in Scotland are not included in the gross margins above. See Page 152.

GRAZING AND REARING CHARGES:
CATTLE AND SHEEP

Grazing charges vary greatly according to the quality of the pasture and local supply and demand. The following figures are typical (estimated for 2011):

Summer Grazing (per head per week)

Store Cattle and in-calf heifers over 21 months, dry cows, and fattening bullocks over 18 months	£3.50 - £4.50
Heifers and Steers, 12-21 months	£2.50 - £3.50
6-12 months Cattle	£2.00 - £2.75
Cattle of mixed ages	£2.50 - £3.50
Ewes	45p - 55p

Winter Grazing (per head per week)

'Strong' Cattle	£2.25 - £3.50
Heifers	£2.00 - £3.00
Sheep...	40p - 50p

Note: the above figures assume the farmer whose land the livestock are on does all the fencing and shepherding. Where the owner of the stock does the fencing, shepherding, etc., the figures may be halved, or be even less depending on local demand.

Grass Keep

Most typically around £75-£185/hectare (£30-£75), with the best £190-£300 (£77-£120) and lower quality keep making £50-£75 (£20-£30).

These figures are highly variable, especially between one part of the country and another, and between one season and another. The charge can be very high where the pasture is good, the supply scarce and the demand strong. Fencing, electricity supply, mains water etc adds a premium to grass keep as does the quality of grassland and any licensor fertiliser applications. Grazing may be offered to livestock keepers at very little or no charge where the need for maintainance of grassland is the driving factor (e.g. amentiy value, requirement to cross comply or meet Agri-environment scheme agreements, value of cattle and sheep to 'clean-up' pasture or to provide beneficial mixed grazing). The length of grazing period offered will also influence the premium of grass keep (e.g. grazing until 30th September or until 31st December).

The new Nitrate Vulnerable Zone (NVZ) rules introduced in 2009 may also increase demand for grass keep in NVZ's where dairy enterprises are commonplace – an additonal acreage may help some producers to keep within the livestock manure loading level.

Winter Keep (Cattle per head per week)

Grazing + 9 kg hay and some straw	£8.50
Full winter keep in yards	£7.00-£10.00
Calf rearing for beef (0 to 12 weeks or 0 to 6 months)..........	£10.00

A typical rental for labour, buildings and maintenance diet would be £6.50 per head per week. These rates apply where feed to achieve maintenance plus some growth is supplied plus labour and buildings and bedding where applicable. A typical rental for labour, buildings and a maintenance diet would be £5 per head per week.

Heifer Rearing Charges

There have historically been two types of arrangements:

1. Farmer X sells calf to Rearer at agreed price; the calf is then Rearer's responsibility and he pays for all expenses and bears any losses. Farmer X has first option on heifers, which he buys back two months before calving. Approximate price: £800 above cost of calf for Holstein Friesians. Rearer fetches calf; Farmer X supplies transport for heifer. *This system is now less common due to low interest rates cheapening borrowing enabling breeders to retain ownership of heifers throughout their life.*

2. Farmer X retains ownership of calf, but sends it to a specialist rearer. Approximate rearer charges range from 105 to 115 pence per head per day although may vary depending upon cattle, system and location. Usually the owner of the cattle is responsible for transport costs and the choice and cost of vaccine programmes. The cost of semen for artificial insemination of the heifers is usually incurred by the owner and paid for over and above the standard rearing charge. The rearer is responsible for all standard rearing costs including for normal veterinary services and worming etc. and any animal losses (unless due to Tb or Bluetongue). *Model agreements are available from industry associations and advisors.*

Contract rearing on behalf of a third party may appeal to some producers who wish to reduce borrowing exposure and / or lower capital investment in a business. A well laid out contract rearing arrangement will also provide greater cost and income clarity to both the rearer and owner and therefore reduce the risk exposure to both businesses. It also enables each business to focus and specialise to achieve optimum performance without being distracted by other enterprises. Biosecurity issues are becoming increasingly paramount where an agreement is set up. In many cases the owner of heifers will require exclusive occupancy of a rearer's farm without cattle owned by the rearer or others being present.

RED DEER

A. **Breeding and Finishing**	Per 100 Hinds
Sales:	£
45 Stags (15-18 months) : 55kg dw @ £3.75/kg..................	9,281
35 Hinds (15-18 months) : 45kg dw @ £3.75/kg	5,906
8 Cull Hinds @ £100..	800
Average Annual Value of Cull Stags.......................	100
Less Average Annual Cost of Replacement Stags.............	200
Output	**15,888**
Variable Costs:	
Concentrates @ 4.0 tonnes @ £180/tonne...............	720
Vet and Med...	495
Miscellaneous...	410
Total Variable Costs	**1,625**
Gross Margin before deducting Forage Costs	**14,263**
Forage Variable Costs (5.5 Hinds per hectare @ £155/ha)............	2,818
Gross Margin per 100 Hinds...............................	**11,444**
Gross Margin per Forage hectare (5.5 hinds/ha)........................	629
Gross Margin per Forage acre (2.2 hinds/ac)............................	255

B. **Selling Store Calves to Finishers**	Per 100 Hinds
Sales:	£
45 Stag Calves @ £95/head (45 kg liveweight).....................	4,253
35 Hind Calves @ £72/head (40 kg liveweight)....................	2,520
8 Cull Hinds @ £100..	800
Average Annual Value of Cull Stags.......................	100
Less Average Annual Cost of Replacement Stags.............	200
Output	**7,473**
Variable Costs:	
Concentrates @ 1.3 tonnes @ £180/tonne...............	234
Vet and Med...	295
Miscellaneous...	210
Total Variable Costs	**739**
Gross Margin before deducting Forage Costs..................	**6,734**
Forage Variable Costs (6.5 Hinds per hectare @ £130/ha)............	2,000
Gross Margin per 100 Hinds...............................	**4,734**
Gross Margin per Forage hectare (6.5 hinds/ha)........................	308
Gross Margin per Forage acre (2.6 hinds/ac)............................	125

Lowland systems assumed. Hind replacements home-reared in systems A and B.

Herd Life: hinds, 12 years; stags, 6 years; 33 hinds per stag. Calves reared per 100 hinds: 90. All schedules for 12 month period.

Purchase price of breeding stock (good quality): hinds £350 plus, yearling hinds £275 plus, stags £500 plus.

C. Finishing Stag Calves

	Per 200 Stags
Sales:	£
195 Stags (15-18 months) : 55kg dw @ £3.75/kg.................	40,219
Less Purchases : 200 @ £94.5 per head.........................	18,900
Output	**21,319**
Variable Costs:	
Concentrates @ 12.0 tonnes @ £180/tonne............................	2,160
Vet and Med..	610
Miscellaneous..	1,000
Total Variable Costs	**3,770**
Gross Margin before deducting Forage Costs..............................	**17,549**
Forage Variable Costs (11.0 Stags per hectare @ £155/ha)............	2,818
Gross Margin per 200 Stags..	**14,731**
Gross Margin per Forage hectare (11 stags/ha).........................	810
Gross Margin per Forage acre (4.5 stags/ac).............................	328

The venison prices reflect projected sales for 2010 to wholesale buyers. Higher prices will be obtained for direct sales to consumers (e.g. farm shops and farmers' markets) and caterers, but extra costs will normally be incurred.

D. Deer Park

	Per 300 Hinds
Sales:	£
120 Stags (15-18 months) : 55kg dw @ £2.80/kg.................	18,480
110 Hinds (15-18 months) : 50kg dw @ £2.80/kg................	15,400
5 Cull Hinds @ £182...	910
5 Live Stag Sales @ £1,000......................................	5,000
Output	**39,790**
Variable Costs:	
Concentrates @ 12.0 tonnes @ £180/tonne............................	2,160
Vet and Med..	510
Miscellaneous..	310
Total Variable Costs	**2,980**
Gross Margin before deducting Forage Costs	**36,810**
Forage Variable Costs (3.0 Hinds per hectare @ £105/ha).............	10,500
Gross Margin per 300 Hinds...	**26,310**
Gross Margin per Forage hectare (3 hinds/ha)...........................	263
Gross Margin per Forage acre (1.2 hinds/ac)............................	106

Sales are based on skin-on carcases bought by a game dealer/butcher.

Forage costs include 200 bales of silage and grass costs.

Sources of further information: The British Deer Farmers Association, PO Box 7522, Matlock, DE4 9BR Tel: 08456 344 758 www.bdfa.co.uk

Acknowledgements: Thanks to - Ali Loder, BDFA; Nigel Sampson, Holme Farmed Venison www.hfv.co.uk

HORSES: LIVERY

The horse industry is now reported to be the second biggest employer in the rural economy and is also one of the fastest growing. Although there are other equine enterprises that farm businesses can operate, by far the most common is providing accommodation for horses; i.e. livery. There are many different forms of livery and the charges, therefore, vary widely also. This is apart from the effects of local supply and demand. However, three fairly standard forms are offered on farms:

Grass Livery. Keep at grass, preferably with shelter, water supply and secure area to keep tack and store feed. Some grass livery will provide an exercise arena and off-road riding. Charges average £25 per week; range £20-£40.

DIY Livery. The owner still has full care of the horse but has the facilities of a stable, grazing, and in some cases an all-weather exercise arena. The owner is responsible for mucking out, turning out, grooming, exercising and all vet./med. care and the cost of all feed and bedding. Charges average £35 per week; range £20-£50.

DIY Plus Livery. As the above, except that the yard manager is responsible for certain tasks, such as turning out and feeding. Charges average £45 per week; range £30-£60.

In addition there is *Full Livery.* The yard supplies a complete service to the horse owner including tasks such as grooming and exercise. Services provided by the yard may be fitted to the needs of a horse/owner. Few farm-based liveries would offer such a high level of management. Full livery charges average £110 per week; with a range of £75-£150.

The above are only guidelines. There is a wide variation both within, and between regions.

Other Costs:

Grazing. Variable costs will average some £50 per horse per year. Average stocking rates are 0·8 ha (2 acres) for the first horse and 0·4 ha (1 acre) for each horse after.

Hay. Average price £3.50 per conventional bale (approximately 20kg) (range £2.50-£5.00), depending on the season. It has to be good quality. Average consumption is one to two bales per horse per week; less in the summer depending on the grass quality/quantity and the work of the horse. Some horses now have haylage; more expensive, dust free and higher fibre and energy/protein levels; less required per head.

Concentrate Feed. Can range from almost nil to 3.0-4.0kg per day depending, amongst other factors, on breed, size and intensity of work. Compound feed 30 to 45p per kg.

Bedding. Averages around £8 per stabled horse per week, with some horses stabled year round and others having significant turnout in the summer, which reduces bedding cost. Typical cost £300-£400 per year. Straw might cost only half as much; however, more expensive, but preferable, alternatives (such as wood shavings, shredded paper and hemp fibre) are now increasingly being used.

Vet. and Med. Averages approximately £150 per horse per year. Some yards include worming of the horse in the livery cost.

Rates. Livery is a non-agricultural use, and therefore any buildings being used for the enterprise are liable to business rates.

The supply of livery yards appears to be increasing, from both farms diversifying and other yards setting up. Filling a yard is, consequently, becoming more difficult. The level of service and facilities expected by customers has increased. There is a trend towards greater professionalism in the running and management of livery yards. Livery contracts should be exchanged showing clearly the responsibilities of each party. Comprehensive third party insurance is also important.

To be successful, a livery enterprise needs higher quality facilities than farm livestock. To the owner the horse can be anything from a highly trained athlete to a family pet. Horses are expensive: even modest quality horses cost between £1,500 and £3,000. Good customer relations and an effective security system (including burglar and fire alarms) are crucial to success, as is good market research and effective advertising.

A full livery yard will require stables, a secure room to store tack, a vermin-proof hard feed store, storage for hay and bedding, a muck heap, a riding arena and parking provision with room for horse boxes. Planning permission is required for the conversion of an existing building to stabling or the erection of new, purpose-built stables. Permission is also required for construction of an all weather arena used for training horses and exercising them in bad weather. Hay and straw should be stored away from the stables and downwind of them to minimise the fire risk. A hard standing area with a water supply and good drainage should be provided for grooming and washing down the horses.

Good ventilation in the stables is crucial as horses are prone to respiratory diseases caused by spores and dust. Provision should be made for owners to soak hay in clean water before feeding it, to reduce respiratory problems.

Fences must be sound and free of protruding nails, wire etc. Ideally fields should be fenced using post and rail, but this is expensive. Barbed wire should be avoided wherever possible or should be 'protected' with an offset electrified fence. Fields should be divided into smaller paddocks to reduce the possibility of fighting between incompatible horses and to separate mares and geldings. Paddocks may be divided using two or more strands of electrified tape or rope but wire is not advisable as it is not easily visible to the horse.

Off-road riding opportunities on the farm are a real asset. The farmer may provide riding trails, a jumping paddock, or a cross country course. An all-weather ménage for exercising horses, possibly with floodlighting, is highly desirable, and some livery yards have horse walkers too. Good facilities can be rented out to individuals or organisations such as pony clubs. It is sometimes possible to link up with nearby farms to increase the length of riding tracks available.

Construction Costs. The cost of conversion of existing buildings will depend on their quality; prefabricated hardwood and steel internal stable partitions can be purchased from upwards of £750 per stable, depending on size and specification. Free standing timber stables cost between £800 and £2,000 (plus base), depending on size and quality. As horses are fairly destructive animals (they both kick and chew) better quality stables will often prove more economic in the long run. All weather arenas (20 metres by 40 metres) cost between £10,000 and £25,000; construction is a specialist job as good drainage is essential; a badly constructed arena is worthless.

Contact*:* Further financial information on horse enterprises, including riding schools and equestrian centres, is available in 'Equine Business Guide', 5th Edition, 2005, edited by Richard Bacon, Warwickshire College; Tel. 01926 318 338.

OSTRICHES

Introduction

Ostrich production was introduced to the UK during the 1990s with breeding stock of very mixed genetics and no production history. Today, production is limited to a handful of small farmers, working individually, selling most meat production through local farmers markets and to the service industry. These farmers have their own breeding stock, incubate and raise their own chicks. Slaughter is carried out under contract in small, dedicated ostrich plants and red meat slaughter plants with a ratite (flightless bird) license. Farmers are responsible for all their own marketing. Ostrich are not sold through livestock auction markets.

Working in low volume presents significant challenges to both maximising revenue and controlling production costs, as it is difficult to achieve economies of scale. Ostrich are produced primarily for their meat, with their skins (for leather), fat and feathers providing additional revenue potential. Skins are generally sold in minimum numbers of 200 so it can require long-term storage to build up sufficient numbers. With the low production levels in the UK, the only market for the feathers and fat are those the farmers can generate from their own value adding.

It is difficult, because of the lack of processing infrastructure to make farming ostrich a viable activity in the UK. It can be done but a prospective farmer needs to thoroughly research the slaughter / processing facilities in their chosen area and be prepared to undertake direct meat marketing. This situation will continue until a substantial investment in production and provision of associated infrastructure is undertaken.

Space constraints restrict detail in the Pocketbook. The tables below provide 3 production scenarios, low, medium and high. Complete explanations and definitions can be viewed at the BDOA web site: www.ostrich.org.uk/johnnix.

Production

Significant variations continue to be reported on production levels and time taken to slaughter – this is a direct reflection of the nutrients fed, management systems and the variable genetics. The following table is an approximate guide to potential production under different production systems.

Breeder Production	Low Production	Medium Production	High Production
Eggs – *per hen per year*	<50	50 - 70	>70
Hatching - %	<65%	65% - 80%	>80%
Surviving Chicks - %	<50%	50%-75%	>75%
Total Chicks *	**< 25**	**25-50**	**> 50**

*Chicks to slaughter or reaching maturity

Slaughter Birds	Very Low Production	Low Production	Medium Production	High Production
Slaughter Age – Days [1]	365-425	425-485	300-365	180-300
Liveweight	85-120	85-130	90-120	90-125
Meat Yield – kilos	20-30	25-45	25-35	35-45
Feed Consumption – kg [2]	650-785	785-925	470-620	230-435
Feed Conversion [3]	5.5:1 – 9:1	6:1 - 11:1	3.9:1 – 7:1	2:1 – 3.5:1

1. 180 days to slaughter with high meat yields will be reached progressively, achieved through a combination of high production rations, good management and genetic improvement.
2. Includes all feed, including grazing and/or silage (when offered).

3. Feed conversion based on liveweight must be used with caution – if birds carry too much fat their meat yields are low despite their high liveweight.

Feeding Rates and Consumption:
The following tables illustrate the food consumption based on 90% dry matter as fed basis and assuming high production rations. Consumption can increase by as much as 30% when rations are nutrient deficient.

Slaughter Bird Age	Ration	Kilos	Cumulative Kilos
1 - 60 Days	Starter	25	25
61 - 140 Days	Grower	107	132
141 - 280 Days	Grower	291	423
281 - 365 Days	Grower	192	615

Breeders	Days	Daily Amount	No. Birds	Total Kilos	No. Birds	Total Kilos
Breeder	252	2.1kgs	2 (Pair)	1058	3 (Trio)	1588
Maintenance	113	2.1kgs	2 (pair)	475	3 (Trio)	712
Total per year	365			1533		2300

Note that feed consumption on low production rations is generally greater than medium and high production rations.

Revenue
Historically skin was the driving product of ostrich. A sustainable meat market offers the greatest potential for growth and commercial success of ostrich. Doubling meat yields and halving time taken to slaughter transforms the overall economics. Meat revenue should attract approximately 75% of revenue, with other products adding valuable additional income. Details of meat yields and muscle sizes are included in the information on the BDOA web site.

Breeder Production Costs/year

Production	Low [1]		Medium	High	
Costs Per Trio:					
Kilos Feed/Trio (kg)	2,300	2,300	2,300	2,300	2,300
Feed Cost/Kilo[2]	£0.22	£0.22	£0.29	£0.34	£0.34
Slaughter Birds/Trio	30	50	70	100	160
Feed Cost/Trio	£509	£509	£672	£783	£783
Other Production Costs/Trio[3]	£110	£110	£110	£110	£110
Total Production Costs/Trio	£619	£619	£782	£893	£893
Costs Per Slaughter Bird:					
Breeder Feed Cost	£16.96	£10.18	£9.60	£7.83	£4.89
Other Production Costs	£3.67	£2.20	£1.57	£1.10	£0.69
Total Breeder Costs per chick	£20.63	£12.38	£11.17	£8.93	£5.58

1. Feed consumption on low production rations can result in increased intake of ± 25%.

2. Based on grain prices as at July 2010 and assuming economies of scale. An additional ±25% should be added if purchasing in bags and/or with low tonnages.

3. Other production costs include a depreciation charge for capital invested in infrastructure. All these costs will vary from farm to farm depending on existing infrastructure and economies of scale.

Gross Margin Per Trio	Low		Medium	High	
Revenue:					
Price Per Chick[1]	£20.5	£12.5	£11.3	£9.30	£6.0
Chicks	£615	£625	£791	£930	£960
Less					
Production Costs	£619	£619	£782	£893	£893
Gross Margin/Trio - High Vol. production	**(£4)**	**£6**	**£9**	**£37**	**£67**
For Low Volume deduct:					
Increased Costs	£189	£189	£189	£189	£189
Additional Chick Price	£6	£3	£2	£1	£1
Total Chick Price	£26	£16	£13	£11	£7

1. The reducing cost per chick with improvements in performance, transferred to production costs of slaughter birds below. Expensive chicks will also be at greater risk of slow growth, higher mortality and poor feed conversion.

Slaughter Bird Costs

Production Level	Low[1]		Medium	High
Days to Slaughter	425	365	300	200
Boneless meat	40kg	40kg	40kg	40kg
Average Meat Revenue/kg	£8/kg	£8/kg	£8/kg	£8/kg
Meat Revenue/bird	£320	£320	£320	£320
Skin	£50	£50	£50	£50
Total Revenue	**£370**	**£370**	**£370**	**£370**
Less – Assuming Low Volume Production				
Cost of Day Old Chick (see breeder Gross Margins)	£26	£16	£13	£11
Feed [2]	£221	£181	£172	£97
Other Rearing Costs [3]	£106	£91	£70	£50
Slaughter, Processing and Packaging	£75	£75	£75	£75
Marketing	£5	£5	£5	£5
Total Expenses	**£434**	**£368**	**£336**	**£238**
Gross Margin Per Bird	**(£64)**	**£2**	**£34**	**£132**

1. Feed consumption on Low Production rations can result in increased intake of ± 25%.

2. Based on feed ingredient prices as at July 2010 and assuming low tonnages. Deduct ±25% if purchasing in bulk with high annual tonnages.

3. Other production costs include a depreciation charge for capital invested in infrastructure. Costs will vary from farm to farm depending on existing infrastructure and size of operation.

Contact: British Domesticated Ostrich Association (BDOA), 33 Eden Grange, Little Corby, Carlisle, CA4 8QW. (Tel.: 01228 562 946); www.ostrich.org.uk

WILD BOAR

Wild Boar are now being farmed in the UK on approximately 50 farms, with a population probably exceeding 1,750 sows. They produce a firm dark meat with a characteristically 'gamey' flavour which is in demand particularly from the hotel and restaurant trade.

Wild Boar come under the Dangerous Wild Animals Act and wild boar farms must be licensed by the Local Authority. There is no uniformity of fee or conditions that have to be met, but typically licences cost £100-£150 and are renewed annually following an inspection of the farm. Enclosures must be secure with strong fencing: a minimum height of at least 1.8m is usually specified and most authorities require 30-80cm below ground plus an additional strand of electric fence inside the main fence. The estimated minimum cost of fencing using approved contractors is from £8 per metre erected plus the hire of a digger. All gates and access areas must be padlocked at all times.

Wild Boars are kept in groups of up to 10 sows per boar. They are nearly always kept outdoors, often on arable land (as outdoor domestic pigs), although rough land with some natural vegetation, such as scrub, or best of all, woodland, is ideal. Good husbandry requires some basic housing, such as arcs. Large arcs are suitable for a group of gestating sows, or sows running with maturing boarlets. Sows should have access to an individual shelter for farrowing and the first few days of lactation. If good vegetation is available sows may make their own farrowing nest away from the main group with satisfactory results.

Stocking rates vary according to the type of land but about a hectare would be needed for a group of 5 sows and a boar. They will forage actively on suitable terrain but this is unlikely to provide a significant part of their diet. They need to be fed a balanced ration (additive free pig concentrate is suitable but specially formulated feeds are available) with supplementary vegetable material. If a good supply of root crops is available this may replace some concentrate. Wild boar mate and farrow naturally and have few health problems, so little if any intervention is needed. Gilts mature at 18 months. In the wild breeding occurs in the autumn and early winter and the sows farrow from February to March after 4 months gestation. One litter per year is the norm. However, most farmed sows maintained at a good nutritional level will give two litters in most years. Young sows produce 2 to 3 boarlets and mature sows 6 to 8. A well-run enterprise should average 7 boarlets per sow per year raised to maturity. Wild boar can live from 12 to 15 years, perhaps more, but in a commercial herd the sows are usually culled at 7 to 8 years old.

The boarlets remain in the family group until they are all weaned together at 8 to 12 weeks (16 at the outside). Although some (usually smaller) producers leave growers to mature in family groups, they are generally separated into grower/finisher groups on rough grass or in open barns. Wild boar will take between 9 and 18 months to reach a slaughter weight of 75-85 kg. This produces a 45-50 kg carcase. They are slaughtered in the same way as pigs. The carcase has more shoulder and less on the hind-quarters than a domestic pig. It can be butchered like a domestic pig or without the skin like venison. The meat from male animals 2 years old or over is too strong, except for sausages, but sows up to 8 years old still have an acceptable carcase and a good cull value. A real problem for some producers is arranging slaughter: abattoirs are currently required to have wild boar specified on their licence and many expect them to be difficult to handle.

Labour requirements are low, owing to the 'hands off' nature of wild boar management. One person might manage a herd of 30-40 sows and fatteners.

In spite of the large and apparently unsatisfied demand for wild boar meat, as with other alternative enterprises, there is no organised marketing system and producers have to develop their own outlets. There are some wholesale butchers and game dealers who will take whole carcase in significant numbers, but many producers organise their own processing into a variety of pre-packed products and arrange their own retailing. Sold at retail the meat commands a considerable margin over the wholesale price, but butchering, packaging and marketing costs have to be considered. Wild boar production can be successful both as a secondary enterprise on a farm or as a stand-alone operation.

Performance:

Finished Boarlets per Sow per Year......................................	7 (6 - 9)
Finished Carcase Weight (over 15 months)............................	45 - 50 kg
Price per kg deadweight..	£3.75 (£3.00-£4.50)

Sales:	£
Meat sales per Sow per Year..................................	1,247
Less Depreciation per Sow per Year (1)........................	30
Output per Sow	**1,217**

Variable Costs:	
Concentrates sow (2)...	205
fatteners (@ £72 each)...................................	504
Bedding...	11
Vet, Med and Licence...	31
Miscellaneous (inc. Water and Electricity)............................	11
Total Variable Costs per Sow	**762**
Gross Margin per Sow	**455**

1. Cost of sow £400, cull value £200, herd life 7 years, plus share of boar

2. Including share of boar

Capital Costs Housing and fencing - £4,000 per hectare (£1,620 per acre); pure-bred boar - £300-£600; pure-bred sow - £250-£500.

Acknowledgement: Thanks to - Dr Martin Goulding www.britishwildboar.org.uk

SHEEP DAIRYING

Performance Level	Low	Average	High
Milk Yield (litres) per Ewe per Year	225	375	450
Sales:	£	£	£
Milk Value (1)......................................	202.5	337.5	405.0
Value of Lambs (2).............................	56.6	56.6	56.6
Wool..	1.5	1.5	1.5
Cull Ewes and Rams (3)......................	4.5	4.5	4.5
Output per Ewe	**265.1**	**400.1**	**467.6**
Variable Costs:			
Concentrates (4).................................		174.3	
Miscellaneous (inc. Vet and Med).......		17.5	
Forage Variable Costs (5)...................		25.0	
Total Variable Costs		**216.8**	
Gross Margin per Ewe	**48.3**	**183.3**	**250.8**
Stocking Rate (Ewes with Lambs per forage Hectare (acre))......................................		11 (4.5)	
Gross Margin per Forage Hectare..............	531	2,016	2,759
Gross Margin per Forage Acre....................	215	816	1,116

1. Price: 90p per litre at farm gate (range from 80p-105p per litre).

2. *Lambing %:* 175%. Assume a 300 Friesland ewe flock. Retain 60 ewe lambs for flock replacements. Sell 390 finished lambs reared from 2 days old (inc. 15% mortality) at £38. If meat-type terminal sires used then cross-bred lamb values per ewe increase to £63.

3. *Cull ewes:* Assumed 18% culled at £25.00 per head (average, including mortality).

4. *Concentrates:* Milking ewes: 200 days at 1.5 kg/head/day, 100 days at 0.5 kg/head/day; cost £200/tonne. Ewe lamb replacements and artificially reared finished lambs at £65/head.

5. *Forage costs:* Quality silage: 1 tonne per milking ewe (or hay equivalent). Grazing: early grass in March/April; good grazing on leys or pasture; similar for dry stock and lambs.

Fixed Costs per Ewe: Labour (paid) £73; Power and Machinery £22; Property Costs £12; Other £13; Total, excluding Finance and Rent, £120.

Capital Costs of Equipment: Complete milking unit for 300 ewes (including yokes, bulk tank, dairy equipment, installation): £12,000-£25,000. A small 50 ewe unit can be put together for under £10,000. Any building works would be additional to the above costs.

Acknowledgement: thanks to - Anthony Hyde, FRICS, FBIAC, ARAgS.

GOAT DAIRYING

Performance Level	Low	Average	High
Milk Yield (litres) per Goat (1)	500	800	1,200
Sales:	£	£	£
Milk Value (2).....................................	200.0	320.0	480.0
Value of Kids (3)................................	2.8	3.6	3.6
Less Livestock Depreciation (4)..................	27.7	27.7	27.7
Output per doe	**175.1**	**295.9**	**455.9**
Variable Costs:			
Concentrates (5)....................................	57.8	92.4	138.6
Miscellaneous (inc. Vet and Med).......	55.0	55.0	55.0
Forage Variable Costs (6)....................	45.0	72.0	108.0
Total Variable Costs	**157.8**	**219.4**	**301.6**
Gross Margin per Doe	**17.4**	**76.5**	**154.3**
Stocking Rate (Goats per Forage Hectare			
(acre) - zero-grazed system).................	6.5 (2.6)	8.0 (3.2)	9.5 (3.8)
Gross Margin per Forage Hectare..............	113	612	1,466
Gross Margin per Forage Acre....................	46	248	593

1. *Yield:* Per 300 day lactation, kidding each year. Autumn kidders tend to yield less.

2. *Price:* 40p per litre; seasonal variation from 33p in June to 53p in November. 12.5% solids delivered.

3. *Kid(s):* Prolificacy relates to age, breed, seasonality and feed level. Assumptions: low 140%; average and high 180%. There is very little trade in kids for meat (£2 per kid assumed).

4. *Culls and Replacements:* Replacements at £180/head; culls £17.50, average life 6 years. Bucks: 1 per 40-50 does. Does normally mate in autumn; gestation 150 days; young goats can be mated from 6 months.

5. *Concentrates:* Average 0.55 kg concentrate per litre, at £210 per tonne.

6. *Forage:* Average 0.9 kg DM forage per litre at £100 per tonne DM (part purchased, part home-grown). Goats can be grazed but are normally storage fed to avoid problems with worms, fencing, milk taints and pneumonia. Farmers able to produce maize silage will have a better forage conversion ratio.

7. *Miscellaneous:* Bedding £12, vet and med. £24 (includes treatment for out-of-season breeding, vaccination against Johnes and humane disposal of unsaleable kids), sundries £19.

8. *Stocking rate:* Based on home-grown forage.

9. *Labour:* 1 full-time person per 100 goats is a guide, but very dependent on technology employed.

10. *Markets:* Herd sizes in the UK range from 50 to 3,000 milking does. Average herd size is growing as established producers expand with the market at about 15% average annual growth. Successful businesses have been built on producer processing and retailing, as bulk purchasers of goats milk are few and far between. Prolificacy and technical improvements allow higher annual growth than the market and there is a cycle in milk and stock prices.

Contact: The British Goat Society (Bovey Tracey, Devon (tel. 01626 833168)) registers pedigree animals and publishes a monthly newsletter.

Acknowledgements: The above information originally supplied by *Dr. T. Mottram*, Silsoe Research Institute, Bedford MK45 4HS, amended since by the author.

ANGORA GOATS

Angora goats produce mohair; angora rabbits produce angora; cashgora is produced by angora cross dairy goats; cashmere is produced by improved feral goats (valuable 'down' has to be separated from guard hairs; thus, with cashmere production, 'yield of down' must not be confused with 'weight of clip' as percentage down is low and can vary widely). Goat meat is called 'chevon'.

UK mohair output is currently around 5 tonnes per year, which indicates a population of between 1500 and 2,000 animals. The figures below are for a commercial enterprise. Many UK angora flocks are kept on a semi-commercial or hobby basis, in which case different criteria may apply – does retained longer, mortality rates lower, doe/buck ratio different. Currently (2010) the world price of mohair is reaching record levels due to a world shortage of Angora Goats and demand from China. The figures used in the calculations are predicted levels for 2011.

Performance:

Kids per Doe per Year (1)	1.4
Fibre: Doe/Buck, 2 clips, 3.2 & 4.5kg/clip respectively (2)	6.8 kg
Kids (1.4), first and second clips (3)	5.0 kg
Whethers/Replacement Does (0.9), third clip (3)	3.15 kg

	£
Fibre Sales:	
Doe/Buck: 6.8kg @ £6.00/kg (3)	40.6
Kids: 5.0kg @ £10/kg (3)	50.4
Whethers/Replacements: 3.2kg @ £7/kg (3)	22.1
Stock Sales:	
Does: 0.5 females sold for breeding @ £100 each (1)(4)	50.0
Whethers: 0.7 males sold for meat @ £40 each (1)(4)	28.0
Culls: 0.17 does @ £40 each (1)(4)	6.8
Skin Sales:	
From cull does and males sold for meat @£10.00	8.7
Less Replacements (Buck only) (4)	1.5
Output per Doe	**205.0**
Variable Costs:	
Concentrates does (plus buck): 90kg @ £200/tonne (5)	18.0
kids (to clip 2): 50kg/hd @ £200/tonne (5)	14.0
replacements: 25kg/head @ £200/tonne (5)	4.5
Vet and Med (6)	8.0
Miscellaneous (6)	18.0
Total Variable Costs per Doe	**62.5**
Gross Margin per Doe before Forage Costs	**142.5**
Forage Variable Costs (10 Does per hectare @ £175/ha) (7)	17.5
Gross Margin per Doe	**125.0**
Gross Margin per Forage hectare	1,250.2
Gross Margin per Forage acre	506.0

1. 1.5 kids born alive per doe mated; 2% mortality to each clip. Of 0.7 surviving doe kids, the majority (0.5) are sold for breeding, the remainder (0.2) are retained for replacements. Culls (0.17) and casualties are equal to the number of replacements (unless the flock size is changing). Progeny are sold after 2 clips for breeding or after 3 clips for meat. Stock may be retained for further shearing. This has become more common, as the demand for breeding stock is small, fibre quality has improved and there is little market for meat.

2. The data for Breeding Does include output and inputs for breeding bucks. Assumes 25 does to one buck.

3. Angora goats are usually clipped twice a year. Yield increases over first four clips, but quality decreases with age. Prices can be volatile, being dependent on fashion and on the world market dominated by South Africa and Texas. Demand and prices are highest for the high quality kid fibre <25 microns in diameter. The following yields and prices have been used:-

   Clip 1: 1.1 kg, £10.00 per kg; clip 2: 2.5 kg, £10.00 per kg; clip 3: 3.5 kg, £7.00 per kg; adult doe: 3.0 kg, adult buck 4.5 kg, £6.00 per kg.

   British Mohair Marketing arranges a collection once a year, currently in September. The fibre is professionally graded and then offered for sale by tender. There is a handling charge of 60p per kg of fibre. Membership of BMM costs £30. (Some producers improve their return by processing and using the fibre themselves or selling to local spinners. Commercial processing costs are significant: combing about £2.50 per kg and spinning about £15 per kg).

4. Stock sales. Breeding stock in commercial flocks are culled after seven years on average. Subsequent shearing stock culled after a further 4 clips. Value of all cull stock: £40 each. Depending on quality, the skin can be worth £10 before curing or up to £120 after curing. Replacement costs: does, £100; bucks, £300. Shearing stock, £20 (as transfer from breeding enterprise). Show quality stock command a premium.

5. Concentrates. Quantities: Kids - 50 kg to clip 2, 15 kg to clip 3; Adults - breeding adults 90 kg per year, shearlings 40 kg per year.

6. Veterinary costs can be high. Miscellaneous costs include £2.50 to £3.50 per shearing per head (it may be more) and bedding materials.

7. Angora goats require more management than sheep. Fencing requirements are similar but housing costs rather higher. Margins are particularly sensitive to the value and number of breeding stock sold, yield and value of fibre, kidding percentage and meat values. There is a market for meat from older animals but no reliable market has yet been developed specifically for younger animals. Angoras are probably most successfully run as a subsidiary enterprise on a farm rather than a stand alone operation.

Contact: *British Angora Goat Society*: www.britishangoragoats.org.uk

Acknowledgements: Stephen Whitley, Corrymoor Angoras, Stockland, Honiton, Devon EX14 9DY socks@corrymoor.com www.corrymoor.com

CAMELIDS

Llamas, alpacas, guanacos and vicunas are collectively known as New World Camelids. Originally they all came from Central America. They are all members of the camelid family and are related to Bactrian and Dromedary camels. Camelids are herd animals and should not be kept in isolation but will live happily with other animals.

Llamas

The llama is the largest of the Camelids, weighing up to 180kg (400lbs) and standing 1.25m (4ft) at shoulder height. Llamas are strong animals traditionally used as pack animals and kept in the UK for trekking or pets. They have a life span of 15-20 years.

Llamas can be kept at stocking rates of 10-12/ha (4-5/acre). They are generally hardy animals but benefit from an open fronted shelter. They eat grass and hay, with occasional supplements. They can be bought from a few hundred pounds.

Alpaca

Alpacas are smaller with a shoulder height of 1m (3ft) and weigh around 70kg (155lb). They produce an outstanding quality fleece. Its fibres are very fine and exceptionally strong. An annual shearing will produce an average fleece of 2.5kg which, when cleaned can sell for;

- Baby Alpaca £8 per kg (22 micron or below)

- Fine Alpaca £5 per kg (23-27 micron)

- Coarse Alpaca £0.75 per kg (28-32 micron)

Alpacas require shearing either annually or biannually, depending on breed type , Huacaya (95% of UK alpacas, tight curly locks) or Suri, (with longer curly locks like a Wensleydale sheep).

Alpacas should be kept at 12–20 per hectare (5-8/acre). They are hardy animals well suited to the UK climate, but require shelter from rain. They graze all year, with additional hay and occasional supplements.

An alpaca can cost anything from £250 for non breeding stock to £15,000. Price will vary according to genetics, age, fertility, fibre quality and colour. The alpaca gestation period is up to 11 months.

The earning potential of an Alpaca is dictated by the quality of its fleece and through breeding as there is no commercial alpaca meat industry in the UK. Animals with low quality fleeces may have a value as pets or even flock guards. Alpaca fleece is a luxury fibre thus only the highest quality fleeces and stock command good prices.

GRAZING LIVESTOCK UNITS

Dairy cows	1.00	Lowland ewes	0.11
Beef cows (excl. calf)	0.75	Upland ewes	0.08
Heifers in calf (rearing)	0.80	Hill ewes	0.06
Bulls	0.65	Breeding ewe hoggets:	
		½ to 1 year	0.06
Other cattle (excl. intensive beef):		Other sheep, over 1 year	0.08
0-1 year old	0.34	Store lambs, under 1 year	0.04
1-2 years old	0.65	Rams	0.08
2 years old and over	0.80		
Breeding sows	0.44	Broilers	0.0017
Gilts in pig	0.20	Other table chicken	0.004
Maiden gilts	0.18	Turkeys	0.005
Boars	0.35	Ducks, geese, other poultry	0.003
Other pigs	0.17	Horses	0.80
Cocks, hens, pullets in lay	0.017	Milch goats	0.16
Pullets, 1 week to point of lay	0.003	Other goats	0.11

Source: as advised by DEFRA for the Farm Business Survey.

1. *Total livestock units on a farm* should be calculated by multiplying the above ratios by the monthly livestock numbers averaged over the whole year.

2. *The ratios are based on feed requirements.* Strictly speaking, when calculating stocking density, allowances should also be made for differences in output (e.g. milk yield per cow or liveweight gain per head), breed (e.g. Friesians v. Jerseys) and quantities of non-forage feed consumed.

FORAGE VARIABLE COSTS

£ per hectare (acre) / year	Grass Dairying (1)	Grass Other (1)	Grass Clover Ley	Forage Maize (2)	Kale
Yield tonnes/ha (tons/acre)	50	45	40 (16)	40 (16)	45 (18)
Seed per year	23 (9)	15 (6)	19 (8)	148 (60)	50 (20)
Fertiliser	179 (72)	129 (52)	42 (17)	143 (58)	144 (58)
Sprays	11 (4)	7 (3)	13 (5)	40 (16)	46 (19)
Total	212 (86)	151 (61)	74 (30)	331 (134)	240 (97)
Cost per tonne fresh weight	4.25	3.35	1.85	8.28	5.34

	Fodder Beet	Forage Rape	Maincrop Turnips	Stubble Turnips	Swedes
Yield tonnes/ha (tons/acre)	70 (28)	35 (14)	65 (26)	35 (14)	70 (28)
Seed	130 (53)	20 (8)	42 (17)	14 (6)	156 (63)
Fertiliser	181 (73)	98 (40)	144 (58)	107 (43)	144 (58)
Sprays	148 (60)	22 (9)	48 (19)	25 (10)	50 (20)
Total	459 (186)	140 (57)	234 (95)	146 (59)	350 (142)
Cost per tonne fresh weight	6.56	4.00	3.61	4.17	5.00

1. *Intensively silaged and grazed grass* may have higher fertiliser costs to as much as £250/ha (100/acre) for some dairying systems (based on N:P:K of 320:40:50). Seed costs vary according to the proportion of permanent pasture and length of leys. Fertiliser is often less on permanent pasture, depending on management style which also affects stocking rates and productive levels per animal.

2. *Contract work on maize:* drilling £43 (17); harvesting £99 (40), or £146 (59) to include carting and clamping.

3. Standing maize crops are typically sold for £600 to £700/ha (£243-283/acre) but can be as high as £850/ha (£350/acre), depending on the potential yield of the crop and local supply and demand.

4. *Labour:* forage and conservation labour, pages 162

5. *Conservation machinery:* page 179.

Whole Crop (feed wheat). Variable costs are as for combined crop (page 5) plus contract harvesting at £175 per ha (£71 per acre). Fresh yield averages 27.5 tonnes per ha (11 tons per acre) harvested in late June at 35% dry matter. Urea treatment (for higher dry matter) for whole-crop alkalage: £6/treated tonne. For urea treated grain, add £13.70 per tonne. Standing wheat in 2010 sold for between £800 (324/ac) and £1,000/hectare (400/ac), on expectations of forage shortages. Normally prices are nearer the lower end of this range.

Plastic wrap for bagged silage = £2.80/bale.

Grass Silage and Hay Costs and Value

Estimated average costs (for 2011) of producing and harvesting, on a full costs basis (i.e. including rental value of the land, all labour, share of general overheads, etc.) are: Hay: £75 per tonne; Silage: £30 per tonne fresh weight.

Approximately half the silage cost is for growing the grass and half for harvesting and storage. The per cent breakdown of total costs is typically as follows:

Proportions of costs of growing and making silage

Variable Costs:	Fertiliser	Seeds and Sprays	Contract	Sundries
Silage.............................	18	2	34	3
Hay.................................	22	3	20	2

Fixed Costs:	Rent	Labour	Tractors	FYM/Lime
Silage.............................	22	6	14	1
Hay.................................	28	7	18	1

Sale Value of hay and (far less common because of its bulk) silage vary widely according to the region and season (supply/demand situation), quality and time of year:

a.   *Hay* (pick-up baled) has an average ex-farm sale value of £80 to £100 per tonne. Seed hay (main range November to May £100 to £120) and £65-£85 for meadow hay (main range November to May £70 to £80); prices are higher in the west than the east and more after a dry summer (giving low yields of grass). Prices tend to be higher for horses. Big bale hay is £20 to £30/tonne cheaper.

b.   *Grass silage* is typically about £35 a tonne delivered (up to £50 when forage is very short in an area and less if it is plentiful), maize silage approx. £30 a tonne.

c.   The dry spring and summer of 2010 (poor silage harvest) and low barley area suggest to some that forage will be dear in 2010/11.

Relative Costs of Grazing, Conserved Grass, etc.

	Yield DM tonnes/ha (acre)	Cost per tonne DM (£)	MJ per kg DM	Pence per MJ of ME in DM
Grazed Grass	10 (4.1)	46	12.8	0.36
Kale (direct drilled)	6.9 (2.8)	69	11.0	0.62
Forage Turnips (direct drilled)	6.9 (2.8)	82	10.2	0.80
Grass Silage............................	10 (4.1)	46	10.9	0.42
Big Bale Silage.......................	10 (4.1)	50	10.8	0.46
Purchased Hay (1)		95	8.8	1.08
Brewers' Grains (2)................		125	11.7	1.07
Concentrates (3)......................		192	12.8	1.50

(1) at £80 per tonne   (2) at £30 per tonne   (3) 14% CP 14% Moisture, delivered in bulk, £160 per tonne

1.   *In interpreting the above figures* for use in planning feed use on farm, it is important to remember that own land, labour and capital for equipment are required for home-produced fodder but not for purchased feed, and much more storage is required

2.   *The consumption of fodder* is limited by its bulk although this very much depends upon its quality/digestibility.

3.   *The cost of forage* will vary enormously depending on growing conditions, soil fertility and type, intensity of farming practice and management ability.

FODDER CROPS, GRASSES, CLOVERS AND ENVIRONMENTAL SEEDS

Seed Prices (Autumn 2010) and Seed Rates

Crop	Price £/Kg	Seed Rate Kg/Ha	Cost £/Ha
Grass Leys			
1 year leys	£2.00-2.50	35-55	70 - 130
2 year leys	£2.00	35	70
3-4 year leys	£2.50	35	85 - 95
4-6 year leys	£2.60	35 - 40	90 - 105
Long-term ley	£2.70	32 - 45	85 - 120
Permanent Grass	£3.00	32.5	100
Mixed and Clover Leys			
White Clover ley	£3.20	30	95
Red Clover ley	£3.30 - 3.40	30	100 - 105
Timothy/M. Fescue ley	£3.20	31kg	100
Fodder Crops			
Fodder Kale	£9.25-£11.50	5-7.5	46 - 70
Swedes	£42.25	Precision drill 0.7	30
		seed drill 3.7	156
Stubble Turnips	£3.80	3.75 kg drilled,	14
		5.0 kg broadcast	19
Maincrop Turnips	£11.25	3.75 kg drilled,	42
		5.0 kg broadcast	56
Rape	£2.00	10	20
Mustard	£2.00	20	40
Rape and Turnip mix	£3.40/kg mix	1.25 kg rape	17
		3.75 kg turnips	
Kale, Swede & Turnips	£14.70/kg mix	1.5 kg kale,	55
		0.5 kg swede,	
		1.75 kg turnips	
Fodder Beet			143 - 153
Cover Mixes, Environmental and Equine			
Game Cover mixture	£3.10	25	80
Game Maize	£2.90	27.5	80
Forage Maize: Silage			130 - 175
Vetch/Tares	£1.55	75 to 125 kg	115 - 205
Quinoa & Kale mix	£8.60	7.5	65
Field Corner mixture	£11.30	25	280
Horse grazing	£2.90 - 4.70	35kg	100 - 175
Gallop mixture	£2.90	100-250	280 - 715

Crop	Price £/Kg	Seed Rate Kg/Ha	Cost £/Ha
Individual Varieties			
Westerwold Ryegrass	£2.00	35 kg	70
Italian Ryegrass	£2.10	35 kg	75
Perennial Ryegrass	£2.80	25 to 40 kg	70 - 110
Hybrid Ryegrass	£2.50	35 kg	87
Cocksfoot	£3.65	20 to 25 kg	73 - 91
Red Clover	£5.20	15	80
White Clover	£5.75	7 kg	40
Timothy	£2.90		
Meadow Fescue	£2.65		
Sweet Vernal	£59.50		
Reed Canary Grass	£14.00	7.5 kg	105
Lucerne	£5.60 (inoculated)	20 kg	115
Sainfoin	£2.65	70 to 90 kg	180 - 240
Millet	£1.96	25	49
Sunflower	£4.50	25	110
Sorghum	£3.60	20	75

Acknowledgement: Particular thanks to - Cotswold Seeds 0800 252 211

3. PIGS, POULTRY, TROUT, RABBIT

PIGS

Breeding and Rearing (to 37 kg liveweight per sow per year and per 37 kg pig reared)

Performance Level	*Average*		*High*	
	per sow	per pig	per sow	per pig
	£	£	£	£
Weaners: (ave) 22.3 (1) @ £49 (3)...........	1093	49.00		
(high) 24.9 (2) @ £49 (3).........			1220	49.00
Less Livestock Depreciation (4)...............	57	2.53	67	2.69
Output	1036	46.47	1153	46.31
Variable Costs:				
Food (5)..	589	26.41	602	24.18
Miscellaneous (6).............................	75	3.36	85	3.41
Total Variable Costs	664	29.77	687	27.59
Gross Margin (per year)	**372**	**16.69**	**466**	**18.72**

1. *Weaners per sow:* - average: 9.90 reared per litter, 2.25 litters per year = 22.3 weaners per sow per year. (The average has now recovered following falls in the early 2000's due to the wasting diseases PMWS and PDNS. Productivity improvements are also being made).

2. *Weaners per sow:* - high: 10.60 reared per litter, 2.35 litters per year = 24.9 weaners per sow per year. For Outdoor Breeding performance figures see page 95.

3. *Price:* assumed pig cycle average. (See General Prices on page 93). Prices for 37kg weaners have varied from £15 to £60 during the past decade. They had been between £30 and £40 for some years prior to mid-2008, but rose with the general improvement in pig prices. They have been above £50 per pig, but some reduction is expected.

4. *Average livestock depreciation* assumes an in-pig gilt purchase price of £195, a cull value per sow of £100 and a 47% replacement rate (i.e. approximately 6 litters per sow life). Sow mortality 4%. Boars (1 per 24 sows) purchased at £700 (40% a year replacement), sold at £100. 'High' compared with 'Average': higher gilt purchase prices, higher replacement rate and slightly fewer sows per boar assumed.

5. *Food:* total food per sow of 2.60 tonnes breaks down as:

	Tonnes	Value £/t	Total Cost
Sow	1.35	185	250
Boar	0.05	185	9
Weaner feed	1.20	275	330
Total	**2.60**	**227**	**589**

High performance: lower sow feed but extra piglet rearing feed for additional weaners. Piglets weaned at average 3.75 weeks, 7.5kg weight.

6. *Miscellaneous Average:* vet. and med. £30, transport £6, straw and bedding £8, miscellaneous £10, electricity and gas £11, and water £10.

7. *Direct Labour Cost* per sow: average £226, good £179; per weaner: average £10.14, good £7.20.   This figure does not include labour used for 'overhead' activities – repairs etc.   For further fixed costs information see page 202.

8. *Building Costs:* see page 212.

Feeding (from 37 kg liveweight): per pig

Average Performance	Pork £	Cutter £	Bacon £
Sale Value......................................	82.90	98.60	111.70
Less Weaner Cost (1)...................................	49.00	49.00	49.00
Mortality Charge................................	1.50	1.60	1.70
Output	32.40	48.00	61.00
Variable Costs:			
Food.......................................	23.50	32.80	41.50
Miscellaneous..	5.50	6.00	6.50
Total Variable Costs	29.00	38.80	48.00
Gross Margin	**3.40**	**9.20**	**13.00**
Liveweight (kg)..	76	90	102
Deadweight (kg)...	56	67.5	77
Killing Out %..	74%	75%	75%
Price per Deadweight (p).............................	148	146	145
Price per Liveweight (p)..............................	109.1	109.5	109.5
Food Conversion Rate..................................	2.65	2.72	2.80
Food per Pig (kg)..	102	143	181
Average Cost of Food per tonne (£) (2)........	£230	£230	£230
Food Cost per Kg l/w Gain (p)....................	60.95	62.56	64.40
Liveweight Gain per Day (kg)......................	0.73	0.76	0.8
Feeding Period (weeks)...............................	7.5	9.9	11.5
Mortality (%)..	3.0	3.2	3.5
Direct Labour Costs per Pig (£)...................	5.60	6.60	7.70

High Performance (same pig price)			
Food Conversion Rate..................................	2.52	2.58	2.65
Food per Pig (kg)..	97	135	171
Food Cost per Pig (£5/t less than ave.).........	21.83	30.48	38.46
Food Cost per Kg l/w Gain (p)....................	56.70	58.05	59.63
Gross Margin per Pig	**4.90**	**11.30**	**15.70**
Direct Labour Costs per Pig.........................	4.40	5.00	5.60

1. *Weaner cost* assumes on farm transfer. If purchased (i.e., feeding only) transport and purchasing costs have to be added: these are very variable but average about £1.75 per weaner.

2. *Average of home-mixed and purchased compounds:* There can be big variations in feed costs per tonne between farms, according to whether the food is purchased as compounds or home-mixed, bought in bulk or in bags, size of unit, etc.

3. *Labour:* see page 162.

4. *Building Costs:* see page 216.

5. *Sensitivity Analysis.* The effect of changes in important variables are as follows:

Change in Gross Margin (£)	Porker	Cutter	Baconer
Price: 5p per kg dw difference 2.80		3.38	3.85
Food Cost per tonne: £10 difference 1.02		1.43	1.81
Food Conversion Rate: 0.1 difference . . . 0.89		1.21	1.48

The effect of differences in the cost per weaner is obvious.

Combined Breeding, Rearing, and Feeding: per pig

	Pork £		Cutter £		Bacon £	
Performance Level*	Ave.	High	Ave.	High	Ave.	High
Sale Value	82.90	82.90	98.60	98.60	111.70	111.70
Sow and Boar Deprcn	2.53	2.69	2.53	2.69	2.53	2.69
Mortality Charge	1.50	1.70	1.60	1.80	1.70	2.00
Output	**78.87**	**78.51**	**94.47**	**94.11**	**107.47**	**107.01**
Food	49.91	45.98	59.21	54.68	67.91	62.68
Miscellaneous	8.86	8.91	9.36	9.41	9.86	9.91
Total Variable Costs	**58.77**	**54.89**	**68.57**	**64.09**	**77.77**	**72.59**
Gross Margin per Pig	**20.09**	**23.62**	**25.89**	**30.02**	**29.69**	**34.42**
Gross Margin per Sow	**448**	**588**	**577**	**748**	**662**	**857**
Labour Costs per Pig	15.74	11.60	16.74	12.20	17.84	12.80
Labour Costs per Sow	351	289	373	304	398	319

*   Performance levels refer to breeding and rearing differences as on the previous 2 pages and, for feeding, differences in food conversion rate, food costs and labour cost only.

Prices - General

Pig prices are notoriously difficult to predict. Over the last three years the GB average pig price (DAPP Eurospec) has ranged from 100p per kg deadweight to over 155ppkg. The majority of UK pigs are now taken to baconer weight. The level shown in the finisher margins for baconers above, of 145p, is an estimated average for late 2010 through 2011. The finished pig price is highly dependent on the £/€ exchange rate.

Further Performance Data

Source: The Meat and Livestock Commission's 'Pig Yearbook 2010' (data for the year ended December 2009).

Breeding	Average	Performance Level Top Third*	Top 10%*
Sow replacements (%)	48.2	48.4	50.0
Sow sales and deaths (%)	46.0	48.7	51.9
Sow mortality (%)	4.0	3.3	3.4
Litters per sow per year	2.25	2.34	2.38
Pigs reared per litter	9.8	10.6	11.5
Pigs reared per sow per year	22.2	24.9	27.2
Weight of pigs produced (kg)	7.6	7.3	7.5
Average weaning age (days)	26.7	26.4	29.0
Sow feed per sow per year (tonnes)	1.28	1.26	1.39
Feed per pig reared (kg)	67	59	55
Sow feed cost per tonne (£)	170	157	165
Sow feed cost per sow per year (£)	227	231	228
Feed cost per pig reared (£)	10.27	9.33	8.56

* selected on basis of pigs reared per sow per year.

Rearing	Average	Top Third*	Top 10%*
Weight of pigs at start (kg)	7.3	7.4	7.1
Weight of pigs produced (kg)	36.6	37.0	38.1
Mortality (%)	2.5	2.7	3.0
Feed conversion ratio	1.80	1.63	1.64
Daily Gain (g)	492	506	525
Feed cost per tonne (£)	277	248	209
Feed cost per kg gain (p)	47.0	39.0	33.0
Feed cost per pig reared (£)	13.30	10.96	8.89

Feeding	Average	Top Third*	Top 10%*
Weight of pigs at start (kg)	38.8	33.6	28.6
Weight of pigs produced (kg)	103.3	105.0	104.2
Mortality (%)	2.8	2.4	2.3
Feed conversion ratio	2.77	2.39	2.13
Daily Gain (g)	819	824	846
Feed cost per tonne (£)	184	172	169
Feed cost per kg gain (£)	49.7	39.4	33.6
Feed cost per pig reared (£)	31.79	28.37	27.49

* selected on basis of feed cost per kg liveweight gain.

Feed conversion ratio for rearing and feeding combined, from 7.5kg to 101kg liveweight is approximately 2.51.

Outdoor v Indoor Performance

Breeding	Outdoor	Indoor
Sow replacements (%).....................................	46.0	49.2
Sow sales and deaths (%)..............................	43.8	47.5
Sow mortality (%)..	3.8	3.9
Litters per sow per year..................................	2.25	2.25
Pigs reared per litter.......................................	9.6	10.1
Pigs reared per sow per year..........................	21.6	22.8
Weight of pigs produced (kg).........................	7.7	7.5
Average weaning age (days)..........................	26.5	26.9
Sow feed per sow per year (tonnes)...............	1.30	1.26
Feed per pig reared (kg).................................	73	60
Sow feed cost per tonne (£)...........................	154	181
Sow feed cost per sow per year (£)	200	243
Feed cost per pig reared (£)...........................	9.39	10.74

1. *Stocking Rate for outdoor pigs* is mainly between 12 and 25 per hectare (5 and 10 per acre), 20 (8) being the most common. Good drainage is essential. A low rainfall and mild climate are also highly desirable. In 2003, MLC's Agrosoft puts the cost of establishing a sow herd on a greenfield site at £1,800 per sow place for an indoor unit and about £600 per sow place for an outdoor unit.

2. *Data on the split* of indoor and outdoor herds is hard to come by. However, it is probable that well over a third of the UK breeding sow herd is now kept outdoors. A somewhat smaller proportion (probably <10%) of pigs are finished outdoors.

Further costing information can be found in 'Pig Production in England 2008-09' produced by Askham Bryan College, York on behalf of Rural Business Research. See www.ruralbusinessresearch.co.uk

Acknowledgement: The main data source for the margins within the Pigs section is the Pig Yearbook 2010 (AHDB), but the pig and feed prices are the author's responsibility.

EGG PRODUCTION

Brown egg layers; 55 week laying period, 2 week changeover period. This reflects current commercial practice

Level of Performance	Cages				Free Range	
	Average		High		Average	
	per bird	per doz eggs	per bird	per doz eggs	per bird	per doz eggs
	£	p	£	p	£	p
Egg Returns......................	15.24	57.5	15.81	57.5	22.75	91.0
Less Livestock Deprcn.....	3.04	11.5	3.04	11.1	3.29	13.2
Output	**12.20**	**46.0**	**12.77**	**46.4**	**19.46**	**77.8**
Variable Costs:						
Food...........................	8.37	31.6	8.37	30.4	10.25	41.0
Miscellaneous.............	1.86	7.0	1.86	6.8	1.81	7.2
Total Variable Costs	**10.23**	**38.6**	**10.23**	**37.2**	**12.06**	**48.2**
Gross Margin	**1.97**	**7.4**	**2.54**	**9.2**	**7.40**	**29.6**

1. *Hen-housed data* are used throughout, i.e. the total costs and returns are divided by the number of birds housed at the commencement of the laying period. IPPC permit charges have not been included. *Large variations* in input costs and returns occur.

Cage Production

3. *Yields assumed* per bird per year are:
   - Average............... 318 (26.5 dozen)
   - High.................. 330 (27.50 dozen)

4. *The price* used, 57.5p per dozen, includes all quantity and quality bonuses. Farmer to shop and consumer prices are well above packer to producer levels and normally 35p and 65p per dozen premiums respectively are required.

5. *Livestock depreciation* - average point of lay pullet is priced at £3.20 (16/17 weeks).

6. *The food price used* is £186 per tonne. The feed cost is dependent on breed, housing and environmental conditions, quantity purchased and type of ration. Quantity of feed used = 45kg.

7. *Direct Labour Costs:* average £1.42 per bird, premium £1.05. See page 176.

8. *Housing Costs:* see page 217. Deadstock depreciation averages about £1.65 per caged bird. Deadstock depreciation is calculated over 57 weeks (55 week laying period plus 2 weeks clean out).

9. *Stocking density*: 550 cm^2 per bird (18.2 birds/m^2)

Free Range Production

10. *Egg yields:* 300 (25 dozen) and *average price:* 91p per dozen.

11. *Quantity of feed* used = 50 kg. Price £205 per tonne.

12. *Livestock depreciation* - the average point a lay pullet is priced at £3.45 (16/17 weeks).

13. *Direct Labour Costs:* average £4.20 per bird, dependent on degree of automation.

14. *Stocking density*: 855cm^2 per bird (11.7 birds per m^2)

REARING PULLETS

Average per bird reared

	£
Value of 16/17 weeks old bird...	3.20
Less Chicks 1.01 (1) @ 64p (including levy).....................................	0.65
Output	**2.55**
Variable Costs:	
Food: 6.25 kg @ £171 per tonne....................................	1.07
Miscellaneous (2)..	0.84
Total Variable Costs	**1.91**
Gross Margin	**0.64**

1. *Chick Value:* Assumes 3 per cent mortality, but 2 per cent allowed in price.

2. *Miscellaneous:* Excluding transport (19p), but including full vaccination costs.

3. *Labour* (40p); *deadstock depreciation* (46p).

TABLE POULTRY

A *Broilers* (per bird sold at 41 days)	p
Returns: 2.2 kg per bird @ 70.0p per kg lw.....................................	154.0
Less Cost of Chick...	30.5
Output	**123.5**
Variable Costs:	
Food: 4.2 kg @ £235 per tonne......................................	98.7
Miscellaneous..	17.3
Total Variable Costs	**116.0**
Gross Margin	**7.5**

1. Capital cost of housing and equipment: £6.65 per broiler space (depreciation cost approximately 5.7p per bird sold). Housing Costs: see page 217.

2. Labour: 5.3p, excluding catching and cleaning out (5.0p) but includes management; see page 176.

3. *Stocking density* 38kg/m^2, 263cm^2/kg

O.R. = Oven Ready

B *All Year Round Turkey* (per bird at 20 weeks, sexed stags)

	£
Returns: 14.3 kg per bird @ £2.58 per kg O.R................................	36.9
Less Cost of Poult..	2.0
Output	**34.9**
Variable Costs:	
Food: 50 kg @ £218 per tonne..	10.9
Miscellaneous..	4.7
Total Variable Costs	**15.6**
Gross Margin	**19.3**

1. 10% mortality allowed in cost of poult figures.
2. Rearing turkeys all the year round now tends to be just in the hands of a few large and vertically integrated companies. Imports have outcompeted many small operators.

C *Christmas Turkey* (Traditional Farm Fresh - indoor reared)

	Light	Medium	Heavy
	£	£	£
Returns per bird sold........................	37.75	42.88	61.26
Less Cost of Poult............................	4.31	4.31	3.62
Output	**33.44**	**38.57**	**57.64**
Variable Costs:			
Food..	6.00	7.59	8.10
Miscellaneous................................	12.37	12.78	13.21
Total Variable Costs	**18.37**	**20.37**	**21.31**
Gross Margin	**15.08**	**18.20**	**36.32**
Killing Age (weeks).........................	18	22	22
Live Weight (kg)...............................	6.6	8.0	12.4
Oven Ready Weight (kg)....................	5.4	6.6	10.2
Food Conversion...............................	3.2	3.4	2.4
Food per Bird (kg).............................	20.8	27.0	29.5
Food Cost per tonne..........................	£288	£281	£275

1. *Mortality:* 7, 8 and 10% mortality allowed for in cost of poult figures for light, medium and heavy weights respectively.
2. *Performance Categories:*
      Light and medium = slow growing sexed hens.
      Heavy = stags (as hatched).
3. *Price per kilogram:*
      Liveweight: small £5.72p/kg, medium £5.36 p/kg and large £4.94p/kg
      Price per kg: hens (smaller) 650-750p range, stags (larger) 550-650p range
      Christmas (fresh, eviscerated): hens 385 - 500p range; stags 250 - 350p range.

4. *Miscellaneous costs* include processing (inc. plucking and eviscerating) and marketing

Note: With both turkey enterprises, considerable variations will occur between individual strains and because of different production systems and feeding regimes. Free range systems for example will show higher costs and returns. The figures should therefore be used only as rough guidelines.

D Large roaster chickens (per bird sold at 12 weeks; Christmas - males only)

	£
Returns: 4.8 kg per bird @ £3.27 per kg O.R.	15.70
Less Cost of Chick..	0.80
Output	**14.90**
Variable Costs:	
Food: 14.3 kg @ £243 per tonne......................................	3.47
Miscellaneous...	1.51
Total Variable Costs	**4.98**
Gross Margin	**9.91**

10% mortality allowed for in cost of chick figures.

E Ducks (Pekin type) (per bird sold at 7 weeks)

	£
Returns: 2.3 kg per bird @ £3.36 per kg O.R..................................	7.73
Less Cost of Duckling...	0.70
Output	**7.03**
Variable Costs:	
Food: 11.3 kg @ £155 per tonne......................................	1.75
Miscellaneous...	2.05
Total Variable Costs	**3.80**
Gross Margin	**3.23**

Day-old costs allow for 10% mortality. There are very few indoor duck farmers left in the UK operating to this system, but they are large-scale.

F Geese (Traditional Farm Fresh - free range and dry plucked)

	£
Returns: 6.5 kg per bird @ £8.00 per kg O.R..................................	52.00
Less Cost of Gosling..	5.40
Output	**46.60**
Variable Costs:	
Food: 64 kg @ £246.25 per tonne....................................	15.76
Miscellaneous...	11.81
Total Variable Costs	**27.57**
Gross Margin	**19.03**

1.   Day-old costs allow for 6% mortality.

2. 16kg feed wheat at £115/t and 48kg goose concentrate at £290/t

3. Farm gate output values used

4. Miscellaneous costs include processing / marketing

   Acknowledgement: The figures in the whole of the poultry section are provided by John Newton, ADAS, Wergs Road, Wolverhampton.

RAINBOW TROUT (FRESHWATER)

	£ per tonne of fish
Returns: 1 tonne of fish @ £2.10 per kg...	2,100
Less 4000 fingerlings @ 6.0p each...	240
Output	**1,860**
Variable Costs:	
Food: 1 tonne @ £1120 per tonne...	1,120
Vet and med;...	130
Miscellaneous...	35
Total Variable Costs	**1,285**
Gross Margin	**575**

1. Fish growing to 350g from fingerlings at 4.5g.

2. Prices are estimated ex-farm to processor or wholesaler. Higher prices of up to £4.20 per kg can be achieved by selling direct to retailers, caterers and consumers at, say farmers markets, but significant additional costs are associated with such sales.

3. Fingerlings price: varies according to quantity ordered and time of year.

4. Average feeding period, 10 months. Mortality, from fingerling to market size, 15%. Food conversion ratio 1.05:1. The price for fish food is for a pigmented high oil expanded pellet.

5. Current capital costs for construction of earth pond unit approximately £80 per cubic metre, to include buildings, holding systems and installation of water supply and services, but excluding land.

6. Labour requirement: the basic norm has in the past been 1 man per 50 tonnes of fish produced per annum on a table fish farm, but to remain competitive farmers now need to produce at least 150 tonnes per annum of table fish per man.

The figures given above must only be considered illustrative and cannot reflect the complexities of trout farming. Trout farming varies across the UK – from Cage Farming in Scottish lochs (freshwater and marine) through to 'traditional' flow through earth/pond/concrete raceway river farming. Trout farming also encompasses both the table and restocking sectors, prices given above relate to the sale of fish for the table market only. As such feed costs, conversion rates etc do vary which obviously has an effect on the costings for the enterprise. Differences in water temperature will also impact significantly on food conversion ratios, growth rates etc.

Acknowledgement: Thanks to - British Trout Association, The Rural Centre, West Mains, Ingliston, Edinburgh, EH28 8NZ. Tel: 0131 472 4080 www.britishtrout.co.uk

MEAT RABBITS

The consumption of rabbit meat in the UK is low, at less than 2oz per person per year, but most of this is imported where production costs are less due to lower welfare standards. There are only very few buyers and processors of meat rabbits in the UK and they do not cover all parts of the country, hence transport costs may have to be allowed for. It is important prospective producers research the market. An individual producer may develop local markets but this will require initiative. The demand for rabbit meat is seasonal - more is eaten in winter than summer, which can pose marketing problems. Producers are advised to adjust their production by 15 to 20% in summer to allow for this. There may be a market for the manure but again this would have to be developed.

Commercial rabbit production is an intensive livestock enterprise and usually requires planning permission and building regulation approval from the Local Authority. The construction or conversion of a building to house rabbits is the main expenditure and must be done in accordance with Defra's Welfare Code. A meat rabbit unit needs a weather- and vermin-proof building, which is insulated, well-drained and has good ventilation, lighting and a water supply. Housing can be fully environment controlled to give good feed conversion rates and better winter conditions for both stock and personnel, or be natural environment, which has lower capital and running costs and possibly keeps animals healthier.

Meat rabbits require a lot of maintenance. Health, hygiene and good stockmanship are crucial to the enterprise. One full time person can look after 250 – 300 does and their progeny. New Zealand White or Californian stock is used. Young does are bought in at 12 weeks and mated at 16-20 weeks. Bucks are bought in at 16 weeks and first mated at 20 weeks. A ratio of one buck to 10-20 does is recommended. Gestation is 31 days. Average litter size is 8-9, of which 6-7 should be successfully fattened. Re-mating can be immediately post-partum or up to 6 weeks afterwards; the average is about 21 days. A doe can have a useful life of 10-12 litters over 18 months; less productive animals may be culled sooner. A mortality rate of up to 12.5% can be expected.

Young rabbits are weaned at 35-42 days at about 2.5-3 lb and then fed *ad-lib* until they are ready for marketing at 5.5-6.5lb liveweight at 11-13 weeks. Food conversion rate, including the doe's feed and a share of the buck's is around 4:1. A balanced ration can be obtained for about £250 per tonne in bulk but may cost up to £350 per tonne. A doe should produce around 50 meat rabbits each year but experienced producers would aim for 60-70.

4. RENEWABLE ENERGY

GENERAL

The rapidly emerging renewable energy industrial sector offers many opportunities to farmers and land based entrepreneurs. Some forms of renewable energy generation such as wind turbines can be located on agricultural land, others, such as bioethanol have a fundamental dependence on agriculture for its raw materials.

Renewable energy is a relatively novel concept in industrial terms even though virtually all technologies are not new and are well understood. Wind power and wood heating clearly have long histories, as has anaerobic digestion having been harnessed by man for centuries. Even biofuels were available for the Second World War and second generation biofuels, whilst well understood are simply prohibitively expensive. What is new is the increasing focus on these technologies as a means to combating climate change.

The Renewable Energy industry is developing in response to incentives to cut the emissions of climate changing green house gases (GHGs) as a result of human activities. The main GHGs are:

- Carbon Dioxide (CO_2), which accounts for up to a quarter of the green house gas effect

- Methane (CH_4) accounts for between 4% and 9% of the effect but is about 25 times more potent by volume than carbon dioxide

- Nitrous Oxide, which, whilst very low in concentration in the atmosphere, is about 300 times more potent than carbon dioxide

- Water Vapour. Whilst this is the most voluminous and causes between a third and two thirds of the green house effect, human activity has a negligible effect on it.

In 2009, human activity in the UK accounted (provisionally) for 575 million tonnes of GHG emissions (CO_2 equivalent), down from 628mt in 2008. Agriculture accounted for 51.4mt CO_2 equivalent, most of which comes from the enteric fermentation of ruminating animals (methane) and the use of (and manufacture) nitrogen fertilisers (nitrous oxides). *Figures are from Defra/DECC.*

RENEWABLE ENERGY POLICY

From 1997 to late 2009, 187 countries signed and ratified the Kyoto Protocol, a commitment to reduce their emissions of GHGs. The UK has a legally binding target under the Protocol to reduce its GHG emissions to 12.5% below 1990 levels between 2008 and 2012. The first commitment period of the Protocol ends in 2012. Another framework will need to replace it. The United Nations Climate Change Conference in Copenhagen in December 2009 was designed to achieve this but progress was not made.

The EU's 2008 Climate Change Package became the 2009 Renewables Energy Directive. It aims to ensure the EU will achieve its self set 2020 climate change targets by setting binding targets:

- a 20% reduction in greenhouse gas emissions,

- a 20% improvement in energy efficiency, and

- a 20% share for renewables in the EU energy mix (the UK national target is 15%)

- of this target, biofuels and electricity should account for 10% of the EU's transport fuel consumption.

The UK 2008 Climate Change Act set legally binding targets for government, to steer it to achieve an 80% reduction of GHG emissions by 2050. It does this through additional targets; a 26% reduction of CO_2 emissions by 2020 and capped emissions over 5 year periods, 3 budget periods set at a time. The 2008 UK Energy Act implements legislation that:

- Strengthens the Renewables Obligation (see later) with ROC bandings to allow greater roll-out of the renewable sector in the UK

- Allowed Government to introduce Feed-in-Tariffs for low carbon electricity projects of up to 5MW

- Enables the Government to establish a financial support mechanism for the provision of renewable heat, the Renewable Heat Incentive, RHI

- Provides Government with the authority to introduce Smart Metering

In July 2009, DECC published The UK's Low Carbon Transition Plan. It is a White Paper laying out the Governments plans for meeting GHG reduction targets. Whilst the UK is expected to reduce emissions by 34% (of 1990 levels) by 2020, agriculture, which accounts for 7% of emissions, is expected to reduce its emissions by only 6%. Government recognises not only the industry is growing, but also will provide the resources for many renewable opportunities and also already stores vast amounts of carbon in soils and woodland.

Also published in July 2009 was the Renewable Energy Strategy which set out how the UK plans to meet its target of delivering 15% of UK energy by 2020.

The Renewables Obligation (RO)

The primary mechanism for encouraging electricity supply from renewable sources in the UK is the Renewables Obligation (RO). Renewables Obligation Certificates (ROCs) are issued to registered electricity generators for producing electricity from renewable sources at between ¼ and 2 per mega watt hour (MWh) depending on the generation type. This so called 'ROC banding' was introduced in April 2009.

Renewables Obligation Target, ROC Value and Non-Compliance Penalty

Year*	Renewables Obligation Target (ROCs per 100MW)	Non-compliance Penalty per MWh (buy-out price)	Average Value of ROCs
2002/03	3.0	£30.00	£47.11
2003/04	4.3	£30.51	£47.68
2004/05	4.9	£31.59	£47.86
2005/06	5.5	£32.33	£40.99
2006/07	6.7	£33.24	£44.78
2007/08	7.9	£34.30	£49.68
2008/09	9.1	£35.76	£52.27
2009/10	9.7	£37.19	£49.31
2010/11	10.4	£36.99	£49.16
Annually thereafter to	+1	Index linked increments	
2015/16	15.4		

ROCs are required by registered electricity suppliers to offset their annual RO target (an annually rising target of ROCs per 100MW of use). If they do not have sufficient ROCs to meet their target, they are charged £30/MWh for the difference (index linked to 2002/03 making £36.99 in 2010/11). This money is re-circulated equally to all certificates after each year-end, meaning ROCs are worth more than the penalty. Thus ROCs have a market value; their average price in June 2010 was £49.16/ROC. Electricity suppliers can fulfil their RO by purchasing ROCs from other generators. Farmers generating renewable electricity can sell the ROCs, having no obligation to keep them.

The introduction of 'ROC banding' meant some renewable electricity generation types 'earn' more ROCs per MWh than others as the next table illustrates. Also, any generator with a capacity of 50kw or less is classified as a micro-generator and earns 2 ROCs per MWh ('double ROCs') if operational pre July 2009.

Number of ROCS per MWh depending on Generation Type (non-exhaustive list)

Generation types	ROCs per MWh
Co-firing of biomass	0.5
Onshore wind	1.0
Hydro-electric	1.0
Co-firing of energy crops	1.0
Energy from waste with CHP	1.0
Co-firing of biomass with CHP	1.0
Standard gasification	1.0
Standard pyrolysis	1.0
Dedicated biomass	1.5
Co-firing of energy crops with CHP	1.5
Anaerobic digestion	2.0
Dedicated energy crops	2.0
Dedicated biomass with CHP	2.0
Dedicated energy crops with CHP	2.0
Solar photovoltaic	2.0
Geothermal	2.0
Existing certificates issued on data from before April 09	1.0

Source: OFGEM

Generators can also claim 1 LEC (Climate Change Levy Exemption Certificate) for each MWh electricity produced. Utilities need to source these LECs so they can exempt business consumers from Climate Change Levy - which in 2010/11 is £4.70 on 1 MWh of electricity.

Feed-in Tariffs (FIT)

Designed to facilitate the administration and subsidy receipts of small-scale electricity generators, the Feed in Tariffs are aimed at encouraging the production of renewable electricity at all levels up to 5MW capacity. This is equivalent to a very large offshore turbine or a very large anaerobic digestion plant. Almost all farm-scale renewable energy schemes would therefore fit within the FIT scheme. The Tariffs work as follows:

- A renewable electricity generator receives a fixed payment for each kWe generated; the 'Generation Tariff'. This is set at different levels depending on technology type, installation size and start date (see below).

- A guaranteed market payment of 3.0 p/kWh is available if required for its export to the wider market; the 'Export Tariff'.

- Generators can opt out of the Export Tariff by either selling electricity directly to an electricity consumer or making use of the electricity themselves.

- The FIT payments are made by the registered Electricity Suppliers, the cost of which is redistributed among all suppliers in a pro-rata manner.

- Generators with capacity below 50kW (known as micro-generators) are eligible for FIT, whilst installations between 50kW and 5MW have the option to choose between FIT and the RO.

- Generators can choose between ROCs or FITs but not claim both.

This was implemented in April 2010. Generation Tariff rates for photo voltaic and wind technologies will reduce in subsequent years for new claimants as technology becomes cheaper. Tariffs are paid for 20 to 25 years after installation depending on technology. Generation and Export Tariffs are index linked.

Generation Tariffs for first 2 years of FITs (2010/11-2011/12)

Generation Terchnology	Scale	Generation Tariff p/kWh		Tariff Lifetime (years)
		to 31/3/11	to 31/3/12	
Anaerobic Digestion	< 500kW	11.5	11.5	20
	> 500kW	9.0	9.0	20
Hydro	< 15kW	19.9	19.9	20
	15-100kW	17.8	17.8	20
	100kW – 2MW	11.0	11.0	20
	2MW-5MW	4.5	4.5	20
Photo Voltaic	< 4kW *New Build*	36.1	36.1	25
	< 4kW *Reterofit*	41.3	41.3	25
	4-10kW	36.1	36.1	25
	10-100kW	31.4	31.4	25
	100kW – 5MW	29.3	29.3	25
	Stand Alone *	29.3	29.3	25
Wind	< 1.5kW	34.5	34.5	20
	1.5-15kW	26.7	26.7	20
	15-100kW	24.1	24.1	20
	100-500kW	18.8	18.8	20
	500-1.5MW	9.4	9.4	20
	> 1.5MW	4.5	4.5	20
Micro Generators moving from the RO		9.0	9.0	To 2027

* Stand Alone Systems are those not attached to a building and not wired to provide electricity to an occupied building.

The Renewable Heat Incentive (RHI)

There is currently no policy incentive to generate heat from renewable sources. This is despite half of all energy used in the UK used for heat production. The value of heat is low (possibly 1-2p/kWh thermal energy) which rarely justifies the capital expenditure in the UK of harnessing heat or generating it from a renewable source. The RHI should change this, with its introduction proposed for April 2011. It will apply to generation of renewable heat of all scales, whether household, community or industrial, and different levels of support will be provided for different types of technology and scales. Technologies producing heat and electricity may be able to claim both FIT and RHI.

Paying the tariffs on a metered basis could encourage the generation of unnecessary heat to claim more RHI support. Also, heat metering is not as simple as electricity metering. Thus, most technologies will be supported according to the amount of heat the instalment is intended and likely to supply. This is known as 'deeming'. The Tariffs are likely to be available for a period of years (10 to 23 years) depending on technology.

Details of the proposed rates are included in the following table although it is noted these figures come from the Government RHI consultation published before the General Election so are likely to change.

Renewable Heat Incentive Proposed Tariff Rates

Technology	Scale (kW)	Proposed Tariff (p/kWh)	Deemed or Metered	Tariff Lifetime (Years)
Small Installations				
Solid Biomass	up to 45	9.0	Deemed	15
Bioliquids	up to 45	6.5	Deemed	15
Biogas on-site combustion	up to 45	5.5	Deemed	10
Ground Sources Heat Pumps	up to 45	7.0	Deemed	23
Air Sourced Heat Pumps	up to 45	7.5	Deemed	18
Solar Thermal	up to 20	18	Deemed	20
Medium Installations				
Solid Biomass	45-500	6.5	Deemed	15
Biogas on-site combustion	45-200	5.5	Deemed	10
Ground Sources Heat Pumps	45-200	5.5	Deemed	20
Air Sourced Heat Pumps	45-200	2.0	Deemed	20
Solar Thermal	20-100	17	Deemed	20
Large Installations				
Solid Biomass	>500	1.6-2.5	Metered	15
Ground Sources Heat Pumps	>350	1.5	Metered	20
Biomethane Injection	All Scales	4	Metered	15

The Renewable Transport Fuel Obligation (RTFO) and Fuel Excise Duty.

In April 2010 a fuel excise duty discount of 20ppl for biofuels was removed. Biofuels now have the same duty payable as mineral fuels for most producers. A 100% duty exemption for small scale biofuel producers those producing up to but not exceeding 2,500l biofuel per year (notionally sufficient for home use) remains in place. The 20p/l duty discount has been maintained for biodiesel produced only from waste cooking oil. This is until April 2012.

The RTFO started in 2008/9 with a target biofuel inclusion rate of 2.5% of aggregate road transport fuel by volume, increasing to 3.25% in 2009/10 (following adjustment after the Gallagher Review), reaching 5.00% in 2013/14. For every litre of biofuel that excise duty is paid on, a Renewable Transport Fuel Certificate (RTFC) is issued. Companies supplying at least 450,000 litres of mineral fuel to the UK market annually (about 14 companies) must participate by either incorporating sufficient biofuel into their sales, buying RTFCs from another biofuel provider or pay a 'buy-out' penalty (fine) of 30p/l.

Fuel Excise Duty:	1-Sep 2009	1-Apr 2010	1-Oct 2010	1-Jan 2011
Mineral Fuel *ppl*	56.19	57.19	58.19	58.95
Bioethanol *ppl*	36.19	57.19	58.19	58.95
Biodiesel *ppl* #	36.19	57.19	58.19	58.95
Rebated gas oil (red diesel) *ppl*	10.80	10.99	11.18	11.33
Biodiesel for non-road use *ppl*	10.80	10.99	11.18	11.33
Natural Gas (inc. biogas) *p/kg* ◊	22.16	23.60	25.05	26.15

Vegetable oil for road fuel qualifies as biodiesel if it meets the relevant specifications. VAT is also payable

◊ *The duty differential applicable to biogas is equivalent to 40.88p on a litre of petrol. It will remain at this level until at least Budget 2012*

Since April 2010, the emphasis has moved from duty exemption to RTFO (buy-out price) as the principal support mechanism for biofuels. As a compelling incentive, the 'buy-out fund' generated is redistributed equally to every RTFC issued by the year-end. This means that the further away the UK is from hitting the annual target, the greater the incentive to incorporate as RTFC values rise. These subsidies are essential to make the industry viable, without them there would be no biofuel industry.

RTFO and Excise Duty Incentives for Biofuels

Biofuel Year[1]	RTFO Obligation [2]	Buy-Out Penalty *ppl*	Duty Discount *ppl* [3]
2007-2008	0.00%	15	20
2008-2009	2.50%	15	20
2009-2010	3.25%	15	20
2010-2011	3.50%	30	0
2011/2012	4.00%		
2012/2013	4.50%		
2013/2014	5.00%		

1 The biofuel accounting year is from 15th April to 14th April

2 The RTFO inclusion obligation is by volume and percentage of fuel sales/use

3 Fuel Excise Duty reduction from fossil fuel Excise Duty per litre

SUPPORT AND GRANTS

The **Energy Crops Scheme** is part of the Rural Development Programme for England and is managed by Natural England. It finances the establishment of Miscanthus and Short Rotation Coppice (SRC of Willow, Poplar, Ash, Alder, Hazel, Silver Birch, Sycamore, Sweet Chestnut and Lime). Applicants submit actual costs of establishment, including materials and suppliers costs as well as on-farm costs such as labour. Since 1 January 2010 the grant rate is increased from 40% to 50% of planting costs. A minimum of 0.5 ha can be claimed. See more on page 153.

The **Bio-energy Capital Grants Scheme** (England only), whilst not part of the Rural Development fund supports the installation of biomass fuelled boilers and CHP (Combined Heat and power) projects. It opens in 'rounds', round 6 closed in March 2010. The scheme provides funding of up to 40% of the difference in cost of installing the biomass boiler or CHP plant compared to installing the fossil fuel alternative, up to a maximum of £500,000. Eligibility extends to biogas for CHP. Future rounds of application are likely.

The **Wood Energy Business Scheme** (Wales) 2008-2013 is a capital grant scheme for wood fuel heating systems, wood powered CHP and equipment for wood fuel supply businesses. Farm and forestry businesses are generally ineligible as it is funded through the Convergence and Competitiveness Structural funds.

The **Bio-energy Infrastructure Scheme** (England) supports biomass feedstock sector (wood-fuel, energy-crops and straw) for heat, power and electricity end users. Producer groups that supply biomass for energy are eligible. Maximum grants are £200,000 per group. Eligible costs include legal and administrative work in setting up the group, rental of office accommodation, purchase/rental of office and IT equipment etc. The scheme doesn't fund planting or growing biomass, or standard items of farm equipment. Round 3 ended in February 2010, and it is not clear if it will reopen again.

LIQUID BIOFUELS

Liquid biofuels are road transport fuels produced from organic materials, including several mainstream farm crops. Biodiesel is produced from oilseed crops such as oilseed rape, soybeans and palm and is a replacement for mineral diesel. Bioethanol is a petrol replacement, produced from starch/sugar-based crops including wheat, maize and sugar beet or cane. Biofuels from cellulosic (woody) feedstock is possible referred to as 'second generation' biofuels. This would enable a higher energy return per hectare and the opportunity to process household, manufacturing and agricultural organic wastes. Its production is not financially viable so may be some years from large-scale commercial production.

Supply

About 40 million tonnes of road fuel is used in the UK (diesel exceeding petrol use by about 55:45). To meet the RTFO target in 2010/11, about 1.4m tonnes of biofuel is required (3.5%). The RTFO does not differentiate between biofuels so one may dominate the market. Splitting the market proportionately would require roughly 775,000 tonnes of biodiesel and 630,000t bioethanol. This would need 1.83m tonnes OSR or equivalent feedstock (at 42% extraction) covering 570,000 hectares (at 3.2t/ha) and 2.1m tonnes of wheat (or equivalent feedstock) covering 255 thousand hectares (at 8.25t/ha).

Farmers' options on whether to grow a crop to supply biofuel facility is simply by allowing the market to decide the buyer: As crops used in biofuel production are, in the most part, mainstream crops that could also be sold to other consumers, the processor that bids the farmer the highest value deal ought to win the contract. Clearly headline price is important, but also other contractual details including the risk of rejection or cost of claims, turnaround times etc should be considered. There are therefore no farm-level gross margins for biofuel crops.

BIOMASS FOR POWER

Energy crops are grown for heat and electricity generation or to produce transport fuels. They are considered 'carbon neutral' which means the carbon released on burning is only what they (recently) took up into the plant when growing, thereby not releasing additional carbon from fossil reserves beyond the requirements for fertiliser and chemicals, mechanical cultivation, harvest and transport to end-use location.

This section covers crops that are grown to be burnt directly to produce heat and/or electricity. The plant material is pelleted, chipped, or baled and is generally either used in boilers in dedicated biomass power stations, or mixed with coal for co-firing in conventional power stations. Biomass includes short rotation coppice, Miscanthus, straw, canary reed grass and switch grass as well as forest residues.

Short Rotation Coppice

Short Rotation Coppice (SRC) is a fast growing species of willow or poplar that when harvested, chipped and dried can be used as a fuel for heat or power generation. In the UK most SRC is willow in part because of problems with mechanically planting poplar.

SRC willow needs ample moisture but grows on any cultivated land. It requires a seedbed similar to that of a conventional arable crop, with particular attention to weed control. Planting is in the spring using un-rooted cuttings at a rate of 15,000/ha. Rabbit (or deer) fencing may be necessary. Pest and weed control is essential until canopy closure is achieved in the second year. In the autumn after planting, most growers cut back the willow to encourage multi-stemmed stools. This allows herbicide application and encourages a more competitive canopy. Some growers omit this cut-back when weed control is good, thereby achieving a commercial harvest sooner. Crops are usually harvested on a 3 year cycle. In poor conditions it may be left for 4 years, but in good conditions possibly every 2 years. In best conditions, stems would grow too thick to harvest if left any longer. Crops should last more than 20 years. Most growers apply some fertiliser post harvest. Sewage sludge is commonly used as are animal manures. In general, approximately 60 kg/ha N is sufficient to maintain growth through the harvest cycle.

The harvested crop can be stored as billets or chips. Many processors grind and pellet the crop, increasing density and improving transport efficiency but adding to costs. Pellets flow better in automated fuel feed systems and are preferred for co-firing (with coal) as the willow has been milled prior to pelleting easing the load on the generator's mills. Pellets command a premium price over billets (6-8 inch lengths) and chips. SRC wood chip sells for around £60/odt (oven dried tonne) delivered, and, depending on contractual details, the consumer may organise delivery to the furnace. The first harvest should yield 10-20odt/ha, subsequent ones 21-27odt/ha.

The following gives a broad indication of likely planting costs and net annual returns. Account has been taken of the Energy Crops Scheme at 50% of costs

SRC Establishment Costs:	*£/ha*
Fencing (optional)...	200
Pre-planting spraying..	33
Post-planting spraying	70*
Fertiliser	40 ˜
Cultivations	150 ∞
Planting..	350 ☐
Cuttings	750
Cut-back	47
Energy Crops Scheme Grant (50%)......................	-820
Total Establishment	*820*

* *This varies from £30 to £140 depending on weed presence and control management.*

˜ *RB209 recommends N:P:K of 90:55:72. This would cost £132/ha. Advisers suggest using biosolid or slurry only.*

∞ *estimate 25% of the site is subsoiled, fully ploughed, power harrowed at least once then rolled twice after planting.*

☐ *including all cold storage of cuttings Haulage & travel for contactor*

Annual Net Returns: Output 25 odt/ha at £60 every third year; £500/year. Harvesting £300/ha plus £50 fuel, transport and handling £10/tonne harvested. Planting costs (including fencing etc) have been amortised over the forecast period of the crop. Use the Amortisation Table in section VIII. SRC land remains eligible for the Single Payment.

Gross Margin for SRC Chips (Amortised over 21 years)

	Per Harvest	Per Established Year	Average/yr over 21 Years
Average Harvest Yield (odt/ha)	25.0	25.0	23.6
	£	£	£
Yield: 25odt/ha at £60/odt	1500	500	471
Output:....................................	**1500** (608)	**500** (203)	**471** (191)
Variable Costs:			
Amortised Planting Cost**	192 (78)	64 (26)	64 (26)
Fertiliser/spray	48 (19)	16 (6)	16 (6)
Harvest	350 (142)	117 (47)	117 (47)
Transport & Handling***	250 (101)	83 (34)	79 (32)
Total Variable Costs..................	840 (340)	280 (113)	275 (111)
Gross Margin per ha (acre).............	**660** (267)	**220** (89)	**196** (79)

* including the rise in yield in early years ** £914 amortised over 21 years at 5% *** £18/odt

Acknowledgement: thanks to – Mark Paulson; Coppice Resources Limited.

Miscanthus (Elephant Grass)

Miscanthus is a perennial energy and fibre crop, indigenous to Africa and Asia, grown commercially in the UK. It differs from short-rotation coppice as it is harvested annually using conventional farm machinery. The crop has a commercial life of 15-20 years.

There is a range of uses for Miscanthus beyond energy generation. After suitable treatment, it makes valuable animal bedding. It can go into paper making and biopolymer manufacture or be used to produce bio-degradable products, such as plant pots.

Miscanthus is grown throughout the UK but the crop is vulnerable to late spring frosts. It is suitable for a wide range of soil types and pH values but is not recommended for drought prone soils. The crop is propagated from rhizomes. Weed control is necessary at establishment and in the following spring. A mature crop suppresses weed growth. So far in the UK there are no significant pathogens and pests. Agro-chemical use is therefore minimal

Fertiliser requirement is low. Leaf mulch recycles nutrient, but cannot replenish that removed from harvest. In the first year, there is little growth so fertiliser is not necessary. Research suggests the mature crop removes 7kg P and 100kg K/ha/year. The plant being deep rooted may access minerals from deeper than most other crops. The mature crop removes about 75kg N/ha/year, some of this is replaced by soil mineralisation and aerial deposition but trials indicate a response from 35-45kg/ha/year. Sewage sludge is an ideal fertiliser. The Miscanthus gross margin below includes fertiliser at 00/05/30kg of $N/P_2O_5/K_2O$ per hectare.

The crop shoots in April, and grows into bamboo-like stems up to 4 metres high by late August. They contain solid pith. The foliage dies after the first frost and stems desiccate to 50% moisture during winter. The leafless canes are harvested in March, before shoots reappear. The robust rhizome network provides a platform for harvesting machinery. The harvest method depends on end use. For energy the crop is cut with a mower conditioner and then baled into 500-600kg Heston bales. For other end uses a modified maize harvester can be used.

In the UK the likely yield of a mature crop should be 12-15 oven dried tonnes (odt)/ha/year. In year 1, only about 50 to 60% of the full yield is obtained. The price for Miscanthus ranges between £45 to £75/odt (ex-farm oven dried tonnes) with £60 fairly standard for energy crop contracts. Note some contracts are for Miscanthus at fresh harvested weight (normally 16% moisture). Horse bedding can retail for as much as £100/tonne in bulk to £240/tonne, de-dusted in 20kg bags.

There are probably about 6,000ha of Miscanthus in the UK although this is difficult to measure. Initially much of the crop was used for propagation material but now it is being planted for both energy and fibre end uses. Small on-farm boilers, to produce heat and energy, have been developed which offer potential for Miscanthus. Very little has been planted in the last 2 years. Planting and establishment costs are in the region of £2,000 per hectare. Some agro-chemicals will probably be required in the first year.

Gross Margin for Miscanthus Amortised over 3 time periods

Crop Longevity (years)	5	15	20
13.0 odt/ha at £60/odt	546	702	722
Income	**546**	**702**	**722**
Variable Costs			
Planting Costs*	231	96	80
Fert/Spray	125	125	125
Harvesting	75	75	75
Bale**	100	129	132
Variable Costs	**531**	**425**	**412**
Gross Margin	**15**	**277**	**309**

* £1,675 less £670 grant amortised at 5% for crop longevity

** £11/tonne per average yield over entire period

Acknowledgement: thanks to - Andrew Riche; Rothamstead.

ANAEROBIC DIGESTION

Anaerobic Digestion (AD) is the digestion of non-woody organic material in the absence of oxygen by micro-organisms to produce biogas (a mixture of 40% carbon dioxide CO_2 and 60% methane CH_4) and digestate (a soil conditioner). The biogas is collected and normally used in a combined heat and power (CHP) generator to produce heat and electricity for use or sale. The biogas can also be purified by removing the CO_2 and contaminant gasses (less than 1%) making biomethane for use as road fuel or in place of natural gas. It is a natural process and is well understood by mankind having been harnessed for many years.

A very wide range of feedstock can be used. Livestock manure provides a cheap supply with high levels of micro-organisms but has a low biogas yield. Energy crops such as maize silage offer high yields and are commonly used in several AD business models but add substantially to operating costs. Non-farm waste streams from food processing companies or separated kitchen wastes offer a high return, with potential to earn revenue from gate fees. Regulatory controls are far greater when importing others' waste streams, especially if animal by products are likely to be included pushing up capital costs.

There are several types of AD plant, all suited to different situations and feedstocks. The rate of turnover of digestate is controlled by the rate at which feedstock enters the digester less the small (usually 3-10%) fall in volume from the production of biogas. Depending on feedstock and system used, digestion can take as little as a week up to 2 months in some circumstances.

Example On-Farm Feedstocks for Anaerobic Digestion

Feedstock	Biogas Yield m^3/t feedstock	Value of Biogas £/t feedstock*
Cattle/pig slurry	15 – 25	4.75 – 7.90
Poultry manure	30 – 100	9.50 – 31.50
Maize silage	190 – 220	60.00 – 66.00
Grass silage	150 – 200	47.50 – 63.00
Whole crop wheat	185	58.50
Maize grain	560	177
Rolled wheat grain	600	190
Crude glycerine	580 – 1,000	180 – 310
Rape meal	620	190
Fats	Up to 1,200	up to 380

* 11.5p/kWh Generation Tariff, 3.0p/kWh Export Tariff, 1p/kWh heat

Policy

When biogas is used to generate electricity, electricity can be sold with Feed in Tariffs (see above) or 2 ROCs can be claimed per MWhe (Mega Watt hour of electricity) as part of the Renewables Obligation (see above). Bio-methane for road transport is technically eligible for RTFCs (see Biofuels section above). AD also benefits from the Climate Change Levy and indirectly the Landfill Directive. AD does not facilitate NVZ implementation regulations.

Economics

The two major costs associated with AD are usually the capital set up and feedstock (if home grown or purchased feed is used). Operating and maintenance costs such as insurance, labour and utilities are usually low. An average size plant (2,500m³ digester and 450kW CHP generator) would cost in the region of £1.5-2 million to build and commission. Depending on feedstock, temperature and other settings, this size plant could digest in the region of 20,000 tonnes of feedstock per year with a 45 day retention time (spent in the digester) or 30,000t with a 30 day retention period.

Revenue from this system digesting 20,000 tonnes using the assumptions from the table above, an average gas yield per tonne of feedstock of $100m^3$/tonne and an efficiency of 90% would return income before costs and without gate fees of about £650,000 with FITs.

HYDRO POWER

Hydro power provides about 40% of all renewable electricity produced in the UK providing about 1,500MW capacity. One major benefit of hydro electricity over many of the other renewable power sources is that power supply is predictable and relatively constant (short of severe drought). Key factors that require careful measurement are the 'head' (total drop of water) and the flow.

Hydro, just like other renewable energy projects is capital loaded, expensive to install but cheap to operate. However, installation costs have fallen in recent years to around £3,000 to £6,000 per kWhe for small 'micro' hydro electric systems. Its price varies as each installation is unique. Capital cost and electrical capacity depend largely on the following:

- The head (maximum vertical fall) of water which is key as the higher the head, the smaller the turbine required to generate the same amount of electricity. Less than 10m is normally considered 'low head'.

- The flow rate of water. For small schemes it is measured in litres per second.

- How much construction is required and how much of it is done 'in-house'.

The cost of construction per kW tends to fall as capacity rises meaning the smallest projects take longest to repay their investment. Operational costs are low, generally 1-2% of capital setup. Access to sites is a factor affecting instalment.

WIND TURBINES

There are currently 2,911 operational wind turbines spread across 264 grid-connected wind farms throughout the UK (July 2010). Small scale turbines can have capacities of as little as 100 watts (W) up to models of 2-3 mega watts (MW) and 6MW for offshore turbines. Wind farms are becoming larger; the average size a decade ago was 7MW and is now 17MW, albeit with considerable offshore wind farm growth.

Wind turbines in good locations produce energy equivalent to their rated capacity for around 30% of the year. For example: for a turbine rated at 40kW this calculates as 40kW x 30% x 8760 (hours in a year) = 105,120 kWh per year (105.12MWh). If this electricity is sold at 27p per kWh with FITs, then a return of £28,382 per year is achieved.

Typical costs for a range of turbine capacities are in the region of the following table. Good quality constructions should have an operational life of 20 years.

Guideline Figures for Capital and Revenue of Wind Turbines

Capacity kW	Capital Cost	Annual Output (kWh)	Revenue/yr using FIT*
5.0	20,000	13,100	£3,900
11	58,000	28.900	£8,600
75	175,000	197,000	£53,000
250	600,000	657,000	£140,000
800	1,000,000	2,100,000	£260,000

* Relevant FIT price as in FIT Table on page 105.

The land surrounding a wind turbine is usually un-affected, apart from access required up to the base of the tower. A minimum wind speed of 5 meters per second (m/s) is required; they operate at their rated capacity at 11-15m/s. Many turbines have automatic shut-down mechanisms when wind speeds exceed about 25m/s to avoid damage. Selection of the correct turbine technology and size is an important decision.

Planning permission is required and consultation with neighbours and stakeholders for all scale turbines. Wind farms (multiple large turbines) are built in association with developers as the costs and expertise required planning and preparing them is very high. Many schemes are operated by developers with land rented to them by the land owner for 20 years. In this situation, a rent will be payable to the landowner, usually at about 2-4% of income (£5,000 to £6,000 per mast per year is not uncommon plus similar construction access fees). Access to the turbines must be possible, but land between the turbines can be farmed normally. Other benefits like road improvements may also be included. An option to develop a site could be worth £1,000 to £5,000 per year.

A 11kW turbine will have a hub (mast) height of 15 to 18 metres, blade diameter of 9 metres and a 63m³ swept area. Tip height will be up to 22.5m. A large (800kW) wind turbine has a standard hub height of 76m, a height at the maximum blade position of 102m, and a blade diameter of 53m. The area of wind captured by this size blade is 0.88ha.

SOLAR POWER

Solar Photovoltaic (PV)

Solar PV panels generate electricity through the direct conversion of daylight. Panels can either be roof mounted, free-standing or integrated as a form of building material though solar slates, tiles or glass laminates.

Supply and installation costs for a 1kWe capacity system start at around £6,000, ranging up to £16,000 for a 4kWe capacity system. Little maintenance is required. The payback period claiming FITs is usually between 7 to 12 years. There are companies that will 'rent' your barn roof for installation of solar PV if you did not wish to invest in equipment yourself.

Approximately 7-8m^2 of PV panels is required to generate 1kW of electricity. A typical panel weighs 13kg per m^2 so additional roof support may be required. Panels may last for 45 years but most manufacturers place a 25 year guarantee on panels and a 5 year guarantee on inverters.

For optimum results, modules should be south facing at an angle of 30-40 degrees and un-shadowed by trees or surrounding buildings. Productivity varies across the UK with levels between 1100 kWh per m^2 in the South West, to 800 kWh per m^2 in the Scottish Highlands. Modules that are not South facing but placed towards the East and the West will drop in efficiency to no less than 85%

In England and Scotland most PV installations do not require planning permission, unless the building is of conservation status, is in a designated area or is a large free standing system. Wales and Northern Ireland will need to seek planning permission from their local planning authority.

Solar Thermal

Solar thermal systems use the sun's energy to warm water through using either evacuated tubes or flat plate collectors fitted to a roof. A conventional or immersion boiler is then used to heat the water further.

Costs of a typical water heating system are £3,000 to £5,000. Most systems come with a 5-10 year warranty and require little maintenance. Savings are modest; the average system can provide one third of water needs, reducing heating bills by approximately £50-£85 per year.

In England most systems will not require planning permission unless the building is listed or within a designated area. Wales, Scotland and Northern Ireland will need to contact their local planning authority.

5.   OTHER ENTERPRISES

MUSHROOMS

The mushroom industry has changed considerably during the past 5 years or so. A significant number of businesses of all sizes and in different parts of the country have ceased production and few if any new growers have entered the business. Less than 75 firms remain in production. Those that remain are either highly efficient enterprises with strong links to supermarkets or small low cost family-run businesses selling largely to wholesalers. The reasons for this are static consumption levels and competition from cheap imports. There are a few organic mushroom producers who sell at a premium.

Among the firms that remain there have also been changes in the method of production. Traditionally, the majority of UK growers employed Phase 1 compost, which they pasteurised and spawn-ran on the premises, to fill moveable trays or shelves in their growing rooms. Currently, the most prevalent system (perhaps 70% of all growers) uses purchased Phase 2 compost (pasteurised, with spawn added). This is supplied in shrink-wrapped blocks but it is also available in plastic bags as well as in bulk. Phase 3 compost (fully spawn-run) in blocks or bags is used by some growers. Organic Phase 2 and Phase 3 compost is also available.

Type of Compost Used	Phase 2	Phase 3
	per tonne compost	
Mushroom Yield/tonne compost	250 kg	300 kg
	£	£
Mushroom Price/kg	1.80	1.80
Spent Compost/tonne	2.00	2.00
Output	**452.0**	**542.0**
Variable Costs:		
Compost (incl. delivery)	95.0	135.0
Casing	15.0	15.0
Operations & growing labour at 6p/kg	15.0	18.0
Supervision & picking labour at 48p/kg	120.0	144.0
Packing materials at 21p/kg	52.5	63.0
Packing labour at 10p/kg	25.0	30.0
Energy costs at 10p/kg	25.0	30.0
Other costs at 15p/kg	37.5	45.0
Total Variable Costs	**385.0**	**480.0**
Margin / tonne compost	**67.0**	**62.0**
Variable Costs / kg mushrooms	1.54	1.60
Margin / kg mushrooms	0.27	0.21

Note: All labour is included but labour for growing, if not picking and packing, could well be regular.

Output: Growers using Phase 2 compost will fill on an 8-week cycle and produce 6.5 crops per year. Phase 3 compost can be filled on a 6-week cycle and allows 8.5 crops per year. Yields are expressed as kg per square metre of bed or kg per tonne of compost. Commercial yields are 25-35kg/sq m of bed area per crop (250-350kg per tonne of compost) using Phase 2 or 3 compost, but only 18-20kg/sq metre (180-200kg/tonne of compost) using Phase 1. Phase 1 compost costs £25/tonne, Phase 2 £85/tonne and Phase 3

£125/tonne plus delivery which can add £6-15/tonne, depending on distance and size of load.

Labour costs: If Phase 2 or 3 compost is used, labour for growing amounts to around 10% of all labour costs while picking is 75% and packing 15%. Using Phase 1 compost labour cost for growing is significantly greater, perhaps 40p/kg or 40% of total labour, but the initial compost is cheaper.

Prices: Mushroom prices are in the range of £2.00/kg supplied to a supermarket to £1.00 or less sold on the wholesale market. Small growers marketing through a producer organisation would get around £1.60/kg delivered. At present 60% of the crop is sold by growers direct to supermarkets. Prices can be volatile and oversupply can lead to mushrooms being sold at a loss. Imports now account for 65% of all mushrooms sold in the UK, and 60% of the value of sales. Almost all imports are from the Netherlands and the Republic of Ireland.

Returns: The data suggest that ex-farm it costs £1.54 to produce 1kg of mushrooms using Phase 2 compost and £1.60 using Phase 3 compost. This does not take into account management or finance costs. The yield of the crop and the number of cycles each year are, of course, crucial.

Establishment Costs: A mushroom farm using Phase 2 compost on an 8-week cycle would require 8 rooms each with a 200sq m capacity. A farm using Phase 3 compost on a 6-week cycle would need 6 rooms of 200sq m capacity. In both cases one growing room would be filled each week using 20 tonnes of compost. To set up such a production system would require a capital investment of £200,000-£300,000 for the rooms, trays or shelves, heating and cooling systems, packing area, hard standings and equipment. If Phase 1 compost is used then buildings and equipment for composting, peak heating and spawning are also required.

Acknowledgement: Mushroom Growers Association, c/o Snowcap Mushrooms, Broadway, Yaxley, Peterborough, Cambs. PE7 3EF: www.mushroomgrowers.org.

LOG CABINS

A renewed interest in British short breaks and holidays has lead to a popularity surge of 'alternative' accommodation over the more traditional cottage rentals or caravan and camping. There are examples where log cabin rentals for tourism and leisure purposes have been extremely successful as farm diversification projects. As with any tourism and leisure based enterprise, location is everything and will determine the success (or failure) of the proposal. It will also determine the rental income and occupancy that can be achieved. There may also be potential for using log cabins as a substitute for 'permanent', traditional buildings for office, storage facilities etc.

Full planning permission will be required before the construction of any log cabin. It is recommended that professional support is sought in this respect prior to any expenditure on equipment / groundwork.

Build Costs

Prices for cabins vary considerably, primarily linked to the size and finish (quality) of the final build and the cost of routing any mains services. The figures below are a guide to log cabin purchase and build costs, but excluding fixtures and fittings which may add £85.00 to £125.00 of additional cost per m². Costs in routing mains services to the cabins will be greatly dependant on remoteness, topography, environmental restrictions etc and the extent of supplies required (bottled gas and septic tanks can be used in place of mains gas and sewage):

| 'Fishing' Log Cabin | 30m² floor space plus sleeping 'loft' | £10,000 - £40,000 |
| 'Holiday let' Log Cabin | 60m² floor space with 2 bedrooms | £20,500 - £52,500 |

For cabins larger than the examples above, add £240.00 to £300.00 per m² for every m² over and above the sizes stated

Rental Potential

Good occupancy rates of the cabins will be paramount to the viability of any investment. Annual occupancy rates will vary depending on location, seasonality of local attractions and level of discount given in the 'off' season. Rental incomes again vary considerably, but typically range from £250 to £1,100 per week, with the higher incomes being achieved where the cabins are located in more desirable locations i.e. near to areas popular for fly and course fishing, mountain biking, walking, coastal activities, tourist attractions etc. Single night stays and short breaks often command a higher income pro rata than weekly lets. The troubles in the wider economy have led to reductions in the more 'typical' tariff rate ranges as businesses realise the importance of maintaining occupancy levels.

COARSE FISHING

Coarse fishing is the most popular pastime in the UK with in excess of 1.5 million people expected to regularly coarse fish in 2010. There have been year-on-year increases in the number of people coarse fishing since 2000. This ongoing demand has lead to many farmers and landowners to explore ways of gaining extra revenue from the letting of fishing rights either on a half day, full day or seasonal basis.

Coarse fishing is a freshwater method of line fishing and in most cases is undertaken by using a rod and real or a 'pole' usually from the banks of a watercourse. Coarse fish species include Rudd, Roach, Bream, Barbel, Tench, Chub, Perch, Pike, Carp etc but exclude sea species and 'game' fish like salmon and trout (the latter of which are usually line caught by 'fly fishing'). Coarse fish are always returned to the water once caught. Freshwater coarse fishing facilities can include rivers, streams, canals and man-made or natural lakes, ponds and drains. The close season for coarse fishing is 15th March to 15th June inclusive each year although most canals and still waters are exempt from the close season. Anyone fishing must have a rod licence (available from the Environment Agency). Fishing permit prices vary widely depending on the location, quality of the fishing, species present etc, but will typically be as follows:

Half-Day Ticket (per rod)	£4.00 to £7.00
Full-Day Ticket (per rod)	£5.00 to £13.00
Season Ticket (per rod)	£50.00 to £180.00

Permit prices will be higher if the water is actively managed to attract more or certain fish species. Ponds and lakes can be initially or routinely stocked. Maintenance and landscaping of the water banks will also add a premium to a facility as will safe, secure car parking and easy access to fishing pegs (platforms). The number of fishing points available along a water (and therefore income potential) will vary, but as a guide spacing of at least 25m per peg is usually required.

GAME SHOOTING

Game shooting remains a popular activity and has in recent years become more accessible to a wider range of people. Game shooting refers to the shooting of game species which include both feathered and fur animals and large mammals in the case of deer. The most common feathered species shot in the UK include pheasant, partridge, duck, woodcock, snipe and grouse. Most feathered game species can be reared in captivity and then released or alternatively populations can be enhanced by different management techniques. There are strict and differing shooting seasons for a range of different species, both game and pests. Shooting activities are widely recognised for their significant contribution to countryside conservation in all areas of the UK.

'Driven' game shooting is the most popular method of game shooting in the UK whereby game birds are 'flighted' towards a standing line of guns. The quality and type of driven shooting available is hugely variable and mostly linked to climatic, landscape and management factors as well as the number of birds present. These variances also have a major impact on the cost of partaking in a shoot. As a guide, a 120 bird day driven shoot will cost in the range of £175 to £500 per gun. It is usual for a driven shoot to have 7 or 8 guns with up to 8 'drives' in a day. An organised driven shoot will usually state how many birds are expected to be shot on a specific day, with any birds shot over and above this charged on a per head basis of circa £24 to £28 per bird in the case of pheasants.

The income potential from running a driven shoot is highly variable depending on the factors outlined above. The expensive nature of most driven game shoots is usually justified by the amount of work and cost involved in running a shoot (buying birds, feeding, structural equipment costs, game plot establishment, game keeper and beater's costs, shoot day hospitality etc) and so margins may be small given the investment required.

Further information: British Association for Shooting and Conservation – www.basc.org.uk

TURF

The market for turf remains reasonably healthy, despite the downturn in the home building industry. Competition within the sector is strong, particularly among the producers of general contract grade turf. The market is now predominantly supplied with seed sown turf or cultivated lawn turf. Pasture turf is still available in certain areas, but overall its importance is small and declining. Suitable pasture for turf lifting is hard to find and it can now be cheaper to grow cultivated turf than treat and prepare existing pasture. Special seed mixtures and cultivation techniques produce a range of types of turfgrass that can be matched to particular sites and uses. In some cases special soil mixes are provided for the site as well as the turf. The Turfgrass Growers Association (TGA) has introduced quality standards and buyers are increasingly specifying the precise type of turf they require. It is estimated that there are around 16,000 ha (40,000 acres) of turfgrass grown in the UK. Although several turfgrass companies were originally set up by farmers, the business has moved away from mainstream farming. However, farms may be involved in the following ways:

Selling existing pasture turf to a turf company

This is the traditional option but it now represents very little of the turf market and its share will continue to decline. The opportunity will be open to very few farmers indeed. The approach may be by the farmer to the company or vice-versa. Minimum 5-6 year ley/pasture generally needed for spring or autumn lifting, 8-10 year grass is better for summer cutting.

Important features: good root structure, number and type of weeds, level, well-drained, stone-free land; good access; timing (farmer wants lifting completed in time to drill next crop).

Payment varies between £750-£1,500 per hectare (£300-£600 per acre), but mainly £900-£1,200 per ha (£360-£480 per acre). There is usually an initial payment plus further payments as turf is lifted. There may be a penalty clause if lifting delays prevent subsequent timely drilling. Lifting can take from two months to even a year. It can be done at any time of year except when there is snow on the ground. The turf company usually sprays against broadleaved weeds, fertilises and mows before lifting; the farmer may do these tasks, for payment. He may graze the land, for a rent, if lifting is delayed.

Apparently the effect on the land is not detrimental; some say there are benefits (removal of accumulated pests, etc. in the top half inch of grass, roots and topsoil).

Some local authorities require planning consent for turf stripping. In some instances it has been refused on the grounds that pasture turf is not an agricultural crop. Cultivated turf, however, is deemed to be an agricultural crop. On tenanted land landlord's permission is necessary to cut pasture turf.

Farmer cutting, lifting and selling pasture turf himself

Extremely uncommon. The turf must be treated, as in option 1. A small turf cutting machine can be hired for about £60 a day. This slices off the turf which must then be cut into lengths and picked up by hand. Two or three workers are required. It is slow going even in good conditions. The wastage figure is commonly 10-20% of the area, perhaps more. To hire a machine which cuts and picks up the turf may be possible but the charge will be considerably more.

Turf has a short life once cut and stacked - a maximum 1 to 2 days in summer, 3 to 4 days in winter, depending on temperature.

Renting land to a turf company for production of cultivated turf

Turf companies rent land for turfgrass production in addition to using their own land. As before, well-drained, stone-free land with good access is required. Typically the land is rented on a per crop basis and one or two crops grown. A turf crop usually takes 12 to 18 months from preparation to harvest but autumn sown crops may be harvested within 12 months. Rent levels depend on the quality of the land, the provision of irrigation and the profitability of competing agricultural enterprises. Currently rents are in the order of £650-£1,200 per hectare per crop (£265-£485 per acre) or £500-£750 per ha per year (£200-£300 per acre).

Cultivated turf production

On their own land turf producers can grow turf continuously, taking a crop every 18 months to two years on average. On rented land (as in option 3), they take one or two crops and move on. Usually they produce a quick growing type of turf which sells quickly on rented land and cultivate more specialist and slower growing turf on their own land. A high level of agronomic expertise and considerable investment in machinery are needed and labour requirements are heavy. As the business is very competitive a high degree of marketing expertise is essential. While the bulk of the trade goes into general landscaping or garden centres there is an increase in the number of contracts where the quality and type of turf is specified. It is estimated that a turf farm would need to be 150-200 hectares (400-500 acres) or more in size to be viable – in order to justify the machinery and equipment necessary and to produce a succession of turf for the market. There are significant economies of scale. The cost of specialist machinery for turf production can be £350,000. The new one-man harvesting machine costs in the order of £120,000-£200,000 but significantly reduces labour costs.

Costs and Returns

Variable Costs plus Rent:	£/ha	(£/ac)
Seed	750-1,100	(300-445)
Fertiliser	400-800	(160-325)
Herbicide	90-150	(35-60)
Fungicide	75-185	(30-75)
Rent (for 15 months)...	650-1,200	(365-525)
Total Costs...	1,965-3,435	(795-1,390)

It may be necessary to irrigate and on occasions use netting to grow the grass through for certain sites.

Labour: Special seed bed preparation (including subsoiling and stone burying), regular mowing (twice a week May/June), picking up clippings, harvesting (2 men on harvester plus one loading lorry) between 0.2-0.4 hectares per day (0.5-1.0 acre). The new one-man harvester can do 2 ha (5 acres) a day.

Total costs of the order of £4,942-£7,413 per ha (£12,000-£3,000 per acre), approximately 56-83p per sq.m. (47-69p per sq.yd.)

Value of Turf (on the field)

	per sq. m	per sq. yd.	per ha*	per acre*
Pasture turf	38-43p	32-36p	£3,420-£3,850	£1,380-£1,570
Hardwearing, domestic general contract	75-95p	65-80p	£6,840-£8,550	£2,755-£3,470
Football, hockey, prestige landscape	115-145p	95-120p	£10,260-£12,825	£4,150-£5,200
High quality/specialist**	190-475p	160-405p	£17,100-£42,750	£6,910-£17,290

*   assuming 90% recovery, but some producers work on 85%.

** for some contracts the price may be higher.

Delivery charges 45-55p per sq.m for a full lorry load. Higher for smaller deliveries.

Acknowledgements: Turfgrass Growers Association, 133 Eastgate, Louth, Lincolnshire, LN11 9QG. Telephone: 01507 607722. www.turfgrass.co.uk. *Robert Laycock,* Dial Cottage, North End, Seaton Ross, York, YO42 4LX. www.robertlaycock.co.uk.

GOLF

Despite the economic recession, golf is still very popular in the UK but the supply of courses comfortably exceeds demand in most areas. According to Sport England, over a million people play golf each month, making it the seventh most popular sport and recreational activity in the country. This equates to 3.5% of the adult population of England playing golf at least once a month.

In the past few years, golf membership has declined from over 900,000 to around 740,000 with the dominance of private members clubs waning and a very large proportion of the market now occupied by proprietary golf clubs (built for profit by individuals or companies).

Over the past year the market has weakened further with some clubs reporting a fall in up to 30% in membership numbers. Few clubs have managed to retain membership numbers but those who have, have adopted ingenious and flexible attitudes to membership fees and the facilities provided.

There are only a few courses under construction, but numerous courses are trying to upgrade old facilities to cope with the new competition. This includes many of private members courses who are having to protect their businesses by investing in courses and facilities to reduce membership attrition. It is virtually impossible to build a new facility for less than the cost of existing trading courses.

Range development has virtually stopped with a declining marketplace.

The need for agricultural land for golf development has ceased in all but a very few situations, such as where hotels wish to add golf to their facilities and need to acquire farmland. In addition, restrictive planning policies on residential development in the countryside make gaining planning permission for all but urban fringe locations extremely difficult.

Financing golf developments has also become more difficult with many overseas investors disappearing from the UK.

Moreover, recent rises in agricultural land values means that the viability of any golf project is threatened by land costs alone, even for hotel companies.

One ray of hope for farmers is the emerging trend for courses within urban areas to be developed for housing. Any displaced club is often cash rich and needs farmland for their new club location. However the planning system has yet to recognise redundant golf courses as a major opportunity for development so this process is still emerging

Type of facility

- 18-hole 7000 yard plus course: 70-80 ha (170-195 acres) with Clubhouse and Pro Shop (600 sq. metres), parking, proper access and maintenance buildings. It takes between 1 and 2 years to construct.
- 9-hole course: 35-40 ha (84-95 acres).
- 9-hole Par 3 course: 7 ha (17 acres).
- 6-hole Par 3 or 4 course: 14 ha (34 acres).
- Driving range: 4 ha (10 acres).
- Pitch and putt course: 1.5 ha (4 acres).

Type of business organisation

To sell land with planning permission: The cost of development of an average new course will be significantly more than the value of the facility when it is complete. There is currently no premium over agricultural value unless the situation or planning consent offers something exceptional.

To let land to a developer/operator: Assuming the latter pays for constructing the course, a long lease will be required. Rental levels will depend on the expected profitability of the facility but currently, in our experience, leases are around £50-80,000 for an 18 hole course

To form a joint company with a developer/operator: This obviously means the farmer shares in the success or failure. The land would be all or part of the farmer's equity. A well constructed agreement is essential.

To develop and operate the course himself: The farmer would need good knowledge of golf and exceptional management ability besides access to substantial capital. In the present circumstances it is not to be recommended.

Construction methods and cost (by a specialist golf course constructor):

- 18-hole course (60-75 ha): £2.5m-£3.5m according to drainage, earthmoving and irrigation, but excluding green keepers building and machinery.
- 9-hole course (35-40 ha): £800,000-£1.2m.
- 9-hole par 3 course (7 ha): £600,000-£900,000.
- 6-hole par 3 or 4 course (14 ha): £500,000-£800,000.
- Driving range (4 ha): £250,000-£800,000, to include offices, storage, equipment, fencing and floodlighting.
- Full inventory of new machinery for 18-hole course: £480,000.
- Clubhouse (600 sq. metres): from £750,000 or £1.9m fitted out.
- Direct labour may reduce costs by around a third.
- Using own farm labour it is possible to reduce costs but it is very risky in terms of resultant course quality.

It is crucial to obtain professional advice at the outset for investment appraisal, feasibility study and a business plan. Changes to the national planning system places some obligation on Local Authorities to make allowance for the needs of all sports in their areas but in many emerging plans such information is often missing.

Large scale developments require Environmental Impact Assessments to be submitted with a planning application. These can cost anything from £80,000 to £150,000 on top of the golf designers and architects fees. The design and environmental fees are all at risk if planning approval is not gained.

Returns

Many existing businesses are seeing none or only marginal growth, whereas a successful well-run golf business has in the past achieved more than a 15% return on capital. These returns on new courses are now extremely rare. It would have to be a special circumstance to recommend the construction of a new stand-alone golf development in the UK today. Some situations exist, but it is very wise to proceed cautiously and be certain of the expected financial returns. Associated residential development could make developments profitable, but even this is now debateable in the current climate.

Acknowledgement: *International Design Group* Studio 5.17, The Paintworks, Bath Road, Bristol BS4 3EH. Telephone: 0117 316 0591. www.idgplanet.com

BED AND BREAKFAST

Although there are no official statistics, it is estimated that up to 2,000 farms across the UK offer B&B. Some are seasonal and informally run but many are open for much of the year, inspected under the auspices of the National Tourist Boards and/or the AA, and are members of a Regional Tourist Board and/or an organisation such as Farm Stay UK.

A bed and breakfast enterprise can be rewarding in both financial and social terms. However, the person running the business should enjoy meeting people, have good social skills and be prepared to work long hours. Other members of the family must be willing to share their home with visitors and to lose a certain amount of privacy. In a crowded market, and with rising customer expectations, the standard of the product is increasingly important. The aim must be to provide a standard of accommodation equal to that found in hotels. This is likely to involve some refurbishment of the farmhouse; either before starting the enterprise, to upgrade an existing B&B to modern standards, or just ongoing repair of wear and tear.

Very little grant assistance is available to cover capital costs in setting-up a B&B. Any support is likely to be on a regional basis. The relevant Regional Development Agency (RDA) should be contacted as a first step. As with all new ventures, it is good practice, and essential if seeking additional finance, to create a well-thought-out business plan containing realistic projections.

Although they are not necessarily onerous for smaller operations, it is vital to know the planning, legislative and financial requirements involved in B&B provision. Details are available from VisitBritain in the *'The Pink Booklet' - a practical guide to legislation for accommodation providers'*. This is now available online at www.accommodationknowhow.co.uk/ Further information can be found on the VisitBritain corporate website at www.visitbritain.org. In addition, a great deal of help and advice is provided by National Tourist Boards – England, Scotland and Wales each have their own organisations. Lastly, there are Regional Tourist Boards, and the Regional Development Agencies.

Marketing is very important. It can be done through a national organisation, in local Tourist Information Centres, in newspapers and magazines, and by word of mouth. Some establishments produce an attractive brochure or card giving details of the B&B, its location, facilities, and quality standards rating. Copies are left at tourist information centres etc and sent to prospective visitors. The internet is an important tool for the promotion of farmhouse B&Bs. Indeed, nowadays it's almost imperative to have a website and e-mail address, whilst many operators are also subscribing to online booking and availability systems.

As there is considerable competition it is useful if the enterprise can offer something special or different such as accommodation for visitors' horses, a welcome for pets, or use of a tennis court or pool. Establishments that can accommodate bigger parties are gaining in popularity. The number of B&Bs offering an evening meal has tended to decline in recent years, but providing locally grown produce can also be a draw. If evening meals are not offered it helps to have good local restaurants and pubs that customers can be directed to.

To join a marketing organisation it is important for the B&B to have a Quality Assurance Standard rating. These are awarded either by the official National Tourist Board inspectorate (which in England is Quality in Tourism), or the AA. The rating is at one of five levels, expressed as stars. It is based on guest care and the quality of what is provided following an unannounced overnight inspection visit. The inspection fee depends on the number of bedrooms and the level of charges. The rated establishment gets a listing in the VisitBritain guides and on their internet site. In some areas membership of a Regional Tourist Board is an option; this confers additional benefits including a reduction in inspection fees, access to legal advice, and discounted rates for promotional activities and training courses.

Prices charged will reflect the quality of accommodation and location but cannot be far out of line with other local B&Bs and small hotels. Prices can also vary depending on length of stay and time of year. The price range for one person per night ranges from £20 to over £40. The average is around £30 on the basis of two adults sharing a room. A higher rate usually applies for single occupancy of a double room. There are regional differences with higher prices generally being charged in the south and east, and lower ones in the west and north.

The receipts from the enterprise can be calculated as follows: If the B&B is open for 40 weeks of the year at £30 per person per night, given a 60% occupancy rate the gross return per bed will be just over £5,000. Most farmhouse B&Bs have 4-6 bed spaces, which would generate a gross return of between £20,000 to £30,000 p.a.

As every farmhouse B&B is different and some costs are difficult to apportion between guests and family, it is hard to provide realistic average costings. The following provides some pointers. Variable costs are food, electricity and heating, laundry, cleaning materials and additional help. There will also be regular redecoration costs, repairs, and replacement and renewal of glassware, china, cutlery, towels and bed linen. Variable costs if no non-family labour is used might average about 20% of the nightly charge. If casual labour has to be included variable costs could amount to 30-35% of the nightly charge.

Fixed costs will include insurance, business rates (if they apply), membership of a marketing organisation, regular advertising, repayments on any loans taken out for building and equipment to start the business and regular labour; they are likely to average 30-35% of charges.

Contact: Farm Stay UK, NAC, Stoneleigh Park, Warwickshire, CV8 2LG. Tel: 02476 696 909. www.farmstayuk.co.uk *VisitBritain,* Thames Tower, Black's Road, Hammersmith, London W6 9EL. Tel: 020 8846 9000. www.visitbritain.org. *Quality in Tourism*, Security House, Alexandra Way, Ashchurch, Tewksbury, Gloucs, GL20 8NB. Tel: 0845 300 6996. www.qualityintourism.com.

CHRISTMAS TREES

About 8 million trees are sold a year in the UK: 7.9 million of them UK grown. Five years ago 80% were Norway Spruce, but this is now down to less than 25%, with Nordman Fir, which retains its needles longer, at 55% (95% in urban areas) and Fraser Fir, a US favourite, 12%. The most popular size has been increasing and is now 5 to 7 feet. Only 5% are sold rooted, although public interest in 'living trees' is now increasing.

Imported trees in the past have accounted for 20% of total sales, but imports for Christmas 2005 fell to a few hundred thousand, and this trend has continued in subsequent years. This has put pressure on supplies and resulting in higher wholesale prices. Christmas trees are not eligible for the Single Payment, and as a result, many growers throughout the EU have grubbed-up trees, or are not replanting. The supply of trees in mainland Europe has therefore been substantially reduced. UK Christmas tree growers, unlike those in other countries, have never received subsidies and have not cut back production significantly. In addition changes in the pound-euro exchange rate has made imports more expensive.

There are some 400 British growers across all parts of the country, with plantations ranging from less than one hectare to 1,000 ha. It is estimated that there are 60 million trees being grown, on some 25,000 ha. The average grower sells 6 to 7,000 a year from about 20 ha. The majority of sales are through the big garden centres, which require a uniform tree, netted and palletised, but there are successful 'choose and cut' operations and the enterprise works well on a farm with a farm shop. Producers need to sell 10,000 to 15,000 a year to justify buying machinery to assist in cultivation

The enterprise is slow to make a return. Norway Spruce is harvested in years 5 to 7, Nordman and Fraser Firs in years 7 to 9, making the enterprise vulnerable to changing market conditions. About 30% of the crop is harvested in the first harvesting year, 40% in the second, 30% in the third. All species need a well-drained site free from late frosts, with good access. As with any crop, the better the land, the better the crop.

	Nordman Fir		Norway Spruce	
	£/ha	(£/ac)	£/ha	(£/ac)
4000 5 to 7 foot trees per ha @ price of . .	£5.50 - 6.00 / ft		£4.50 / ft	
Output (average)	138,000	(55,848)	108,000	(43,707)
Variable Costs:*				
Plants	2,950	(1,194)	2,360	(955)
Planting	830	(336)	830	(336)
Fertiliser	1,140	(461)	850	(344)
Weed control	1,930	(781)	1,930	(781)
Pesticides	830	(336)	1,230	(498)
Pruning and shaping	5,010	(2,028)	2,720	(1,101)
Harvesting	4,680	(1,894)	4,130	(1,671)
Marketing	13,800	(5,585)	10,800	(4,371)
Total Variable Costs	31,170	(12,614)	24,850	(10,057)
Gross Margin (whole period)	106,830	(43,234)	83,150	(33,650)
Gross Margin per year over 8 & 6 years . .	**13,354**	**(5,404)**	**13,858**	**(5,608)**

1. *Labour* assumed to be casuals.

2. *Rabbit fencing:* (£2 per m) and possibly deer fencing (£5.50 per m) are pre-requisites. Spacing is possible from 60cm x 60cm to 1.8m x 1.8m, but 1.2m x 1.2m is recommended. This gives 5,500 plants per ha allowing for 80% land loss for headlands, access, etc. Losses of 5 to 10% in the first year means 300-500 replacements are needed in second year. Norway Spruce transplants 30p-50p each, Nordman Fir 40-60p. Planting, by hand or machine, 12-15p/per plant.

3. *Variable Inputs:*

   Fertiliser in a split top dressing of 350 kg/ha 12:11:18 + Mg and TE in late March and mid-September.

   Herbicides for weed control: residual herbicide, as cereals, in first year; subsequently an over-spray in October/November plus spot weeding until the canopy closes over. Weed control costs have been affected by rising herbicide costs and are likely to be 35p/per plant over the life of the tree.

   Pesticides: aphicide three times a year for Norway Spruce, once for Nordman Fir at £35 per ha per application. Acaricide from year 3 to harvest: £200 per ha per year for Norway Spruce, £110 for Nordman Fir.

4. *Pruning and Shaping*: This is essential to produce the shape of tree the market demands. Norway Spruce: shaping 16.5p per tree per year from year 3 or 4. Nordman Fir: basal pruning in year 3 or 4 at 20p per tree plus shaping in the same year at 15p per tree and bud-rubbing every year except harvest at 5-10p per tree per year.

5. *Harvesting:* Done over 3 to 6 weeks, for dispatch Nov 20th to Dec. 12th. A full-time person is needed per 3,000 trees sold, or one person per week per 400-500 trees. Cost: Norway Spruce 65-85p per tree, Nordman Fir 75-100p; Norway Spruce may be dipped or sprayed to reduce needle drop. Marketing costs around 10% of output.

6. *Machinery:* Inter-row plantation tractors £15,000-£65,000; stump clearing machines £7,000-£25,000; palletiser £13,000-£14,000; mist blowers £8,000-£10,000; hydraulic netting funnel £8,000-£10,000; manual netting funnel £175.

7. *Labour:* Planting and pruning can be done in January/February and tagging for height and quality in October/November. Thus it fits in well with combinable cropping.

The gross margins given are high, but these will only be achieved by a high level of expertise and commitment and the long period before any return is obtained must also be stressed, together with the risk this entails.

Acknowledgement: Thanks to - British Christmas Tree Growers Association, 13 Wolrige Road, Edinburgh, EH16 6HX. Tel: 0131 664 1100 www.bctga.co.uk.

OTHER DIVERSIFICATION

Well calculated diversification should be encouraged. Non-agricultural enterprises managed in conjunction with the farming operation can offer several benefits to the business. These include:

- Spreading risks of returns; if the economics of agricultural production declines, revenue from non-commodity based enterprises may boost business income.

- Resource efficiency; most farm systems have quieter and busier periods for staff and management which may be switched into other roles for examples.

- Increasing profit.

Any new enterprise will have its own risks associated with it. These must be clearly and objectively calculated (this will be a requirement if borrowed money is necessary). Each resource employed will have its own opportunity cost (what could it be earning if it was not being used for this new venture?). Cash (return on capital) is the obvious one, what could it earn in a high interest account? Labour is less straight forward. For example, a B&B might require minimal new capital under some circumstances, but tie somebody to the house at key times of the day, restricting other employment opportunities.

Before any major investment or change in business structure to incorporate new diversifications, business plans and market research to assess the likely income potential are critical. Most new enterprises require new skills (such as different production systems, new marketing and sales techniques). These take time and dedication to acquire. Developing new ideas and expanding a novel business venture can be exciting and time consuming; maintaining sufficient management time on the existing farm business is a common problem.

Nevertheless, many ventures exist where entrepreneurial skills have achieved notable success. Conversion of surplus farm buildings, for offices, workshops, retail and storage, has been the primary farm diversification activity up to date. A DEFRA survey found that 51% of farms had diversified activity in 2008/09, but if letting farm buildings is stripped out the percentage of diversified farms falls to 28%. It also shows that arable farms tend to be more diversified than livestock and farms in the South East are more diversified than elsewhere in the UK.

Some 'diversification' enterprises have been included above. There are many others, which include;

Novel Crops/Livestock
- Alpacas
- Herbs
- Carp and Crayfish
- Llamas
- Alpacas
- Quails
- Snails

Sporting
- Fisheries
- Game Shooting
- Stalking
- Clay Pigeon Shooting

Horses
- Riding School
- Trekking

Adventure Games
- Motor Sports
- Go-carting

Tourism
- Caravans / Camping
- Holiday Cottages

Barn Conversions
- Business Lets
- Dwelling Let

Vertical integration
- Yoghurt, Ice cream, etc.
- Meat sales
- Farm Shop

6.   FORESTRY

ESTABLISHMENT COSTS (BEFORE GRANT)

Unit Cost of Operations

Year/s	Operation	Estimated Cost (£)
1.	Trees for planting	
	(i) Bare rooted:	
	Conifers	180-220 per 1,000
	Broadleaves	360-440 per 1,000
	(ii) Rooted in small peat blocks:	
	Conifers	170-300 per 1,000
	Broadleaves	350-430 per 1,000
1.	Tree Protection	
	(i) Fencing (materials and erection)	
	Rabbit	5.31-6.49 per metre
	Stock...	4.05-4.95 per metre
	Deer	7.02-8.58 per metre
	Deer and Rabbit	9.00-11.00 per metre
	Split post and rail	5·50-8.50 per metre
	(ii) Tree guards/shelters	
	Spiral and canes (450mm)	23-28 per 100
	Plastic tubes (1,200mm).................	85-110 per 100
	Stakes...	45-55 per 100
1.	Spot spraying	40-60 per 1,000 trees
1.	Hand planting	
	Conifers	180-220 per 1,000 trees
	Broadleaves *	135-165 per 1,000 trees
	Machine planting (loams and sand based on	
	2250 plants per ha).......................	225-450 per ha
2-3.	Replacing dead trees **	
	Operation......................................	60-120 per ha
	Plant supply	75-100 per ha
1-4.	Weeding per operation	
	Herbicide ***	45-55 per ha weeded
2.	Inter-row mowing.......................................	225-275 per ha

Costs specific to location		Upland	Lowland
1. Ground Preparation:	ploughing	132-209 per ha	66- 99 per ha
	mounding	275-385 per ha	275-385 per ha
1. Drainage		88-110 per ha	—
1. Fertilising		132-297 per ha	—

*   Includes cost of erecting guards/shelters.

**   Replacing dead trees (beating up) may be necessary, once in the second year and again in the third year. Costs depend on number of trees.

***   Up to 2 weeding operations may be necessary in each of the first 4 years in extreme situations. Costs are inclusive of materials.

Access roads may need to be constructed and can typically cost between £13,500 and £33,000 per kilometre (£21,700 to £53,000 per mile) depending on availability of road stone and the number of culverts and bridges required.

Total Establishment Costs up to Year 3

1. *Conifer—Lowland Sites:* On a fairly typical lowland site, requiring little or no clearing or draining, the approximate cost before grant of establishing a conifer plantation would be in the range £2,000-£3,500 per hectare. Up to 8 separate weeding operations may be required.

2. *Conifer—Upland Sites:* Establishing a similar conifer plantation on an upland site could cost £2,200 to £3,800 per hectare. Normally some form of site preparation and drainage is required but only one weeding operation may be necessary. Overall costs tend to be £110-£220 per ha less than on lowland sites.

3. *Hardwoods:* Costs of establishing hardwood plantations are highly dependent on the fencing and/or tree protection required. If tubes are needed the overall costs will be influenced by the number of plants per hectare. Costs could be in the range £2,000-£5,000 per ha. Site conditions normally mean that hardwoods being grown for timber production are restricted to lowland sites.

4. *Farm Woodlands:* Establishment costs for farm woodlands may be lower than those indicated for hardwoods in (iii) above if lower planting densities are used. Initial establishment costs in the first year of about £2,800 per ha for woods under 3 ha and £2,500 per ha for woods of 3 to 10 ha would be typical.

5. *Size Factor:* Savings in fencing and other economies of scale may reduce average costs per ha by 10 to 20% where large plantations are being established; conversely costs for small woods may easily be 25% higher per ha established.

6. *Method of Establishment:* A range of organisations and individuals undertake forestry contracting work and competitive tendering can help to control costs.

Re-Stocking Costs

Once trees on a site have been felled, the Forestry Commission usually requires the site to be restocked as a condition of awarding a felling licence. This can be done by replanting or through natural regeneration, leaving a proportion of the trees standing and using seed from these trees to re-stock. Minimal site preparation is usually required for natural regeneration. There is no longer any grant for restocking woodland, although grant is available for 'regeneration' where the species mix is being altered. (see Grant section). The costs of establishment given above, and those for maintenance given below, are estimates for England. Costs in Scotland tend to be lower.

MAINTENANCE COSTS

Once trees have been established they normally require some maintenance and management work each year. For trees being grown primarily for timber production on a large scale, operations required may include ride and fence maintenance, pest control, fire protection, management fee and insurance premiums. Costs are normally £40-£60 per ha per annum depending on the size of the plantation and the complexity of management. In upland areas, fertiliser is occasionally applied once or more times in the first 20 years of the tree's life depending on the quality of the site. Estimated cost £110-£275 per ha, depending on elements applied. For trees being grown for sporting and amenity purposes, annual maintenance costs are likely to be less and may range up to about £11 per ha.

A brashing operation which involves removing branches up to two metres may be required for access reasons as the crop matures. Opening up inspection racks over 5-10% of the crop may cost £44-£77 per ha. Brashing 40-50% of the crop costs £176-£396 per ha.

PRODUCTION

Production is usually measured in terms of cubic metres (m³) of marketable timber per hectare and will vary according to the quality of the site, species planted and thinning policy. Sites in lowland Britain planted to conifers typically produce an average of 12 to 18 m³ of timber per ha per year over the rotation as a whole and would accordingly be assessed as falling in yield classes 12 to 18. Under traditional management systems, thinning begins 18 to 25 years after planting and is repeated at intervals of approximately 5 years until the wood is clear-felled at between 40 and 60 years. Approximately 40-45% of total production will be from thinnings. Broadleaves typically produce an average of between 4 and 8 m³ of timber per hectare per year and fall in yield classes 4 to 8. A felling licence must be obtained from the Forestry Commission before any felling takes place, unless a Forest Management Plan has already been approved by them. Grants are available for preparing a Forest Management Plan which covers a 20 year period (see Grants section).

Prior to a thinning sale the trees normally have to be marked and measured at an estimated cost of 75p - £1 per m³, which is equivalent to £175-£300 per hectare depending on species, crop density and age. For a clear-felling sale the cost can range from £300 to £400 per ha, or about £1.50 per m³ where a full tariff applies, i.e. where each tree is counted and sample measurements of individual trees are taken.

PRICES

Prices for standing timber are extremely variable, depending on species, tree size and quality, ease of extraction from site, geographical location (nearness to end user), quantity being sold, world market prices and effectiveness of marketing method used. The use of wood for energy generation is beginning to open up a new market for poorer quality hardwood and conifer logs and forest residues.

Conifers

Average prices paid for standing coniferous timber sold from Forest Enterprise areas in the year to 31st March 2010, were:

Harvesting stage	Average tree size (m³)	Price (£ per m³)		
		England	Scotland	Wales
1st Thinning	Up to 0.074......................	12.47	2.56	0.89
	0.075-0.124	9.19	2.67	5.95
Subsequent	0.125-0.174	9.44	3.25	7.26
Thinnings	0.175-0.224	11.22	9.22	5.56
	0.225-0.274	9.06	3.35	17.02
	0.275-0.424	13.30	7.03	10.83
	0.425-0.499	15.74	12.44	18.01
Clearfelling	0.500-0.599	14.03	7.16	11.37
	0.600-0.699	12.76	11.07	8.10
	0.700-0.799	16.50	10.49	0.00
	0.800-0.899	14.58	3.29	13.98
	0.900-0.999	17.01	9.21	19.64
	1.000 and over.................	18.71	7.92	10.62

Source: Forest Enterprise.

Hardwoods

The hardwood trade is very complex. Merchants normally assess and value all but the smallest trees on a stem by stem basis. Actual prices fetched can show considerable variation depending on species, size, form, quality and marketing expertise of the seller. Felling usually takes place in the winter months.

Some indicative prices for hardwoods are given below, but it is important to note that actual prices fetched can vary quite widely. Wood quality is particularly important in determining prices.

Harvesting stage	Tree size range (m³)	Price range £ per m³ standing	Possible use
First thinnings	<0.13	0-16	Firewood, board products and pulp wood. Poles for refineries and turnery.
Subsequent Thinnings	0.13-0.3	5-20	Smaller sizes and lower quality material may go for fencing or for use in the mining industry.
	0.3-0.6	8-22	
	0.6 -1.0	10-70	
Clearfellings	1.0-2.0	15-120	Trees over 30 cm in diameter and of better quality may go for planking, furniture or joinery. High quality material may go for veneers and can fetch between £150 and £300 per m³ depending on species and specifications.
	2+	25-220	

Prices for Oak, Sycamore, Cherry and Elm tend to be significantly higher than for Beech, which seldom exceeds about £45 per m³ standing even for stands containing significant volumes of first quality planking. The market for Ash has been historically weak for the past 5-7 years.

TIMBER MARKETING

In-house marketing by the owner or agent can be cost effective but only if they have detailed, up-to-date knowledge of timber buyers in the market place. The alternative is marketing through a forestry manager or management company.

Nationwide electronic sales of timber by auction and tender are now available for all types and quantities of timber.

MARKET VALUE OF ESTABLISHED PLANTATIONS AND WOODS

The value of woods depends on many factors, such as location, access, species, age and soil type. The table on the following page gives an indication of the range of current (2008) market values of commercial woodlands of different ages, based on recent market sales.

From years 20 to 25 onwards prices of commercial woods will also be increasingly influenced by the quantity of merchantable timber they contain. Depending on the time of clear-felling, the timber may be worth between £900 to £6,000 per hectare (£360 to £2,500 per acre).

Woods that are relatively small with high amenity or Ancient Woodland status can often command a premium over prices fetched for commercial woodlands as can those that are freehold and include minerals and sporting rights. This is particularly the case in southern England. Conversely conservation designation can restrict value by preventing economic forest management.

The value of woods containing mature hardwoods will depend on the quality and value of the timber they contain and the quality of access.

Market Value of Commercial Sitka Spruce Woodlands

Age of Commercial Woods and Plantations	Price Range for crop and land	
	£/ha	£/acre
0-5 years	1,000-2,000	(400-800)
6-10 years	1,500-2,750	(600-1,100)
11-15 years	2,500-3,500	(1,000-1,400)
16-20 years	3,000-4,500	(1,200-1,800)
21-25 years	3,500-6,000	(1,400-2,400)

WOODLAND GRANTS

Each part of the United Kingdom has its own woodland grant scheme, administered by the Forestry Commission. In England it is called the English Woodland Grant Scheme, in Scotland there are grants for woodlands offered as part of the Rural Development Programme, and in Wales they are offered under the Better Woodlands for Wales (BWW) programme. Details of all the schemes can be obtained via the Forestry Commission's website (www.forestry.gov.uk). Previous grant schemes are now closed to new entrants.

English Woodland Grant Scheme

The English Woodland Grant Scheme (EWGS) is the Forestry Commission's suite of grants designed to develop the co-ordinated delivery of public benefits from England's woods. EWGS is supported via the Rural Development Programme for England (RDPE).

In order to be eligible for the grant scheme, woodlands need to be registered on the Rural Land Register and the owner must hold a Single Business Identifier. There are six components of the scheme as follows:

1. *Woodland Management Planning Grant:* available as a contribution towards the cost of producing plans for existing woodlands, and which meet the UK Woodland Assurance Standard. Rates of grant contribution are £20 per hectare for the first 100 hectares and £10 thereafter. There is a minimum payment of £1,000 for plans covering more than 3 hectares but less than 30 hectares.

2. *Woodland Assessment Grant:* available as a contribution towards the costs of obtaining additional information about the woodland in relation to ecology, landscape, historic and heritage assessments, and to determine stakeholder interests. Grant varies from £2.80 per ha - £5.60 per ha with a minimum payment of £300.

3. *Woodland Management Grant:* aid for providing public benefits and to undertake sustainable woodland management. Potentially eligible activities include public access, maintaining boundaries, protecting archaeological features, management of old wood habitat and open space, soil and ground water protection, controlling non-native species, pest control, woodland health and monitoring sustainability. The rate of grant is in line with ELS payments at £30 per hectare per year.

4. *Woodland Regeneration Grant:* a contribution towards the cost of regenerating woodland after felling. The aim is to promote the replacement of felled woodland whilst changing woodland types for increased public benefit. Grant rates depend on the type of wood being felled and the type of wood which replaces it:

Type of woodland felled	Type of woodland being regenerated	Grant (£/ha)
Conifer plantation	Native species	1,100
	Broadleaved species	950
	Conifer species	360
Broadleaved plantation	Native species	1,100
	Broadleaved species	950
	Wide spaced broadleaves	350
Conifer plantation on Ancient Woodland Site	Native species	1,760
	Broadleaved species	950
	Conifer species	0
Broadleaved plantation on Ancient Woodland Site	Native species	1,760
	Broadleaved species	950
Ancient and other semi-natural woodland	Native species	1,100

5. *Woodland Improvement Grant:* a contribution towards the cost of work to improve the quality of woodland for social, environmental, and economic benefits. The rate of grant is set between 50% - 80% of standard costs in a five-year plan. The focus is on improving access, biodiversity, and protecting SSSIs. Regions can choose to vary the rate of contributions or priority areas to reflect regional differences.

6. *Woodland Creation Grants:* aids the establishment of new woodlands. This element of the EWGS is competitive and will be assessed on a points-scoring system with the applications that giving the greatest benefits being selected. Woodland creation may be by natural regeneration or by direct seeding/planting. The rates of grant will depend on the type of woodland; Standard (3 ha or more), Small Standard (less than 3 ha), Native Species Only, Community (designed for public access), or Special Broadleaved (species appropriate for growth at wide spacing). Planting density requirements, percentage open space and percentage of shrub element are set for for each woodland type. Rates of grant are as follows:

Woodland category	Broadleaves £/ha	Conifers £/ha
Standard, Native and Community	1,800	1,200
Special Broadleaved	700	n/a

In addition to the above grant an extra £500 per ha is paid for woodland established within five miles of 100,000 people or within the National Forest Area, or where there is an agreement to provide for public access and there is an identified need. Woodland meeting both of these requirements will be eligible to claim £1000 per ha. An additional £2,000 per ha is also available for woodland planted within target areas located throughout the country.

Payment is made 80% on the completion of the work, with the final 20% payable after 5 years as long as the plantation is maintained. Applications usually have to be made prior to a 30th September deadline prior to the winter/spring when the planting will take place.

Planting on Agricultural Land: Annual payments are available under the Farm Woodland Payment for converting agricultural land to woodland (similar to the old FWPS). Payments will continue for 15 years when new woodlands comprise more than 50% broadleaved species, and 10 years when the percentage broadleaves is less than 50% (or fast growing broadleaved species such as poplar). Payment rates will depend on the agricultural land use category being converted to woodland. Current rates are set out below, although they may be subject to revision in future years;

Payments available under the Farm Woodland Payment

Agricultural Land Category	Annual payment (£ per ha)
Arable Land in the Lowlands..................	300
Other improved land in the Lowlands....	200
Unimproved or land in the Uplands.......	60

More details of the EWGS are available on the Forestry Commission website (www.forestry.gov.uk). There are deadlines for the submission of application forms for the different components of the scheme as funding is limited. Early discussion with one of Forestry Commission England Conservancy offices is advised. Help and advice can also be obtained from the EWGS helpline Tel: 01223 346 004.

WOODLAND SINGLE PAYMENT & CARBON FUNDING

Landowners who are eligible for the Farm Woodland Payment can also continue to claim Single Payment on the same land. The Forestry Commission will not fund applications for new woodland creation that include carbon co-funding if there is any link between the proposals and use of the term 'offsetting'. The Forestry Commission will, however, allow co-funding provided certain criteria are met and appropriate language is used.

WOODLAND TAXATION

Income from commercial woodlands is not subject to income tax, and tax relief cannot be claimed for the cost of establishing new woodlands. In general EWGS grants are tax free but annual Farm Woodland Payments are regarded as compensation for agricultural income forgone and are liable to income tax. The sale of timber does not attract Capital Gains Tax, although the disposal of the underlying land may give rise to an assessment.

Woodlands which are managed commercially or which are ancillary to a farming business may be eligible for either Business Property Relief or Agricultural Relief for Inheritance Tax purposes if owned for more than two years.

Acknowledgement: The above estimates are based in part on information supplied by Justin Mumford FICFor CEnv of Lockhart Garratt Ltd (Tel: 01536 408840).

7. ORGANIC FARMING

The Organic Sector:

The total organic land area fell in the UK from 2008 to 2009 by 1%. Throughout 2009, 4.0% of UK agricultural land (excluding common grazing) was in organic production on 4,946 (5,383) holdings. In 2009 the area (in hectares) devoted to organic production was as follows:

	Fully Organic	In conversion	Total	% of Agric. Area	of UK Organic Area	% of UK Organic Producers
England	311,176	67,588	378,764	4.0	51.3	62
Wales	88,566	36,800	125,366	8.4	17.0	20
Scotland	209,256	12,039	221,295	4.0	30.0	12
N. Ireland	10,270	3,015	13,284	1.3	1.8	5
2009	*619,268*	*119,442*	*738,709*	*4.2*	*100*	*100*
2008	*594,413*	*149,103*	*743,516*	*4.2*		
2007	*524,303*	*157,893*	*682,196*	*3.9*		
2006	*498,646*	*121,137*	*619,783*	*3.6*		
2005	*533,902*	*85,951*	*619,853*	*3.6*		

Following a sharp rise in organic demand and therefore production in recent years, the demand for organic foods has waned over the last 2 years (12.8% fall in organic demand in 2009) as shoppers tighten their belts. Some claim the organic movement has been confusing its marketing messages to the cost of market share. At the same time, the rise of other, sometimes less expensive food brandings have been stealing the 'ethical crown' such as Fairtrade, free range and local produce. There have never been so many organic promotions and deals in the grocery sector. Farm gate organic premiums over conventional foods have fallen over the last 18 months, squeezing organic margins.

There is grant aid to help producers during the required conversion period (see next page). Some organic farmers have reverted to conventional production primarily because of declining premiums. Imports of organic fruit and vegetables, are especially high, indeed, over half of organic produce consumers in the UK is imported.

Many hill and upland livestock farms have converted to organic production – with inputs already low, management changes need only be small. Similar factors have meant that a sizeable number of extensive lowland beef and sheep producers have also embraced organic production. This contributes to the explanation why organic farms are less productive than conventional.

Below are the land use estimates of producers of organic and in conversion crop areas and livestock numbers for the applicable years:

| *Organic Land Use according to Crop Type (UK)* | | | | | *year on year* |
'000 ha	*2005*	*2006*	*2007*	*2008*	*2009*	*% change*
Cereals	47.7	47.5	51.5	57.2	60.0	4.8
Other crops	10.8	10.2	11.3	11.2	11.2	0.2
Fruit & Nut	1.7	1.8	2.0	1.9	2.2	16.9
Vegetables & Pots	13.7	15.5	16.9	19.8	18.9	-4.4
Herbs & Ornam.s	0.8	0.7	0.6	5.5	5.8	4.5
Temporary pasture	98	102.7	125.1	130	126	-2.8
Permanent pasture	429	422.6	452.0	496	496	0.3
Woodland	6.7	8.2	11.5	5.9	7.2	21.9
Other	12.1	10.6	11.2	17.9	11.6	-35.4
Total area ha	*620*	*619*	*682*	*744*	*739*	*-0.6*

| *Organic Livestock Numbers (UK)* | | | | | *year on year* |
'000 head	*2005*	*2006*	*2007*	*2008*	*2009*	*% change*
Cattle	214.3	244.8	250.4	*319.6*	*331.2*	*3.6*
Sheep				*n/a*	*884.8*	*n/a*
Pigs	30.0	32.9	50.4	*71.2*	*48.2*	*-32.4*
Poultry	3,439	4,421	4,440	*4,363*	*3,959*	*-9.3*
Goats	0.5	0.6	0.5	*0.4*	*0.1*	*-67.5*
Other Livestock	1.5	4.3	3.4	*4.3*	*3.3*	*-25.2*

The economics to the farmer depend primarily upon the:

- relative yield compared with conventional farming;
- price premium compared with conventional farming.

In the case of cereals both research and experience suggests that yields of organic crops are typically between 60% and 70% of those of conventionally produced crops, but the much higher prices obtained have compensated for this to date, with feed wheat prices around £180 ex-farm and feed beans £230 per tonne ex-farm, in addition to the obvious saving in fertiliser and spray costs. Hence the gross margin is normally much higher as long as a high yield is achieved. However, there are also the wider whole farm effects to be considered, e.g., unless the farm already has a substantial percentage of its area down to leys this will probably have to be increased in order to maintain yields and this extra grass has to be utilised profitably – which is far from easy, and the extra capital requirements could be heavy.

Furthermore, there is a two year 'conversion period' to undergo before full price premiums can be claimed; (though note the aid scheme, below). Also, in the case of vegetable crops, quality (in the sense of appearance) can be badly affected by pests and diseases.

As regards relative cultivation costs, in one ADAS monitored study, these were reported to be 15% higher on the organically grown wheat (approximately £20 more per ha (£8 per acre) at present costs). However no spraying is required. Survey data have indicated overall labour requirements to be 10-30% higher than on conventional farms, with machinery costs generally similar.

In the case of livestock, premiums have been highly attractive. In some sectors, such as milk, this led to many producers converting to organic, creating an excess of supply over demand. This then collapsed the organic premium. It is a demonstration of the need to consider markets fully in a 'niche' sector like organic. Organic production of grazing livestock is generally speaking of greater value to the larger farm, especially on land that favours grass rather than cash crops, where the reduction in stocking rate caused by the lack of bagged nitrogen fertilizer is less important or crop requirement can be met with alternatives. Concentrate feed costs per tonne are much higher.

Aid for Organic Farmers:

In England, support for organic farmers is through the Organic Entry Level Stewardship (OELS) (see Section III). In summary, this provides relatively high levels of support per hectare for the two-year conversion period. Rates then drop to a 'stewardship' level thereafter. Similar schemes, but with different categories and payment rates, are available in Wales and in Scotland.

Further Information:

No gross margin data for organic enterprises are included in this section because a specialist publication is available on the subject: the '2009 Organic Farm Management Handbook', (8th Ed - Sept 2008) by Nic Lampkin, Mark Measures and Susanne Padel, University of Wales, Aberystwyth. Tel: 01970 622 248.

Additional information may be available from the following organisations:

DEFRA (Organic Food and Industrial Crops Division)
Nobel House, 17 Smith Square, London, SW1P 3JR.   0207 238 5605

Organic Farmers and Growers Limited
The Elim Centre, Lancaster Road, Shrewsbury, Shropshire, SY1 3LE.   01743 440 512

Soil Association
Bristol House, 40-56 Victoria Street, Bristol, BS1 6BY.   0117 929 0661

Elm Farm Research Centre
Hamstead Marshall, Newbury, Berkshire, RG20 0HR.   01488 658 298

Biodynamic Agricultural Association
The Secretary, Painswick Inn, Stroud, Glos. GL5 1QG.   01453 759 501

Organic Food Federation
1 Turbine Way, EcoTech Business Park, Swaffham, Norfolk, PE37 7XD.01760 720 444

Organic Centre Wales
University of Wales, Aberystwyth, Ceredigion, SY23 3AL.   01970 622 248

Tesco Centre for Organic Agriculture
Nafferton Farm, Stocksfield, Northumberland, NE47 7XD.   01661 830 222

Scottish Agricultural College
Organic Farming Unit, Craibstone Estate, Bucksburn, Aberdeen,
AB21 9YA   01224 711 293

8.   SUMMARY OF GROSS MARGINS

This page summarises the key figures of the gross margins over the previous pages. There are well in excess of 100 gross margins in the Pocketbook and additional data for other enterprises too. They cannot be directly compared on a like for like basis, as different resources are required in order to produce each one and some offer whole farm benefits beyond the gross margin. Some, for example require higher quality land than others and some will require more overheads in terms of machinery, labour, buildings or working capital than others. Management requirement varies from one enterprise to another.

Summary of Arable Crop Gross Margins

Crop (£/Ha)	Price	Yield	Output	Variable Costs	Gross Margin
Winter Feed Wheat	£120	8.35	£1,002	£387	£615
Winter Milling Wheat	£134	7.70	£1,032	£426	£606
Spring Milling Wheat	£132	5.75	£758	£304	£454
Winter Feed Barley	£115	6.90	£794	£308	£486
Winter Malting Barley	£130	5.85	£761	£283	£478
Spring Malting Barley	£135	5.45	£736	£232	£504
Winter Oats	£110	6.40	£704	£236	£468
Spring Oats	£110	5.50	£605	£207	£398
Winter Rape	£260	3.40	£884	£339	£545
Spring Rape	£260	2.00	£520	£201	£319
Linseed	£299	1.75	£523	£210	£313
Winter Beans	£162	4.00	£686	£214	£472
Spring Beans	£174	3.70	£682	£190	£492
Blue Peas	£170	3.75	£676	£255	£421
Marofats	£190	3.40	£684	£297	£387
Lupins	£220	3.00	£698	£296	£402
Rye	£120	6.20	£744	£338	£406
Triticale	£115	5.00	£575	£264	£311
Naked Oats	£160	5.50	£880	£284	£596
Durum Wheat	£170	6.20	£1,054	£366	£688
Borage	£2,500	0.40	£1,000	£258	£742
Crambe	£160	2.50	£400	£243	£157
Hemp	£130	7.50	£975	£422	£553
Grain Maize	£145	7.50	£1,088	£351	£737
Millet	£230	3.00	£690	£247	£443
Poppies		2.00	£800	£268	£532
Soya	£325	2.50	£813	£265	£547
Sunflower	£350	2.00	£700	£253	£447
Vining Peas	£253	4.75	£1,200	£412	£788
Maincrop Potatoes	£140	45.00	£6,300	£2,839	£3,461
Early Potatoes	£190	23.00	£4,370	£1,994	£2,376
Sugarbeet	£27.78	66.00	£1,834	£815	£1,018

Summary of Livestock Gross Margins

Livestock		Output	Variable Costs	Gross Margin /Head	Gross margin £/Ha
Dairy					
Friesian Holsteins	per Cow	£1,604	£679	£924	£1,849
Channel Island	per Cow	£1,230	£562	£668	£1,602
Ayreshire	per Cow	£1,420	£591	£829	£1,989
Friesian Followers	per Head	£1,060	£420	£640	£882
Channel Followers	per Head	£870	£369	£501	£872
Ayreshire Followers	per Head	£770	£363	£407	£708
Beef Cattle					
Bucket Reared Calf 3 month	per Calf	£122	£86	£36	
Bucket Reared Calf 6 month	per Calf	£252	£165	£87	
Spring calving lowland suckler	per Cow	£278	£227	£51	£92
Autumn calving lowland suckle	per Cow	£352	£290	£62	£103
Spring calving upland suckler	per Cow	£261	£209	£52	£83
Autumn calving upland suckler	per Cow	£345	£273	£72	£90
Summer Store Finishers	per Head	£198	£114	£84	£336
Winter Store Finishers	per Head	£211	£182	£30	£266
Winter finished sucklers	per Head	£370	£242	£128	£1,025
Grass finished sucklers	per Head	£303	82	£221	£886
Overwintered & grass finished	per Head	£314	£218	£95	£357
Grazed and yard finished	per Head	£331	£206	£126	£502
Winter finished dairy stores	per Head	£262	£229	£33	£197
Grass finished dairy stores	per Head	£203	82	£121	£484
Overwintered & grass finished	per Head	£256	£233	£23	£80
Grazed and yard finished dairy	per Head	£388	£255	£133	£464
Continental Cereal beef	per Head	£450	£469	-£19	
Holstein Cereal Beef	per Head	£544	£469	£75	
18 month Beef	per Head	£626	£468	£158	£538
Silage Beef	per Head	£612	£514	£98	£781
Sheep					
Lowland Spring Lamb	per Ewe	£69	£38	£30	£303
Early Lambing	per Ewe	£86	£68	£17	£224
Upland Flocks	per Ewe	£52	£40	£12	£107
Hill Flocks	per Ewe	£41	£22	£19	
Store Lambs	per Ewe	£12	£11	£1	£26

Summary of Livestock Gross Margins (Continued)

Livestock		Output	Variable Costs	Gross Margin /Head	Gross margin £/Ha
Pigs					
Weaners	per Sow	£1,036	£664	£372	
Pork	per Pig	£32	£29	£3.40	
Cutter	per Pig	£48	£39	£9.20	
Bacon	per Pig	£61	£48	£13.00	
Combined Pork	per Pig	£79	£59	£20.09	
Combined Cutter	per Pig	£94	£69	£25.89	
Combined Bacon	per Pig	£107	£78	£29.69	
Poultry					
Caged Eggs	per Bird	£12.20	£10.23	£1.97	
Free Range Eggs	per Bird	£19.46	£12.06	£7.40	
Pullets	/bird reared	£2.55	£1.91	£0.64	
Broilers	p/bird	123.50p	116.00p	7.50p	
All year turkey	£/Bird	£34.89	£15.60	£19.29	
Christmas Turkey	£/Bird	£38.57	£20.37	£18.20	
Large Roaster Chickens	£/Bird	£14.90	£4.98	£9.91	
Ducks	£/Bird	£7.03	£3.80	£3.23	
Geese	£/Bird	£46.60	£27.57	£19.03	
Other Livestock					
Breeding & Finishing Deer	per 100 hinds	£15,888	£4,349	£11,538	£635
Deer Calves	per 100 hinds	£7,473	£2,621	£4,852	£315
Finishing Stag Calves	per 200 hinds	£21,319	£6,480	£14,838	£816
Ostriches	per Bird	£356	£324	£32	
Wild Boar	per Sow	£1,217	£762	£455	
Dairy Sheep	per Ewe	£400	£217	£183	£2,016
Dairy Goats	per Doe	£296	£219	£77	£612
Angora Goats	per Doe	£205	£63	£143	£1,250
Trout	per tonne fish	£1,860	£1,285	£575	
Rabbit	per 50 does	£7,884	£5,242	£2,642	

III. GOVERNMENT SUPPORT

1. INTRODUCTION

Agricultural support to farmers and the rural economy is largely provided through the European Union's Common Agricultural Policy (CAP), and delivered in the UK by the devolved Governments of England, Wales, Scotland and Northern Ireland. The World Trade Organisation (WTO) provides a higher tier in the hierarchy of agricultural support policy and has driven the past changes in the CAP. With the collapse in July 2008 of the WTO Doha Development Round no immediate further WTO driven changes are anticipated. The Doha Round was working towards an agreement that would have meant the EU reducing barriers to imports (mainly tariffs and tariff quotas) and this could have had the effect of reducing prices to UK farmers. Now the existing tariff regime largely continues and it is likely to be several years before changes are agreed and implemented.

The CAP has two main budgets (or pillars). Pillar 1 includes the Single Payment Scheme (SPS) which provides direct aid to farm businesses and also Market Support for agricultural produce – once the mainstay of CAP support, but now much reduced in importance. Pillar 2 is support through the Rural Development legislation which is increasing in importance in the EU and provides direct support to farmers and also to rural communities. As an indication of the relative importance of Pillar 1 and Pillar 2 support to English farmers it is estimated that in the period 2007-13 Pillar 1 will amount to approximately 73% and Pillar 2 27%. Market support (which is not paid direct to farmers) is not included but is now a very small proportion of total CAP support.

Further details of the main CAP mechanisms are given in the following paragraphs: in individual situations businesses should always check with the latest legislation and their devolved administrations' publications.

2. SINGLE PAYMENT SCHEME

Major reforms of Pillar 1 of the CAP were agreed in 2003. They came into effect, for the most part, on the 1st January 2005. Then in November 2005 a major reform of the Sugar Regime was agreed including price cuts and compensation to farmers starting with the 2006 sugar beet crop. In 2007 a reform of the Fruit and Vegetable regime was agreed. These subsequent reforms have now been incorporated into the Single Payment legislation and there have been some significant simplifications. The latest reforms were in 2008 when the 'Health Check' of the CAP was agreed. This was not a radical reform. The main points affecting the UK are summarised below and include:

- the permanent end to set-aside – although English farmers have had some 'mitigation' measures put in place for 2010 – see later

- the €45 Aid for Energy Crops was abolished from 2010 onwards. The €55 Protein Crop will go before 2012

- milk quotas will end by 2015. Producers will receive an increase in quota of 1% for five years starting on 31st March 2009

- minor changes to cereals and milk intervention systems

- changes to modulation rates (only affecting very few large Welsh farms)

- option to move to a flat-rate regional payment system

- changes to the National Envelope Measures (Article 68)

- changes to SPS rules including minimum claim size and to entitlements for 2010 onwards (set-aside and national reserve entitlements have become normal/standard)

The implications of the Health Check are expanded on in the sections below.

SINGLE PAYMENT SCHEME BASICS

The major, essential change of the 2003 reforms was ***decoupling***. This means that farm support is no longer linked to what is being produced on the farm during the year, i.e. to the crops being grown or the livestock kept. The 'Single Payment' (still often referred to as the 'Single Farm Payment') is being made according to what was being produced, by each individual farmer who made the claims, during the three years 2000-2002 (the reference period), expressed on a £ per hectare basis. While it was originally conceived (by most people at least) that these would be paid directly to the individuals who originally made the claims ('historic entitlements') an alternative method of distributing the total entitlements gained increasing support during the later months of 2003: paying it as a flat-rate regional average payment per hectare. Various 'hybrids' – combinations of the two methods – were also advocated.

The governments in the various EU member states finally made widely different decisions regarding the distribution of the payment: often varying in different regions within their countries. Differences even occurred within the UK. Essentially (with some relatively small variations), Scotland and Wales decided to adopt an individual historic entitlements basis, Northern Ireland a static hybrid.

For England the government opted for what may be regarded as a complex 'sophisticated' method: generally referred to as a 'dynamic hybrid' or 'delayed flat-rate'. It consists of some of each, historic and regional average, with the proportions changing over an eight-year period: starting mainly historic and changing in annual steps to become entirely a flat rate regional average, as follows:

Transitional Percentages from Historic to Regional Component in English SPS

Year	2005	2006	2007	2008	2009	2010	2011	2012
% historic	90	85	70	55	40	25	10	0
% regional	10	15	30	45	60	75	90	100

The regional payments in England will differ according to topography, with three types: lowland (or non SDA), non moorland severely disadvantaged areas (SDAs) and moorland SDA. Payments for the second of these will be approximately 80% of those in the lowland and those for moorland about 14% (i.e. about a sixth of those in non-moorland SDAs).

In order to receive payment recipients will have to be farming 'eligible' land (see below). They must also satisfy 'cross-compliance' rules, which are in two parts: 'Statutory Management Requirements' (directives, largely already in force, on public and plant health, animal welfare and the environment) and keeping the land in 'Good Agricultural and Environmental Condition'. They apply to the entire holding. The rules in England include no cultivating, fertilising or spraying within two metres of the centre line of any hedge or ditch (after July 2005), no hedge cutting between 1st March and 31st July and providing a soil management plan. The area of permanent pasture in each region must be maintained (this is a government responsibility to monitor not an individual farmer responsibility).

A claimant's total reference amount (or historic entitlement) was calculated by multiplying the area and headage claims in the reference period by the 2005 aid rates in euros per hectare, per head or per litre. These were as follows:

2005 Aid Rates used for Calculating Reference Amount

Arable Area: €/ha		Livestock: €/head	
England	371.07	Suckler Cow Premium	237.5
Scotland non-LFA	357.21	Beef Special Premium (steers) .	150
Scotland LFA	328.23	Beef Special Premium (bulls) . .	210
Wales non-LFA	325.71	Slaughter Premium	80
Wales LFA	318.15	Extensification (lower rate) . . .	40
N.Ireland non-LFA	328.86	Extensification (higher rate) . . .	80
N.Ireland LFA	316.89	Sheep Annual Premium (SAP) .	21.79
Other Crops:		SAP LFA Supplement	7
Hops	480.00	*Dairy: (€/litre)*	
Dried Fodder Aid (€/tonne) . . .	68.83	2005	0.02435
		2006	0.03654

Sugar: Compensation for sugar reform price cuts increased farmers' reference amounts on the basis of their contract tonnage for the 2005 crop. For 2006 the whole amount of £6.58 per tonne was paid separately after receipt of the Single Payment, subject to modulation deductions. For 2007 onwards compensation has been incorporated into the recipient's reference amount and will be subject to the increasing deductions (only 10% remaining in 2011) under the English regional average scheme.

OTHER SINGLE PAYMENT POINTS

The other important points are as follows:

- As the payments are calculated in euros the pound:euro exchange rate remains important, as pre-2005. The rate used is that prevailing on 30th September each year. For the first three years the rate was €1 = 68-69p. There was an increase in 2008 to 79p and a further increase in 2009 to €1 = 91p. For 2011 onwards the rate used in the Pocketbook is 85p.

- Initial entitlements were awarded to the IACS claimant of agricultural land in 2005. They are transferable/tradable: and can be sold with or without land, or if leased only with an equivalent area of land.

- In 2005 only, farmers could opt for the historic payments to which they were entitled to be paid in full on a smaller area of land than that previously farmed. This provision applied in England, and to a much lesser extent elsewhere.

- Most farmland is 'eligible', comprising arable land and permanent pasture but excluding woodland and land in non-agricultural use. Initially 'permanent crops' (essentially orchards and vineyards) were excluded, but new legislation allows this land to be eligible. The land has to be 'at the farmer's disposal', initially for at least ten months (the 10 month rule), but from 2008 the land has to be at the farmer's disposal for just 15th May (the application deadline).

- From 2008 land growing soft fruit, vegetables and potatoes (fvp crops) can activate any entitlements (this applies to all UK land). This change removed the need for 'FVP Authorised Entitlements' in England.

- Set-aside Entitlements were issued to farmers in 2005, in Scotland and Wales at 10% of the Arable Area Payment claims in the years 2000-02. In England they were based on 8% in English lowland (1.3% in non-moorland SDA) of arable land in 2005. Now that compulsory set-aside has been abandoned by the EU under the Health Check set-aside entitlements have been converted into 'normal' entitlements. They no longer need to be activated by 'arable land' that is in set-aside although they still retain their existing values.

- Following the ending of set-aside, English ministers had intended to introduce, as a cross compliance measure under the SPS, a compulsory area of cultivated land in environmental management. This has not been implemented. Instead Hilary Benn decided to give the voluntary approach, advocated by the CLA and NFU, time to prove it can recapture the environmental benefits of set-aside. The vehicle for this will be the 'Campaign for the Farmed Environment' (CFE). Various targets have been set by Defra, for example to double the current uptake of in-field options under ELS to 40,000 Ha, and farmers not in ELS to enter at least 30,000 Ha into voluntary environmental management. Farmers are encouraged to do what they can to help make the CFE a success.

- A Dairy Premium was introduced in 2004 as compensation for intervention price cuts. Details of the payments in 2005 and 2006 are given on the previous page. These were decoupled in 2005 and added to reference amounts based on quota held at 31st March 2005. In England, as with all other payments, the annual historic element will be calculated by multiplying the relevant annual percentage, and therefore worth less than in Wales and Scotland.

- There are supplements (euros/ha) for protein crops (€55.57) and energy crops (€45). Following the Health Check, the Energy Crops Premium ended after the 2009 scheme year. The Protein Crop Supplement will end by 2012. Member States have the option to end it earlier. In England the Supplement will continue until 2011 after which it will be included in the regional payments. In Scotland the Supplement finished in 2009, those who have been growing proteins will have their entitlement values increased. In Wales the payment will continue until 2012.

DEDUCTIONS TO THE SINGLE PAYMENT

Initial deductions: A 'National Ceiling', based on past national subsidy receipts led to a 0.17% reduction in England only. Across the UK 4.2% was deducted for the 'National Reserve', to provide payments for special cases, e.g. new entrants since the end of 2002 and purchasers of extra land. These two deductions were made before issuing the initial entitlements in 2005. Up to 10% of direct aids from each sector can be deducted to set up a 'National Envelope' to support specific types of farming or improve product quality/marketing; in the UK this is only being used in Scotland (for beef).

Modulation: There is compulsory 'Modulation' (for all EU member states) to fund EU-wide Rural Development projects; this was 3% in 2005, 4% in 2006 and 5% in 2007 and initially agreed to be 5% thereafter. But following the Health Check this has been increased by 2% in 2009 and then by 1% for the next three years, taking it to 10% in 2012. Additionally, from 2009 there will be an extra 4% on top of the normal EU rate for the element of Single Payment exceeding €300,000. From the amount raised through Modulation, Member States get at least 80% of its modulated funds back for use in Rural Development programmes and there is an element of compulsory match-funding by Member States. The first €5,000 of aid on every farm is exempt.

Member States may also levy 'voluntary' (National) modulation, and the UK has levied this at different rates in the devolved administrations from 2005. The Health Check

(HC) limited the increases applying from 2009. Effectively the new 'total' modulation rate will be the higher of either the pre HC EU rate + national voluntary or the new higher EU rate. For the UK the agreed modulation rates for payments under €300,000 are shown below for each devolved administration;

Agreed Total UK and EU Modulation Rates and the New Higher EU Rate

%	2005	2006	2007	2008	2009	2010	2011	2012
Scotland	6.5	8.5	10	13	13.5	14	14	14
Wales	4.5	4.5	5	7.5	9.2	10.8	11.5	11.5
N.Ireland	3	8.5	9.5	11	12	13	14	14
England	5	10	17	18	19	19	19	19
New Higher EU Rate > €300,000					11	12	13	14

The new higher EU rates will apply in Wales only from 2009 for the element of payments in excess of €300,000.

Financial Discipline: EU Farm Ministers decide annually what percentage reductions are needed to keep spending within stipulated budget thresholds; as with EU modulation the first €5,000 of aid per farm will be exempt. No Financial Discipline has been deducted so far and none is expected for 2010, but for budgeting it may be prudent to allow 1% for both the 2011 and 2012 years.

WINNERS AND LOSERS

The gradual change to a flat-rate area payment in England is clearly creating winners and losers. By 2012 a farm in 100% combinable crops will lose around €17/ha (from approximately €343/ha to €326/ha), probably increasing to around €89/ha after deductions. The loss in euro terms is being offset at current conversion rates by the weak pound. Growers of unsupported crops in the past, such as potatoes and soft fruit, will gain the whole of the payment, though at the cost of having to obey cross-compliance rules. Sugar beet growers saw their single payments increase in 2006, but there will be a steep decline after 2009 to the regional average rate in 2012.

In the case of dairy farmers the higher their historic milk yield and stocking rate the more they will lose, especially if they have a flying herd, i.e. no followers. A low-yielding, extensively stocked dairy farm with many followers may lose little or even gain. Intensive beef producers could lose considerably; a low stocking rate suckler herd could be no worse off. Lowland sheep would have to be stocked at a very high rate historically to lose from the new system; most should gain, some significantly.

TOTAL PAYMENTS PER FARM

It is obvious from the above that every farm will have a different total payment per hectare each year as far as the historic payments are concerned. In Wales and Scotland these differences will persist until they change from the wholly historic system which is likely after 2012. In England the differences will gradually iron out as a higher and higher proportion becomes a flat-rate per hectare across all 'lowland' (or all non-moorland SDA or all moorland SDA in the case of the other two areas).

The following are estimates of the flat-rate area payments in 2012 in the three areas (or sub-regions) of England, with €1 = 85p from 2010 onwards. 'Lowland' covers all non-SDA (Severely Disadvantaged Area) land, which is more than 84% of farmed land. The estimates are made by Andersons and include allowance for the inclusion of Dairy Premium and Sugar Beet compensation in the flat-rate area payments.

Estimated 2012 Flat Rate Area Payments in England

	Lowland	Non-Moorland SDA	Moorland SDA
	£/ha (acre)	£/ha (acre)	£/ha (acre)
Payments before deductions....	275 (111)	225 (91)	39 (16)
Payments after deductions	223 (90)	183 (74)	33 (13)

   SDA = Severely Disadvantaged Area

Arable Example: As a first example, let us take a 100% combinable cropping farm in England. Assuming the same currency conversion and deductions as above, the table below gives actual figures up to 2009 and estimates for 2010 onwards: payments increased in 2009 due to currency, they are expected to fall in 2010 and then decline only marginally by 2012.

Single Payment Calculation for Example Arable Farm

	A. Before Deductions			B. After Deductions
	Historic Part	Flat-rate Part	Total	Total
Year	£/Ha	£/Ha	£/Ha	£/Ha
2005	215	19	234	223
2006	200	31	231	209
2007	169	66	235	197
2008	151	112	263	218
2009	126	173	299	244
2010	74	206	280	229
2011	29	248	277	227
2012	0	275	275	223

Beef Example: in the next example, a lowland farm has intensive or semi-intensive beef, giving a gross historic payment of approximately £400/ha (at 2005 exchange rate). The example also applies to very intensive dairy farms (i.e. high yield and high stocking rate), except the figures would be higher in 2006 than 2005 (because the dairy premium rises, before levelling off). The rate of the loss compared with pre 2005 increases over time more quickly than the first example, in spite of the currency gain from 2009.

Single Payment Calculation for Example Lowland Beef Farm

	A. Before Deductions			B. After Deductions
	Historic Part	Flat-rate Part	Total	Total
Year	£/Ha	£/Ha	£/Ha	£/Ha
2005	348	19	367	350
2006	324	31	355	320
2007	274	66	340	284
2008	245	112	356	294
2009	204	173	352	307
2010	119	206	325	266
2011	47	248	296	241
2012	0	275	275	223

Lowland Sheep Example: Finally, as a third example, let us assume a lowland sheep farm extensively stocked, giving an historic payment of only £100/ha (at 2005 currency rate). In this example the farmer gains from the new system increasingly over time, and this is accelerated by the currency gain from 2009.

Single Payment Calculation for Example Lowland Sheep Farm

| | A. Before Deductions | | | B. After Deductions |
| | Historic Part | Flat-rate Part | Total | Total |
Year	£	£	£	£
2005	89	19	108	104
2006	83	31	114	104
2007	71	66	137	115
2008	63	112	175	145
2009	52	173	225	185
2010	31	206	237	194
2011	12	248	260	213
2012	0	275	275	223

IMPLICATIONS OF DECOUPLING ON PRODUCTION

Reasons for Little Change: Despite the enormity of the change made in the gross margins – and even more so in net margins, or profits – of the major enterprises affected, the impact on production (areas planted and number of livestock reared) would appear to have been relatively small so far. They may be greater in subsequent years, although with the high prices received in the arable sector in 2007 there was an increase in production. Changes like those seen in the arable sector are not as easy when considering livestock. There has been a steady exodus from the livestock sector, but firmer prices received recently in the meat sector have steadied the decline, although the introduction of EID, Bovine TB and Blue Tongue will all have a negative impact. Low confidence in the dairy industry coupled with weak milk prices and NVZ regulations may trigger further declines in this industry.

There are a number of reasons for the small impact so far:

- The changes, though considerable, will take time to 'register' for many producers. The instinct to 'wait and see' is be strong. Simple inertia will also play a part.

- Many will continue to sow and to rear as in the past because 'it is what they do': it is what their farm life (which is often the major part of their life) is about. The Single Farm Payment, in many (perhaps most) cases at least will enable this to be done – even if it could be regarded as subsidising unprofitable production.

- If ones own labour, whether manual or managerial, capital and land is charged at 'the going rate', or opportunity cost, most enterprises that might previously have shown a profit, with an area and headage payment, will no longer do so. However, if one stays farming (or even if one does not) many of these costs will still have to be borne, i.e. they are unavoidable, or inescapable by reducing, or even stopping, production. On many farms, especially small and medium sized ones, little would be saved in the way of 'fixed' costs: they really *are* largely, 'fixed'. Hence even a low gross margin may still be leaving an addition to the net income that one would otherwise not have.

- The same point as above needs also to be remembered when considering leaving poorer fields fallow while still cropping the rest. The only actual costs saved on those fields may be the variable costs (primarily seed, fertiliser and sprays) and some fuel and repairs, a total for cereals of around £386/ha (£156/acre), which would be covered by a wheat yield of only 3.2 tonnes/ha (1.7t/acre) at £120/tonne. However, there would be benefits of greater timeliness on the rest in difficult seasons and casual labour and 'catch up' contract work may be saved on some farms.

- Many arable farmers made heavy investments in expensive new machinery following the high prices for the 2003 and the 2007 harvest crops, many of them with a view to farming more land, particularly in contract farming arrangements; they are unlikely to want to see such investments wasted. Similarly, well established farmers will not want to lose their skilled workers.

Reasons for Change: The recent volatility in both output prices and input costs may be the trigger for a bigger withdrawal from production in some circumstances. Much will depend on future profitability in the various sectors and on other factors such as bovine TB. A number of other situations have led to change and these may increasingly be important:

- An increasing number of farmers, particularly those who are older, with no obvious successors, or others simply tired of the work involved, the uncertainties and the paperwork, can opt for a simpler system of farming, with very low inputs, taking care to abide by cross-compliance rules.

- Those who have most of their farm operations done by contractors, will be in a different position than those described above with truly 'fixed' costs. Clearly the contractor's cost is saved if one ceases production, which could be crucial, especially where yields are only average or below.

- The higher the crop yields, or present levels of enterprise profitability, the more clearly it will pay to continue to farm similarly as in the past. Those in the opposite situation who are still farming and either have very low (escapable) fixed costs or another source of income, will be among those likely to turn to more extensive farming, as described above.

- More farmers are expected to introduce, or expand existing, diversification enterprises, partly, even entirely in some cases, replacing farm enterprises. For many, however, this is easier said than done, and the current recession generally makes diversification more risky.

- With regard to the so called 'variable' costs, primarily seed, fertiliser and sprays, the initial thought might be to reduce them. However, if the right (economic) level of these was being applied before (where, as an economist would put it, marginal cost roughly equates to marginal revenue) then it remains the right amount. Reducing these costs will reduce the net margin (or remaining gross margin) from the crop, with or without an aid payment. The exception might be some economies, cutting out waste, but these should already have been attended to, regardless of policy changes.

3. MARKET SUPPORT

Market support measures are the other part of Pillar 1 funding, including intervention buying, export subsidies, quotas/set-aside and tariff barriers. Most of these mechanisms are being phased out and are of little significance directly to farmers. The main exception is tariffs which are unlikely to change much in the short term following the collapse of WTO talks – see the introduction to this section. Milk quotas still remain, although they will end by 2015. Individual UK producers have seen their quota increase by 0.5% at the end of each of the 2005/06, 2006/07 and 2007/08 milk years. A further 2% allocation was made at the end of the 2007/08 milk year. As a result of the Health Check individual quotas are increasing by 1% for another five years as from 31st March 2009.

Sugar prices are still supported within the EU. Following the 2006 reforms 'institutional' sugar prices have been cut over four years to reach a minimum EU beet price of €26.4 per tonne in 2009 until 2012. For 2011 at €1=85p this would give a price of about £22.44 per tonne before transport and late delivery bonus (LDB). Actual prices paid are determined through the Inter-Professional Agreement (IPA) between British Sugar (BS) and the NFU (refer to page 33).

British Sugar reduced contract offers to growers by 10% for 2008 in anticipation of further EU restructuring and this will be the final 'institutional' led cut of contract tonnage. Compensation was paid for the recent cut based on contract tonnage held for each of the growing seasons 2005, 2006 and 2007. Payments were made in June 2009 at a rate of €2.18 per tonne converted into sterling on 1st June 2009 giving a sterling price of £1.90 per tonne.

4. RURAL DEVELOPMENT

Rural Development or Pillar 2 of the CAP supports environmental protection and improvement of the countryside, and encourages sustainable enterprises and thriving rural communities. A range of support measures are allowed under four 'axes', with a minimum percentage of each Member State's budget in each:

- Axis 1 Competitiveness (min 10%): includes training young farmers, advice, food quality, production groups etc.

- Axis 2 Land Management (min 25%): includes agri-environmental schemes, hill farming (LFA support), forestry and animal welfare.

- Axis 3 Diversification (min 10%): includes grant aid for non-farming business, tourism, rural services etc.

- Axis 4 LEADER schemes (min 5%): funds local partnership programmes to address specific problems in certain areas.

Each country has a 7-year Rural Development programme running from 2007-13. A brief description is given below. For further details contact the relevant agency in England, Wales, Scotland and Northern Ireland.

ENGLAND

The stated strategy for the Rural Development Programme England (RDPE) is:

- To build profitable, innovative and competitive farming, food and forestry sectors, that meet the need of consumers and make a net positive contribution to the environment.

- To improve the environment and countryside.

- To enhance opportunity in rural areas in a way that harnesses and builds on environmental quality.

The overall budget for the RDPE for the period 2007-2013 is 5,185 million made up of 3,217 million (62%) from EU funds and voluntary modulation and the remainder (38%) from national funds. The total funding split into axes is given below:

		%
Axis 1 – Competitiveness	448m	9
Axis 2 – Land Management	4,183m	81
Axis 3 – Diversification	334m	6
Axis 4 – Leader	220m	4
	5,185m	100

Axis 2 Schemes

The vast majority of spending in England is in Axis 2 or the Land Management Schemes. These are being administered by Natural England (NE) and the Forestry Commission. The available schemes are:

- Environmental Stewardship Scheme (ESS)

- England Woodland Grant Scheme (EWGS)

- Energy Crops Scheme (ECS)

Environmental Stewardship Scheme (ESS)

The Environmental Stewardship Scheme was launched in 2005 to replace the Environmental Sensitive Areas, Countryside Stewardship and Organic Farming schemes. The scheme now comprises four elements:

- Entry Level Stewardship (ELS)

- Organic Entry Level Stewardship (OELS)

- Higher Level Stewardship (HLS)

- Uplands Entry Level Scheme (UELS)

A review of the ESS was undertaken in 2009. A few adjustments have been made to the scheme. The third edition of the Environmental Stewardship Handbooks is available; it includes new ELS options and details of the new Uplands strand of the ELS. It is the basis for all new Agreements from 1st February 2010.

ELS: is intended to encourage a large number of farmers across a wide area to adopt simple environmental management practices such as hedgerow management, stone wall maintenance, low input grassland, buffer strips and arable options. The scheme is non-competitive and open to all as long as scheme requirements are met. Points are awarded for each management option adopted. There is a large range of management options including hedgerow management, one side 11 points/100m, both sides 22points/100m; 2m, 4m, 6m buffer strips attracting 300, 400 and 400 points/ha respectively; overwintered stubbles gain 120 points/ha and beetle banks 580 points/ha. Applicants have to achieve a minimum number of 30 points per hectare to be accepted into ELS. An annual payment of £30 per hectare will be made. ELS agreements last for five years. Above the moorland line in the LFAs the payment is £8 per hectare for parcels of land over 15ha.

OELS: is open to all organic farmers with land which is registered as organic or in conversion and not currently receiving aid under the Organic Farming Scheme (closed to new applicants). OELS has similar options to those under ELS and participants will receive annual payments of £30 per hectare for carrying out the organic options on the organic land plus an additional £30 per hectare for farming the land organically. There will also be an option to apply for organic conversion with a payment of £600 per hectare per year for top fruit orchards and £175 per hectare for improved land. To participate in this latter option land must not already have been converted to full organic production and applicants must have registered the land with an organic inspection body. OELS agreements last for five years. Where a business has a mix of organic and conventional land a single OELS must be made and payments will be at £30 per hectare on the ELS eligible land and £60 per hectare on the organic land.

HLS: is targeted towards achieving significant environmental benefits in high priority areas with the objectives being wildlife conservation, protecting historic environments, maintaining and enhancing landscape quality, encouraging public access and resource protection. Applicants have to produce a Farm Environment Plan (FEP) and will usually have to participate in ELS. Only applications that give the best value in meeting the scheme aims will be accepted. Payment will depend on the management options adopted, and can include a mix of capital items and per hectare payments. HLS agreements will normally be for ten years with a break clause for either party after five years. NE is now operating a pre-application screening process so that potential applicants do not get involved in unnecessary work and expenditure. In autumn 2008 NE announced 110 target areas for HLS covering 4.8 million hectares. Farmers in one of these target areas will need to perform one or more of the land management activities specified for that area. Farmers outside these target areas are not excluded from HLS applications, but must contribute to achieving specified themes for their region.

UELS: replaced the Hill Farm Allowance (HFA) scheme (see below) from the 2010 year. The UELS is an additional strand to the ELS, with similar rules and principles. The scheme will be open to all farmers who farm within the Severely Disadvantaged Areas (SDAs). Farmers will need to have an ELS Agreement over all of their land and enter all their SDA land into the UELS. There are different points targets depending on the classification of the land, see the table below. Producers have to achieve the combined total.

Land Category	ELS Points/ha	UELS Points/ha	Combined Points/ha
SDA Moorland Parcels			
15ha and above	8	15	23
Below 15ha	30	32	62
SDA Land Below the Moorland Line	30	32	62

Similar to the ELS, applicants have to achieve the points target. Once achieved the points equate to the level of payment. SDA Moorland parcels 15ha and above will receive £23/ha; all other SDA land will receive £62/ha.

Points are obtained through meeting a number of 'requirements' and also by selecting from a menu of 'options'. There are different requirements for Moorland and Non-Moorland. By meeting the requirements on Moorland parcels above 15ha applicants receive 15 points per ha. By meeting the requirements on Moorland parcels below 15ha and other SDA land the producer receives 11 points per ha. The additional points needed to reach the target must be made up by using the 'options' menu.

The scheme is not available to farmers who have other agri-environmental scheme agreements still running e.g. CSS and ESA schemes. In order that these farmers do not lose out now the HFA has finished, from 2011 there will be an Uplands Transitional Payment. This will be similar to the existing HFA. It is expected to have broadly the same payment rates, taper at 350ha and a cut off rate at 700ha (see below).

Hill Farm Allowance (HFA) Scheme (Closed in 2010)

This scheme provided support for beef and sheep farming in the Less Favoured Areas. The last payments under the scheme were received in March/April 2010. It has now been replaced by Uplands Entry Level Stewardship (UELS) scheme (see above). Payments were made to farmers who extensively grazed eligible land with sheep breeding flocks and suckler cows but not dairy farming or other enterprises such as deer farming.

Payments were made up of a Basic Payment and an optional Environmental Enhancement:

Basic HFA Payments:

£/ha	2007	2008	2009	2010
Moorland	13.32	14.12	*14.14*	*14.14*
Common Land	13.32	14.12	*14.14*	*14.14*
Other SDA Land	35.20	37.31	*37.34*	*37.34*

DA = Disadvantaged Area, SDA = Severely Disadvantaged Area

Full rate was paid on the first 350ha, half rate on the next 350ha. No payment was paid on land in excess of 700ha. As from 2008 no payment was made on Disadvantaged Land.

England Woodland Grant Scheme (EWGS)

The previous Woodland Grant Scheme (WGS) and the Farm Woodland Premium Scheme (FWPS) have been replaced by the England Woodland Grant Scheme (EWGS), administered jointly by Natural England and the Forestry Commission. Details of the scheme are set out in the Forestry section at page 133.

Energy Crops Scheme (ECS)

The Energy Crops Scheme provides aid for the planting of Short Rotation Coppice (SRC) and Miscanthus (elephant grass). Poplar, willow, ash, alder, hazel, silver birch, sycamore, sweet chestnut and lime have been added to the list of trees that are eligible for the SRC grant. Any land is eligible for the ECS, either agricultural or non-agricultural, but not land already under forestry, energy crops, or common land. There is a minimum application size of 3 hectares. Agreements are normally for five years. Producers must be able to demonstrate that there is an end-use for the crop.

Grant aid is paid at 50% of the actual expenditure. Applicants have to submit invoices showing their actual costs. Applicants will be required to provide estimates of likely costs as part of the application process if these estimates are consistent with an Independent Verification of typical costs then the application can be accepted on a single quote. Where estimated costs are higher than the Independent Verification applicants will be required to provide written evidence to explain the variation – this may also involve getting further quotes. Grant is paid in full on submission of costs.

No English Woodland Grant Scheme payments are available on these crops. Land planted to these crops remains eligible for the Single Payment in addition to payments under this scheme. See also page 107.

Axes 1,3 and 4 Schemes

This part of the RDPE is administered by eight Regional Development Agencies (RDAs). Each RDA has its own priorities and schemes. Support is in the form of capital grants to fund a percentage of eligible expenditure. There may also be funding for training and advice, including individual farm business advice, but this varies between RDAs. Funding is limited and applications competitive. Compared to previous programmes, RDAs are mostly looking for fewer, larger projects, and have a tendency to encourage collaboration and cooperation. Schemes cover the following broad areas:

- Adding value to farming and forestry products

- Diversification of farming businesses

- Collaboration/cooperation between land-based businesses

- Renewable energy and water conservation and management

For scheme details the relevant RDA should be contacted at www.englandsrdas.com.

WALES

The stated strategy for the Wales Rural Development Programme (WRDP) is:

- To stimulate a dynamic and innovative agricultural sector.

- Encourage sustainable production methods with a view to improving the environment.

- Improve the quality of life in rural areas and encourage diversification of the rural economy.

- Build capacity and innovation in rural areas.

The overall budget is a total of €985 million made up of €377 million (38%) from EU funds and voluntary modulation and the remainder (62%) from national funds. The total funding split into axes is given below:

		%
Axis 1 – Competitiveness	122m	12
Axis 2 – Land Management	722m	73
Axis 3 – Diversification	94m	10
Axis 4 – Leader	47m	5
	985m	100

Axis 2 Schemes

There have been five environmental schemes in Wales but this is changing to a single scheme in 2010/2011 as follows:

- Tir Gofal, which means 'land in care'. This is an integrated agri-environmental scheme, with 10 year agreements with a 5 year break clause. The whole farm must be entered and there is a combination of mandatory and optional land management payments, and capital grants. This scheme is now closed to new entrants – see below.

- Tir Cynnal, is a whole farm entry level type scheme introduced in 2005. Application is via the Single Application Form (SAF). Applicants enter their whole farm with a 10 year agreement with a 5 year break clause. Payments are made per hectare in bands with the first 20 hectares at £45 per hectare reducing to any area over 200 hectares at £2 per hectare. This scheme is now closed to new entrants – see below.

- The Organic Farming Scheme (OFS) is a five year agreement covering land in conversion and/or fully organic.

- Better Woodlands for Wales (BWW) helps fund the improved management of existing woodland and funds the creation of new woods in Wales. The scheme is run in conjunction with the Forestry Commission.

- Tir Mynydd makes payments for land in the LFA areas as entered on the previous year's SAF. Under the 2010 scheme, payments per hectare were £24 for DA land and £28 for SDA land. Reduced rates are paid above 140 hectares but there is no upper limit. Above 640 hectares the percentage paid is 30% of the full payment. (see below)

A new scheme is to be introduced called Glastir, rationalising the current suite of schemes into one. The Tir Gofal and Tir Cynnal schemes (see above) are now closed to new entrants. All existing scheme agreements will end on 31st December 2013 unless they expire earlier. Transitional arrangements will be put in place for those who are still in these schemes in 2012 and 2013.

The last full payment under Tir Mynydd will be made in March 2011. Under transitional arrangements farmers will be able to claim 60% of their 2011 payment in 2012 and 30% in 2013. After which there will no longer be a dedicated measure for the Less Favoured Areas, but the payment (see below) for all LFA farmers entering the all-Wales part of Glastir will be increased by 20%, including dairy farmers who are currently not included under Tir Mynydd. Funds for organic farmers will be available through Glastir. Interim funds will be available under the OFS for those converting to organic in the period 2010 – 2012 subject to a formal offer. BWW will continue, although the Welsh Assembly Government is working with the Forestry Commission on a simpler way for farmers to obtain grant aid for forestry in Wales.

Glastir will have two main elements; The All-Wales Element and the Targeted Element. The first will be open to all farmers in Wales and the second element will be targeted at those areas that can deliver important environmental benefits. The new scheme will commence in 2012 with transitional arrangements in place until 2014. Application packs will be sent in September 2010 to those wishing to enter in 2012 and who expressed an interest on their 2010 Single Application Form (SAF). These must be returned by 31st October 2010.

The All-Wales Element is a whole farm entry level management scheme. Contracts will be for five years and applicants must enter all the eligible land they will have full management control of for the full five years. Applications will be via the annual SAF application, the next application date will be on the 2011 SAF for a 2013 start date. Applicants have to obtain a points threshold for their farm which is 28 x total hectarage. To reach the threshold applicants choose from a number of management options. Each option is allocated a set number of points. Producers can also opt to choose from a list of options in the Regional Package. These are considered to offer the greatest environmental value for their area. If the regional options are chosen the applicant will receive 10% more points per option.

Payment for the All-Wales Element will be a flat rate of £28 per hectare for all land entered into the scheme. Land within the LFA will receive £33.60 per hectare. Claim for payment will be made annually on the SAF. The first claim will be in 2012.

The All-Wales Element will also include:

- A Common Land Element – for those who hold rights on Common Land and who have joined together to establish a Grazing Association

- An Organic conversion fund (details not yet available). Those already holding an organic certification will only have to score 50% of the points that a conventional farm will have to score

- Agricultural Carbon Reduction and Efficiency Scheme (ACRES). This will provide capital grants aimed at reducing the carbon emissions of agricultural and horticultural holdings.

To be eligible for the scheme, producers also need to comply with the Whole Farm Code - 13 standards of environmental practice. This attracts an additional payment of:

0 – 20 hectares	£15/ha
21 – 50 hectares	£8/ha
51 - 100 hectares	£2.75/ha

The Targeted Element aims to address concerns over soil carbon management, water quality, water quantity management, biodiversity, the historic environment and improving access. Land will be assessed against target maps. At this level management will be of a prescribed nature, payments will vary consisting of both capital and non-capital items.

Note: Glastir is still subject to approval by the European Commission therefore the above details and payment rates are subject to change.

Axes 1, 3 and 4 Schemes

The WRDP covering these three axes has an emphasis on collaboration and co-operation in the whole food chain. At the centre of the strategy is the processing and marketing grant scheme (PMGS) which covers food and forestry. Grant is available for adding value to agricultural products and for marketing. The rate of Grant is 40% of eligible costs (50% in some designated areas). Eligible expenditure includes erection of buildings as well as product development, market research etc. There will also be assistance for diversification and tourism and farm business advice through Farming Connect.

In 2010 a revised new entrants scheme started called The Young Entrants Support Scheme (YESS). It will run for five years or until funds are exhausted. It is available to young farmers (less than 40 years) who are setting up as head of a holding for the first time or have set-up as head of a holding for the first time within the last 12 months. It will provide grant aid of 50% of agreed eligible expenditure up to a maximum of £15,000 whichever is less. It will also provide sign posted access to funded mentoring services from established farmers and or processors.

SCOTLAND

The overall strategy for the Scotland Rural Development Programme (SRDP) is to:

- support business viability

- add value to the rural economy and facilitate increased market orientation.

- Support a coherent and integrated approach to meet environmental objectives.

- Encourage private enterprise and entrepreneurship, improve services and infrastructure at local level and support Scotland's cultural opportunities.

- Support capacity building and innovation.

The overall budget from the SRDP is €2,131million of which €676 million (32%) is from European funds and voluntary modulation and the remainder (68%) from national funds. The total funding split into axes is given below:-

	€	%
Axis 1 – Competitiveness	306m	14
Axis 2 – Land Management	1,469m	69
Axis 3 – Diversification	248m	12
Axis 4 – Leader	108m	5
	2,131m	100

Rural Development Contracts

The SRDP is delivered through a single mechanism known as Rural Development Contracts (RDCs), and is divided into three tiers:-

Tier I: The Single Payment Scheme – through the cross-compliance requirements a basic level of environmental protection, food safety and animal welfare is provided.

Tier II: Land Manager's Options - Farmers choose from a menu of options with application at the same time as the Single Application Form (SAF).

Tier III: Rural Priorities – This element is discretionary and competitive and it covers the areas that were previously aided under schemes such as the Rural Stewardship Scheme (RSS), Organic Aid Scheme (OAS), Farm Business Development Scheme (FBDS) and Forestry Support. Now a New Entrants scheme has been added, there is also aid for processing and marketing which is available at the farm level through the SRDP, but larger scale projects are funded directly by Scottish Government.

A review of the workings of the SRDP took place in 2009 and some changes were announced. There will two new Land Managers Options (LMOs) for 2011. There have been changes to the Rural Priorities (RP) scheme. These include streamlining the application process, but also providing additional support to New Entrants, renewable energy projects, and slurry handling facilities.

Less Favoured Area Support Scheme (LFASS) 2010 - 13

Hill Farming Support (LFASS) is outside the RDCs. It is recognised that there is a problem with destocking in the remotest hill areas. Various policy options have been looked into but the decision has been made to continue the LFASS on a similar basis to 2008 but to increase payment rates in the fragile and very fragile areas. For the LFASS 2010 – 2013 there has been an update to the historic reference on which payments are based. Subject to EU approval, from 2011 those farmers in the standard areas will also see their payments increase (see below). At the same time a new grazing category will be introduced for land not currently designated and a new variable minimum stocking rate to ensure payments are targeted towards active producers.

The LFASS is applied for on the annual SAF application. Eligible hectares are adjusted for non-ring fenced dairy land, minimum or maximum stocking density restrictions, grazing category and an enterprise mix multiplier. The adjusted hectares are then paid at the payment rates below depending on the grazing category and location of the land.

£ per adjusted Hectare	2010		2011 (est)	
Grazing Category	A & B	C & D	A & B	C & D
Very Fragile	71.35	63.00	71.35	63.00
Fragile	62.10	54.51	62.10	54.51
Standard	37.80	332.50	45.00	35.17

There is a minimum payment of £385

Whole Farm Review

The other main support for farmers in Scotland outside the RDCs is the Whole Farm Review, which grant aids a business review, action plan and implementation up to a maximum of £2,400.

NORTHERN IRELAND

The strategy for the Northern Ireland Rural Development Programme (NIRDP) is to:

- Focus on vocational training, farm modernisation and supply chain improvements
- Support for less favoured areas and agri-environment and forest environment measures
- Diversification of rural economy, cultural heritage and promotion of tourism, to be supported by the local communities through a bottom up approach.

The overall budget from the NIRDP is €647million of which €328 million (51%) is from European funds and voluntary modulation and the remainder (49%) from national funds. The total funding split into axes is given below:-

		%
Axis 1 – Competitiveness	61m	10
Axis 2 – Land Management	456m	70
Axis 3+4 – Diversification/Leader	130m	20
	647m	100

CLOSED SCHEMES

There are many schemes across the UK that are now closed to new applicants but are still providing annual payments to some farmers. Some were available across all the devolved regions such as the Environmentally Sensitive Areas (ESA) schemes and support for farmers in the LFAs. The other major agri-environmental schemes include the Countryside Stewardship (CSS) in England, Tir Gofal and Tir Cynnal in Wales, and Rural Stewardship (RSS) in Scotland. The table below summarises the latest payments made for these closed schemes and for the schemes that are still open.

Environment Schemes Payments, 2008 (provisional)

		£ million
England:	Organic Farming Scheme (c)	0.5
	Environmentally Sensitive Areas (c)	53.3
	Countryside Stewardship (c)	84.9
	Hill Farm Allowance (c)	27.2
	Environmental Stewardship Scheme	222
Wales:	Organic Farming Scheme (c)	6.0
	Environmentally Sensitive Areas(c)	1.9
	Tir Mynydd	29.7
	Tir Gofal (c)	22.0
	Tir Cynnal (c)	6.3
Scotland:	Organic Aid Scheme	5.3
	Environmentally Sensitive Areas (c)	5.9
	Rural Stewardship (c)	18.0
	Less Favoured Area Support Scheme	61.0
	Land Management Contract Scheme	20.0
N. Ireland	Organic Farming Scheme	0.3
	New Environmentally Sensitive Areas	7.7
	Countryside Management Scheme	18.5
	Less Favoured Area Compensatory Allowances	22.0

Source: DEFRA, SGRPID, DARD, WAGDEPC. Agriculture in the UK 2009.
   (c) Schemes that are now closed to new entrants.

IV.   LABOUR

1.   LABOUR COST

STATUTORY MINIMUM WAGE RATES

The following rates are taken from the proposed Agricultural Wages Board (AWB) Order for the year from 1st October 2010. They are subject to ratification. The minimum weekly rates relate to a 39-hour standard week of normal hours worked on any five days between Monday and Saturday. The recently announced abolition of the AWB will not be implemented before these proposals but could lead to major changes in 2011/12.

Normal Hours (Standard Rates)

Grade		39 Hr Weekly Rate	Hourly Rate	Overtime per Hour
		£	£	£
1.	Initial Grade Over 16 years	232.05	5.95	8.92
	..................Under 16 years	-	2.98	4.47
2.	**Standard Worker**............	**256.62**	**6.58**	**9.87**
3.	Lead Worker	282.36	7.24	10.86
4.	Craft Grade......................	302.64	7.76	11.64
5.	Supervisory Grade...........	320.97	8.23	12.35
6.	Farm Management Grade	346.32	8.88	13.32
Apprentice:	Year 1.............................	139.23	3.57	5.36
	Year 2 ~ 16-18 years	141.96	3.64	5.46
	Year 2 ~ 19-21 years	191.88	4.92	7.38
	Year 2 ~ 22 years and over	232.05	5.95	8.93

Night work rates are £1.29 per hour; dog rates £7.21 per week.

Flexible Working

Grade		Number of days basic hours worked	Weekly Rate	Hourly Rate	Overtime per Hour
			£	£	£
1	Initial Grade (16+ only)	4 to 5	243.75	6.25	8.93
		6	248.43	6.37	8.93
2.	Standard Worker...........	4 to 5	269.49	6.91	9.87
		6	274.56	7.04	9.87
3.	Lead Worker.................	4 to 5	296.40	7.60	10.86
		6	302.25	7.75	10.86
4	Craft Grade...................	4 to 5	309.27	7.93	11.33
		6	323.70	8.30	11.64
5	Supervisory Grade	4 to 5	336.96	8.64	12.35
		6	343.59	8.81	12.35
6	Farm Management Grade	4 to 5	363.48	9.32	13.32
		6	370.50	9.50	13.32

1. *The structure* comprising six grades was introduced in 2005. Flexible working rates were set for each of the six new grades. In 2006 the Basic Trainee Grade was renamed

the Initial Grade. All age differentials were abolished apart from the under 16 category in the Initial Grade.

2. *Standby duty days* are to be renamed *'on call'* so the payment will be called *'on call allowance'*. It will be calculated as 2 hours overtime pay. If a worker is called to work, he will be paid overtime rate (with a minimum of 2 hours)

3. *A deduction* up to £32.27 a week or £4.61 a day for non-house accommodation can be made. There are specified provisions for sick pay, paid bereavement leave and paid paternity leave.

4. *Full details* are available from the Agricultural Wages Board for England and Wales (Telephone: 0800 917 2368).

Holiday Pay

Holidays with pay. The number of days holiday that workers are entitled to in a year depends on the number of days worked each week. Those working full-time, 5 days a week, have 23 days per year. There are rules as to timing. For part-time workers the number of days worked per week is based on the total hours worked over the 12 months ending on the last 5th April.

TYPICAL ANNUAL LABOUR COST

Estimated for the 2010/11 year (from 1st October), based on a Standard Worker.

	Average Annual Cost(1)	Average Weekly Cost	Average Hourly Cost(2)
	£	£	£
Minimum Wage (basic standard worker rate)	13,344	256.62	7.60
National Insurance Contribution and Employers Liability Insurance	1,842	35.41	1.05
Minimum Cost	15,186	292.03	8.65
Overtime, average 10 hrs per working week (45) @ £9.60 (+ NIC, ELI)	5054	97.2	
	20,240	389.23	11.53
'Premium' over basic rate average £46.00 per week (+ NIC, ELI)	2,722	52.35	
Total Cost (3,4)	22,962	441.58	13.08

1. NIC = National Insurance Employer Contribution = 12.8%;

2. ELI = Employer's Liability Insurance = 1%

3. *Estimated average annual cost* higher than 2010 AWB rate as figures based on calendar year rather than Oct-Oct AWB year.

4. *Hours, excluding overtime*, based on 45 weeks (of 39 hours) per year = 1,755 hours, i.e. statutory holidays (23 days), public holidays (8 days) and illness (4 days), have been deducted.

5. *Annual cost of cottages* (or net value), value of perquisites, contribution towards payment of the council tax, etc., would have to be added where appropriate.

6. *Total average worker's gross earnings* on the above assumptions = £20,178 a year, £388.04 a week, £9.15 an hour including overtime.

2. LABOUR HOURS AVAILABLE FOR FIELD WORK

per man per month

	Total Ordinary Hours (1)	Adjusted Ordinary Hours (2)	% Workable	Available Ordinary Hours (3)	Available Overtime Hours (4)	**Total Available Hours**	Total Available Days' (5)
January	177	148	50	74	28 (61)	102 (135)	13 (17)
February	160	134	50	67	33 (55)	100 (122)	12½ (15)
March	172	149	60	89	69 (82)	158 (171)	20 (21½)
April	161	139	65	90	86	176	22
May	171	151	70	106	110	216	27
June	170	150	75	112	112	224	28
July	177	157	75	118	113	231	29
August	169	150	75	112	104	216	27
September	172	152	70	106	82 (89)	188 (195)	23½ (24½)
October	177	153	65	99	63 (83)	162 (182)	20 (23)
November	172	144	50	72	26 (59)	98 (131)	12 (16½)
December	161	135	50	67	25 (65)	92 (132)	11½ (16½)

1. *Ordinary Hours:* 40 hour week, less public holidays. No deductions have been made for other holidays because they may be taken at various times of the year.

2. *After deducting* (a) for illness (10 per cent Nov. to Feb., 7½% March, April and Oct., 5% May to Sept.), and (b) for contingencies and non-delayable maintenance (½ hour per day).

3. *Available Ordinary Hours:* Adjusted Ordinary Hours x percentage Workable.

4. *Available Overtime Hours:* Maximum 4 hours overtime per summer day, 3 hours winter, and 12 to 14 hours at weekends, according to season. Same adjustments for illness and percentage workable as ordinary hours. Figures in brackets indicate hours available if headlights used, up to limit of overtime stated. The percentage overtime (without headlights) available from weekend work as opposed to evenings = (January to December): 100, 78, 58, 50, 40, 40, 41, 42, 53, 67, 100, 100.

5. *Total Available Days:* Total available hours ÷ 8.

Additional Notes

6. *Figures relate to medium land.* The percentage workability will be higher with light soils, less with heavy soils. On heavy soils the land may be virtually 100% unworkable between late November and early March (or later, according to the season), particularly if undrained. A rough estimate of variations in workability according to soil type (compared with the figures above) is as follows.

    Heavy land - March, October, November: 30% less; April: 20% less; September: 10% less; May to August: no difference. Light land — October to April: 15% more; May and September: 10% more; June to August: no difference.

7. *It must be remembered that indoor work,* e.g. livestock tending or potato riddling, can be continued over the full working week, i.e. the hours available are the Adjusted Ordinary Hours, plus overtime. Also, some handwork in the field has to continue even in rain, e.g. sprout picking.

8. *Percentage workability* varies according to the particular operation, e.g. compare ploughing and drilling.

9. *Some operations* are limited by factors other than soil workability, e.g. combine-harvesting by grain moisture content.

3.   SEASONAL LABOUR REQUIREMENTS

CROPS AND GRASS

On the following pages, data on labour requirements for various crops and types of livestock are given. Two levels are shown: average and premium. The average figures relate to the whole range of conditions and farm size, i.e. small and medium-sized farms as well as large; the figures give all farms equal weight. The premium rates do not denote the maximum rates possible, for instance by the use of especially high-powered tractors under ideal conditions, but relate to rates of work estimated to be obtainable over the whole season, averaging good and bad conditions, with the use of wide implements, relatively large tractors (over 90 kW / over 120 hp) and high capacity equipment in 8 hectare fields and over, where no time is wasted. Most farmers with more than 200 hectares (500 acres) of arable land aught to achieve at least the premium levels shown. Those with over 400 hectares (1,000 acres) will have still bigger machines and therefore faster work rates, and thus require 15 to 25% less labour than even the premium levels given.

The rates of work include preparation, travelling to fields, allow for minor breakdowns and other stoppages. They relate broadly to medium and medium-heavy land; some jobs, such as ploughing, may be done more quickly on light soils. Operations such as combine harvesting can obviously vary according to many factors to do with the topography and other natural features of the farm.

The usual times of year when each operation takes place are shown; these relate to lowland conditions in the south-eastern half of Britain. They will obviously vary between seasons, soil types, latitude and altitude. In particular, light land can be ploughed over a longer winter period and a high proportion of cultivations for spring crops may be completed in February in many seasons. All such factors must be allowed for in individual farm planning. Conditions in different seasons will also affect, for instance, the number and type of cultivations required in seedbed preparation. Typical monthly breakdowns of requirements are given for various crops.

To illustrate the type of questions that need to be asked for full details of seasonal labour requirements on the individual farm, critical questions affecting timing are listed for cereals. Similar questions would, of course, need to be asked for other crops.

Winter Cereals

Operations	Labour-hours per hectare		Time of Year
	Average	Premium	
Plough (1)	1.4	1.0	July to October (according to previous crop)
Cultivate (often power harrow).	1.0	0.7	September to October (according to previous crop) (½ Aug if ploughed in July)
Drill (often with power harrows) followed by roll	1.1	0.7	Mid-September to 3rd week October (according to previous crop and soil)
Apply Fertiliser	0.3	0.2	
Spray	0.3	0.2	October-November
Top Dress (three times [2])	0.9	0.6	March and April
Spray (three or four [2])		1.0	0.5 Spring/early summer
Combine, Cart Grain, Barn Work	2.5	1.9	Mid-Aug to approx. 10th Sept
Later Barn Work (3)	0.7	0.4	September to June
Total	**9.2**	**6.2**	
Straw: Bale	1.3	0.8	Mid-August to end
Cart	3.5	2.6	September

Typical Monthly Breakdown

Month	Average	Premium	Notes
October	2.4	1.7	Approx. 60% of Ploughing,
November	—	—	Cults., Drill, Harrow
December	—	—	
January	—	—	
February	—	—	
March	0.4	0.2	Part Top Dress
April	0.8	0.5	Part Top Dress, Spraying
May	0.3	0.2	Spraying
June	0.3	0.2	Spraying
July	—	—	
August	1.7 (+2.4 Straw)	1.3 (+1.7 Straw)	⅔ of harvesting (4)
September (harvest)	0.9 (+2.4 Straw)	0.6 (+1.7 Straw)	⅓ of harvesting (4)
September (prepn. drill)	1.7	1.1	40% of Ploughing, Cults., Drill, Harrow

1. *Some cereal crops* are direct drilled or drilled after reduced, or minimal, cultivations, i.e. without traditional ploughing. Direct drilling reduces man-hours per hectare by about 2.5 (average) or 1.8 (premium), and minimal cultivations by about 1.2 (average) and 0.9 (premium).

2. *This is for winter wheat;* winter barley will often have one less top dressing and spraying and oats two less. Also see next page for harvest times for winter barley and oats.

3. *Later barn work* is excluded from monthly breakdown.

Spring Cereals

Operations	Labour-Hours per hectare		Time of Year
	Average	Premium	
Plough (1)	1.4	1.0	July to October (according to previous crop and soil type)
Cultivate (often power harrow)...	1.0	0.7	March (½ in second half February on light land)
Apply Fertiliser	0.3	0.2	
Drill (often with power harrow), plus roll	1.2	0.8	March (½ at end February on light land)
Top Dress (once, some possibly twice)	0.4	0.2	
Spray (two or three)	0.7	0.3	May
Combine, Cart Grain, Barn Work	2.4	1.8	Last ¾ of August (affected by variety and season)
Later Barn Work (2)	0.6	0.4	September to June
Total	**8.0**	**5.4**	
Straw: Bale (unmanned sledge)	1.3	0.8	Mid-August to end
Cart	3.5	2.6	September

Typical Monthly Breakdown

Month	Average	Premium	Notes
October	0.4	0.3	Ploughing. How much in
November	0.8	0.5	October depends on area
December	0.2	0.2	W. Wheat, Potatoes, etc.
January	—	—	
February	—	—	
March	2.4	1.6	All Cults. Drilling, Rolling, (nearly half in February on light land)
April	—	—	
May	1.1	0.6	Spray and Top dress
June	—	—	
July	—	—	
August (3)	2.4	1.8	Harvesting
	(+2.6 Straw)	(+1.8 Straw)	
September	—	—	
	(+2.2 Straw)	(+1.6 Straw)	

1. *Autumn drilling* preferable if possible to allow frost to crumble soils

2. *Later barn work* excluded.

3. *This is for spring barley*; spring wheat and oats partly September.

Crop Timings in a Normal Season:

Winter Wheat

Drilling mid-September to 3rd week October.
Harvesting mid-August to approx. 10th September.

Winter Barley

As for winter wheat, except that:
- Ploughing unlikely to start before cereal harvest, as usually follows a cereal crop.
- Harvesting some weeks earlier: mid July to approx. 10th August.

Winter Oats

As for winter wheat, except that:
- Drilling usually first full half of October.
- Harvesting earlier (late July or first half of August).

Spring Barley

Drilling end of February to end of March or early April.
Harvesting last half to ¾ of August.

Spring Wheat

As for spring barley, except that:
- Drilling on average 1-2 weeks earlier (should finish in March) - lose more if later than barley.
- Harvesting, on average, 2 weeks later: last week August/first half of September (two-thirds in September).

Spring Oats

As for spring barley, except that:
- Drilling usually a little earlier.
- Harvesting is later than spring barley, earlier than spring wheat: end of August/beginning of September.

Critical Questions affecting Timing for Spring-sown Cereals

1. Previous crops.
2. Will the crop be ploughed traditionally, chisel ploughed, subsoiled, minimally cultivated, or direct drilled?
3. Months when winter ploughing is possible, on average (where relevant).
4. Is spring ploughing satisfactory (where relevant)?
5. Average period of cultivations and drilling.
6. Earliest dates for starting and finishing spring cultivations/drilling and latest dates for starting and finishing cultivations/drilling, ignoring extreme seasons (1 year in 10).
7. Effect on yield if drilling is delayed.
8. Is the crop rolled (a) within a few days of drilling or (b) later?
9. (a) Average period of harvesting.
   (b) Earliest dates for starting and finishing harvest, and latest dates for starting and finishing harvest, ignoring extreme seasons (one year in ten).

Critical Questions affecting Timing for Autumn-sown Cereals

1. Previous crops (affects time available and need for ploughing and cultivations).

2. Will the crop be ploughed traditionally, chisel ploughed, subsoiled, minimally cultivated, or direct drilled?

3. Earliest and latest drilling date, by choice.

4. Effect on yield if drilling is delayed.

5. Autumn weed control?

6. In the spring: (a) whether crop is rolled, and when,

                      (b) whether crop is harrowed, and when,

                      (c) time of top dressings,

                      (d) number of spray applications.

7.   (a) Average period for harvesting.

       (b) Earliest dates for starting and finishing harvest, and latest dates for starting and finishing harvest, ignoring extreme seasons (1 year in 10).

Maincrop Potatoes

Operations	Labour-Hours per hectare		Time of Year
	Average	Premium	
Plough	1.4	1.0	September to December
Cultivating, Ridging, De-stoning/			
Clod sep. (as required)	6.5	5.0	March, early April
Plant and Apply Fertiliser (1)	4.5	3.5	Last quarter of March, first
Apply Herbicide	0.3	0.2	three-quarters of April
Spray for Blight (av. 6 times)	1.2	0.9	July, first half August
Burn off Haulm	0.3	0.2	End September, early
			October
Harvest, Cart, Clamp (2).............	15.0	10.0	End September, October
Work on Indoor Clamp...............	4.8	3.2	November
Riddle, Bag, Load.......................	40.0	30.0	October to May
Total..	**74.0**	**54.0**	

1. *Automatic planter.* Hand-fed planters: approx. 12 hrs plus 8 (could be casual labour).

2. *Mechanical harvester,* excluding up to 25 hours for picking off on harvester - usually casual labour. None may be needed on clod and stone-free soils. Hand harvesting: additional approx. 80 hours of casual labour.

Typical Monthly Breakdown

Month	Average	Premium	Notes
October..	12.2	8.2	80% of harvest, ½ burn off
November.....................................	5.9	4.0	Clamp work and ¾ plough
December	0.3	0.2	¼ plough
January	—	—	
February	—	—	
March	7.8	6.0	All fert', ½ cults', ¼ plant
April	3.5	2.7	½ cult's, ¾ plant
May	—	—	
June	—	—	
July..	0.9	0.7	3 blight sprays
August	0.3	0.2	1 blight spray
September.....................................	3.1	2.0	20% harvest, ½ burn off

These figures exclude casual labour and riddling.

Early Potatoes

Operations	Labour-Hours per hectare		Time of Year
	Average	Premium	
Plough	1.4 (1)	1.0 (1)	September to December
Cultivating, etc	6.5 (1)	5.0 (1)	Late February, early March
Plant and Apply Fertiliser	4.5 (1)	3.5 (1)	Late February, early March
Apply Herbicide	0.3 (1)	0.2 (1)	1st half March (some in February on light land or in early season)
Further Spraying	0.3 (1)	0.2 (1)	
After-Cultivation/Spray	0.3 (1)	0.2 (1)	April, early May
Harvest, bag, load	30.0 (1)	25.0 (2)	2nd week June onwards. All June or till mid-July

1.   Excluding 80 hours picking—usually casuals.

2.   Excluding 60 hours picking—usually casuals.

Second Early Potatoes

Operations	Labour-Hours per hectare		Time of Year
	Average	Premium	
Plough	1.4 (1)	1.0 (1)	September to December
Cultivating, etc	6.5 (1)	5.0 (1)	March
Plant and Apply Fertiliser	4.5 (1)	3.5 (1)	March
Apply Herbicide	0.3 (1)	0.2 (1)	Half 2nd half March, half 1st half April
Further Spraying	0.9 (1)	0.7 (1)	End April, May, early June
Harvest	15.0 (1)	10.0 (2)	Mid-July to end August

1.   *Spinner or elevator-digger*, excluding picking and riddling—usually casual labour.

2.   *Mechanical harvester*, excluding picking off on harvester/riddling - usually casual.

Sugar Beet

Operations	Labour-Hours per hectare		Time of Year
	Average	Premium	
Plough	1.4	1.0	September to December
Seedbed Cults	3.2	2.2	Mainly March (some early April. Some late February in good seasons)
Load, Cart, Apply Fertiliser	0.7	0.4	
Drill (and Flat Roll)	1.8	1.1	Between mid-March and mid-April
Spray (herbicide: pre- and post-emergence)	0.6	0.3	Late March/April
Spray (x 2)	0.6	0.3	May/June
Spray (aphis)	0.3	0.2	July
Harvest (machine)	14.0	9.0	End September, October, November
Load	3.4	2.5	End September to early January
Total	**26.0**	**17.0**	

Typical Monthly Breakdown

Month	Average	Premium	Notes
October............................	7.2	4.6	45% harvest; + loading
November	8.2	5.3	45% harvest; ¾ ploughing; + loading
December	1.0	0.8	¼ ploughing; + loading
January	0.5	0.4	Loading
February	—	—	
March	3.8	2.3	Fert., most cults., some drilling
April	2.5	1.7	Some cults., most of drilling
May	0.3	0.2	Spray
June	0.3	0.15	Spray
July.................................	0.2	0.15	Spray
August	—	—	
September.......................	2.0	1.4	10% harvesting; + loading

Vining Peas

Operations	Labour-Hours per hectare		Time of Year
	Average	Premium	
Plough	1.4	1.0	September to December
Cults, Fert. and Drill..................	2.3	1.6	Mid-Feb. to April
Post Drilling and Spraying..........	1.5	0.8	
Harvesting	19.0	14.0	July and early August
Total..	**24.2**	**17.4**	

Drilling is staggered in small areas through the season, ranging from early varieties to late varieties.

Dried Peas

Month	Labour-Hours per hectare		Notes
	Average	Premium	
October..	1.2	0.8	
November....................................	0.8	0.5	Stubble cult., Plough
December	—	—	
January	—	—	
February	0.2	0.1	Cult. x 2, harrow; drill & fert.
March	2.8	1.9	(80% March); light harrow
April	0.6	0.4	roll; and spray
May	2.5	1.2	
June	0.2	0.2	Scare pigeons; spray
July..	1.8	1.1	Possible spray desiccant;
August	2.2	1.3	combine and cart, dry
September.....................................	0.5	0.3	Stubble cult.

Assumes direct combining.

Field Beans

Winter Beans

Operations	Labour-Hours per hectare		Time of Year
	Average	Premium	
Broadcast Seed	0.6	0.4	
Apply Fertiliser...........................	0.3	0.2	
Plough	1.4	1.0	September/October
Power Harrow............................	1.0	0.8	
Spray (pre-emergence)	0.3	0.15	
Spraying (two or three times)	0.8	0.35	Spring
Combine and cart and			
Barn-work...................................	3.0	2.4	August

Spring Beans

Operations	Labour-Hours per hectare		Time of Year
	Average	Premium	
Plough	1.4	1.0	September to December
Cultivate (often power harrow)...	1.0	0.7	
Apply Fertiliser...........................	0.3	0.2	
Drill, Roll	1.2	0.8	End Feb, early March
Spray (two or three times)	0.8	0.4	
Combine and cart and			
Barn-work...................................	3.0	2.4	September

Winter Oilseed Rape (*Desiccated*)

Month	Labour-Hours per hectare		Notes
	Average	Premium	
October............................			
November........................	0.6	0.3	Spray herbicide and
December			insecticide if necessary
January	—	—	
February	—	—	
March			
April	0.8	0.4	Top dress twice
May	—	—	
June	—	—	Desiccate (1st half July);
July..................................	2.4	1.7	combine (½ 2nd half July
August	2.0	1.4	½ 1st half Aug.); dry
August	1.6	0.9	Cults. (x 2), spray, drill, fert.;
September	1.6	0.9	harrow, roll, barn work (0.5)

Herbage Seed (first production year)

Undersown

Operations	Labour-Hours per hectare		Time of Year
	Average	Premium	
Undersown	0.6	0.4	March, April
	(0.6	0.4)	Straight after drilling
Roll... {	0.4	0.3	September
	0.4	0.3	Late February, March
Harvest (by Combine): Mow	1.4	0.9	3 to 4 days before combining
Combine and Cart.......................	4.5	3.5	Ital. Ryegrasses and Early *Perennials: late July.* *Intermed. Perennials: late July/early August.* *Late Perennials/White Clover: mid-August*
	6.0	4.5	Meadow Fescue: early July
	7.0	5.0	Cocksfoot: early July
	10.0	7.0	Timothy: mid-August Red Clover: late September

Direct Drilled in Autumn

Operations	Labour-Hours per hectare		Time of Year
	Average	Premium	
Plough	1.4	1.0	
Seedbed Cults.............................	2.2	1.6	Depends on previous crop—
Load, Cart, Apply Fertiliser........	0.3	0.2	Usually July or August
Drill (with harrows behind)	0.8	0.6	As early as previous crop allows. This may be up to mid-Sept for ryegrass without detriment to the yield.
Roll (soon after drilling).............	0.6	0.4	Meadow fescue and cocksfoot are best sown no later than July and it is risky to sow Timothy much later than this.

Grass

Production

Operations	Labour-Hours per hectare		Time of Year
	Average	Premium	
Plough	1.4	1.0	Autumn drilling: may not
Seedbed Cults.............................	2.2	1.6	
Load, Cart, Apply Fertiliser........	0.3	0.2	
Drill*	0.7	0.5	Mid-March to mid-April (1) or end July to mid-Sept.
Roll...	0.6	0.4	Soon after drilling
Load, Cart, Apply Fertiliser* (three lots)	0.9	0.6	March to mid-August (2)
Top*	1.3	0.8	Mid-June to mid-July; if grazed only.

1. * These operations apply only where the seeds are undersown in a spring cereal crop soon after drilling. One extra harrowing and rolling is needed if undersown in an autumn-sown cereal crop.
2. *Spring drilling* may continue to mid-May to enable extra cleaning cultivations or the application of farmyard manure.
3. *P. and K.* may be applied in September—especially on undersown ley in year sown.

Conservation

Operations	Labour-Hours per hectare		Time of Year
	Average	Premium	
Plough	1.4	1.0	Autumn drilling: may not
Hay (5.5 tonnes per hectare)			
Mow	1.2	0.9	
Turn, etc	2.6	1.9	Two-thirds June, one-third
Bale	1.3	0.9	July
Cart......................................	6.0	4.5	
Total per hectare	11.1	8.2	
Total per tonne............................	2.0	1.5	
Silage (17 tonnes per hectare)			
Mow	1.2	0.9	
Turn, etc	0.7	0.5	Two-thirds May, one-third
Load......................................	2.3	1.7	June
Cart......................................	3.0	2.3	
Clamp...................................	2.3	1.7	
Total per hectare	9.5	7.1	
Total per tonne............................	0.56	0.42	

Specialised Equipment Prices for Grass Conservation: see page 163.

Typical Monthly Breakdown

Production (figures averaged over the life of the ley)

	1-year ley undersown in spring		3-year ley undersown in autumn (1)		1-year ley drilled		3-year ley drilled	
	Ave.	Prem.	Ave.	Prem.	Ave.	Prem.	Ave.	Prem.
March	0.9	0.5	0.7	0.5	0.6	0.3	0.6	0.3
April	0.9	0.5	0.7	0.5	0.6	0.3	0.6	0.3
May	0.6	0.3	0.6	0.3	0.6	0.3	0.6	0.3
June	0.6	0.3	0.6	0.3	0.6	0.3	0.6	0.3
July.............	0.6	0.3	0.6	0.3	0.6	0.3	0.6	0.3
August	0.3	0.2	0.3	0.2	5.0	3.4	1.9	1.4
September...	0.6	0.3	0.3	0.2	3.2	2.2	1.4	1.0

1. *If ploughed after a cereal crop,* drilled early August to mid-September.

	1-year ley drilled in autumn (1)		3-year ley drilled in spring		Permanent Pasture	
	Ave.	Prem.	Ave.	Prem.	Ave.	Prem.
March	3.0	2.1	1.4	1.0	0.6	0.3
April	1.8	1.2	0.9	0.7	0.6	0.3
May	0.3	0.3	0.6	0.3	0.6	0.3
June	0.6	0.3	0.6	0.3	0.6	0.3
July...................	0.6	0.3	0.6	0.3	0.6	0.3
August..............	0.3	0.2	0.2	0.2	0.3	0.2
September.........	—	—	—	0.2	0.2	0.2
October.............	0.9	0.5	0.6	0.3	—	—
November.........	1.4	1.0	1.0	0.3	—	—
December	0.7	0.5	0.6	0.2	—	—

Conservation

	Hay				Silage			
	per hectare		per tonne		per hectare		per tonne	
	Av.	Prem.	Av.	Prem.	Av.	Prem.	Av.	Prem.
May	—	—	—	—	6.3	4.7	0.37	0.28
June	7.4	5.6	1.3	1.0	3.2	2.4	0.19	0.14
July................	3.7	2.6	0.7	0.5	—	—	—	—

Kale

Production

	Labour-Hours per hectare		
Operations	Average	Premium	Time of Year
Plough	1.4	1.0	September onwards
Seedbed Cults.............................	2.2	1.6	March, April, early May
Fertiliser	0.3	0.2	April, early May
Drill..	1.3	1.0	May
Roll...	0.6	0.4	Straight after drilling
Spray (weed killer)	0.3	0.2	6 weeks after drilling

Catch Crop

Kale may be drilled up to the first week of July; the crop will be smaller but either an early bite or silage crop may have been taken from a ley earlier in the year, or the ground may have been fallowed and thoroughly cleaned during the spring and early summer. The smaller crop is also easier to graze using an electric fence.

The above operations will still apply although the times of the year will obviously be different, but there may be an additional three or so rotavations and two or three heavy cultivations if fallowed for the first half of the year or ploughed after an early bite. This means approximately an extra 10 (average) or 8 (premium) man-hours per hectare in April, May, June.

FIELD SCALE VEGETABLES

(Labour hours per hectare unless otherwise stated)

Cabbage Transplanting	Hand 150-160. Spring cabbage, Sept.-Oct.; summer, April; autumn, May-June Machine (3.5 gang). Spring cabbage 75, summer 85, autumn 100. Pulling and dipping plants. 20 per hectare transplanted.
Cabbage Harvesting	Early spring cabbage, 210, Feb.-April; hearted spring, 250, April-June; summer, 220, June-July; autumn, 220, Oct.-Dec.
Brussels Sprouts Transplanting	45 (machine) to 55 (hand), May-June.
Brussels Sprouts Picking	320-400: picked over 3-5 times, maximum approx. 3 hectares per picker per season. Early sprouts, Aug.-Dec.; late, Nov.-Mar.
Peas Hand Pulling	475-525 (150 per tonne). Early, June; maincrop, July-Aug.
Runner Beans (Picked)	Harvesting. 625 (175 per tonne), July-Sept.
Runner Beans (Stick)	Harvesting. 675, July-Sept.
Runner Beans (Stick)	Erecting Canes and String. 100-150, May-June.
Carrot Harvesting.	Elevator-digger: 260 (1 man + 12 casuals, 20 hours per hectare). Earlies, July-Aug.; maincrop, Sept.-Feb. Harvester: 30 (3 men, 10 hours per hectare). Riddle and Grade: (1° per tonne), Dec.-Feb.
Beetroot Harvest and Clamp.	25, Oct.-Dec. 12-15 man-hours per tonne to wash and pack.

Source: The Farm as a Business, Aids to Management, Section 6: Labour and Machinery (M.A.F.F.). (N.B. This data is now very dated, but it is still the latest known to the author.)

LABOUR FOR LIVESTOCK

Dairy Cows

Time Required per Cow Depending on Yield.

Yield of Cow	5,500	7,000	8,000	9,000
	hours per cow per month			
January	2.0	2.5	3.1	3.8
February	1.9	2.5	3.1	3.8
March	1.8	2.5	3.1	3.8
April	1.6	2.4	3.0	3.8
May	1.6	2.1	2.7	3.5
June	1.6	2.1	2.6	3.2
July	1.6	2.1	2.6	3.2
August	1.6	2.1	2.6	3.2
September	1.6	2.2	2.8	3.5
October	1.8	2.4	3.1	3.8
November	1.9	2.5	3.1	3.8
December	2.0	2.5	3.1	3.8
Total per Cow per Year	21	27.9	34.9	43.2
Average Seconds per Litre	*13.7*	*14.3*	*15.7*	*17.3*

No time is allocated here for dairy young stock. This schedule is based on a 100-cow herd. Low yielding cows tend to spend more time at grass and less housed. High milk yielders take more management time.

13.7 seconds per litre = 1 man per 725,000L
17.3 seconds per litre = 1 man per 575,000L

The most labour efficient milk producing operations in the UK achieve over 800,000 litres per employed man.

Hours staff Requirement per Cow per Year.

	Cow Annual Milk Yield (L)			
	5,500	7,000	8,000	9,000
Cows per Herd				
60	21.9	29.1	36.4	45.0
100	21.0	27.9	34.9	43.2
150	20.0	26.6	33.2	41.1
300	17.5	23.3	29.1	36.0
500	15.0	19.9	24.9	30.9

Labour Cost Per Litre

	Cow Annual Milk Yield (L)			
ppl	5,500	7,000	8,000	9,000
Cows per Herd				
60	3.86	4.02	4.41	4.85
100	3.70	3.86	4.23	4.65
150	3.53	3.68	4.03	4.43
300	3.08	3.22	3.52	3.88
500	2.64	2.76	3.02	3.32

Earnings. The average earnings of 'dairy herdsmen' in 2010/11 is estimated to be £26,852 a year and working 2770 hours (10 hours for 277 days). This includes relief milking etc but no cover for young stock or fieldwork, such as hay and silage making

Dairy Followers and Beef

No recent survey work has been published on labour requirements for beef animals and dairy followers. The following data is therefore only 'best estimates'. They are for average performance and average conditions, excluding fieldwork. Substantial variations occur, e.g. through differing management styles or economies of scale with differing herd sizes.

Calves (per head, early weaning)

Age Group	Labour hours per month	
	Average	Premium
0-3 months..	2.3	1.6
3-6 months..	0.9	0.6
(av. 0-6 months...	1.6	1.1)
6-12 months, yarded......................................	1.1	0.8
6-12 months, summer grazed...........................	0.3	0.2
(av. 0-12 months, during winter (1).................	1.3	0.9)
(av. 0-12 months, during summer (1).................	0.9	0.6)

1. Assuming 6 to 12-month olds housed in winter and grazed in summer, and calvings or calf purchases fairly evenly spaced throughout the year.

Stores (per head)

	Average	Premium
Yearling, housed....................................	1.0	0.7
2 year olds and over, housed.....................	1.4	0.8
Out-wintered store................................	0.7	0.5
12 months and over, summer grazed............	0.2	0.1

Dairy Followers

(Per 'replacement unit', i.e. calf + yearling + in-calf heifer.) (1)		
During winter...	2.9	2.0
During summer..	1.2	0.8

1. Assuming calvings fairly evenly spaced throughout the year and heifers calving at 2 to 2.5 years old.

Beef Finishing (per head)

Housed...	1.8	1.2
Summer Grazed.......................................	0.2	0.1
Intensive Beef (0-12 months).....................	1.3	1.0

Suckler Herds (per cow)

Lowland Single suckling (av. whole year)....... .	0.9	0.6
Lowland Multiple suckling (av. whole year)...	2.9	2.1
Upland/Hill Single suckling (av. whole year)...	1.1	0.7

Sheep (per Ewe)

	Labour hours per month	
	Average	Premium (4)
January..	0.3	0.2
February...	0.3	0.2
March..	1.0 (1)	0.7
April...	0.4	0.25
May..	0.3	0.2
June..	0.4 (2)	0.3
July..	0.2	0.15
August...	0.2	0.15
September..	0.25	0.15
October..	0.25	0.15
November...	0.2	0.15
December...	0.2	0.15
Total..	4.0 (3)	2.75

1. Assuming mainly March lambing.
2. 0.3 if shearing is by contract.
3. A full-time shepherd, i.e. one who did no other work on the farm, would have to have a flock of at least 600 ewes for the average 4 hours per ewe per year to be achieved, assuming full-time assistance during lambing time.
4. In a national survey conducted in 1999 the average annual requirement for flocks exceeding 500 ewes was 2.9 hours.

Pigs

	Labour hours per month	
Age Group	Average	Premium
Breeding and Rearing, per sow...............................	1.5	1.20
(Average 130 sows per worker, Premium 160)		
Feeding only, per 10 pigs.......................................	1.6	1.25
No. at a time, per worker:		
Average 1,200 per man, Premium 1,600		
No. per year, per worker:		
Average: 6,000 porkers, 4,800 cutters, 4,450 baconers		
Premium: 8,000 porkers, 6,400 cutters, 5,750 baconers		
Breeding, Rearing and Feeding, per sow (with progeny)		
Porkers, average 90 sows per worker, premium 110.........	2.4	2.0
Cutters, average 80-85 sows per worker, premium 100-105	2.6	2.1
Baconers, average 75-80 sows per worker, premium 95-100	2.8	2.2

Poultry (large scale, automated)

	Labour hours per month
Laying hens: battery cages (18,000 per full-time worker)	1.1 per 100
free range	4 per 100
Broilers: 32,500 at a time per full-time worker*	
(225,000 a year)	1.0 per 100

* additional help needed for catching and cleaning out (included in labour hours/ month)

4.   STANDARD MAN DAYS

The Standard Man Day (SMD) estimates are drawn from the labour use figures above, and are based on a standard 8-hour day. Most of these SMD figures are based on limited data only - though all that is available; these are subject to substantial variations with scale and production methods. Little research has been done recently to update these figures.

Crops (per hectare)	S.M.D.s
Winter Feed Wheat	
Winter Milling Wheat	
Spring Wheat	
Winter Feed Barley	1.15 /
Winter Malting Barley	1.75 (1)
Spring Malting Barley	
Winter Oats	
Spring Oats	
Winter Oilseed Rape	1.10
Spring Oilseed Rape	1.00
Linseed	1.00
Winter Field Beans	0.90
Spring Field Beans	0.95
Dried Peas	1.60
Lupins	1.50
Vining Peas	3.00
Maincrop Potatoes	9.25 (2)
Early Potatoes	5.50 (2)
Sugar Beet	3.00
Herbage Seed (Ryegrass)	1.40
Hops	9.50 (2)
Kale (grazed)	1.40
Silage:~ one cut	1.60 (3)
two cuts	2.80 (3)
Grazing only	0.40 (3)
Hay for sale	1.80 (3)
Let Keep	0.40 (3)
Bare fallow / set-aside	0.20
Rough Grazing	0.20

Notes Overleaf

Livestock (per head) (4)

Dairy Cows	4.00
Bulls	3.50
Beef Cows (single suckler including calf):	
lowland	1.35
upland/hill	1.68
Cereal Beef (0-12 months) (5)	1.90
18-month Beef (5)	1.60
Grass Silage Beef (5)	1.90
Finishing Suckler bred stores:	
Grass	1.10
Winter	1.10
Calves; to 6 months (5)	1.20
Ewes:lowland	0.50
upland	0.45
hill	0.40
Rams	0.50
Winter Finishing Store Lambs	0.30
Sows (including weaners to 30kg)	2.25
Boars	2.00
Other Bacon Pigs	0.25
Laying Birds:battery cages	0.017
free range	0.06
Pullets reared (5)	0.005
Broilers (5)	0.002

1. 1.15 if straw ploughed in; 1.75 if straw harvested. Highly mechanised larger farms will require no more than 0.75 S.M.D./ha of direct labour for cereals and other combinable crops (assuming straw ploughed in).

2. Excludes casual labour for harvesting.

3. Excludes any reseeding carried out – this is likley to be around 0.6 S.M.D./ha in the year reseeding is carried out.

4. Note that for grazing livestock, the S.M.D.s per head exclude field work, e.g. grass production and silage making, i.e. the labour for these has to be added to give total labour for these enterprises.

5. For these livestock, S.M.D. per annum should be based on numbers produced (sold) during the year. For all other livestock, average numbers on the farm at any one time during the year should be used (i.e. average of numbers at end of each month).

7. 'Other Cattle' can refer to both beef animals and dairy followers (ref. detail on page 175).

V. MACHINERY

1. AGRICULTURAL MACHINERY PRICES

This schedule of prices is estimated for spring 2011 purchase of new machinery, net of discounts and ex. V.A.T. Machinery inflation has been subdued over much of the last decade compared with most other benchmark inflation indicators (mainstream and agricultural). Over the seven years between 1997 and 2003, machinery inflation totalled only 1.1 per cent. Since then, inflationary pressures have affected machinery prices by much more, with overall rises in 2004 of 4.6%, 2005 of 5.2%, 2006 of 1.4%, 2007 of 4.9% 2008 of 7.5% and 2009 of 5.1%. Over the forthcoming year, it is expected that the cost of machinery is likely to increase by a smaller margin. As a general rule, prices are increased in this schedule by between 2 and 4%.

Tractors   £

(a)	Two-Wheel Drive	
	43-49 kW (57-66 hp)...	21,000-25,000
	50-56 kW (67-75 hp)...	22,200-28,100
	57-66 kW (76-89 hp)...	25,500-31,000
	67-75 kW (90-100 hp)...	28,100-33,400
(b)	Four- Wheel Drive	
	43-50 kW (57-67 hp)	20,400-29,700
	56-65 kW (75-87 hp)...	28,100-33,600
	66-75 kW (88-100 hp)...	34,600-40,200
	76-90 kW (101-120 hp)...	38,500-48,500
	94-105 kW (125-140 hp).......................................	46,600-58,000
	115-134 kW (154-180 hp).....................................	57,800-70,300
	140-165 kW (187-220 hp).....................................	67,800-74,500
	170-200 kW (228-268 hp).....................................	86,400-99,000
(c)	High Road Speed (50 Km /hour)	
	15-130 kW (155-175 hp).......................................	62,900-77,400
	140-165 kW (188-221 hp).....................................	77,400-90,300
(d)	Crawlers	
	175-225 kW (230-300 hp) rubber track........................	138,500-152,000
	225-300 kW (340-400 hp) rubber track........................	160,000-186,000
	336-410 kW (450-550 hp) rubber track........................	193,000-213,000

Cultivating Equipment   £

(a) Ploughs	Fixed width	Variable width	
		Mechanical Adjustment	Hydraulic Adjustment
Reversible:			
3-furrow............	7,700-8,700	8,700-10,900	—
4-furrow............	9,100-10,300	10,000-13,500	13,500-19,800
5-furrow............	10,300-11,600	11,600-15,400	15,900-20,500
6-furrow............		15,000-19,300	18,600-22,500
6-furrow (semi-mounted).............		17,600-20,400	20,200-19,900
7-furrow (semi-mounted).............		19,100-21,800	21,000-26,700
8-furrow (semi-mounted).............		24,300-27,200	25,100-30,500

9-furrow (semi-mounted)		29,200-35,400

(b) *Furrow Presses*

1.6-1.8 m double row	3,000-3,800
2.0-2.4 m double row	3,500-4,800
2.6-3.0 m double row	4,600-6,800
3.2-3.6 m double row	6,800-8,500
3.8-4.0 m double row	8,100-9,500
Front Press Arm – hydraulic	1,550-1,650

(c) *Front Presses (excluding linkage)*

1.5 m single row	2,370-2,680
3.0 m single row	3,600-5,150
4.0 m single row — hydraulic folding	5,450-6,700

(d) *Front Press Linkage*

1.5 to 2.0 tonne	2,050-2,370
3.5 to 5.5 tonne	2,790-3,500

(e) *Other Cultivating Equipment*

Sub Soiler 2-3 leg		2,680-3,400
Soil Looseners	(3 m)	6,300-7,600
	(4 m)	9,800-11,100
Vibrating Compaction Breaker	(2-2.5m)	7,100-8,600
	(3 m)	9,800-11,100
Straw Incorporating Disc Cultivator	(2.5-3 m)	7,900-9,300
Stubble Cultivator	(3 m):	5,500-6,300
(heavy duty)	(4 m): hydraulic folding	9,800-11,100
	(6 m): hydraulic folding	14,100-16,900
Spring-tine Cultivator	(3-4 m):	2,270-3,300
	(5-6 m): hydraulic folding	6,300-7,500
Combination Harrows	(2.5-4 m)	4,750-7,400
	(5-6 m): hydraulic folding	12,500-13,400
Levelling Harrows	(2.5-4.2 m)	1,650-2,680
	(3.7-6.1 m): hydraulic folding	3,400-5,160
Disc Harrows	(2.7-3.6 m): trailed	12,700-13,900
	(4.25-6.25 m): trailed, , folding	22,400-32,700
Harrows (5-6 m): light-medium, hydraulic folding		2,170-2,580
Rotovator	(up to 100 kW tractor)	7,400-8,800
	(150 kW tractor)	12,100-13,500
Power Harrow (with packer roller)		
	(2.5-3 m)	6,700-7,600
	(3.5-4m)	9,600-11,100
	(5-6m): folding	21,100-23,700
Rolls: triple gang, hydraulic folding	(6 m)	7,400-8,800
five gang, " "	(12m)	17,800-19,600

Fertiliser Distributors, Seed Drills, Sprayers £

(a) *Fertiliser Distributors*

Mounted Spinners	
(500-750 litre)	1,650-2,170

		(700-1,200 litre): twin disc, hydraulic control1	2,370-2,990
		(1,300-1,700 litre): twin disc, hydraulic control.........	3,900-4,300
		(1,650-2,300 litre): twin disc, electronic control	6,700-7,300
		(3,200 litre): twin disc, electronic control	8,600-8,900
		Bag lifter (850-1,000kg)	1,650-1,950

(b) *Seed Drills*

Grain: mounted	3 m, gravity fed, 25 row	6,700-8,300
	3-4 m, pneumatic, 24-32 row ..	13,700-16,700
	6 m, pneumatic, 48 row...........	27,300-32,200

(c) *Combined Cultivator and Pneumatic Drill*

| | 3-4 m, 24-32 row..................... | 19,400-23,300 |
| | 6 m, 48 row .... | 39,100-44,200 |

(d) *Combined Power Harrow and Pneumatic Drill*

| | 3-4 m, 24-32 row..................... | 20,600-27,800 |
| | 6 m, 48 row .... | 37,700-55,000 |

(e) *Direct Drill*

6m, 32 chisel openers... 68,100-75,300

(f) *Sprayers*

Mounted, 600-800 litre tank, 12 m boom.............................	3,900-4,440
Mounted, 1,000-1,300 litre tank, 20-24 m hydraulic boom ..	16,500-20,800
Mounted, Air assisted, 1,000 litre tank, 18 m boom.............	23,300-27,900
Trailed, Air assisted, 2,500-3,000 litre tank, 24 m boom......	41,700-48,000
Trailed, 2,500-3,000l tank 18-24 m boom...........................	31,000-34,700
Trailed, 3,000-3,500l tank 24-30 m boom...........................	36,000-41,700

Self-propelled sprayers,

3,200-4,200l, 24-36 m boom, 4-wd...........................	98,000-107,300
6,000-7,500l tank, 40m boom, 240hp	139,000-149,500
8,000-12,000l tank, 42m boom, 3 axle, ...	£185,000

Grass Conservation and Handling Equipment   £

(a) *Silage Equipment*

Forage Harvester: trailed, precision chop	26,500-35,100
Self-propelled (3 m pick-up 280-375 hp)	133,000-152,000
Maize attachment, 4-6 row..	26,500-34,600
Silage Trailer, 12 tonne, tandem axle	7,200-8,800
Silage Trailer, 14 tonne, tandem axle	8,000-10,300
Silage Trailer, 16 tonne, tandem axle	10,200-11,600
Buckrake (push off)..	2,070-2,370

(b) *Haymaking Equipment*

Mowers

1.5-1.8 m, 1-2 drum......................................	2,480-3,300
2.0-2.4 m, 5-6 disc.......................................	4,500-5,200
disc conditioner, mounted (2.4-3.2 m).........................	9,300-10,700
disc conditioner, trailed (2.8-3.2 m)	14,700-16,000

Rakes,

| Single/double rotor, 3.2m-4.5m range........................ | 3,100-7,400 |
| multiple rotors 10-13m range.................................... | 14,400-31,000 |

Tedder/swather
5-7 m, 4-6 rotors	4,540-7,200
13-17m multiple rotors	24,400-29,900

Balers and Bale Handling: see 5(c) and (d) below

(c)   *Silage Handling Equipment*
Silage shear bucket (1-1.2 m)	2,370-3,500
Silage grab	1,750-2,270
Big Bale Silage Feeder, mounted	6,700-8,700
Diet-feeder Wagon (8-14 m)	23,300-28,100
Clamp Silage Mixer (12-18m^3)	22,600-28,800

Grain and Straw Harvesting and Handling Equipment   £

(a)   *Combines*

Engine size kW (hp)	Cutterbar width metres (feet)	
150-165 (200-220)	4.5-5.0 (14-16)	110,000-115,000
165-185 (220-249)	4.5-5.5 (14-18)	118,000-160,000
186-223 (250-299)	5.4-6.1 (18-20)	128,000-174,000
223-298 (300-399)	6.0-7.7 (20-25)	155,000-245,000
Over 300 (400 up to 530)	9.0-9.15 (25-30)	233,000-360,000

(b)   *Yield monitoring/mapping*   7,500-9,500

(c)   *Pick-up Balers (twine tying)*
Small rectangular bales	10,500-11,800
Small rectangular bales, heavy duty models	13,100-15,700
Big round bales, twine tying and net wrap	18,400-22,300
High density rectangular bales	71,000-79,500

(d)   *Bale Wrappers*
Big Bale Wrapper: mounted/trailed	10,300-11,700
Big Square Bale Wrapper: mounted	15,800-17,100
Combined Baler and Wrapper	41,300-50,000
Bale Trailers, 5-8 tonne	3,200-4,350
Accumulator, flat 8, mechanical	2,170-2,800
Big bale accumulator	9,500-10,500
Loader, flat 8	900-1,240
Big Bale Spike	250-330
Big Bale Handler	670-1,030
Big Bale Shredder, silage or straw	6,600-7,800

(e)   *Drying, Handling, Food Processing Equipment*
Grain driers and Grain storage:	*see pages 163 and 181*
Cleaner/grader, 10-20 tonnes/hour	9,900-13,900
Grain augers 100 mm, 3.3-7.3 m	620-800
Grain augers 150 mm, 6-8.5 m, with trolley	1,960-2,500
Grain conveyors, (25-50t/hour)	1,450-1,970 + 145-185 per m
Specific gravity separator, (5-10t/hour)	15,800-18,700
Bucket elevator, (25-50t/hour)	2,060-2,800 + 185-245 per m
Hammer mill, 7.5-15 kW	3,600-4,000
Roller mill, 4-5.5 kW	3,100-3,600

Mixer, 750-1000 kg		4,000-4,750
Mill and mixer, 1,000-1,300kg, 3.7-5.5 kW		6,500-7,900
Grain weigher, 25 tonne/hour		1,960-2,270

Potato, Sugar Beet and Vegetable Machinery   £

(a) *Potato Machinery*

Stone separator, 1.6 m (1 bed)		44,200-50,000
Bedformer, 2 row		3,900-4,300
Bed cultivator, 1.7-1.8 m (1 bed)		8,300-9,000
Planter:	2 row mounted	10,700-13,300
	4 row mounted	33,400-37,800
Haulm pulveriser:	2 row	6,700-7,500
	2 row cross conveyor	10,300-10,500
Elevator-Digger,	2 row	6,700-7,500
Harvesters (trailed):	2 row, elevator manned/unmanned	73,000-86,500
	2 row, 6 tonne bunker	95,000-111,000
	4 row, self-propelled	131,000-188,000
Store loader (heavy duty)		25,000-29,400
Flat belt conveyor, 3-8 m		2,270-3,700
Soil elevator (rubber belt)		6,900-7,500
Self-unloading hopper, 3-5 tonnes		10,100-11,400
Clod separator		10,100-11,300
Sizer, 5-30 tonnes/hour		10,100-15,100
Sponge drier, 0.9-1.2m		13,800-15,100
Barrel washer, 8-10 tonnes/hour		20,200-22,700
Roller inspection table, 1.2 x 2.4 m		3,700-4,300
Weigher, automatic, 8-10 tonnes/hour		6,300-7,500
Box tipper with cross conveyor		17,700-20,300
Box filer, automatic		15,100-16,400
Bag stitcher (hand held)		980-1,240
Complete out of store grading line:	20 tonnes/hour	37,900-46,400
	30 tonnes/hour	88,000-95,000
Box filler (30 tonnes/hour)		13,900-17,000

(b) *Sugar Beet Machinery*

Precision Drill:	6 row (pneumatic)	10,700-12,600
	12 row-18 row (pneumatic)	21,500-33,200
Hoe:	6 row-12 row (heavy duty)	7,800-13,300
Harvesters:	Trailed, 2 row, tanker	67,000-74,000
	Trailed, 3 row, tanker	81,000-88,000
	Trailed, 4 row, tanker	94,000-101,000
Self-propelled, 6 row, 18 tonne tank		320,000-365,000
Cleaner-loader, with engine, 1-3 tonnes per minute		26,500-30,300
Fodder beet harvester		7,300-8,100

(c) *Vegetable Machinery*

Onion windrower		9,900-11,400
Root crop digger:	1 webb	6,900-7,500
	2 webbs	8,000-9,400

Top lifting vegetable harvester:	single row, bunker............	52,600-60,500
	twin row, bunker/elevator	93,400-113,000
	four row, elevator.............	120,000-140,000
	four row, self-propelled....	320,000-348,000
Leek harvester (mounted)......................................		20,000-33,200

General

	£
Trailer, 4 tonne tipping..	2,500-2,900
Trailer, 5-6 tonne tipping; grain/silage	3,300-4,100/4,100-4,600
Trailer, 10t tipping, tandem axle; grain/silage	6,100-6,500/7,300-8,000
F.Y.M. Spreaders, (6 - 8 tonne)................................	5,300-6,700
F.Y.M. Spreaders, (10 - 12 tonne).......................................	7,400-10,400
F.Y.M. Spreaders, (12 - 14 tonne).......................................	9,500-13,600
Loaders, front mounted	4,600-5,400
Pallet loader, self levelling (1,000-1,600 kg)........................	5,400-6,600
Materials Handler, telescopic boom (2.5-3.0 tonne).............	42,900-50,500
Skid steer loader (500-600 kg)	17,600-20,200
Slurry Stores (metal), including base for 120 day storage period for:	
100 cows..	£263 per cow
200 cows..	£243 per cow
400 cows..	£212 per cow
Vacuum Tankers (5,000-6,000 litre)	5,300-5,900
Low Ground Pressure Tankers (9,000-11,000 litre)	11,400-13,400
Slurry pump	4,000-4,700
Cattle crush	1030-1,450
Cattle crush with weigher.......................................	2,060-2,370
Cattle trailer (twin-axle)...	2,370-3,100
Yard scrapers	680-870
Rotary brush (2-2.5 m)..	1,860-2,370
Grassland roll, ballastable (2.5-3 m)	1,140-1,350
Pasture topper (2.0-3.0 m)......................................	2,370-3,300
Hedge cutter:	
hydraulic angling; flail head	12,000-14,900
7.6m reach, 1.3m flail head, double sided.................	26,800-34,000
Ditcher: fully slewing..	9,500-10,700
Carrier box	660-770
Post hole digger/driver	1,240-1,600/1,960-3,100
Saw bench..	1,960-2,270
Log splitter..	770-980

2. TYPICAL CONTRACTORS' CHARGES, AVERAGE FARMERS' COSTS, AND RATES OF WORK FOR FARM OPERATIONS

Contractors' charges vary widely according to many factors: these are estimates for 2011. Farmer-contractors often charge less than dedicated contractors, since their overheads and machinery fixed costs are largely *considered* covered by their own farming operations, but the service may not always be so complete, including specialist advice.

Farmers' own costs (including the value of the farmers' own manual labour) vary even more widely; those given (for 2011) are averages in every respect - different types of soil, size of farm, and so on; they are based on accounting cost procedures in that labour, tractor and machinery fuel, repairs and depreciation are included - no allowance has been added for general farm overheads, interest on capital, supervision/management or under-occupied labour during slack times. They assume four-wheel drive 75-90 kW (100-120 hp) tractors for ploughing, heavy cultivation and other work with a high power requirement. Four-wheel drive 55-65 kW (75-87 hp) tractors are assumed to be used for most other operations. The figures should not be used for partial budgeting.

For a typical set of farm operations, excluding harvesting, the breakdown of the farmers' costs averages very approximately one third each for labour, tractors and implements/machines. The larger the farm, the lower the labour element and the higher the machine element are likely to be and vice versa. However the input from contractors may affect these costs.

The contract charges and average farmers' costs are put side-by-side for tabular convenience, not to facilitate comparisons. Apart from the fact that contractors' charges must cover expenses omitted from the farmers' cost, the advisability or otherwise of hiring a contractor for a particular job depends on many factors, varying widely according to farm circumstances; furthermore, there are advantages and disadvantages not reflected in a cost comparison alone.

Assumptions: Contractors' costs are particularly sensitive to many factors. These include input costs, capital machinery prices, and demand versus local competition. Of these, fuel has risen by almost a quarter in the preceding 12 months and at the time the data was struck, was at 52ppl for tractor diesel. The average price inflation of machinery is forecast to be minimal for the year to September 2011 following the considerable rises in years prior to 2010. Fuel is included in the contractors' costings.

Machinery rings. Prices charged by farmers offering services through machinery rings are extremely variable but are generally between average farmers' costs and contractors' charges. There are exceptions, which mainly relate to relatively expensive items of machinery (e.g. precision drills, destoners and combine harvesters), where the charges for services offered through machinery rings are close to and often less than average farmers' costs.

Four-wheel drive 120-150 kW (150-200 hp) tractors are assumed where appropriate to achieve the 'premium' rates of work (which will be achieved on most farms with more than 200 hectares (500 acres) of arable land); obviously, still larger wheeled tractors and crawlers could achieve still faster rates of work, particularly on light land. The rates of work include preparation, travelling to and from the fields and allow for minor breakdowns and other stoppages. All charges and costs below are per hectare unless otherwise stated.

Average Contractors and Farmers Costs of Performing Certain Mechanical Operations.

Operation	Contract Charge £/ha	Farmer's Average Cost £/ha	Rate of Work (Ha per 8 hour day)	
			Average	Premium
Cultivations:				
Ploughing (light/heavy soils)	48.80-54.90	54-70	5-6½	7½-9
with furrow press	Extra £6.40	62-83	4½-6%	7-8½
Deep Ploughing (over 300 mm)	58.00	86-106	3-3¾	5-6½
Rotovating ploughed land	58.00	93	4½	6
grass	58.00	140	3	4
Subsoiling	56.10	49	6	10
Mole Ploughing Single Leg	68.00			
Twin Leg	113.70			
Stubble Cultivating	33.30	27	12	16
Heavy Disc Cultivating	37.90	39	10	15
Disc Harrowing	30.75	20	12	16
Chain Harrowing	15.30			
Power Harrowing	38.55	37	10	15
Spring tine Harrowing	20.50	20	12	18
Seedbed Harrowing	17.80	17	12	20
Pressing	29.40			
Rolling ~flat (Grassland)	18.40	28	6	10
~ ring, (Seedbeds)	13.80	15	15	25
Fertiliser Distributing *(including loading and carting)*:				
Broadcast (125-375 kg/ha)	9.75 (fert. in field)	7.80	30	60
Broadcast (500-750 kg/ha)		12.50	22.5	45
Broadcast (1,000-1,250 kg/ha).		18.80	15	30
Pneumatic (125-375 kg/ha)		18.00	25	40
Liquid Fertilising	12.60			
Drilling:				
Cereals : conventional	31.75	26.20	14	18
Cereals : combi-drilling	49.40	46.60	10	14
Direct Drilling	44.50			
One-pass tillage train	46.30			
Rape Drilling inc Flat lift Subsoiler	40.40			
Grass Broadcasting	19.30	19.10	11	15
Roots/Maize (inc. fertiliser)	41.90	78.90	3½ (4 row)	5 (6 row)
Sugar Beet - precision drill	40.80	47.00	6 (6 row)	10 (12 row)
Destoning potato land	210.00	235	3.25	4
Potato Planting automatic	66.70	150	2½ (2 row)	3½
Potato Ridging	50.70	36.30	5½	7

Operation	Contract Charge £/ha	Farmer's Average Cost £/ha	Rate of Work (Ha per 8 hour day)	
			Average	Premium
Spraying *(excl. materials):*				
(extra £3.00 for < 20ha)				
ATV Spraying	19.80			
Low volume (to 175 l/ha)		9.90	35	75
Medium vol.(200-300 l/ha)	10.90	11.50	30	60
High vol. (over 800 l/ha)		20.50	25	50
Slug Pelleting	7.70			
Tractor Hoeing Sugar Beet		45.80	5	8
Combine Harvesting:				
Combine Harvesting Cereals:			(hectares per hour)	
100 ha/year		151	¾-1	1-1¾
200 ha/year	76.90	98	1	1½
300 ha/year		85	1½	2
600 ha/year		74	2¾	3¼
Grain carting (per hour)	31.60	23.30/hr		
Straw Chopper incorporated	5.40			
Seed Autocast on combine	14.80			
Straw chopping (separately)	37.10			
Combining:				
Oilseed rape (windrowed)	74.40	as cereals + 10%	⅔-1	¾-1¼
Oilseed rape (direct)	75.10			
Beans	76.50	as cereals + 10%	⅔-1	¾-1¼
Peas	78.50	As cereals	¾-1	1-1½
Windrowing Oilseed Rape	42.00		1.2	1.4
Potato Harvesting				
2-row unmanned	581		0.75	2
2-row manned inc. carting	976			
Sugar Beet Harvesting				
Excluding Carting	222	210	4.0	4.5
Extra for Carting	34.50	47.00		
Baling *(Inc. string):*				
small	40p/bale	27.0p/bale	0.8	1.25
80x70cm	2.90/bale			
120x70cm	4.50.bale			
120x130cm	5.60/bale			
Round (120cm)	2.30/bale	2.23/bale		
Bale wrapping:	4.80/bale			
Round 4-layer	3.30/bale			
Round 6-layer	4.70/bale			
Square 6-layer	4.40/bale			
Square 8-layer	6.50/bale			

Operation	Contract Charge £/ha	Farmer's Average Cost £/ha	Rate of Work (Ha per 8 hour day)	
			Average	Premium
Crop Drying *(inc. intake and pre-cleaning):*				
Cereals:		*per tonne*		
by 6 per cent	14.90	9.25		
by 10 per cent	16.90	11.35		
Oilseed Rape:				
by 5 per cent	18.60	9.00-12.00		
by 10 per cent	22.00	12.0-16.00		
Cleaning without drying (£/t)	9.00			
Mobile Seed Cleaning				
(cereals inc. SPD)	57-65/t	plus royalty		
Grain Storage (/tonne/week)	35p	(see page 201)		
Handling into store (/tonne)	2.00	£1.50		
Handling out of store (/tonne)	2.00	£1.50		
Grass Mowing/Topping:				
Grass Mowing	25.30	28.30	8	12
Topping	24.70	31.50	6	9
Swath Turning/Tedding	14.50	19.00	11	15
Raking	14.20	20.00	10	15
Forage Harvesting:				
First cut	54.70	44-55	16	20
Other cuts	52.30			
Forage harvesting,				
Forage wagon only	47.00			
Harvesting, carting and ensiling grass				
First cut	107.00			
Other cuts	101.30			
Complete Service – mow, rake plus above	133.40			
Harvesting, carting and ensiling maize, 25-30t/ha	148.30			
Manure Handling etc.				
F.Y.M.: Tractor and Spreader	37.00/hr	48.20/hr		
F.Y.M.: Tractor and Loader	28.75/hr	34.80/hr		
Slurry Spreading ~ Tanker	35.75/hr	46.00/hr		
Umbilical Top Spreading	63.70/hr			
Umbilical Trailing Shoe	£70/hr			
Slurry Injection	55.40/hr			
Lime Spreading /tonne	4.15/t			
General Rural Maintenance				
Hedge Cutting ~ flail	28.60/hr	34.50		
~ saw blade	40.90/hr			
Hedge Laying (per metre run)	11.00/m			

Operation	Contract Charge	Farmer's Average Cost	Rate of Work (Ha per 8 hour day)	
	£/ha	£/ha	Average	Premium
Fence Erection per metre				
Post & Wire inc wire	3.45/m			
Post & netting inc. netting	4.45/m			
Post & rail inc. wood	13.00/m			
Ditching 360° digger	31.00/hr			
Tractor inc. driver and fuel	31.55/hr	23.30/hr (60 -120hp)		
Trailer (with driver and tractor)	27.70/hr	add £6.20 to above		
Forklift/Telehandler & operator	31.20/hr	28.40/hr		

Livestock Husbandry

Sheep Shearing ~ ewes	1.40/head
~ rams	2.80/head
Sheep Dipping inc chemicals	85p/head
Sheep Jetting inc chemicals	75p/head
Sheep Crutching	60p/head
Foot Trimming ~ Sheep	65p/head
~ Cattle	12.70/head
Sheep Ultrasound	50p/head
Cattle Ultrasound	2.00/head
General Sheep Husbandry	12.00/hour
General Cattle Husbandry	12.00/hour

Acknowledgement. The above estimates for contractors' charges are based in part on information kindly supplied by the National Association of Agricultural Contractors.

Contract Charge for All Operations

(Cereals and Combinable Break Crops, 'stubble to stubble' i.e. up to and including combine harvesting and carting the grain to store): £240 to £320/ha (£100-130/acre). Variations depend upon such factors as distance away, area contracted, size of fields, type of terrain, quality of soil and level of inputs (as affecting weight of crop to be harvested and carted) and local competition.

Management Agreements.

Generally these are formalised with a written agreement which sets out the terms for the "Farmer" (who can be a landowner or tenant) and a "Contractor". The "Contractor" can be a neighbouring farmer or traditional contractor. "Contractor" remuneration includes a guaranteed basic payment (fee) and share of a surplus calculated by an agreed formula set out in the agreement. The basic payment is usually between £210 and £275/ha (£85-£110/acre) for combinable crops.

Following deduction of agreement running costs (drying etc) and the Farmers Basic Payment which is often slightly lower these days the balance is split between the 2 parties. The split may typically be 70%-80% to the contractor and 20%-30% to the landowner. In arrangements where lower basic payments are made, a second band of payment rate may be introduced.

One sometimes sees farmers' total power and machinery costs compared with stubble to stubble contractors' charges. It has of course to be remembered that the former include many cost items not included in the latter, e.g. the cost of farm vehicles, fixed plant such as grain stores and general farm maintenance.

3.   TRACTOR HOURS

per annum

Crops	per hectare	
	Average	Premium
Cereals	9	7
Straw Harvesting	3.5	2.5
Potatoes	25	15
Sugar Beet	20	12
Vining Peas	20	12
Dried Peas	10	8
Field Beans	9	7
Oilseed Rape	9	7
Herbage Seeds:		
1 year undersown or 3 year direct drilled	7	5
1 year direct drilled	11	8
Hops (machine picked)	125	—
Kale (grazed)	8	6
Turnips/Swedes: folded/lifted	12/35	10/25
Fallow	12	7
Ley Establishment:		
Undersown	2	1
Direct Seed	7	4
Making Hay	12	8
Making Silage:		
1st Cut	12	8
2nd Cut	9	6
Grazing:		
Temporary Grass	3	2.5
Permanent Grass	2	1.5

Livestock	per head Average
Dairy Cows	6
Other Cattle over 2 years	5
Other Cattle 1-2 years	4
Other Cattle ½-1 year	2.25
Calves 0-½ year	2.25
Housed Bullocks	3
Sheep, per ewe	1.25
Store Sheep	0.8
Sows	1.75
Other Pigs over 2 months	1
Laying Birds	0.04

1. *For livestock,* annual requirements are the per head requirements above multiplied by average numbers during the year (i.e. average numbers at end of each month).

2. *As with labour,* the number of tractors required by a farm depends more on the seasonal requirements and number required at any one time than on total annual tractor hours. These can be calculated from the seasonal labour data provided earlier in this book. The soil type and size/power of tractors purchased are obviously other relevant factors.

Tractor Power Requirements

		hp/acre		hp/ha		kW/ha	
		av.	prem.	av.	prem.	av.	prem.
Combinable crops:	heavy land	0.75	0.65	1.85	1.5	1.4	1.1
	light land	0.5	0.45	1.25	1.0	0.95	0.75
Mixed cropping:	heavy land	1.0	0.75	2.5	1.85	1.85	1.4
	light land	0.7	0.5	1.75	1.25	1.3	1.95

UK Agricultural Tractor Sales per Year *(over 50 HP)*

Year	Average Tractor Size kW (HP)	Number of Units Sold	Per Cent change y/y
2002	88.48 (118.6)	13,878	+20.4%
2003	94.0 (126.0)	14,445	+4.1%
2004	96.1 (128.8)	14,750	+ 2.1%
2005	95.2 (127.6)	13,068	-11.4%
2006	95.7 (128.3)	13,566	+ 3.8%
2007	100.0 (134.0)	15,540	+14.6%
2008	103.0 (138.1)	17,104	+10.1%
2009	107.0 (143.4)	15,013	-12.2%
2010 (to June)		*7,772*	*-15.7%*

(data from the Agricultural Engineers Association).

GRAIN HAULAGE COSTS

The average costs per tonne of grain (and oilseed) haulage in Great Britain over the past six seasons are summarised by the HGCA's haulage survey carried out each December. The summarised results for the years 2004 to 2009 are tabulated below:

Summary table of the HGCA Haulage Survey Results

	2004	2005	2006	2007	2008	2009
10 miles	£4.05	£4.29	£4.09	£4.18	£4.83	£4.24
20 miles	£4.52	£4.77	£4.57	£4.69	£5.35	£4.81
40 miles	£5.47	£5.74	£5.53	£5.72	£6.40	£5.95
60 miles	£6.42	£6.71	£6.50	£6.74	£7.45	£7.09
100 miles	£8.31	£8.65	£8.43	£8.78	£9.54	£9.38
150 miles	£10.68	£11.08	£10.84	£11.34	£12.16	£12.23

4.   TRACTOR COSTS

	Two-Wheel Drive 43-49 kW (56-66 h.p.) £24,150		Four-Wheel Drive 56-65kW (75-85 h.p.) £34,650	
Initial Cost...............................	per year	per hour	per year	per hour
	£	£	£	£
Depreciation...........................	1,449	2.90	2,166	4.33
Insurance................................	281	0.56	368	0.74
Repairs and Maintenance........	966	1.93	1,386	2.77
Fuel and Oil..........................	2,101	4.20	3,353	6.71
Total......................................	4,797	9.59	7,273	14.55

	Four-Wheel Drive			
	76-90 kW (101-120 h.p.) £49,350		115-134 kW (154-180 h.p.) £66,150	
Initial Cost...............................	per year	per hour	per year	per hour
	£	£	£	£
Depreciation...........................	3,208	6.42	4,631	9.26
Insurance................................	488	0.98	610	1.22
Repairs and Maintenance........	1,974	3.95	2,646	5.29
Fuel and Oil..........................	4,642	9.28	6,447	12.89
Total......................................	10,312	20.62	14,334	28.67

	Crawlers			
	60 kW (80h.p.) £30,030		200 kW (266h.p.) £152,250	
Initial Cost...............................	per year	per hour	per year	per hour
	£	£	£	£
Depreciation...........................	2,102	4.20	10,658	21.32
Insurance................................	314	0.63	1,315	2.63
Repairs and Maintenance........	1,201	2.40	6,090	12.18
Fuel and Oil..........................	3,301	6.60	11,003	22.01
Total......................................	6,918	13.84	29,066	58.13

Figures are estimates for 2011. Depreciation assumes small two-wheel drive tractors are sold for 40% of their original value after ten years and small, medium and large four-wheel drive tractors (including crawlers) are sold for 37.5, 35 and 30% respectively of their original value after ten years. Annual repair costs have been calculated at 4% of initial cost for all tractors. No interest on capital has been included. Fuel is charged at 52p/litre.

The hourly figures are based on a use of 500 hours per year. A greater annual use than this will mean higher annual costs but possibly lower hourly costs. On large arable farms and contracting businesses, many tractors do over 750 hours per year, even 1,000 in some cases. Earlier replacement at a given annual use will increase depreciation costs per hour but should reduce repair costs. The hourly figures are averages for all types of work: heavy operations such as ploughing obviously have a higher cost than light work.

5. ESTIMATING ANNUAL MACHINERY COSTS

Annual machinery costs consist of depreciation, repairs, fuel and oil, contract charges, and vehicle tax and insurance. These can be budgeted in three ways;

1) using information on past machinery costs on the farm,

2) per hectare, by looking up an average figure for the district, according to the size and type of farm. Approximate levels are shown in the tables of whole farm fixed costs (page 202). This is obviously a rough and ready measure.

3) Fully detailed calculation, costing and depreciating each machine in turn, including tractors, estimating repairs and fuel costs for each, and adding the charges for any contract work. The following tables give, for different types of machine, estimated life, annual depreciation, and estimated repairs according to annual use.

ESTIMATED USEFUL LIFE OF POWERED MACHINERY IN NORMAL USE

Estimated Useful Life (years)	Annual Use (hours)				
Equipment	25	50	100	200	300
Group 1:					
Ploughs, cultivators, toothed harrows, hoes, rolls, ridgers, potato planting attachments, grain cleaners	12+	12+	12+	12	10
Group 2:					
Disc harrows, corn drills, grain drying machines, food grinders and mixers	12+	12+	12	10	8
Group 3:					
Combine harvesters, pick-up balers, rotary cultivators, hydraulic loaders	12+	12+	12	9	7
Group 4:					
Mowers, forage harvesters, swath turners, rakes, tedders, hedge cutting machines, semi-automatic potato planters and transplanters, unit root drills, mechanical root thinners	12+	12	11	8	6
Group 5:					
Fertilisers, combine drills, FYM spreaders, elevator potato diggers, spraying machines, pea cutter windrowers	10	10	9	8	7
Miscellaneous:					
Beet harvesters	11	10	9	6	5
Potato harvesters	—	8	7	5	—
Milking machinery	—	—	—	—	20 +

	Annual Use (hours)				
	500	750	1,000	1,500	2,000	2,500
Tractors	12+	12	10	7	6	5
Electric motors	12+	12+	12+	12+	12	12

DEPRECIATION: AVERAGE ANNUAL FALL IN VALUE

(per cent of new price)

Age of Machine	Complex. High Depreciation Rate e.g. potato harvesters, mobile pea viners, etc.	Established machines with many moving parts, e.g. tractors, combines, balers, forage harvesters	Simple equipment with few moving parts, e.g. ploughs, trailers
	%	%	%
1	40	30	20
2	27½	20	15
3	20*	16*	12½
4	17½†	14½	11½
5	15‡	13†	10½*
6	13½	12	9½
7	12	11	9
8	11	10‡	8½†
9	(10)	9½	8
10	(9½)	8½	7½‡

* Typical frequency of renewal with heavy use.

† Typical frequency of renewal with average use.

‡Typical frequency of renewal with light use.

DEPRECIATION: PERCENTAGE RATES

Straight-Line

Trade-in, Second-hand or Scrap Value as % of New Price

Years Retained	5%	10%	20%	25%	33%	40%	50%	60%
3	—	—	—	—	—	20	16	13
4	—	—	—	—	17	15	12	—
5	—	—	—	15	13	12	—	—
6	—	—	13	12	11	10	—	—
8	—	11	10	9	—	—	—	—
10	9	9	8	—	—	—	—	—
12	8	7	—	—	—	—	—	—
15	6	—	—	—	—	—	—	—

Example: If a machine costing £10,000 is retained for 8 years, at the end of which the trade-in value is 20% of the new price (i.e. £2,000), the average depreciation per annum has been £8,000 over 8 years = £1,000 (i.e. 10% per year of the new price).

Formula to calculate percentage = ((NP − TiV) / AoM) / NP x 100

NP   New Price

TiV   Trade in Value

AoM   Age of Machine

Diminishing Balances

Trade-in, Second-hand or Scrap Value as % of New Price

Years Retained	5%	10%	20%	25%	33%	40%	50%	60%
3	—	—	—	—	—	26	21	16
4	—	—	—	—	24	20	16	—
5	—	—	—	24	20	17	—	—
6	—	—	23	20	17	14	—	—
8	—	25	18	16	—	—	—	—
10	25	20	15	—	—	—	—	—
12	22	17	—	—	—	—	—	—
15	18	—	—	—	—	—	—	—

Example: If a machine costing £10,000 is retained for 4 years, at the end of which the trade-in value is 40% of the new replacement price, the annual depreciation on the diminishing balances method is:

Year 1, £2,000 (i.e. 20% of £10,000);

Year 2, £1,600 (i.e. 20% of £8,000 [the written-down value]);

Year 3, £1,280 (i.e. 20% of £6,400); Year 4, £1,024 (20% of £5,120).

The total written-down value at the end of Year 4 is therefore £4,096 (i.e. £10,000 less the total depreciation of £5,904). This is approximately 41% of the new price. (Taking the percentages in the above table to decimal places would give the trade-in prices stated more precisely).

ESTIMATED ANNUAL COST OF SPARES AND REPAIRS

These figures are based on a percentage of purchase price* at various levels of use

	Annual Use *(hours)*				Additional 100 hours
	500	750	1,000	1,500	use add
	%	%	%	%	%
Tractors..	5.0	6.7	8.0	10.5	0.5

	Annual Use *(hours)*				Additional 100 hours
	50	100	150	200	use add
Harvesting Machinery:	%	%	%	%	%
Combine Harvesters, self-propelled and engine-driven...........................	1.5	2.5	3.5	4.5	2.0
Combine Harvesters, p.t.o. driven, metered-chop forage harvesters, pick-up balers, potato harvesters, sugar beet harvesters.....................	3.0	5.0	6.0	7.0	2.0
Other Implements and Machines:					
Ploughs, Cultivators, Toothed harrows, Hoes, Elevator potato diggers......................................	4.5	8.0	11.0	14.0	6.0
Rotary cultivators, Mowers, Pea cutter-windrowers..................	4.0	7.0	9.5	12.0	5.0
Disc harrows, Fertiliser distributors, Farmyard manure spreaders, Combine drills, Potato planters with fertiliser attachment, Sprayers, Hedge-cutting machines..	3.0	5.5	7.5	9.5	4.0
Swath turners, Tedders, Side-delivery rakes, Unit drills, Flail forage harvesters, Semi-automatic potato planters and transplanters, Down-the-row thinners.............................	2.5	4.5	6.5	8.5	4.0
Corn drills, Milking machines, Hydraulic loaders, Potato planting Attachments.............................	2.0	4.0	5.5	7.0	3.0
Grain driers, Grain cleaners, Rolls, Hammer mills, Feed mixers Threshers.................................	1.5	2.0	2.5	3.0	0.5

* When it is known that a high purchase price is due to high quality and durability or a low price corresponds to a high rate of wear and tear, adjustments to the figures should be made.

SUMMARY OF MACHINERY COSTS

The percentage composition of the total cost (based on Cambridge, Reading and Wye Farm Business Survey data) varies with size and type of farm but averages the following. This method may be used as a check on the per hectare calculation:

Depreciation	Repairs	Fuel/Elec.	Contract	VTI*
34	22	20	19	5

*Vehicle tax and insurance.

6. FIELD DRAINAGE

(Estimated for 2011)

1. Installation (costs per metre of excavating a trench, supplying and laying the pipe and backfilling with soil).

Plastic pipes:	60mm diameter	1.80—2.00
	80mm diameter	2.10—2.70
	100mm diameter	3.00—3.25
	125mm diameter	4.00—4.35
	150mm diameter	4.50—5.10
	300mm diameter	12.10—13.60

The above rates apply to schemes of 5 hectares or more; smaller areas and patching up work can cost up to 50% more.

Supplying and laying permeable backfill to within 375mm of ground level will add between £2.65 and £3.40 per metre to costs.

Digging new open ditches (1.8m top width, 0.9m depth) costs £2.00-£2.50 per metre compared with improving existing ditches at £1.40 to £2.00 per metre.

Subsoiling or mole draining will cost in the region of £55-£60 per hectare.

2. *Total Costs* per hectare for complete schemes will vary depending on the distance between laterals, soil type, size of area to be drained, region of the country and the time of year when the work is to be undertaken. The cost of a scheme with 20m spacing between laterals and using permeable backfill will typically be in the range £2,500 to £3,000 per hectare (£1000-£1,200 per acre).

Backfilling with soil, rather than with permeable material such as washed gravel, may reduce the cost by almost half but is only possible on certain types of soil. Equally, certain soil types which are particularly suitable for mole drainage may permit spacing between laterals to be increased to 40m or even 80m in some instances. Where this is possible costs will be reduced proportionately.

7. IRRIGATION COSTS

Estimated for 2011

Capital Costs

1. Pumps (delivering from 20 to 200 cubic metres per hour from a surface water source, all with portable suction and delivery fittings)

Tractor pto shaft driven c/w monitoring equipment	£3,000-5,700
Diesel engine driven c/w monitoring equipment	£5,300-23,000
Electric motor driven (c/w switch gear)	£2,800-40,000
Optional remote/wireless monitoring controls	£2,300-5,700

2. Pipelines (averages per m)

Portable: (excl. valve take offs) 50mm, £2.80; 75 mm, £3.35; 100 mm, £5.00; 125 mm, £6.00; 150 mm, £8.60; (incl. valve take offs) 75 mm, £5.20; 100 mm, £6.60; 125 mm, £7.60; 150mm, £11.00.

Permanent Underground P.V.C. pipe 12.5 bar rating (supply and laying) per metre: 75 mm, £5.00; 100 mm, £6.20; 150/160 mm, £8.50; 200 mm, £12.00; 250mm, £16.20.

Hydrants: 100 mm x 100 mm, £225; 150 mm x 125 mm, £275.

3. Application Systems

   (a) Traditional portable hand move sprinkler systems

   75mm (3 inch) diameter. Sprinkler line assemblies:

1 move/day/six day cycle	£880/ha
2 moves/day/six day cycle	£460/ha
3 moves/day/six day cycle	£320/ha

   (b) Solid set sprinkler lines – semi-permanent systems

   63mm dia. pipework assemblies at

18m x 18m triangulated spacing	£1,535/ha
As above but infra-red automated hand-held controls	£1,750/ha

   (c) Drip irrigation systems

   16.5mm non-recoverable tape (excluding header mains, control valves and filtration equipment)   £420/ha

   (d) Hose reel systems using rain guns (average cost per machine)

		Manual controls	Electric Controls
Small	6-15m³/hr	£4,400	–
Medium	20-40m³/hr	£11,000	£12,900
Large	40-80m³/hr	£15,700	£17,300

   (e) Hose reel systems using irrigation booms (average cost per unit)

Small including	20m boom	£ 8,000
Medium including	40/50m boom	£15,000
Large including	70/80m boom	£30,000

   (f) Pivot and linear systems

Small pivot	200m radius (12.5ha)	£1,450/ha full circle
Large pivot	600m radius (113ha)	£870/ha full circle
Linear machine (dependent on length)		£1,660-2,350/ha

4. Total

If no source works are needed, as with water from a river, or pond, total capital costs are likely to vary between £1,150 and £2,250 per hectare requiring irrigation at regular intervals, depending on the levels of sophistication and automation of the system installed.

Water Sources

An abstraction licence is required if more than $20m^3$ (4,000 gallons) of water per day are taken from surface or underground sources. If abstracting more than $10m^3$ per day in Scotland, you must obtain authorisation from SEPA. If abstracting less than $10m^3$ per day in Scotland, and comply with certain General Binding Rules (GBR) you do not require authorisation.

Abstraction charges vary widely (and have risen sharply for 2010/11) calculated by a formula combining the following factors together:

- Volume – annual licensed
- the Source Factor; whether the source is Environment Agency unsupported, supported or tidal
- The Season Factor; summer, winter or all year round
- A minimum charge of £25

There were 32 regions 'supported' by the Environment Agency in 2010/11. Abstraction from these rivers is 3 times dearer than 'unsupported' sources. Abstraction from tidal sources costs 20% of 'unsupported' sources.

Winter abstraction charges (authorised for abstraction between 1 November to 31 March) cost 16% of all-year abstraction charges. Summer charges (1st April to 31 October) are 160% of the all-year charge.

An application charge of £135 and advertising administration charge of £100 is due, alongside a standard unit charge (SUC), a charge for the region in which the abstraction is authorised to be made and an Environmental Improvement Unit Charge (EIUC). For 2010/11 they are:

Region (£/1000m³)	Standard Unit Charges	Environmental Improvement Unit Charge (EIUC)
Anglian	26.71	4.26
Midlands	14.95	2.51
Northumbria	25.98	0.00
Yorkshire	11.63	0.62
North West	13.22	0.76
Southern	19.13	3.59
South West including Wessex	19.71	4.80
Thames	13.84	0.83
EA Wales	13.89	2.42

Water Costs

A typical extraction cost for a non-tidal, non supported farm in East Anglia for 25mm per hectare (250m³ per hectare) would be £1.24/ha for winter abstraction only (0.5p/m³), £7.74 for all year abstraction (3.1p/m³) and £12.39/ha (summer only abstraction) (5.0p/m³). The same for an acre-inch would equate to £0.51, £3.18 and £5.09 respectively. This is clearly just the cost for the water. The capital invested and the labour and any power requirement should also be accounted for which will vary according to individual circumstances. Mains water at 130p per m³ would cost £325 per application of 25mm per hectare (£134/acre).

New time limited abstraction licences are difficult to obtain, especially for summer abstraction. Hence there is an increasing trend towards constructing reservoirs that can be used to store water abstracted during the winter months. The cost of clay-lined reservoirs varies widely but would typically be in excess of £1 per m³ of water stored. This price could double if the reservoir is lined and fenced.

Overall Operating Costs

Because of variations in individual farm circumstances in terms of source works and the irrigation system used, the overall cost of applying 25mm per hectare can range widely, from £65 to £125. Very sophisticated systems distributing mains water over intensive specialist crops could be much more expensive.

Conversions and Calculations

The (approximate) imperial equivalents for metric values commonly used in irrigation are as follows:

- 1 cubic metre = 1,000 litres = 220 gallons (1 million gallons = 4,546 cubic metres).

- A pump capacity of 100 cubic metres per hour is equivalent to 22,000 gallons per hour (366 gallons per minute).

- 1,000 cubic metres is sufficient to apply 25 millimetres of water over 4 hectares, which is approximately equivalent to applying 1 inch over 10 acres. An acre inch is therefore 100 cubic meters (22,000 gallons), or a hectare centimetre is 100 cubic meters.

- The cost/volume conversion from a hectare of 25mm depth to an acre-inch is 0.411 or 2.433 from an acre-inch to a hectare 25mm.

8.   GRAIN DRYING AND STORAGE COSTS

Estimated for 2011

Drying

Capital Costs: vary widely according to type and capacity of drier. A standard 20 tonne per hour heated air drier, suitable for a 350 hectare arable unit would cost in the region of £113,000 including the wet bin and associated handling requirements (to feed drier and empty it). Over 10 years, this capital cost represents £5.00 for every tonne of grain regardless of drying requirements. Over 16 years it will fall to £3.15. Amortised (including finance) at 6% and assuming only 75% of the grain requires drying, over the 16 year period, this figure rises to £6.65/tonne dried. This figure changes dramatically by changes to throughput and longevity. At 20 tonne per hour operating for 12 hours a day 7 days a week for 6 weeks could theoretically cope with 10,080 tonnes of grain. Under this 'full' capacity, the amortised capital cost per tonne over 16 years falls to £1.11/tonne.

Annual fixed costs: being fitted and immobile, grain dryers have a low resale value. *Depreciation* is calculated as the capital value divided by the longevity and tonnes per year. This ranges from £5.30 to £1.30 per tonne. *Maintenance* tends to be low at around 2% of purchase value, rising as the dryer ages. *Insurance*; £12 per £1,000 of current value.

Running costs: *Fuel*: A useful 'rule of thumb' is 1 litre of fuel per 1% moisture per tonne. Thus drying each tonne by an average of 6% points at 52ppl makes £3.12 per tonne. *Electricity* use is 17.5Kw/hr for the burner and dischargers, as much again for the handling apparatus, totalling 35Kw/hr. Over a season, (approximately 150 hours use) at 10p/kWh is £294. This represents 18p per tonne grain. Little labour is required for modern automatic driers unless grain has to be passed over the drier several times.

Central grain stores have grain drying services of about £6.00 to £12.00 per tonne for 5% moisture drying for members and non-members respectively.

Storage

Capital Costs: from approximately £110 per tonne (on-floor storage in a purpose-built building) to over £300 per tonne for an elaborate plant, including pit, elevator, conveyors, ventilated storage bins, catwalk etc. in a new building. *Typical costs* are given on page 195.

Depreciation and Interest: £250/t depreciated over 22 years is £11.36/t per year. Interest/opportunity cost of £250 at 6% is £15/year. *Fuel and Repairs:* £2.50 per tonne (1%).

Extra Drying: Additional drying costs will be borne if storage necessitates further moisture reduction. Average £5.75 per tonne where own drier, £7.50 if dried on contract, for an additional 4% moisture extraction.

Interest on Grain Stored: 60p/month at £120/t grain at 6% interest to £1.00/month at £135/t grain, at 9% interest.

Contract Storage: typically £2.00/t per month with a handling charge of around £2.00 per tonne for loading into store and out of store.

VI. OTHER FIXED COSTS DATA

1. WHOLE FARM FIXED COSTS

The following are a broad indication of the levels of fixed costs per hectare (acre) for various types and sizes of farm, estimated for 2011, including the value of unpaid family manual labour, including that of the farmer and his wife. The figures are based on the actual results from the Farm Business Survey (FBS) for the 2008-09 year, adjusted for subsequent changes in costs. The FBS is based on a sample of farms which does change over time, so there is not a consistent sample. This just emphasises that the costs given below should be used only as an indication and must be adjusted according to individual situations; see also further notes on the use of this data below.

The FBS is conducted by a consortium of Universities and Colleges across England on behalf of DEFRA. Although the survey is limited to England, the figures within this section are likely to be broadly applicable to most parts of the UK. The FBS has undergone an overhaul in recent years. Specific regional reports are no longer published - although they can be accessed via the FBS website (see www.farmbusinesssurvey.co.uk). In addition, the farm types have been standardised across the country. They are now based on DEFRA's standard farm classifications. This has meant that some categories of farm have disappeared (mainly the 'mixed' ones such as dairy & arable, and arable & lowland livestock). All of these costs can of course vary very widely according to many factors, especially the intensity of farming, e.g. the number of cows per 100 hectares on dairy farms, or the hectares of intensive crops on general cropping farms.

The figures provided are averages. 'Premium' farms of the same level of intensity can have labour, machinery and general overhead costs at least 20% lower. However, the most profitable farms are often more intensive. They therefore have higher fixed costs associated with the great intensity - but with substantially higher total farm gross margins. Thus it is the net amount (Gross Margin – Fixed Costs) that matters.

The 'small' farm categories relate only to full-time holdings and do not include very intensive holdings occupying very small areas.

The term 'fixed costs' is used here as it is in gross margin analysis and planning; a full explanation of the differences between fixed and variable costs in this context is given on pages 1 and 2. Note that all casual labour and contract work has been included under fixed costs. In calculating enterprise gross margins on the individual farm these costs are normally allocated as variable costs if they are specific to a particular enterprise and vary approximately in proportion to its size, i.e. are approximately constant per hectare of a particular crop or per head of livestock. Otherwise they are included as fixed costs. In both cases, however, they could be regarded as substitutes for regular labour and/or the farmer's own machinery - which are both items of fixed cost. It is therefore simpler if both are included, fully, as fixed costs. If one is comparing results from accounts set out on a gross margin basis, and some or all of the casual labour and contract work have been included as variable costs (especially on cropping farms, e.g. for potato harvesting using casual labour or a contractor's machine), the necessary adjustments need to be made in making the comparisons.

Notes on the Schedules

1. *Unpaid Labour:* Refers to the value of unpaid family manual labour, including that of the farmer and his wife.

2. *Machinery Depreciation:* This is based on current (i.e. replacement) cost. This gives a truer reflection of the real loss of value of machinery (as is apparent when replacement becomes necessary). It also allows easier comparison between different businesses.

However, many farm accounts calculate depreciation on the 'historic' (i.e. original) cost of the machinery. This will tend to produce a lower figure. Depending on the age of the machine, and bearing in mind recent strong increases in machinery prices, the historic method may underestimate depreciation by 10-20%. Note that both the Depreciation item and Repairs include vehicles.

3. *Leasing Charges:* The capital element, but not the interest, is included in depreciation; the proportion paid as interest varies according to the rate of interest paid and the length of the leasing period, but is typically 7 to 10 per cent.

4. *Machinery Running Costs:* This includes fuel, oil, repairs, servicing and vehicle tax and insurance. Separate figures for these elements are no longer available. As a general rule, fuel might make up a little over half of all such costs.

5. *General Overheads:* include general farm maintenance and repairs, office expenses, water, insurance, fees, subscriptions, etc.

6. *Rent & Interest:* Rent now only relates to the actual rent paid by the average farm in that particular category. It is no longer an imputed rent for all land farmed by the business; thus, a fully owned-occupied farm will have no rental costs. Interest used to be excluded but now actual interest paid by the average farm in that particular category is shown.

In making comparisons with fixed costs taken from farm accounts it is important to note that in the figures below unpaid manual labour is included; farm accounts will rarely include unpaid labour. Also the figures below include average rent and interest; in farm accounts these will vary widely depending on the farm tenure and borrowing. Very low 'target' figures given in press articles often omit these items and can therefore be misleading; usually, too, they relate only to large, very well appointed farms. If an 'opportunity cost' for owner-occupied land (often fully paid for many years ago) is included, then the cost level rises further. Note too that the figures given below do not include management, whether paid or unpaid. The margin after deducting the fixed costs below from the total gross margin plus any other farm receipts represents the total return to management and own capital in the business.

Labour, machinery and buildings are the main items of 'fixed' costs subject to change with major alterations in farm policy. Each has a separate section in this book.

Mainly Dairying

	Under 75 ha (Under 185 acres)		75 - 125 ha (185 - 310 acres)		Over 125 ha (Over 310 acres)	
Regular Labour (paid)	75	(30)	110	(45)	210	(85)
Regular Labour (unpaid)	650	(263)	430	(174)	235	(95)
Casual Labour	25	(10)	25	(10)	30	(12)
Total Labour	**750**	**(304)**	**565**	**(229)**	**475**	**(192)**
Machinery Depreciation	125	(51)	125	(51)	125	(51)
Machinery Running Costs	140	(57)	140	(57)	145	(59)
Contract	95	(38)	110	(45)	115	(47)
Total Power & Machinery...	**360**	**(146)**	**375**	**(152)**	**385**	**(156)**
Farm Maintenance	30	(12)	35	(14)	50	(20)
Water & Electricity	140	(57)	130	(53)	120	(49)
General Overhead Expenses ..	85	(34)	80	(32)	65	(26)
Total Overheads	**255**	**(103)**	**245**	**(99)**	**235**	**(95)**
Rent & Interest	145	(59)	145	(59)	165	(67)
Total Fixed Costs	**1510**	**(611)**	**1330**	**(538)**	**1260**	**(510)**

Mainly Cereals

	Under 175 ha (Under 430 acres)		175 - 300 ha (430 - 740 acres)		Over 300 ha (Over 740 acres)	
Regular Labour (paid)	50	(20)	60	(24)	100	(40)
Regular Labour (unpaid)	250	(101)	180	(73)	110	(45)
Casual Labour	15	(6)	10	(4)	15	(6)
Total Labour	**315**	**(127)**	**250**	**(101)**	**225**	**(91)**
Machinery Depreciation	95	(38)	100	(40)	105	(42)
Machinery Running Costs	90	(36)	105	(42)	90	(36)
Contract	70	(28)	65	(26)	45	(18)
Total Power & Machinery...	**255**	**(103)**	**270**	**(109)**	**240**	**(97)**
Farm Maintenance	20	(8)	25	(10)	30	(12)
Water & Electricity	65	(26)	60	(24)	55	(22)
General Overhead Expenses ..	65	(26)	60	(24)	55	(22)
Total Overheads	**150**	**(61)**	**145**	**(59)**	**140**	**(57)**
Rent & Interest	85	(34)	90	(36)	95	(38)
Total Fixed Costs	**805**	**(326)**	**755**	**(306)**	**700**	**(283)**

Large-Scale Cereal Farms (over 500 ha (1,250 acres))

Data from the Farm Business Survey indicates there are further economies of scale for cereals farms at even larger farm sizes. There are likely to be wide variations depending on the precise scale of these businesses (some of which are very large). The following figures may be used as a guide; Labour - £140 per ha (of which paid labour £100); Power & Machinery - £220 per ha; Other Overheads - £120 per ha; Rent & Interest - £95 per ha. This totals £575 per ha (£233 per acre).

Data for larger-scale General Cropping farms (see below) is not so conclusive. Costs on a 'per ha' basis do not necessarily seem to fall as farm size increases. This may be due to the larger proportion of (higher cost) root crops and vegetables seen on larger farm sizes. The 2007/08 medium sized sample appears also to have more intensive cropping.

General Cropping

	Under 150 ha (Under 370 acres)		150 - 225 ha (370 - 560 acres)		Over 225 ha (Over 560 acres)	
Regular Labour (paid)	65	(26)	100	(40)	130	(53)
Regular Labour (unpaid)	330	(134)	220	(89)	150	(61)
Casual Labour	25	(10)	30	(12)	50	(20)
Total Labour	**420**	**(170)**	**350**	**(142)**	**330**	**(134)**
Machinery Depreciation	115	(47)	115	(47)	125	(51)
Machinery Running Costs	130	(53)	135	(55)	140	(57)
Contract	85	(34)	95	(38)	85	(34)
Total Power & Machinery...	**330**	**(134)**	**345**	**(140)**	**350**	**(142)**
Farm Maintenance	20	(8)	25	(10)	30	(12)
Water & Electricity	85	(34)	75	(30)	80	(32)
General Overhead Expenses ..	50	(20)	80	(32)	60	(24)
Total Overheads	**155**	**(63)**	**180**	**(73)**	**170**	**(69)**
Rent & Interest	120	(49)	135	(55)	130	(53)
Total Fixed Costs	**1025**	**(415)**	**1010**	**(409)**	**980**	**(397)**

With potatoes and/or sugar beet and/or field vegetables; grade 1 or 2 land.

Mainly Sheep/Cattle (lowland)

	Under 90 ha (Under 220 acres)		90 - 125 ha (220 - 310 acres)		Over 125 ha (Over 310 acres)	
Regular Labour (paid)	30	(12)	45	(18)	45	(18)
Regular Labour (unpaid)	420	(170)	270	(109)	250	(101)
Casual Labour	10	(4)	10	(4)	15	(6)
Total Labour	**460**	**(186)**	**325**	**(132)**	**310**	**(125)**
Machinery Depreciation	70	(28)	70	(28)	75	(30)
Machinery Running Costs	75	(30)	80	(32)	75	(30)
Contract	45	(18)	40	(16)	45	(18)
Total Power & Machinery...	**190**	**(77)**	**190**	**(77)**	**195**	**(79)**
Farm Maintenance	20	(8)	15	(6)	20	(8)
Water & Electricity	65	(26)	55	(22)	50	(20)
General Overhead Expenses ..	45	(18)	40	(16)	30	(12)
Total Overheads	**130**	**(53)**	**110**	**(45)**	**100**	**(40)**
Rent & Interest	65	(26)	75	(30)	90	(36)
Total Fixed Costs	**845**	**(342)**	**700**	**(283)**	**695**	**(281)**

	Mainly Sheep/Cattle (upland)					
	Under 130 ha (Under 320 acres)		130 - 230 ha (320 - 570 acres)		Over 230 ha (Over 570 acres)	
Regular Labour (paid)	25	(10)	25	(10)	40	(16)
Regular Labour (unpaid)	325	(132)	220	(89)	170	(69)
Casual Labour	5	(2)	5	(2)	10	(4)
Total Labour	**355**	**(144)**	**250**	**(101)**	**220**	**(89)**
Machinery Depreciation	55	(22)	45	(18)	45	(18)
Machinery Running Costs	55	(22)	50	(20)	55	(22)
Contract	25	(10)	20	(8)	15	(6)
Total Power & Machinery...	**135**	**(55)**	**115**	**(47)**	**115**	**(47)**
Farm Maintenance	10	(4)	15	(6)	15	(6)
Water & Electricity	35	(14)	30	(12)	30	(12)
General Overhead Expenses ..	20	(8)	20	(8)	20	(8)
Total Overheads	**65**	**(26)**	**65**	**(26)**	**65**	**(26)**
Rent & Interest	45	(18)	45	(18)	60	(24)
Total Fixed Costs	**600**	**(243)**	**475**	**(192)**	**460**	**(186)**

Other Farm Types

The other main DEFRA farm types are *'Mixed'*, *Pigs*, *Poultry and Horticulture*. As the name suggests, the Mixed category includes all farms where one enterprise is not sufficiently dominant for it to be allocated to one of the categories above. As it includes many different mixes of enterprises, the figures are unlikely to be useful for budgeting purposes.

Due to the intensity and variability of the Pig, Poultry and Horticultural farm types, the presentation of average 'per ha' figures would not be useful. Detailed historic FBS data for the different pig, poultry, and horticulture systems found in England are published on line at the addresses given on page 4. For pigs, Askham Bryan: for poultry and horticulture, Reading, or go to www.farmbusinesssurvey.co.uk.

2.   RENTS

One of the main factors affecting the rental level of agricultural land is the type of tenancy it is let on. There are three main types of agricultural tenancy in England and Wales: Full or Agricultural Holdings Act (AHA) 1986, Farm Business Tenancies (FBTs, under the 1995 Act) and Seasonal Lets of less than 1 year. Since the introduction of the 1995 Act no new AHA tenancies can be created.

The influence of the Single Payment Scheme provisions which started in 2005 also needs to be taken into account when comparing rent levels. The situation will vary from farm to farm and differ between the different regions of the countries of the UK. The tenant is the only person who can claim the Single Payment (SP), except in some seasonal agreements where the landlord may be able to claim. In an AHA tenancy agreement the rental is struck independently of the Single Payment in that the tenant will have been awarded the Single Payment entitlements in 2005 and at the end of the tenancy the ownership remains with the tenant or his/her successors. With FBTs the assumption is that the tenant is claiming a 'full' SP, and if land becomes available without SP entitlements then rental levels will be lower than those shown below.

Unless otherwise stated the figures in this section relate to farms let with a combination of crops, grass and rough grazing in England; they include housing and buildings, as available.

Agricultural Holdings Act Tenancies:

It should be borne in mind that rough grazing may be included in the figures given in the table below and the figures relate to the 2008/09 (Feb-Feb) year mainly covering 2008. Some farms are likely to be let at below competitive rates, for various reasons. Rents for land had been tending to fall up to 2007 but this was offset by higher rents for housing and buildings so that overall per hectare rents were stable. The surge in many commodity prices in 2007 and 2008 has now affected rental levels. Where rentals were reviewed in 2007 increases of up to 20% were sometimes obtained. By mid 2008 with rapid input cost increases (especially fuel, fertiliser and feed) much lower settlements were made, usually in the range of 5-10%. In 2009 with continued pressure on arable and dairy profitability AHA rents drifted lower.

The average rent for lowland, excluding woodland and rough grazing for farms under full Agricultural Tenancies is likely to be approximately £173 per ha, £70 per acre, in 2010. The levels on large mixed arable farms (i.e. including potatoes, sugar beet and/or vegetables) on very good soil, or well-equipped dairy farms, will tend to average £185 to £245 per hectare, £75 to £100 per acre. Rents on moderate, below average, quality farms, particularly with full repairing and insuring leases are likely to average £125 to £140 per hectare, £50 to £55 per acre.

Farm Business Tenancies:

On average FBT rents will remain higher than those above for AHA tenancies. Although, not always the case especially for lowland cattle and sheep land and dairy land. Farmers who already own land, with little or no mortgage, can afford to offer a higher figure than bidders with no other farms. For cereals land of reasonable quality recent offers have tended to follow the price of a tonne of wheat per acre, but offers of over £400 per hectare (£160 per acre) have been reported for 3-5 year agreements. However typically FBT rentals for arable land are much lower and a 2010 opinion based survey from RICS reported below, gives the average for England and Wales for arable FBT rents at £249 per hectare, £101 per acre.

Farm Business Survey 2008-2009:

The figures are rounded to the nearest 50p/ha or 25p/acre.

Average Rent by Type of Agreement:	£/ha (acre)
Full Agricultural Tenancies	136 (55.00)
Farm Business Tenancies for 1 year and over	160 (64.75)
Seasonal Lets of less than one year	107 (43.50)

Average Rent by Farm Type: (£ per ha [acre])	Full Agricultural Tenancies	Farm Business Tenancies*
Cereal	138 (55.75)	158 (64.00)
General Cropping	164 (66.25)	222 (89.75)
Dairy	167 (67.50)	152 (61.50)
Cattle and Sheep (Lowland)	123 (49.75)	96 (38.75)
Cattle and Sheep (LFA)	54 (21.75)	65 (26.25)
All	136.00 (55.00)	160 (64.75)

*for a year and over

Source of Data

DEFRA (Farming Statistics): Farm rents 2008 – England. In the past DEFRA rental statistics were collected via the Tenanted Land Survey (TLS) and these were reported on in previous editions of the Farm Management Pocketbook. Following a review in early 2009 DEFRA decided that the Farm Business Survey (FBS) data should be the main source and the Tenanted Land Survey (TLS) should be discontinued. The FBS is an annual survey conducted by trained Interviewers. The FBS collects data at business level and collects data for up to 15 agreements per business, with a sample of around 1,900 farm businesses. The next publication is due in January 2011 for the 2009-10 survey.

RICS Rural Land Market Survey :

Published in July 2010 the following were average rents for England and Wales for the first half of 2010 but should be treated with caution as they are opinion based, and reflect recently struck rental levels.

Average Rent	Full Agricultural Tenancy £ per Ha (acre)	Farm Business Tenancy £ per Ha (acre)
Arable	157 (64)	249 (101)
Pasture	128 (52)	180 (73)

3.   LAND PRICES

SALE VALUE OF FARMLAND, ENGLAND AND WALES

Auction Sales (with Vacant Possession only) :
Oxford Institute/Savills(1) series, 1937-2000

Year	Current Prices		Real Values(2)		Index (3)	Year	Current Prices		Real Values(2)		Index (3)
1937-9	0	(24)	2030	(822)	33	1982	4557	(1844)	8373	(3389)	136
1945	111	(45)	2246	(909)	37	1983	5145	(2082)	9041	(3659)	147
1955	198	(80)	3274	(1325)	53	1984	4888	(1978)	8180	(3310)	133
1960	198	(80)	2643	(1070)	43	1985	4781	(1935)	7542	(3052)	123
1965	304	(123)	3608	(1460)	59	1986	4193	(1697)	6398	(2589)	104
1970	581	(235)	5857	(2370)	95	1987	4944	(2001)	7242	(2931)	118
1971	605	(245)	4872	(1972)	79	1988	6716	(2718)	9376	(3794)	153
1971	647	(262)	4761	(1927)	77	1989	6558	(2654)	8493	(3437)	138
1972	1473	(596)	9603	(3886)	156	1990	6346	(2568)	7505	(3037)	122
1973	1871	(757)	11793	(4773)	192	1991	6007	(2431)	6708	(2715)	109
1974	1572	(636)	8529	(3452)	139	1992	5441	(2202)	5859	(2371)	95
1975	1332	(539)	5817	(2354)	95	1993	5456	(2208)	5783	(2340)	94
1976	1814	(734)	6798	(2751)	111	1994	5028	(2035)	5204	(2106)	85
1977	2449	(991)	7922	(3206)	129	1995	6140	(2484)	6140	(2485)	100
1988	3279	(1327)	9794	(3964)	160	1996	8797	(3560)	8591	(3477)	140
1979	4371	(1769)	11513	(4659)	188	1997	8065	(3263)	7636	(3090)	124
1980	4265	(1726)	9521	(3853)	155	1998	7250	(2934)	6637	(2686)	108
1981	4272	(1729)	8525	(3450)	139	1999	13920	(5634)	12565	(5085)	205
						2000	7895	(3196)	7125	(2885)	116

(1) Savills after 1988. (2) At 1995 general price levels. (3) Real Values, 1995 = 100.

From 1970, figures were based on sales reports in the Estates Gazette and the Farmers Weekly, plus some unpublished sales, with a minimum size of 10 hectares. This series was discontinued after 2000.

Current Agricultural Land Prices

A CALP/RICS Farmland Price Index (England and Wales) began in 1995. It covers sales of vacant possession land in England and Wales, excluding residential value where more than 50% of total sale price; value of milk quota excluded. It is calculated by dividing total value of sales by total area sold. Figures for the most recent quarters are subject to revision as further information becomes available.

In 2006 twice as much land was sold as in 2005 and that year saw an increase of 30% compared to 2004. The higher area sold in 2006 did not see lower prices reflecting a strong market. Since then there has been a similar level of sales. Strong commodity prices during 2007 and up to mid 2008 meant that farmland prices were the last to react to the downturn in the economic climate. 'Lifestyle' purchasers were replaced by farmers keeping the demand for and the price of land high. But with the increase in farm inputs and the fall in commodity prices farmland prices fell in the first half of 2009. Although tight supplies and rising demand saw prices rebound in the second half. Prices fell again in the first half of 2010, although this is more due to the residential component in the transaction reflecting the slowdown in the wider housing market, rather than actual farmland prices. The RICS opinion based measure, which just considers bare land prices actually increased by 6%.

An increase in price is expected to continue through 2010 and 2011 especially in the commercial farmland secor.

CALP/RICS Farmland Price Index 1995-2010 – Transaction based.

		Number of Sales	Area sold '000		Weighted Average Price £		Index 1995
			Ha	(acres)	Ha	(acres)	=100
1995	Q1	73	3.9	(9.6)	5,187	(2,099)	100
1998	Q1	113	5.2	(12.8)	7,364	(3,033)	145
	Q2	133	5.5	(13.6)	7,545	(3,053)	146
	Q3	164	7.1	(17.5)	6,411	(2,594)	124
	Q4	149	7.9	(19.5)	6,812	(2,757)	131
1999	Q1	84	3.6	(8.9)	6,376	(2,580)	123
	Q2	138	4.5	(11.1)	7,337	(2,969)	141
	Q3	152	9.0	(22.2)	7,186	(2,908)	139
	Q4	15	6.9	(17.0)	7,204	(2,915)	139
2000	Q1	90	3.9	(9.6)	7,660	(3,100)	148
	Q2	120	4.9	(12.1)	7,211	(2,918)	139
	Q3	134	7.2	(17.8)	7,082	(2,866)	137
	Q4	128	5.9	(14.6)	6,461	(2,615)	125
2001	Q1	73	4.5	(11.1)	7,273	(2,943)	140
	Q2	70	4.3	(10.6)	7,967	(3,224)	154
	Q3	137	7.5	(18.5)	7,169	(2,901)	138
	Q4	130	5.8	(14.3)	7,327	(2,965)	141
2002	Q1	71	3.0	(7.4)	7,906	(3,200)	152
	Q2	87	3.4	(8.4)	7,579	(3,067)	146
	Q3	135	6.6	(16.3)	7,694	(3,114)	148
	Q4	154	6.0	(14.8)	6,390	(2,586)	123
2003	Q1	69	2.5	(6.2)	7,817	(3,163)	151
	Q2	80	3.4	(8.4)	7,910	(3,201)	152
	Q3	67	3.3	(8.2)	7,629	(3,087)	147
	Q4	85	4.1	(10.1)	8,367	(3,386)	161
2004	Q1	46	1.8	(4.4)	9,526	(3,855)	184
	Q2	75	2.8	(6.9)	9,255	(3,745)	178
	Q3	53	2.1	(5.2)	10,670	(4,318)	206
	Q4	89	2.6	(6.4)	9,828	(3,977)	189
2005	H1	141	6.0	(14.8)	8,967	(3,629)	173
	H2	164	8.7	(21.5)	9,647	(3,904)	186
2006	H1	173	9.4	(23.2)	9,408	(3,807)	181
	H2	234	15.0	(37.1)	10,376	(4,199)	200
2007	H1	141	7.0	(17.3)	11,153	(4,513)	215
	H2	230	10.8	(26.7)	14,138	(5,721)	273
2008	H1	233	8.9	(21.9)	15,824	(6,404)	305
	H2	278	11.7	(28.9)	16,342	(6,713)	315
2009	H1	181	6.3	(13.8)	15,199	(6,151)	293
	H2	256	11.4	(28.2)	16,126	(6,526)	311
2010	H1	293	5.5	(14.0)	15,177	(6,142)	293

Other Land Price Series

In past editions of the Pocketbook, Inland Revenue and Valuation Office (VO) land price returns have been published, covering 30 years up to 1996/97 and 1993-2004 respectively. These series contained detailed splits between vacant possession and tenanted land, farms (including houses and buildings) and bare land, and also by size, land class and region. This information is still available from past editions of the Pocketbook (available at the same contact details). Data in the VO series does not continue beyond 2004, although limited information is available on the website, www.voa.gov.uk

Much of the data included in this section is available in **Farmland Market**, a Farmers Weekly publication in association with RICS, and includes other land and rental statistics, articles and opinion.

SALE VALUE OF FORESTS AND WOODLANDS

Forests

The figures in this section relate to planted land sold (over 25 hectares) so that values include the value of the property (land) and the timber. Timber prices have continued to fall over the last year along with most world commodities but forest property values have held their own, only declining slightly. Moreover an increase in the demand for wood is expected with potential for improvement into 2011. Investors still see land and trees as a safe haven during the difficult economic climate.

The number of transactions increased significantly to the year September 2009 with the area sold almost double the area sold in 2008 at 14,600ha. The total market value for 2009 was almost double the 2008 market at £48.2m

Average forest prices were down 8% in the year to September 2009 compared to 2008 to £3,300 per Ha. The figures below are for the UK and are predominantly upland with at least 50% coniferous content. Values vary with many factors and only size of block and age are recorded here, but yield class is also important..

Value of Forestland:

By Size Range (approx.)	2008	2009
	£/ha (£/acre)	£/ha (£/acre)
Below 51 hectares............................	5,700 (2,307)	6,000 (2,428)
51 to 100 hectares............................	3,100 (1,254)	3,600 (1,457)
101 to 200 hectares..........................	3,300 (1,335)	3,500 (1,416)
Above 200 hectares	3,600 (1,457)	2,900 (1,174)

By Age Band	2008	2009
	£/ha (£/acre)	£/ha (£/acre)
Young (1 to 10 years)	2,050 (830)	1,850 (749)
Mid-rotation (11 to 20 years).........	2,650 (1,072)	3,450 (1,396)
Semi-mature (21 to 30 years).........	3,350 (1,356)	2,750 (1,113)
Mature (over 30 years)...................	4,550 (1,841)	3,150 (1,275)
Mature (over 40 years)...................	5,150 (2,084)	4,950 (2,003)

Woodlands

Small woodland values continued to increase, attributable to the general rise in land values and keen demand for amenity, sporting and development hope value. Values are at their highest adjacent to centres of population and for properties of high amenity value. Sales in the South of England are often recorded in the £8-12,000/ha range, whereas £2-5,000/ha is more typical for more remote properties, or where amenity values are lower. Woodlands are sometimes being split and marketed in very small blocks and have often been sold in the £8-12,000 per ha range throughout the UK.

Source: UPM Tilhill and Savills, Forest Market Report (2009)

4. BUILDINGS

BUILDING COSTS

Building costs are notoriously variable. Many factors influence a contractor's price, including distance from his yard, size of contract, site access, site conditions, complexity of work, familiarity with the type of work and his current work load. There will also be differences in efficiency and standard of work between contractors and, as is often the case with farm buildings, the absence of detailed specification by the client may mean different contractors will not have quoted for identical buildings. The number of extras that are found to be required after a contract has been agreed will also vary.

The costs given below are an approximate guide. They refer to new buildings, erected by contractor on a clear level site and exclude VAT and grants that may be available. The costs were provided by SAC Buildings Design Services, Aberdeen, in mid 2010. More detailed information is available in the following publications. The books and journals giving general building cost information generally assume knowledge of how to take off quantities for building work.

Specialised Information on Farm Buildings

- Farm Building Cost Guide. Published by SAC Building Design Services, Aberdeen.

- Standard Costs. Published by the Scottish Government. Used when claiming government grants on a standard-cost basis. It can be found at www.scotland.gov.uk/Resource/Doc/158202/0042819.pdf

- The Farm Buildings Handbook. Published by the Rural and Industrial Design and Building Association, Stowmarket.

General Building Cost Information

Books are produced by a number of publishers with annual or more frequent new editions and updates. Examples are Laxton's Building Price Book, Spon's Architects' and Builders' Price Book, and Wessex Comprehensive Building Price Book. Regularly updated cost information is also given in several professional and trade journals.

Constituent Parts

Frame, Roof and Foundations   *per m² floor area*

1. Open-sided timber framed pole barn with round pole uprights on concrete bases, sawn timber rafters and purlins, high-tensile galvanised steel cladding to roof and gable ends above eaves, hardcore floor, eaves height 4.8 m, 9 m span, no side cladding, rainwater drainage to soakaways.   £70

2. Open-sided steel portal-framed building with fibre-cement or plastic coated steel cladding to roof and gables above eaves, hardcore floor, eaves height 4.8 m, no side cladding, rainwater drainage to soakaways.

9 m span	£120
13.2 m span	£105
18 m span	£100

3. Cost breakdown of 2 above;
    Materials: portal frame and purlins   26%

	foundations	3%
	roofing	16%
	rainwater and drainage	3%
	hardcore and blinding	2%
	Total Materials	**50%**
Erection:	portal frame and purlins	19%
	foundations	2%
	roofing	19%
	rainwater and drainage	5%
	hardcore and blinding	5%
	Total Erection	**50%**

Roof cladding   *per m²*

1. Natural grey fibre-cement, 146 mm corrugations fixed with drive screws

Materials	£14.00	
Fixing	£12.50	
Total		£26.50

2. Extra for coloured sheet   £2.50

3. Deduct for translucent sheets   £0.50

4. Deduct for PVC-coated steel   £3.00

5. Deduct for high-tensile corrugated galvanised steel sheeting   £4.00

                                                                                             per m run

6. PVC 150 mm half-round gutter on fascia brackets, including stop-ends and outlets   £25.00

7. PVC 100 mm rainwater pipe with fixings, swan-neck and shoe   £44.00

8. Fibre-cement close-fitting ridge   £37.00

9. Fibre-cement ventilating ridge   £42.50

Walls and Cladding   *per m²*

1. Concrete blockwork, fair faced and pointed both sides

150 mm thick	£45.00
215 mm thick	£65.00
215 mm thick hollow blocks	£66.00
215 mm thick hollow blocks, filled and reinforced	£82.50

2. Extra for rendering or roughcast to blockwork on one side   £22.50

3. Vertical spaced boarding 21x 145 mm with 19 mm gaps including horizontal rails, all pressure treated   £26.00

4. Fibre-cement vertical cladding, including rails   £40.00

5. Corrugated high-tensile steel side cladding, including rails   £33.50

6. Wall element: 215 mm thick blockwork, including strip foundation (base 750 mm below ground level), 2.5 m height above ground level   £164 per m run

Floors   *per m²*

1. Concrete floor 100 mm thick, Gen 3 mix, on 150 mm hardcore,
   including excavation: £32.55

   Breakdown:
   (a) excavate, level and compact   £2.95
   (b) hardcore   £4.65
   (c) blinding   £2.20
   (d) damp-proofmembrane   £2.00
   (e) premixed concrete spread and compacted   £17.00
   (f) float finish   £3.75

2. Extra to above for
   (a) 150 mm instead of 100 mm   £5.35
   (b) laying concrete to falls   £1.55
   (c) broom or textured finish   £1.90
   (d) Carborundum dust non-slip finish   £3.25
   (e) insulating concrete   £10.00

3. Reinforced concrete slatted floors for cattle
   (a) cattle loading   £72.00
   (b) tractor loading   £79.00

4. Reinforced concrete slats for pigs   £52.00

5. Insulating floor, including excavation and base
   (a) 27 mm expanded polystyrene, 38 mm screed   £46.50
   (b) insulating concrete with lightweight aggregate   £38.00
   (c) as (b) with 20 mm screed   £47.00

6. Form channel in concrete   £4.50 per m run

7. Excavate for cast 1 m3 in-situ concrete bases for stanchions   £125.00 each

Services and Fittings   *per m²*

1. Drainage: 100 mm PVC pipe laid in trench, including 750 mm
   deep excavation and backfil   £25.50 per m run
   Breakdown:
   (a) excavate and backfill   £16.00
   (b) 100 mm PVC pipe laid   £9.50
   Extras:
   (c) add to (a) for 1 m deep   £3.50
   (d) add to (b) for 150 mm pipe   £6.50

2. Excavate soakaway and fill with stones   £105 each

3. Trap and grid top, 100 mm PVC   £25 each

4. Yard gully with heavy duty road grating 400 x 300 mm £190 each

5. Inspection chamber 900 mm deep, 450 x 600 mm opening and   £375 each
   medium duty cast iron cover

6. Above-ground vitreous enamel slurry tank on concrete base, £50,000 each
   1000 m³

7. Reception pit, 20 m³   £4,750 each

8. Slurry channel beneath (not including) slats, 1.8 m deep,
   3m wide   £435 per m run

9.	Lighting: 1.5 m 60W single fluorescent unit, including wiring and switch	£130 each
	Extras:	
	(a) PVC conduit	£6.00
	(b) screwed steel conduit	£11.00
10.	Power: 13A switched outlet	£22.50 each
11.	Diagonal feed fence, fixed, including posts (painted)	£120 per m run
12.	Tombstone feed fence, fixed, including posts (painted)	£125 per m run
13.	Feed bunker	£70 per m run
14.	Hay rack, wall fixing	£80 per m run
15.	Cubicle division, galvanised, fixed in place	£100 each
16.	Fencing: three-rail timber with posts, all pressure treated	£27.50 per m run
17.	Gate, 3 m wide, galvanised steel, including posts set in concrete	
	(a) medium duty	£230 each
	(b) heavy duty	£300 each
	Deduct for painted instead of galvanised finish	£30

Complete Buildings

Fully Covered and Enclosed Barn

Portal frame, 18 m span, 6 m bays, 6 m to eaves, 3 m high blockwork walls with sheet cladding above, 6 m sliding doors at either end, 150mm thick concrete floor	£175 per m² floor area

Cows and Cattle Housing

1.	Covered strawed yard, enclosed with ventilated cladding, concrete floor, pens only, with 4.0 m² per head floor area	£700 per head
2.	Extra to 1 for 4.0 m wide double-sided feeding passage, barrier and troughs	£285 per head
3.	Kennel building	£425 per head
4.	Portal framed building with cubicles	£1,400 per head
5.	Extra to 4 for feed stance, feeding passage, barriers and troughs	£585 per head
6.	Extra to 4 for slatting of cubicle passages	£600 per head
7.	Covered collecting yard, 1.1 m² per cow	£210 per head
8.	Milking parlour building, example: 5.5 x 11.5 m for 8/16 parlour	£17,500
9.	Parlour equipment, herringbone parlours:	
	(a) low level, 1 stall per point	£3,600 per point
	(b) pipeline	£3,250 per point
	(c) extra for meter and auto cluster removal	£2,000 per point
	(d) auto feed dispenser	£830 per point
10.	Dairy building	£310 per m² floor area
11.	Bulk tank and washer	£8.00 per litre
12.	Loose box, 16 m² floor area laid to falls, rendered walls	£300 per m² floor area
13.	Bull pen and open run	£12,000

14.	Cattle crush and 20 m race	£5,750
15.	Slatted floor cattle building for 120 growing cattle (1.7 m² pen space per head) with drive-through feed passage/troughs	£1,400 per head

Silage   *per tonne stored*

1.	Timber panel clamp on concrete base with effluent tank	£70
2.	Precast concrete panel clamp with effluent tank	£95
3.	Glass-lined forage tower and unloader	£225

Waste Storage   *per m³ stored*

1.	Lined lagoon with safety fence	£39.00
2.	Glass-lined steel slurry silo	
	small (400 m³)	£54.00
	medium (1,200 m³)	£48.50
	large (3,600 m³)	£44.00
3.	GRP below-ground effluent tank, encased in concrete	
	small (12 m³)	£460
	large (36 m³)	£400

Sheep Housing

1.	Penning, troughs, feed barriers and drinkers installed in suitable existing building	£33.50 per ewe
2.	Purpose-built sheep shed with 1.35 m² pen space per ewe concentrate troughs, feed passage and barrier for forage feeding	£210 per ewe
	Extras:	
	(a) softwood slatted floor panels, materials only	£8.00 per m²
	(b) slatted panels as (a), made up, plus supports	£28.50 per m²

Pig Housing   *per sow and litter*

1.	Farrowing and rearing	
	(a) Prefabricated farrowing pens with crates, side creep areas, part-slatted floors, including foundations, electrical and plumbing work	£3,250
	(b) Steel-framed farrowing house with insulated blockwork walls, part-slatted pens with side creeps in rooms of eight with off main passage	£3,600
	(c) Flat-deck rearing house 3-6 weeks with fully perforated floors to pens, 0.25 m² per pig pen area	£140 per weaner
	(d) Prefabricated verandah house including foundations, electrical and plumbing work, 0.3m² per pig internal lying area	£110 per weaner

2. Finishing   *per baconer*

    (a) Prefabricated fattening house with part-slatted floors, trough feeding   £240

    (b) Prefabricated fattening house with part-slatted floors, floor fed   £225

    (c) Steel framed building with insulated blockwork walls, part-slatted floors, trough fed   £100

    (d) Automatic feeding systems for items (a), (b) and (c) above:

        dry-feed system with ad-lib hoppers   £625

        dry on-floor feeding   £14.50

        wet feeding   £20

3. Dry sows and boars   *per sow*

    (a) Yards with floor feeding   £340

    (b) Sow cubicle system   £565

    (c) Yards with electronic feeders   £950

    (d) Yards with individual feeders   £1,050

    (e) Two-yard system with flat-rate feeding   £1,200

    (f) Boar pens as part of sow house   £2,500 each

4. Complete pig unit

Building costs calculated on basis of three-week weaning, 23 pigs per sow per year to bacon, excl. external slurry or dung storage, feed storage and handling/weighing facilities:

    (a) Breeding and rearing only   £1,900 per sow

    (b) Breeding with progeny to bacon   £3,400 per sow

Poultry Housing and Equipment   *per bird*

1. Intensive enriched cages with automatic feeding and egg collection; (new traditional cages were banned from 1st January 2003;only enriched cages complete with nest box, perches and scratching area are now allowed)   £21.00-£25.00

2. Perchery/barn   £20.00-£24.00

3. Free Range: new sites stocked at 9 birds per m²,   £24.50-£32.00

    existing sites stocked at 11.7 birds per m²   £20.00-£26.00

    smaller mobile units will cost   £29.00 plus

4. Broiler Breeders, deep litter, 0.167 m² per bird   £26.00

5. Pullets (cage and floor reared)   £14.00

6. Broilers, deep litter, 0.05 m² per bird   £8.00-£9.00

7. Turkeys, 20,000 pole barn fattening unit (cost varies with size of unit and degree of automation)   £19.00-£25.50

Grain Storage and Drying   *per tonne stored*

1. Intake pit, conveyor, elevator, overhead conveyor and catwalk, storage bins within existing building   £200

    extra for low volume ventilation of bins   £80

2.	As 1 in new building	£300
3.	Portable grain walling for on-floor storage in existing building	£50
4.	On floor grain storage in purpose-built building	£110
	Extras:	
	(a) low volume ventilation	£8.00-£9.00
	(b) on-floor drying with above-ground main duct and laterals	£120
	(c) add to (b) for below-ground laterals	£15.00
5.	Sealed towers for moist grain, including loading and unloading equipment	£145-£180

Potato Storage		*per tonne stored*
1.	Pallet-box store with recirculation fans	£215
	Pallet boxes, 1 tonne	£75
2.	Bulk store, building only	£200
	Ventilation system: fans, main duct, below-floor lateral ducts	£50

Roads and Fences	*per m length*
3.2 m wide hardcore road with drainage ditches using locally excavated material	£30.00
using imported hardcore (£6.15/m³)	£45.00
extra for bitumen macadam surfacing, two coats	£50.00
Traditional 7-wire stock fence	£7.00
High tensile 7-wire stock fence	£5.00

Construction Equipment Hire	*hourly rate, with driver*
Excavator	£25.00-£32.50
Tipping lorry	£35.00-£50.00
10-tonne crane	£40.00
	weekly rate
Concrete mixer, 100 litre (5/3)	£42
Compressor and heavy breaker	£125

STANDARD COSTS

Standard costs are published by the Scottish Government on the basis of the cost of farm or casual labour and new materials. They do not include an allowance for overheads and profit: in most cases building contractors would add 15-30% to cover them. Standard costs are therefore usually lower, sometimes by a larger percentage than this, particularly where the labour content of the item is high. The following examples are based on standard costs issued for 2002. Farm buildings costs generally will have risen by about 40% between that year and mid-2009. Crown copyright material is reproduced from 'Standard Costs' with permission of the Controller of HMSO and the Queen's Printer for Scotland.

per m² floor area

Open-sided framed building with cladding to roof and gable peaks only, hardcore floor, rainwater drainage to soakaways:

9 x 18 m	£35
13.2 x 24m	£32.50

per m² wall or roof

Corrugated cladding to roof or walls, including supports (purlins or rails):

fibre cement sheeting	£16.80
extra for coloured sheeting	£0.80
extra for PVC coated steel instead of fibre cement	£0.60
deduct for metallic coated (e.g. galvanised) steel	£4.90
Spaced boarding	£18.80
Wall element, concrete block-work 190-324 mm thick with strip foundation (base 750 mm below ground level) and 2.5 mm height above ground level	£92 per m run
Extra for rendering block-work on one side	£6.50 per m²
Concrete floor, 100 mm thick, including excavation, hardcore and waterproof membrane	£11.50 per m²
Concrete floor, 150 mm thick as above	£15.50 per m²
Reinforced concrete slats for cattle (supports not included)	£47.50 per m²
Yard gully with heavy grating	£251 each
Drainage pipes, 100 mm, jointed in UPVC, clay-ware or spun concrete including 900 mm trench and backfill	£10.70 per m run
Drainage pipes 150 mm as above	£19.00 per m run
Tank for water, effluent etc., 20 m³	£2,966 each
Gate, 3 m wide, steel, including posts concreted in: light duty	£106.40 each
cattle yard type	£141.90 each

per m² floor area

Fully covered enclosed building with concrete floor, and rainwater drainage to soakaways

10 x 18 m	£72.50
15 x 24 m	£54.60

STORAGE REQUIREMENTS

Bulk (cubic metres (feet) per tonne):

Beans		1.2	(43)
Wheat, peas		1.3	(46)
Barley, rye, oilseed rape, linseed, fodder beet		1.4	(50)
Oats		1.9	(68)
Potatoes		1.6	(57)
Dry bulb onions		2.0	(71)
Concentrates:	meal	2.0	(71)
	cubes	1.6	(57)
Grass silage:	18% DM	1.3	(46)
	30% DM	1.6	(57)
Maize silage		1.3	(46)
Silage: large round bales		2.5	(88)
Wheat straw ⎤		13.0	(464)
Barley straw ⎬ small bales		11.5	(411)
Hay ⎦		6.0	(214)
Wheat straw ⎤		20.0	(714)
Barley straw ⎬ large round bales		18.0	(643)
Hay ⎦		8.0	(286)
Brewers' grains		0.9	(32)

(With straw and hay the storage requirement clearly depends on the packing density; the above are simply typical averages).

Boxes (floor area in square metres (feet) per tonne):

Potatoes:	0.5 tonne boxes, 5 boxes high	0.52	(5.6)
	1.0 tonne boxes, 4 boxes high	0.52	(5.6)
	1.0 tonne boxes, 5 boxes high	0.45	(4.8)

Bags (floor area in square metres (feet) per tonne):

Feedstuffs:	2 bags high	1.6	(17)
Fertiliser:	6 bags high	1.1	(12)
	10 bags high	0.7	(8)

VII.   TAXATION

Note: no responsibility can be taken for any errors or omissions in the information presented in this section or for any action taken on the basis of the information provided. Professional advice should always be sought before taking any decision that may affect your tax position.

1.   INCOME TAX

RATES OF INCOME TAX (2010-11)

	Income Band	Dividends	Interest	Other Income
Starting rate	Up to £2,440*	10	10	20
Basic rate	£2,441 to £37,400	10	20	20
Higher rate	£37,401-150,000	32.5	40	40
Additional rate	over £150,000	42.5	50	50

*   For 2010-11 the lower rate of 10% still applies to other savings income (primarily bank and building society interest) up to a limit of £2,440. This 10% rate is not available if taxable non-savings income exceeds £2,440.

ALLOWANCES AND RELIEFS (2010-11)

Personal Allowance

This is £6,475 (£9,490 if aged 65 to 74 and £9,640 if aged over 75 on 5th April 2011, subject to total income not exceeding the statutory income limit (£22,900 for 2010-11)).

The basic personal allowance for income tax will be gradually reduced to nil for individuals with adjusted net incomes in excess of £100,000. The reduction is £1 for every £2 over the limit.

Married Couples Allowance

This was abolished from the tax year ended 6th April 2001 except for couples where at least one spouse was born before 6th April 1935. From 2005-06 the allowance is available to couples in a civil partnership where at least one partner was born before 6th April 1935. The relief is given as a reduction in income tax restricted to the lower of 10% of the allowance (£2,670 for 2009-10) or the total tax liability.

Personal Pension Schemes

Tax relief is obtainable for contributions to a pension. The rules on maximum contributions have been simplified; there is an annual allowance of £255,000 for 2010-11 (£245,000 for 2009-10) and a lifetime allowance of £1,800,000 in 2010-11 (£1,750,000 in 2009-10). Maximum contributions under the simplified Stakeholder Pension rules are £3,600 per year. The 2009 Budget announced anti-forestalling legislation which will impact on any individuals with total income exceeding £150,000 who increase their normal pension contributions after 22nd April 2009. The 2009 December Pre-Budget report reduced the income level to £130,000 with effect from 9th December 2009. Any high income individuals who are looking to change their pension contributions should seek professional advice.

2.   PRIVATE COMPANY TAXATION

RATES OF CORPORATION TAX (2010-11)

The rates set out in the table below apply to profits made in any financial year (FY) ending 1st April to 31st March. FY11 therefore covers 1st April 2010 to 31st March 2011. Profits are chargeable at the following rates;

Corporation Tax Bandings

	Profits band	per cent tax	
		FY10	*FY11*
Small companies' rate	Up to £300,000	21	*21*
Upper marginal rate	£300,000 to £1.5m	29.75	*29.75*
Main companies' rate	Over £1.5m	28	*28*

Note: The marginal rates shown above are divided by the number of associated companies.

COMPANY TAXATION – OTHER ISSUES

Capital Gains

Capital gains of companies are charged at the appropriate rate of Corporation Tax. The indexation allowance is still available to reduce capital gains made by Companies.

Quotas

Milk quota purchased by a company after 1st April 2002 will attract Corporation Tax relief at the rate of depreciation selected in the accounting policies of the company or 4% per year if not depreciated in the accounts of the company.

Distributions

Dividends are not deductible in arriving at the amount of Corporation Tax profit. However, the recipient of distributions will be credited with a tax payment of 10% of distributions received, which will be deemed to discharge the liability of basic rate (20%) taxpayers. Higher rate taxpayers are liable to pay tax at 32.5% on that part of their dividend income falling above the higher rate limit. Taxpayers with income in excess of £150,000 will be liable to tax on dividends at 42.5%.

Losses

Carry back restricted to one year. However the 2009 Budget introduced an extension to the loss relief provisions for two years. Where a company makes a trading loss in its accounting periods ending in the period 24th November 2008 to 23rd November 2010 the trading loss can be carried back and offset against profits of the 3 preceding years. The amount of losses that can be carried back to the first preceding year remains unlimited. After carry back to the preceding year, a maximum of £50,000 of the balance of the unused losses is available for carry back to the earlier two years. The £50,000 limit applies separately to the unused losses of each 12 month period.

Losses can be carried forward and offset against profits of the same trade.

3. AGRICULTURAL BUSINESSES: OTHER ITEMS

ASSESSING SELF-EMPLOYED PROFITS

Self-employed people are assessed for tax in any tax year on the basis of the profits recorded in the annual accounts which end in that tax year, i.e. on a 'current year basis'.

LIVESTOCK

Dairy cows or breeding livestock may be treated on the herd basis or on a trading stock basis;

Herd Basis

Under the herd basis valuation changes are not included in the trading account, nor are additions to the herd, but sales from the herd and replacements are. On the sale of all or a substantial proportion (normally taken as 20% or more) of the herd, no tax is paid on any profit over the original cost price, nor is there any relief for loss.

Editorial Note: The high values of cattle at present make it less likely that a new farming business will want to elect for the herd basis although each case must be judged on its merits.

Trading Stock Basis

Purchases, sales and valuation changes are all included in the trading account. Under this method stock should be valued at the lower of cost (or cost of production) and net realisable value. Where animals are home-produced and it is not possible to ascertain actual costs from farm records the 'deemed' cost may be used. This is 60% of market value for cattle and 75% for sheep and pigs.

STOCK VALUATION: CROPS

Crops should generally be valued at the cost of production (or net realisable value, if lower). Costs which are directly attributable to buying, producing and growing the crops should be included. The deemed cost method allows 75% of market value to be used although this method should only be used where it is not possible to ascertain actual costs.

ALLOWANCES FOR CAPITAL EXPENDITURE

Machinery and Plant

1. The same rules apply whether the machinery and plant is new or second hand. An annual writing down allowance of 20% p.a. is available on a reducing balance basis on capital expenditure incurred on the provision of plant and machinery. Qualifying expenditure is added to the asset 'pool' and the writing down allowances are given on the residue of expenditure in that pool.

2. The Annual Investment Allowance ('AIA') was introduced from 6th April 2008 (1st April 2008 for companies). This gives 100% relief for the first £100,000 (£50,000 from 6th April 2008 to 5th April 2010) of qualifying expenditure incurred in an accounting period. The limit is proportionally increased or decreased where the chargeable period is longer or shorter than a year. A group of companies can only receive a single allowance. Expenditure on cars does not qualify, although expenditure on long life assets, or on 'integral features' can be claimed.

3. The 2009 Budget introduced a First Year Allowance of 40% on any expenditure incurred in the year ended 5th April 2010 for individuals, 31st March 2010 for companies. The first year allowance is available on expenditure above the Annual Investment Allowance of £50,000, or on which the Annual Investment Allowance has

not been claimed, which would otherwise qualify for writing down allowances at 20% in the general plant and machinery pool.

4. A new 10% rate applies to expenditure incurred on certain listed 'integral features' in a building and on long life assets on or after April 2008. Long life asset expenditure brought forward will obtain the 10% rate (6% up to April 2008).

5. 100% first year allowances can be claimed for expenditure incurred by any business on designated energy-saving plant and machinery and environmentally beneficial technologies and products. The lists of items which qualify can be found on the Government's Energy Technology Product lists which is at www.eca.gov.uk.

6. For chargeable periods beginning on or after 6th April 2008 (1st April 2008 for Companies), a Writing Down Allowance of up to £1,000 can be claimed in respect of the main pool and/or the special rate pool where the unrelieved expenditure in that pool is £1,000 or less.

Cars

Motor cars purchased before 1st April 2009 for companies and 5th April 2009 for unincorporated businesses, costing more than £12,000 are included in a separate 'pool' in the year of purchase, on which a 20% writing down allowance is available. The allowance is restricted to a maximum of £3,000 for motor cars with a written-down value of more than £12,000. Special rules apply where a motor car is only partly used for business purposes. There is a 100% first year allowance for new cars with emissions of less than 110g/km CO_2 (120g/km for expenditure incurred before 1st April 2008). This applies to cars registered after 16th April 2002.

For expenditure on motor cars purchased after 1st April 2009 for companies and 5th April 2009 for unincorporated businesses, the regime for cars costing over £12,000 is abolished. Cars with CO_2 emissions exceeding 160gm/km will be allocated to the 10% special rate pool. All other cars will go into the general pool. For unincorporated businesses, cars will have their own separate pools where there is an element of private use.

Machinery Leasing

Tax allowances for rental payments on financial leases are spread to reflect the commercial depreciation of the asset. This may mean that full tax relief for rental payments may not be gained in the years in which the payments are made.

Buildings

Farm buildings, fencing, drainage and other improvements (including up to one-third of farmhouses) used to qualify for a writing-down allowance of 4% annually, given equally over 25 years. These annual allowances are now phased out by the end of this 2010-11 tax year. For 2010-11, the rate has been reduced by 50% to 1%. Where an accounting period spans the financial year (31st March for companies, 5th April for individuals and partnerships), time apportionment applies to determine the amount of the allowance.

Editorial Note: *The 2007 Budget announced of the phased withdrawal of Agricultural Buildings Allowances. The change includes the withdrawal of allowances on expenditure previously incurred. The changes make it even more important that any items of plant and equipment are identified in a building and the appropriate allowances claimed.*

The new Annual Investment Allowance (AIA) makes the planning of capital expenditure more important where expenditure can be brought forward or deferred. Businesses who consistently spend in excess of the £50,000 pa AIA will need to review their spending policies to ascertain whether leasing or contract hire may be more efficient.

The 2010 Post-election Budget announced proposals to reduce the level of expenditure qualifying for the Annual Investment Allowance to £25,000 with effect from April 2012. In addition, it is proposed that the rate of writing down allowances on the main pool will reduce from 20% to 18% and the rate of allowances on the special rate pool will reduce from 10% to 8% also from 6th April 2012.

LOSSES

Losses can normally be set off against other income in the year they are incurred and in the prior year. If other income is insufficient in the year when the loss occurs and in the prior year, any unrelieved losses can be carried forward and set off against future profits from the same trade. Special rules apply to prevent abuse of loss relief provisions by 'hobby' farmers who are not running their farms on a commercial basis with a view to producing a profit: normally losses are disallowed against other income after 5 consecutive years of loss. Trading losses may be set against capital gains in the same year as the loss.

The 2009 Budget introduced an extension to the loss relief provisions for two years. Where an unincorporated business makes a trading loss in the 2008-09 and/or 2009-10 tax years, the trading loss can be carried back and offset against profits of the 3 preceding years. The amount of losses that can be carried back to the first preceding year remains unlimited. After carry back to the preceding year, a maximum of £50,000 of the balance of the unused losses is available for carry back to the earlier two years. The £50,000 limit applies separately to the unused losses of each tax year.

PROFIT AVERAGING

This relief is to enable farmers, other than companies, to average their taxable profits over two consecutive years. Where the difference between the profits of two consecutive years is 30% or more of the higher profits, the total profits for the two years are equally divided between the two years. Marginal relief is available where the difference is less than 30% but more than 25% of the higher profits. Profit for the purposes of tax averaging calculations is after the deduction of capital allowances. There is a two year limit in which to make the claim.

4.   CAPITAL GAINS TAX

APPLICATION AND RATES

Applies to capital gains made by an individual. Capital gains accruing to companies are chargeable to Corporation Tax. A capital gain is the difference between the acquisition value and the sale price. The first £10,100 of capital gains realised by an individual in a tax year are covered by their annual exemption.

The rate of capital gains tax for disposals between 6th April 2008 and 22nd June 2010 is 18%. Disposals of non-business assets on or after 23rd June 2010 will attract capital gains tax of 18% for basic rate taxpayers or 28% for higher and additional rate taxpayers. The rate of CGT is 18% where total taxable gains and income, after taking into account all allowable deductions including losses, personal allowances and the CGT annual exemption, are less than the upper limit of the income tax basic rate band. The 28% rate will apply to gains or any parts of gains above this limit.

Exempt assets include a principal private residence (e.g. farm house, if non-exclusive business occupation applies) if occupied as such, normal life assurance policies, animals and tangible movable property (i.e. chattels) disposed of for £6,000 or less.

Capital Gains Tax is chargeable only on the disposal (including gifts) of assets. Capital Gains Tax is not payable on death.

Payment of Capital Gains Tax is due on 31st January following the tax year of disposal on the self-assessment return.

RELIEFS

Losses

Should a transaction produce a loss, this may be set against any long term chargeable gains arising in the same year or, if these are insufficient, those accruing in subsequent years. Losses brought forward will be used only to the extent necessary to reduce untaxed gains for the year to £10,100.

Where a trading loss can be set against other income in the same or prior year for income tax purposes, any unused loss can be set against capital gains for those years.

Improvements

Spending that has increased the value of the asset can be offset against any gain. In the case of agricultural property, allowance would be made for any capital expenditure undertaken to improve the property.

Indexation and Taper Relief

Indexation and Taper relief for individuals has now been abolished for any disposals taking place on or after 6th April 2008. Indexation allowance is still available for capital gains arising in companies.

Entrepreneurs Relief

Entrepreneur's relief applies to certain disposals of business assets by an individual. The relief, which must be claimed, gives a reduced effective rate of Capital Gains Tax of 10% for eligible gains of up to £2m for disposals between 6th April 2010 and 22nd June 2010. Gains arising in the period from 6th April 2008 to 5th April 2010 are subject to a limit of £1m. For qualifying disposals on or after 23rd June 2010, a 10% rate of tax now applies on the first £5m of lifetime gains. The limit is a lifetime limit per individual. The assets which qualify for entrepreneurs' relief are in line with those which qualified for business asset taper relief. This covers:

- a trading business carried on by an individual alone or in partnership;
- assets of such a trade following cessation;
- shares or securities in a trading company where the individual owns 5% or more and is an officer or employee

The conditions for the relief must have been satisfied throughout a qualifying period of a year before the disposal. The relief operates by reducing the amount of qualifying gains by four-ninths to arrive at the effective rate of 10% for gains arising before 22nd June 2010. For gains arising on or after 23rd June 2010, a new rate of 10% now applies.

Editorial Note: The new rules for Entrepreneur relief are complex, particularly in cases of disposals of part of the business. The rules are similar to the previous retirement relief and are particularly tricky in cases of disposals of farmland and related assets and trade. It is recommended that professional advice is sought where it is anticipated claiming this relief, particularly as given the increase in the lifetime allowance combined with the increase in tax rate for non-business assets, the tax savings can be greatly increased.

Rollover

Payment of tax may be deferred on gains accruing from the sale of business assets (including land and buildings occupied and used for trade purposes, fixed plant and machinery, milk quotas, and from the sale of shares in a family business) if part or all of the proceeds are spent on acquiring new qualifying assets. The tax is deferred by deducting the gain from the acquisition price of the new asset. It can only be claimed if the new asset is acquired within 12 months before and 3 years after the disposal of the old assets.

Disposal and acquisition dates for Capital Gains purposes are generally contract, not completion, dates.

Holdover

Payments of tax may be deferred where disposal is by gift. This relief only applies to gifts of business assets, land which qualifies for agricultural property relief at either the 100% or 50% rate under Inheritance Tax (see next section) and gifts which lead to an immediate charge to Inheritance Tax (e.g. gifts into a discretionary trust). The amount of the chargeable gain which would normally have accrued to the donor will be held over; the value at which the donee is deemed to acquire the asset will be its market value reduced by the amount of the donor's chargeable gain held over. Where deferral is not available, payment of tax by interest bearing annual instalments over 10 years will be allowed for gifts of land, controlling share holdings and minority share holdings in unquoted companies.

5. INHERITANCE TAX

APPLICATION AND RATES

This tax is charged on lifetime gifts and transfers on death. Rates for 2010-11 are as follows;

Slice of Chargeable Transfer	Rate per cent
£1- 325,000	0%
Over £325,000	40%

The nil rate band is potentially increased for surviving spouses or civil partners who died on or after 9th October 2007. From this date the nil rate band may be increased by the unused proportion of the deceased spouse or civil partners nil rate band.

Outright gifts to individuals are exempt from tax at the time of the gift. If the donor lives for a further seven years then the transfer is fully exempt. Gifts into accumulation and maintenance trusts and interest in possession trusts no longer receive special treatment - all other gifts will be taxed at half the above rates at the time of the transfer.

Tax is charged on the value of an individual's estate at death plus the value of all gifts made within seven years of death. Allowance is made for any tax paid on lifetime gifts included in the value of the estate on death. Relief is given for outright gifts made more than three years before death according to the following scale:

Years between gift and death	Percentage of the full charge to tax
0-3	100
3-4	80
4-5	60
5-6	40
6-7	20

Exemptions include: transfers between husband and wife; the first £3,000 of gift made by a donor in the income tax year and separately up to £250 per year to any number of persons; gifts made out of income which form part of normal expenditure; marriage gifts within limits of £5,000 for a parent, £2,500 for a lineal ancestor and £1,000 for other donors.

RELIEFS

Agricultural Property Relief

Relief may be available for agricultural land. Subject to a general rule that the agricultural land must have been occupied by the transferor (or by his controlled company) for two years, or owned by the transferor for 7 years and occupied for agricultural purposes by someone else before any relief is granted. The relief is at two different rates. If the basis of valuation is vacant possession (or there is the right to obtain it within 12 months), the taxable value of the land is reduced by 100%. If the basis of valuation is tenanted value, the taxable value of the land is reduced by 50% of that tenanted value. Ownership and occupation periods normally include prior periods of ownership or occupation by husbands and wives. From 1st September 1995, 100% relief applies to new lettings of agricultural land as Farm Business Tenancies.

The 2009 Budget extended Agricultural relief to include agricultural land situated in the European Economic Area (EEA).

Editorial Note: There has been much publicised activity and tax cases concerning APR claims, particularly attempts by the Inland Revenue to reduce or deny the relief on claims for farmhouses. Care must be taken to protect the relief particularly where the attached land is either let out on a Farm Business Tenancy or under a contract farming arrangement.

Business Property Relief

Relief is also available in respect to 'business property' transferred during lifetime or on death. The relief extends to the business assets of a proprietor and the interest of a partner or controlling shareholder in the business capital of a company. The value of such property, providing certain tests are satisfied (e.g. it has been owned by the transferor for two years preceding transfer), is reduced by 100%. Where a partner or controlling shareholder owns assets (e.g. land) that the business uses, the value will be reduced by 50%. Shareholdings in unquoted companies receive a 100% reduction in market value.

Lifetime gifts of property eligible for Agricultural and Business Property Relief have to be retained (or replaced by similar property) until the death of the donor (or earlier death of the donee) if those reliefs are to be available when the tax (or additional tax) becomes payable subsequent to the donor's death

In the case of the transfer of property eligible for APR and BPR, the tax can be paid by annual instalments over ten years free of interest.

6. STAMP TAXES

STAMP DUTY

Stamp Duty is charged at 0.5 per cent of consideration paid on the transfer of shares and securities.

STAMP DUTY LAND TAX

Stamp duty land tax is charged on the transfer of an interest in land; both sales and leases. With sales of property the tax is levied on a percentage of the sale value of the property (special rules apply to land in disadvantaged areas). The rates applicable to transactions from 1st January 2010 are:

Residential property	Rate	Non-residential and mixed use	Rate
Value up to £125,000...........	nil	Value up to £150,000..............	nil
£125,001 to £250,000..........	1%	£150,001 to £250,000..............	1%
£250,001 to £500,000..........	3%	£250,001 to £500,000..............	3%
£500,001 or more................	4%	£500,001 or more....................	4%

Stamp Duty Land Tax is payable on leases calculated according to the net present value of the rent payable over the term of the lease.

7.   VALUE ADDED TAX

Agricultural businesses with a turnover of taxable goods and services in excess of £70,000 per annum from 1st April 2009 (£68,000 from 1st May 2009 to 31st March 2010), are required to register for VAT. Businesses with a turnover below this limit may apply for voluntary registration. The standard rate of VAT is 17.5% from 1st January 2010 until 4th January 2011 when it will increase to 20%. Most agricultural products are zero rated for VAT purposes. VAT has to be paid on certain inputs. Registered businesses are eligible to reclaim the tax paid where the goods or services purchased have been used in the production of zero-rated supplies.

A flat rate scheme is available to farmers as an alternative to registering for VAT. Farmers under the flat rate scheme do not have to submit tax returns or account for VAT and consequently cannot reclaim tax. They can, however, charge (and keep) a flat rate addition of 4% when they sell to VAT registered customers goods and services which qualify. This addition is not VAT but acts as compensation for losing input tax on purchases. The registered person paying the flat rate amount to the farmer can recover it as if it were VAT, subject to the normal rules for reclaiming. The local VAT office may refuse to issue a certificate to participate in the flat rate scheme if this would mean the farmer would recover substantially (£3,000) more than through the normal system.

A new flat rate scheme operates for small businesses generally and is an alternative that farmers can use if they have taxable supplies of no more than £150,000 and a total business income of no more than £187,500. This scheme operates in a different way to the flat rate scheme for farmers in that a business charges the normal rate of VAT on sales. However, the VAT which the business has to remit to Customs and Excise is calculated by multiplying the value of gross sales by a rate specified for each particular trade sector. The rate for agriculture is 6% from 31st December 2009 except for businesses supplying agricultural services, when the rate is 10%.

Editorial Note: *Farmers and landowners must always consider the VAT implications when considering any new or more farming activities on the land or within the buildings, particularly where supplies are made the public who cannot recover any VAT which may be charged on the service or goods provided from the farm.*

8. NATIONAL INSURANCE

The tables below set out the National Insurance contributions for the 2010-11 year;

Class 1 (not contracted out)

Employee's weekly earnings	Employee	Employer
£110.00 or less....................................	Nil	Nil
£110.01 to £844.00............................	11%	12.8%
Over £844.00.....................................	1%	12.8%

Class 2

Self-employed flat rate .... £2.40 a week

Class 3

Non-employed (voluntary) flat rate .... £12.05 a week

Class 4

Self-employed. On profits or gains
between £5,715 and £43,875 .... 8%
over £43,875... 1%

It is proposed that each class of National Insurance will increase by 1% from 6th April 2011.

Acknowledgement: The Author is grateful to *Howard Worth Chartered Accountants Agricultural Department* (Tel: 01606 369 000) for their assistance in updating this section of the Pocketbook.

VIII. FARM BUSINESS MANAGEMENT

1. DEFINITIONS OF FARM MANAGEMENT TERMS

VALUATIONS AND CAPITAL

Valuations

Valuation is essentially a process of estimation. Alternative bases are possible, according to the purpose intended. The basis should be consistent throughout the period of any series of figures.

1. *Saleable crops in store.* At estimated market value less costs still to be incurred, e.g. for storage and marketing. Both may be estimated either at the expected date of sale or at the date of valuation.

2. *Growing crops.* Preferably at variable costs to the date of valuation, although estimated total cost can alternatively be used.

3. *Saleable crops ready for harvesting* but still in the ground. Preferably as valued in point 1 above, less estimated harvesting costs, although they can alternatively be treated as described in point 2 above.

4. *Fodder stocks (home-grown).* Preferably at variable costs when calculating gross margins. Alternatively at estimated market value (based on hay-equivalent value according to quality). Fodder crops still in the ground, e.g. kale, treated as point 2 above.

5. *Stocks of purchased materials (including fodder).* At cost (net of discounts).

6. *Machinery and equipment.* Original cost (net of investment grants), less accumulated depreciation to date of valuation – this gives a valuation on the 'historic' cost basis. Alternatively at estimated market value.

7. *Livestock.* At current market value, less cost of marketing. Fluctuations in market value expected to be temporary should be ignored.

Capital

Tenant's Capital. The estimated total value of capital on the farm, other than land and fixed equipment. There is no easy way of determining this sum precisely and estimates are made in several ways depending on the information available and the purpose for which the estimate is required. One method is to take the average of the opening and closing valuations (at either market value or cost) of livestock, crops, machinery and stores (feed, seed, fertilisers). See also pages 234 (following section).

Landlord's Capital. Value of the land and fixed equipment (including buildings).

OUTPUT TERMS

Revenue (or Income). Receipts adjusted for debtors at the beginning and end of the accounting period. Items such as CAP support, revenue grants, contract receipts and wayleaves are included.

Returns. Revenue adjusted for valuation changes (add closing, deduct opening, valuation).

Gross Output. Returns plus the value of produce consumed in the farmhouse or supplied to workers for which no payment is made, less purchases of livestock, livestock products and other produce bought for resale.

Enterprise Output. The total value of an enterprise, whether sold or retained on the farm. It therefore equals Gross Output of the enterprise plus the market value of any of the products kept on the farm (transfers out). Following 'decoupling' the Single Payment should not be apportioned to individual enterprises, but coupled support such as protein and energy crop per ha payments should be. Products transferred from another enterprise to be used in the production of the enterprise whose output is being calculated are deducted at market value (transfers in). Instead of the accounting year the "harvest year" can be used for crops which means valuations may not be relevant.

(Enterprise) Output from Forage. Primarily the sum of the enterprise outputs of grazing livestock, but includes keep let and occasional sales, e.g. of surplus hay, together with an adjustment for changes in the valuation of stocks of home-grown fodder. However, fortuitous changes in stocks caused by yield variations due to the weather, the severity or length of the winter, or minor changes in livestock numbers or forage area can be either ignored (if small in relation to total annual usage) or included in miscellaneous output.

Adjusted Forage (Enterprise) Output is Output from Forage less rented keep and purchases of bulk fodder.

Standard Output. The average enterprise output per hectare of a crop or per head of livestock calculated from either national or local average price and average yield data.

INPUT TERMS

Expenditure. Payments adjusted for creditors at the beginning and end of the accounting period. Capital expenditure is not included.

Costs. Expenditure adjusted for valuation changes (add opening, deduct closing, valuation), with the following adjustments. Add: depreciation on capital expenditure including machinery, any loss made on machinery sales (add to depreciation) and the value of payments in kind to workers if not already included in their earnings. Deduct: purchases of livestock, livestock products and other produce bought for resale, any profit made on machinery (deduct from depreciation), allowance for private use of farm vehicles (deduct from machinery costs), the value of purchased stores used in the farmhouse (e.g. electricity) or sold off the farm (deduct from the relevant item).

Inputs. Costs with the following adjustments, made in order to put all farms on a similar basis for comparative purposes. Add: the value of unpaid family labour, including the manual labour of the farmer and his wife, and, in the case of owner-occupiers, an estimated rental value (based on average rents of similar farms in the area), less any cottage rents received. Deduct: any mortgage payments and other expenses of owner-occupation, interest payments and the cost of paid management. A proportion of the rental value of the farmhouse may also be deducted.

Fixed Costs. See pages from 202 whole Farm Fixed Costs.

Variable Costs. See page 1.

MARGIN TERMS

Management and Investment Income. Gross Output less Inputs. It represents the reward to management and the return on tenant's capital invested in the farm, whether borrowed or not. It is mainly used for comparative purposes, all farms having been put on a similar financial basis by the adjustments made to costs in calculating Inputs.

Net Farm Income. Management and Investment Income, less paid management, plus the value of the manual labour of the farmer and his wife. It represents the return to all tenant's type capital and the reward to the farmer for his manual labour and management.

Profit (or Loss). Gross Output less Costs. This represents the surplus or deficit before imputing any notional charges such as rental value or unpaid labour. In the accounts of owner-occupiers it includes any profit accruing from the ownership of land.

Farm Business Income. This term is increasingly being used in FBS costings, and is similar to 'Profit' above. It represents the return to all unpaid labour and to all their own capital in the farm business including land and farm buildings.

Gross Margin. See page 1.

Net Margin. A term sometimes used to denote Gross Margin less direct labour and machinery costs charged to an individual enterprise. This is not, however, nationally accepted terminology. Increasingly Net Margin in the enterprise context is being used to denote the profit of an enterprise by taking its gross output less its 'complete enterprise costs', but see page 2.

AREA TERMS

Total Hectares. All hectares comprising the farm.

Hectares. Total hectares less areas of woods, waste land, roads, yards, buildings, etc.

Adjusted Hectares. Hectares reduced by the conversion of rough grazings into the equivalent hectares of average quality grassland. This is the figure often used for lowland farms when calculating "per hectare" results.

Forage Hectares. Total hectares of forage crops grown, less any hectares exclusively used by pigs or poultry and the area equivalent of any home-grown fodder fed to livestock reared in cereal systems. Also, the area of rough grazings is converted to its grassland equivalent (see Adjusted Hectares). Forage crops are all crops including grass, rough grazing, maize and whole crops grown specifically for grazing livestock, but excluding catch crops and crops harvested as grain and pulses.

Adjusted Forage Hectares. Forage hectares adjusted as follows. Add area equivalent of keep rented, deduct area equivalent of keep let; deduct the area equivalent of occasional sales of fodder, e.g. surplus hay, and seed cuts (note: hay and seed grown regularly for sale should be regarded as cash crops, not forage crops); add or deduct the area equivalent of planned changes in the valuation of stocks of home-grown fodder (fortuitous changes in stocks resulting from weather conditions may be ignored); convert rough grazings into their grassland equivalent if not already done. The following adjustments also may be made: add the area equivalent of catch crops and of grazing from cash crops of hay or seed: add the area equivalent of purchased fodder.

In calculations such as Gross Margins per Forage Hectare, Adjusted Forage Hectares are usually used. If the area equivalent of purchased fodder has been added the cost of purchased fodder must not be charged as a variable cost: this is probably the best calculation for comparative purposes. Alternatively, when considering all the grazing enterprises taken together, purchased fodder can be deducted as a variable cost and no addition made for its area equivalent.

2. CAPITAL REQUIREMENT AND RETURN

TENANT'S CAPITAL

1. *Machinery.* Costs of new machinery are given on pages 179. Written-down values in 2010 are likely to be averaging £500-600 per hectare (£200-243 per acre) taking all farm types together. Average values for different farm types are given on the next page.

2. *Breeding Livestock.* The 2011 average of breeding livestock value per hectare will vary from zero to over £1,500 (£600) for an intensive dairy farm. Approximate average market values of various categories of breeding livestock (of mixed ages in the case of adult stock) are as follows (actual value will vary according to average age and weight, quality and breed):

Average market values of various breeding livestock

Holstein/Friesian Dairy Cows:	£1,150
Channel Island Dairy Cows:	£800
Other Dairy Cows:	£900
Beef Cows:	£900

	Holstein Friesians	Replacements Ayrshires and C.I. Breeds	Beef Cattle
In Calf Heifers	£1,500	£950	£1,050
1-2 years	£950	£750	£800
6-12 months	£600	£475	£575
Under 6 months	£300	£225	£325

	Other Livestock
Ewes (young ewes)	£90
Rams (good quality, young rams)	£350
Sows and In-Pig Gilts	£175
Boars	£500

3. Working Capital. This is defined as the current assets of a business less its current liabilities. It is the liquid capital needed to finance the cash flow through the production cycle, the length of which varies considerably between different crop and livestock enterprises and different combinations of these enterprises. It can include the cost of purchased fattening stock, feed, seed, fertilisers, regular labour, machinery running costs, general overhead costs, rent and living expenses. This capital may be only £250 per hectare (£100 per acre) or so on an all-dairying farm but £900 or more per hectare (£365 per acre) on an all-cereals farm where the crop is stored until the spring. Specialist root crop and vegetable farm businesses will have significantly higher working capital requirements. The only accurate way to estimate working capital requirement is to complete a full cash flow estimate for the production cycle of the business.

Average Tenants Capital per Hectare

Average Tenant's Capital per hectare (acre) for different farm types, for 2011:

Farm Type Group	Average No. Hectares	Livestock	Crops, Cultivns., Stores	Machinery and Equipment*	Total Tenant's Capital	
		£	£	£	£	£
Mainly Dairying:						
under 75 ha..........	60	1200	185	860	2245	(909)
75 to 125 ha.........	90	1250	195	760	2205	(892)
Over 125 ha.........	170	1300	220	825	2345	(949)
Mainly Cereals:						
under 175 ha.........	170	30	460	550	1040	(421)
175 to 300 ha.......	220	45	475	600	1120	(453)
over 300 ha..........	575	48	485	580	1113	(450)
General Cropping:						
under 150 ha.........	110	-	410	660	1070	(433)
150 to 225 ha........	190	-	560	745	1305	(528)
over 225 ha..........	475	-	425	760	1185	(480)
Mainly Sheep/Cattle (Lowland):						
Under 90 ha.........	90	410	80	410	900	(364)
90 to 125 ha............	135	370	85	430	885	(358)
Over 125 ha.........	250	355	70	300	725	(393)
Mainly Sheep/Cattle (Upland LFA):						
under 130 ha.........	115	345	35	320	700	(283)
130 to 230 ha........	180	360	35	250	645	(261)
over 230 ha..........	320	380	30	210	620	(251)

* Based on current (i.e. replacement) costs.

The above (deliberately rounded) data is based on Farm Business Survey results compiled annually by University/Colleges centres (as listed on page 4). The values of milk quota and Single Payment entitlements are excluded as are other assets not named above, such as debtors.

RETURN ON CAPITAL

Tenant's Capital.

Return on tenant's capital is calculated by taking the management and investment income (MII) of a business as a percentage of the tenant's capital (see definitions in VIII.1). Because MII is before deduction of any interest, this return is 'gross', i.e. before allowing for cost of finance. However, it should be borne in mind that MII includes no charge for management but that a rental value for owner-occupied land and the value of the unpaid labour of the farmer and wife have been deducted.

Landlord's Capital

The return on landlord's capital is calculated by taking the rental income, less any ownership expenses (mortgage, insurance, repairs etc.), expressed as a percentage of the land value. With farmland in 2011 averaging, possibly £15,000 per hectare (£6,070 per acre) (see page 209) with vacant possession (assuming no special amenity or house value), an average lowland rent of, say, £173 per hectare (£70 per acre) (see p. 207), and assuming ownership expenses at £65 per hectare (£26 per acre), the (net) return (£108 per hectare (£44 per acre) averages 0.72 per cent. If land is taken at its tenanted value, with a vacant possession premium of say one-third, the return increases to 1.08 per cent. If farm business tenancy rents were paid, at say 40% above the average level for established tenants (i.e. £240/ha [£97/acre]), the return would average 1.6 per cent with land at the vacant possession price assumed and 2.4 per cent with land at the tenanted value assumed. Full repairing and insurance leases clearly raise the returns above these levels. Above average quality farms acquire higher rents but also obviously command higher prices than the average levels quoted above.

Return on Capital to Individual Enterprises

On a mixed farm it is almost impossible to ascertain the return on enterprise capital, except perhaps for a full-time pig or poultry enterprise, nor would it be of very much use even if it could be determined. It would require the arbitrary allocation both of costs and capital inputs that are common to several, in some cases all, of the enterprises on the farm.

What is relevant and important is the extra (net) return from an enterprise either to be introduced or expanded, as calculated by a partial budget, related to the extra (net) capital needed. The 'net' in brackets relates, as regards return, to the addition to gross margins less any addition to (or plus any reduction in) 'fixed' costs, bearing in mind that another enterprise may have to be deleted or reduced in size; and, as regards capital, to the fact that deletion or reduction of another enterprise may release capital.

In most cases of 'marginal' substitution, it is differences in the value of breeding livestock and differences in variable costs that are particularly relevant, but the timing of both inputs and sales are also obviously very important.

'Marginal' Capital Requirements

These are for small changes in crop areas or livestock numbers and can be estimated as follows:

- Crops: variable costs till sale.
- Dairy Cows and Egg Production: value of the cow* or hens, plus food until payment of product.
- Other Breeding Livestock: average value of stock*, plus variable costs to sale (payment) of the progeny (e.g. lambs) – or their transfer to another enterprise (e.g. weaners to the pig fattening enterprise).
- Rearing Breeding Livestock (e.g. heifers, tegs, gilts, pullets): cost of the calf, lamb, weaner or chick, plus variable costs till they produce their first progeny/eggs.
- Fattening Livestock and Production of Stores: cost of stock, plus variable costs till sale.

* Value of breeding stock, including dairy cows: either the average value over their entire breeding or milk producing life (see table on page 234) or their value when they first produce progeny can be taken. The latter will give the lower return on (marginal) capital and is thus the severer test.

Home-reared stock: where stock to be used for milk or egg production, breeding or fattening are home-reared, there are two possibilities:

(a) either they can be valued at variable costs of production when they are transferred from the rearing to the 'productive' enterprise; in this case the return on (marginal) capital will be estimated over the combined rearing and 'productive' enterprise.

(b) or they can be valued at market value at point of transfer. This is the procedure if one wishes to work out a return on (marginal) capital for the rearing and the 'productive' enterprises separately.

Return on 'Marginal' Capital.

This is sometimes expressed as the gross margin less fuel and repair costs of the enterprise expanded as a percentage of the 'marginal', or extra, capital. However, two points have to be remembered:

(a) If another enterprise has had to be reduced in size to enable the enterprise under consideration to be expanded, the capital released and the gross margin forfeited by reducing the size of the first enterprise must be brought into the calculation in estimating the net result of the change.

(b) All the above statements on 'marginal' capital refer to small changes. If the change is large enough to cause changes in labour, machinery or building requirements the capital changes brought about may be considerably greater.

Return on Investments in Medium-Term and Long-Term Capital.

This calculates the Rate of Return and the Discounted Yield.

Example: If a £5,000 investment results in an annual net return of £500 (after deducting depreciation, but ignoring interest payments):

$$\text{Rate of Return on Initial Capital} = \frac{500}{5,000} \times 100 = 10\%$$

$$\text{Rate of Return on Average Capital} = \frac{500}{2,500} \times 100 = 20\%$$

It is more accurate to calculate the '*Discounted Yield*', which is the discount rate that brings the present value of the net cash flows (which means ignoring depreciation) to the value of the investment. The tables on pages 243 may be used.

'Short-Cut' Estimates of the Discounted Yield on Depreciating Assets

The Discounted Yield falls between the simple Rates of Return on Initial and Average Capital. In fact, for investments lasting 5 to 15 years, when the Rate of Return on Initial Capital is 10 per cent and on Average Capital 20 per cent, the Discounted Yield will be almost exactly halfway between, i.e. about 15 per cent. However, this is only so providing the anticipated annual net cash earnings are fairly constant — or fluctuate unpredictably around a fairly constant level.

There are three circumstances when the Discounted Yield will get closer to the Rate of Return on Initial Capital (i.e. the lower per cent return) and further from the Rate of Return on Average Capital:

(a) The longer the life of the investment.

(b) The higher the Rate of Return.

(c) The higher the net cash flow is in the later years of the investment compared with the earlier years.

When the opposite circumstances obtain, the Discounted Yield will be closer to the Rate of Return on Average Capital (i.e. the higher per cent return).

Granted that there are inevitably varying degrees of estimation and uncertainty in calculating future net annual earnings of investments, the following short-cuts might reasonably be used where the annual net cash earnings are expected to be fairly constant —

or fluctuate unpredictably (e.g. through weather effects on yields) around a fairly constant level. (W.O. period = write-off period; R.R.I.C. = rate of return on initial capital).

1. Where

    (i)   the W.O. period is 5 years or less,

    (ii)   the W.O. period is 6 - 10 years and the R.R.I.C. is 15 per cent or less,

    (iii) the W.O. period is 11 - 20 years and the R.R.I.C. is 10 per cent or less,

    calculate the Return on Capital as being approximately midway between the Rates of Return on Initial and Average Capital, i.e. by calculating the Rate of Return on 2/3 of the original investment.

    For example, following the earlier example above:

$$\frac{500}{3,333} \times 100 = 15\%.$$

2. Where

    (i)   the W.O. period is 6 to 10 years and the R.R.I.C. exceeds 15 per cent,

    (ii)   the W.O. period is 11 to 20 years and the R.R.I.C. is between 10 per cent and 25 per cent,

    (iii) the W.O. period exceeds 20 years and the R.R.I.C. is 10 per cent or less,

    calculate the Return on Capital on 80 per cent of the original investment.

    For example, again following the earlier example:

$$\frac{500}{4,000} \times 100 = 12.5°\%.$$

3. Where

    (i)   the W.O. period is 11 to 20 years and the R.R.I.C. exceeds 25 per cent,

    (ii)   the W.O. period exceeds 20 years and the R.R.I.C. exceeds 10 per cent, take the Return on Capital to be the R.R.I.C.

In borderline cases, use method 1 rather than 2, or 2 rather than 3 if there is a tendency for the cash flow to be higher in the earlier years, e.g. because of tax allowances on machinery. Take 2 rather than 1, and 3 rather than 2, if the likelihood is that the cash flow will be lower in earlier years and increase in later years.

However, where the annual cash flow is expected to vary (apart from unpredictable fluctuations) it is safer to make the full D.C.F. calculation. This is particularly so where the variation is both up and down and where further periodic investments are to be made during the life of the project.

3.   INTEREST RATES

Rate of interest on Bank Loans.

Typically 2.5% to 3.0% above Base Rate. Main range is 1.5% above to 4.0% above. Extremes are likely to be 0.8% above (minimum) and 7% above (maximum). Since the banking crisis and the reduction in Base Rate to 0.5% in 2008, interest rates have become more variable depending often on the relationship with the bank. Banks seem to be asking for wider margins generally and low margins over base are becoming extremely rare.

Annual Percentage Rate (APR)

This is the effective rate of interest calculated on an annual basis and should be used when seeking to make a true comparison between interest charges on money borrowed from different sources. The APR allows for the fact that when interest is applied to accounts at half yearly, quarterly or monthly intervals an element of compounding will arise.

For example, £100 borrowed for one year at a quoted annual nominal interest rate of 6% (e.g. 5.5% over base rate of 0.5%) with interest charged quarterly, will lead to an accumulated interest charge of £6.136 (i.e., giving an APR of just under 6.14%). The higher the annual nominal interest rate and the more frequently the interest charges are applied to the account, the more pronounced the compounding element becomes. For example, an annual nominal interest rate of 10% produces an APR of 10.25% with half yearly charging, 10.38% with quarterly charging and 10.47% with monthly charging.

In the case of some loans and hire purchase agreements, interest charges may be quoted as a flat rate on the original amount borrowed. The APR will be considerably greater than the flat rate if the loan is repaid by equal periodic instalments, comprising part capital and part interest, so that the borrowing is completely repaid by the end of the agreed term. For example, the APR for a loan at a flat rate of interest of 8% repaid by monthly instalments over 5 years will be 15%. The shorter the repayment period, and the more frequent the payments, the higher is the APR compared with the flat rate.

The Real Rate of Interest.

When preparing simple profit and loss budgets to estimate how worthwhile an investment in a fixed asset (machinery, buildings, land) is, it is usual to price inputs and outputs at present-day values even when most costs and returns are expected to rise due to inflation over the life of the investment. Where this real terms approach is adopted a more realistic estimate of the effect on profitability can be gained by basing charges for capital on the real rate of interest rather than the APR.

The real rate of interest is the APR adjusted for the annual rate at which prices relevant to the investment are expected to increase. A crude estimate of the real rate of interest can be obtained by simply subtracting the expected rate of price increase from the APR; for example, if the APR were 8% and the expected rate of inflation 3%, the real rate of interest would be $8 - 3 = 5\%$.

4. FINANCIAL RATIOS

Common Ratios

The following ratios are often quoted as rough guidelines:

		% of Gross Output
Variable Costs		30-40%
Labour	15-17½%	⎫
Machinery	15-17½%	⎬ 30-40%
Sundry Fixed Costs	5%	⎭
Rent & Interest		15%
Margin*		15%

* to cover drawings, tax, capital repayments, reinvestments

It has to be borne in mind that these are indeed only rough guidelines and need to be considered with great care. Values vary, with type of farming and size of farm. It is often unclear how certain items are being measured, especially whether unpaid manual labour of the farmer and family has been included or whether a rental value has been allowed for owner-occupied land. In the table above variable costs at 30% or less would be found on cereals type farms, leaving 40% for labour, machinery and sundry fixed costs. On intensive livestock farms variable costs of 40% would be expected, leaving only 30% for fixed costs.

Farm Survey Ratios

The following are rounded averages based on farm surveys in recent years on a large sample of all types of farm, assuming a Management and Investment Income (see page 232) of 10% of Total Output is made. It is to be noted that Total Output includes the market value of any production retained for use/consumption on the farm (e.g. cereals for feed or seed), Unpaid Labour (value of manual labour supplied by the farmer and spouse) is included. Rent includes the rental value of owner-occupied land and Interest charges are not included in the costs. Casual labour and all Contract work are included in fixed costs. Obviously, costs are a lower proportion and the margin a higher proportion in profitable years, and vice-versa in low profit years. Obviously, too, within years the more profitable farms have lower percentage costs, leaving higher percentage margins and vice-versa.

Average Financial Ratios from Farm Business Survey

	% Total Output	% Total Gross Margin	% Total Fixed Costs
Variable Costs:			
(excl. casual labour and contract work)	32.5		
Fixed Costs:			
Labour: Paid (inc. casuals) ⎱	20	30	33
Labour: Unpaid ⎰			
Power & Machinery			
(inc. contract work)	20	30	33
Labour & Machinery	40	60	66
Rent/Rental Value	12.5	19	21
General Overheads	7.5	11	13
Total Fixed Costs	60	90	100
Margin	**7.5**	**10**	-

Total Gross Margin = 67.5% of Total Output

Lending Criteria

Another set of standards widely used by lending and leasing institutions looks at total Finance Charges (rent, interest, leasing charges, etc.), as a percentage of Gross Output and Gross Margin;

Finance as a % of Gross Output	Finance as a % of Gross Margin	Lending Criteria
0-10%	0-15%	Normally very safe
11-15%	16-22.5%	Common range, should be safe
16-20%	23-29%	Care required
20% plus	30% plus	Potentially dangerous

As lenders will be well aware, however, these ratios too must be regarded with caution and in conjunction with the farm's level of net worth (% equity) and its trend in recent years, recent trends in its profitability and the potential borrower's record of expenditure both on and off the farm, together with his or her character and potential. Also, of course, some enterprises / types of farming are more risky than others.

DISCOUNTING TABLE

Discount Factors for Calculating the Present Value of Future (irregular) Cash Flows

Year	Percentage																
	3%	4%	5%	6%	7%	8%	9%	10%	11%	12%	13%	14%	15%	16%	18%	20%	25%
1	0.971	0.962	0.952	0.943	0.935	0.926	0.917	0.909	0.901	0.893	0.885	0.877	0.870	0.862	0.847	0.833	0.800
2	0.943	0.925	0.907	0.890	0.873	0.857	0.842	0.826	0.812	0.797	0.783	0.769	0.756	0.743	0.718	0.694	0.640
3	0.915	0.889	0.864	0.840	0.816	0.794	0.772	0.751	0.731	0.712	0.693	0.675	0.658	0.641	0.609	0.579	0.512
4	0.888	0.855	0.823	0.792	0.763	0.735	0.708	0.683	0.659	0.636	0.613	0.592	0.572	0.552	0.516	0.482	0.410
5	0.863	0.822	0.784	0.747	0.713	0.681	0.650	0.621	0.593	0.567	0.543	0.519	0.497	0.476	0.437	0.402	0.328
6	0.837	0.790	0.746	0.705	0.666	0.630	0.596	0.564	0.535	0.507	0.480	0.456	0.432	0.410	0.370	0.335	0.262
7	0.813	0.760	0.711	0.665	0.623	0.583	0.547	0.513	0.482	0.452	0.425	0.400	0.376	0.354	0.314	0.279	0.210
8	0.789	0.731	0.677	0.627	0.582	0.540	0.502	0.467	0.434	0.404	0.376	0.351	0.327	0.305	0.266	0.233	0.168
9	0.766	0.703	0.645	0.592	0.544	0.500	0.460	0.424	0.391	0.361	0.333	0.308	0.284	0.263	0.225	0.194	0.134
10	0.744	0.676	0.614	0.558	0.508	0.463	0.422	0.386	0.352	0.322	0.295	0.270	0.247	0.227	0.191	0.162	0.107
11	0.722	0.650	0.585	0.527	0.475	0.429	0.388	0.350	0.317	0.287	0.261	0.237	0.215	0.195	0.162	0.135	0.086
12	0.701	0.625	0.557	0.497	0.444	0.397	0.356	0.319	0.286	0.257	0.231	0.208	0.187	0.168	0.137	0.112	0.069
13	0.681	0.601	0.530	0.469	0.415	0.368	0.326	0.290	0.258	0.229	0.204	0.182	0.163	0.145	0.116	0.093	0.055
14	0.661	0.577	0.505	0.442	0.388	0.340	0.299	0.263	0.232	0.205	0.181	0.160	0.141	0.125	0.098	0.078	0.044
15	0.642	0.555	0.481	0.417	0.362	0.315	0.275	0.239	0.209	0.183	0.160	0.140	0.123	0.108	0.084	0.065	0.035
20	0.554	0.456	0.377	0.312	0.258	0.215	0.178	0.149	0.124	0.104	0.087	0.073	0.061	0.051	0.037	0.026	0.012
25	0.478	0.375	0.295	0.233	0.184	0.146	0.116	0.092	0.074	0.059	0.047	0.038	0.030	0.024	0.016	0.010	0.004
30	0.412	0.308	0.231	0.174	0.131	0.099	0.075	0.057	0.044	0.033	0.026	0.020	0.015	0.012	0.007	0.004	0.001

Example: The Present Value of £500 received 10 years from now, at 12 per cent discount rate of interest = 500 x 0.322 = £161.

Conversely, £161 invested now, at 12 per cent compound interest, will be worth £500 in 10 years' time.

DISCOUNTING TABLE B

Discount Factors for Calculating the Present Value of Future Annuity (i.e. Constant Annual Cash Flow) Receivable in Year 1 to n inclusive.

Year	Percentage																
	3%	4%	5%	6%	7%	8%	9%	10%	11%	12%	13%	14%	15%	16%	18%	20%	25%
1	0.971	0.962	0.952	0.943	0.935	0.926	0.917	0.909	0.901	0.893	0.885	0.877	0.870	0.862	0.847	0.833	0.800
2	1.913	1.886	1.859	1.833	1.808	1.783	1.759	1.736	1.713	1.690	1.668	1.647	1.626	1.605	1.566	1.528	1.440
3	2.829	2.775	2.723	2.673	2.624	2.577	2.531	2.487	2.444	2.402	2.361	2.322	2.283	2.246	2.174	2.106	1.952
4	3.717	3.630	3.546	3.465	3.387	3.312	3.240	3.170	3.102	3.037	2.974	2.914	2.855	2.798	2.690	2.589	2.362
5	4.580	4.452	4.329	4.212	4.100	3.993	3.890	3.791	3.696	3.605	3.517	3.433	3.352	3.274	3.127	2.991	2.689
6	5.417	5.242	5.076	4.917	4.767	4.623	4.486	4.355	4.231	4.111	3.998	3.889	3.784	3.685	3.498	3.326	2.951
7	6.230	6.002	5.786	5.582	5.389	5.206	5.033	4.868	4.712	4.564	4.423	4.288	4.160	4.039	3.812	3.605	3.161
8	7.020	6.733	6.463	6.210	5.971	5.747	5.535	5.335	5.146	4.968	4.799	4.639	4.487	4.344	4.078	3.837	3.329
9	7.786	7.435	7.108	6.802	6.515	6.247	5.995	5.759	5.537	5.328	5.132	4.946	4.772	4.607	4.303	4.031	3.463
10	8.530	8.111	7.722	7.360	7.024	6.710	6.418	6.145	5.889	5.650	5.426	5.216	5.019	4.833	4.494	4.192	3.570
11	9.253	8.760	8.306	7.887	7.499	7.139	6.805	6.495	6.207	5.938	5.687	5.453	5.234	5.029	4.656	4.327	3.656
12	9.954	9.385	8.863	8.384	7.943	7.536	7.161	6.814	6.492	6.194	5.918	5.660	5.421	5.197	4.793	4.439	3.725
13	10.635	9.986	9.394	8.853	8.358	7.904	7.487	7.103	6.750	6.424	6.122	5.842	5.583	5.342	4.910	4.533	3.780
14	11.296	10.563	9.899	9.295	8.745	8.244	7.786	7.367	6.982	6.628	6.302	6.002	5.724	5.468	5.008	4.611	3.824
15	11.938	11.118	10.380	9.712	9.108	8.559	8.061	7.606	7.191	6.811	6.462	6.142	5.847	5.575	5.092	4.675	3.859
20	14.877	13.590	12.462	11.470	10.594	9.818	9.129	8.514	7.963	7.469	7.025	6.623	6.259	5.929	5.353	4.870	3.954
25	17.413	15.662	14.094	12.783	11.654	10.675	9.823	9.077	8.422	7.843	7.330	6.873	6.464	6.097	5.467	4.948	3.985
30	19.600	17.292	15.372	13.765	12.409	11.258	10.274	9.427	8.694	8.055	7.496	7.003	6.566	6.177	5.517	4.979	3.995

Example: The Present Value of £500 a year for the next 10 years, at 12 per cent discount rate of interest = 500 × 5.650 = £2,825. This is the same answer that would be obtained by multiplying 500 by each discount factor (at 12 per cent) in Table A for each year from 1 to 10, and adding together the ten resulting figures.

To obtain the Discounted Yield of a constant annual net cash flow, divide this into the original investment and look up the resulting figure in the table above, against the number of years. Example: an investment of £1,000 is estimated to produce £80 a year additional profit over 10 years (before charging interest). Add £100 depreciation a year = £180 annual net cash flow. 1000 /180 = 5.56. This equals just over 12 per cent (the 10 years /12 per cent figure being 5.650).

243

COMPOUNDING TABLE

The Future Money Value of £1 after n Years with no additional payments made

Rate of Interest

Year	3%	4%	5%	6%	7%	8%	9%	10%	11%	12%	13%	14%	15%	16%	18%	20%	25%
1	1.03	1.04	1.05	1.06	1.07	1.08	1.09	1.10	1.11	1.12	1.13	1.14	1.15	1.16	1.18	1.20	1.25
2	1.06	1.08	1.10	1.12	1.14	1.17	1.19	1.21	1.23	1.25	1.28	1.30	1.32	1.35	1.39	1.44	1.56
3	1.09	1.12	1.16	1.19	1.23	1.26	1.30	1.33	1.37	1.40	1.44	1.48	1.52	1.56	1.64	1.73	1.95
4	1.13	1.17	1.22	1.26	1.31	1.36	1.41	1.46	1.52	1.57	1.63	1.69	1.75	1.81	1.94	2.07	2.44
5	1.16	1.22	1.28	1.34	1.40	1.47	1.54	1.61	1.69	1.76	1.84	1.93	2.01	2.10	2.29	2.49	3.05
6	1.19	1.27	1.34	1.42	1.50	1.59	1.68	1.77	1.87	1.97	2.08	2.19	2.31	2.44	2.70	2.99	3.81
7	1.23	1.32	1.41	1.50	1.61	1.71	1.83	1.95	2.08	2.21	2.35	2.50	2.66	2.83	3.19	3.58	4.77
8	1.27	1.37	1.48	1.59	1.72	1.85	1.99	2.14	2.30	2.48	2.66	2.85	3.06	3.28	3.76	4.30	5.96
9	1.30	1.42	1.55	1.69	1.84	2.00	2.17	2.36	2.56	2.77	3.00	3.25	3.52	3.80	4.44	5.16	7.45
10	1.34	1.48	1.63	1.79	1.97	2.16	2.37	2.59	2.84	3.11	3.39	3.71	4.05	4.41	5.23	6.19	9.31
11	1.38	1.54	1.71	1.90	2.10	2.33	2.58	2.85	3.15	3.48	3.84	4.23	4.65	5.12	6.18	7.43	11.64
12	1.43	1.60	1.80	2.01	2.25	2.52	2.81	3.14	3.50	3.90	4.33	4.82	5.35	5.94	7.29	8.92	14.55
13	1.47	1.67	1.89	2.13	2.41	2.72	3.07	3.45	3.88	4.36	4.90	5.49	6.15	6.89	8.60	10.70	18.19
14	1.51	1.73	1.98	2.26	2.58	2.94	3.34	3.80	4.31	4.89	5.53	6.26	7.08	7.99	10.15	12.84	22.74
15	1.56	1.80	2.08	2.40	2.76	3.17	3.64	4.18	4.78	5.47	6.25	7.14	8.14	9.27	11.97	15.41	28.42
20	1.81	2.19	2.65	3.21	3.87	4.66	5.60	6.73	8.06	9.65	11.52	13.74	16.37	19.46	27.39	38.34	86.74
25	2.09	2.67	3.39	4.29	5.43	6.85	8.62	10.83	13.59	17.00	21.23	26.46	32.92	40.87	62.67	95.40	264.7
30	2.43	3.24	4.32	5.74	7.61	10.06	13.27	17.45	22.89	29.96	39.12	50.95	66.21	85.85	143.4	237.4	807.8

COMPOUNDING TABLE B

The Future Money Value of £1 after n Years*

Year	Rate of Interest																
	3%	4%	5%	6%	7%	8%	9%	10%	11%	12%	13%	14%	15%	16%	18%	20%	25%
1	1.03	1.04	1.05	1.06	1.07	1.08	1.09	1.10	1.11	1.12	1.13	1.14	1.15	1.16	1.18	1.20	1.25
2	2.09	2.12	2.15	2.18	2.21	2.25	2.28	2.31	2.34	2.37	2.41	2.44	2.47	2.51	2.57	2.64	2.81
3	3.18	3.25	3.31	3.37	3.44	3.51	3.57	3.64	3.71	3.78	3.85	3.92	3.99	4.07	4.22	4.37	4.77
4	4.31	4.42	4.53	4.64	4.75	4.87	4.98	5.11	5.23	5.35	5.48	5.61	5.74	5.88	6.15	6.44	7.21
5	5.47	5.63	5.80	5.98	6.15	6.34	6.52	6.72	6.91	7.12	7.32	7.54	7.75	7.98	8.44	8.93	10.26
6	6.66	6.90	7.14	7.39	7.65	7.92	8.20	8.49	8.78	9.09	9.40	9.73	10.07	10.41	11.14	11.92	14.07
7	7.89	8.21	8.55	8.90	9.26	9.64	10.03	10.44	10.86	11.30	11.76	12.23	12.73	13.24	14.33	15.50	18.84
8	9.16	9.58	10.03	10.49	10.98	11.49	12.02	12.58	13.16	13.78	14.42	15.09	15.79	16.52	18.09	19.80	24.80
9	10.46	11.01	11.58	12.18	12.82	13.49	14.19	14.94	15.72	16.55	17.42	18.34	19.30	20.32	22.52	24.96	32.25
10	11.81	12.49	13.21	13.97	14.78	15.65	16.56	17.53	18.56	19.65	20.81	22.04	23.35	24.73	27.76	31.15	41.57
11	13.19	14.03	14.92	15.87	16.89	17.98	19.14	20.38	21.71	23.13	24.65	26.27	28.00	29.85	33.93	38.58	53.21
12	14.62	15.63	16.71	17.88	19.14	20.50	21.95	23.52	25.21	27.03	28.98	31.09	33.35	35.79	41.22	47.50	67.76
13	16.09	17.29	18.60	20.02	21.55	23.21	25.02	26.97	29.09	31.39	33.88	36.58	39.50	42.67	49.82	58.20	85.95
14	17.60	19.02	20.58	22.28	24.13	26.15	28.36	30.77	33.41	36.28	39.42	42.84	46.58	50.66	59.97	71.04	108.7
15	19.16	20.82	22.66	24.67	26.89	29.32	32.00	34.95	38.19	41.75	45.67	49.98	54.72	59.93	71.94	86.44	137.1
20	27.68	30.97	34.72	38.99	43.87	49.42	55.76	63.00	71.27	80.70	91.47	103.8	117.8	133.8	173.0	224.0	428.7
25	37.55	43.31	50.11	58.16	67.68	78.95	92.32	108.2	127.0	149.3	175.8	207.3	244.7	289.1	404.3	566.4	1318
30	49.00	58.33	69.76	83.80	101.1	122.3	148.6	180.9	220.9	270.3	331.3	406.7	500.0	615.2	933.3	1418	4034

* Equal payments made at the beginning of each year.

AMORTISATION TABLE

Annual Charge to write off £1,000

Write-off Period	Rate of Interest															
	3	4	5	6	7	8	9	10	11	12	13	14	15	16	18	20
5 years	218	225	231	237	244	250	257	264	271	277	284	291	298	305	320	334
6	185	191	197	203	210	216	223	230	236	243	250	257	264	271	286	301
7	161	167	173	179	186	192	199	205	212	219	226	233	240	248	262	277
8	142	149	155	161	167	174	181	187	194	201	208	216	223	230	245	261
9	128	134	141	147	153	160	167	174	181	188	195	202	210	217	232	248
10	117	123	130	136	142	149	156	163	170	177	184	192	199	207	223	239
11	108	114	120	127	133	140	147	154	161	168	176	183	191	199	215	231
12	100	107	113	119	125	133	140	147	154	161	169	177	184	192	209	225
13	94	100	106	113	120	127	134	141	148	156	163	171	179	187	204	221
14	89	95	101	108	114	121	128	136	143	151	159	167	175	183	200	217
15	84	90	96	103	110	117	124	131	139	147	155	163	171	179	196	214
16	80	86	92	99	106	113	120	128	136	143	151	160	168	176	194	211
17	76	82	89	95	102	110	117	125	132	140	149	157	165	174	191	209
18	73	79	86	92	99	107	114	122	130	138	146	155	163	172	190	208
19	70	76	83	90	97	104	112	120	128	136	144	153	161	170	188	206
20	67	74	80	87	94	102	110	117	126	134	142	151	160	169	187	205
25	57	64	71	78	86	94	102	110	119	127	136	145	155	164	183	202
30	51	58	65	73	81	89	97	106	115	124	133	143	152	162	181	201
40	43	51	58	66	75	84	93	102	112	122	131	141	151	160	180	200

Example: £3,000 is borrowed to erect a building. The annual charge to service interest and capital repayment on the £3,000, repayable over 10 years at 12%, is 3 x £177 = £531. Where the write-off period of the building (10 years) is equal to the repayment period of the loan, then the average annual depreciation and interest will also equal £531.

The proportion of the total annual charge representing the average amount of capital repaid per annum can be readily determined by dividing the sum borrowed by the number of years of the loan: (in the above example this is £3,000 ÷ 10 = £300/year). The remainder is clearly the average amount of interest paid per annum: (in the above example, £531 — £300 = £231/year). The year to year variations between the two items (i.e. capital repaid and interest) are shown in the tables on pages 228 to 230, which demonstrate the way in which the capital repayment part increases and the interest part decreases over time.

SINKING FUND TABLE

The sum required to be set aside at the end of each year to make £1,000

Rate of Interest

No. of Years	3	4	5	6	7	8	9	10	11	12	13	14	15	16	18	20
5	188	185	181	177	174	170	167	164	161	157	154	151	148	145	140	134
6	155	151	147	143	140	136	133	130	126	123	120	117	114	111	106	101
7	131	127	123	119	116	112	109	105	102	99	96	93	90	88	82	77
8	112	109	105	101	97	94	91	87	84	81	78	76	73	70	65	61
9	98	94	91	87	83	80	77	74	71	68	65	62	60	57	52	48
10	87	83	80	76	72	69	66	63	60	57	54	52	49	47	43	39
11	78	74	70	67	63	60	57	54	51	48	46	43	41	39	35	31
12	70	67	63	59	56	53	50	47	44	41	39	37	34	32	29	25
13	64	60	56	53	50	47	44	41	38	36	33	31	29	27	24	21
14	59	55	51	48	44	41	38	36	33	31	29	27	25	23	20	17
15	54	50	46	43	40	37	34	31	29	27	25	23	21	19	16	14
16	50	46	42	39	36	33	30	28	26	23	21	20	18	16	14	11
17	46	42	39	35	32	30	27	25	22	20	19	17	15	14	11	9
18	43	39	36	32	29	27	24	22	20	18	16	15	13	12	10	8
19	40	36	33	30	27	24	22	20	18	16	14	13	11	10	8	6
20	37	34	30	27	24	22	20	17	16	14	12	11	10	9	7	5
25	27	24	21	18	16	14	12	10	9	7	6	5	5	4	3	2
30	21	18	15	13	11	9	7	6	5	4	3	3	2	2	1	1
40	13	11	8	6	5	4	3	2	2	1	1	1	1	—	—	—

MORTGAGE REPAYMENT DATA

Items per £1000 invested; where I = Interest, P = Principal repaid, L = Loan outstanding

Loan of	4%			5%			6%			8%			10%			12%		
	I	P	L	I	P	L	I	P	L	I	P	L	I	P	L	I	P	L
5 years																		
1	40	185	815	50	181	819	60	177	823	80	170	830	100	164	836	120	157	834
2	33	192	623	41	190	629	49	188	635	66	184	645	84	180	656	101	175	670
3	25	200	424	31	200	424	38	199	435	52	199	447	66	198	458	80	197	469
4	17	208	216	21	210	220	26	211	224	36	215	232	46	218	240	56	221	248
5	9	216	0	11	220	0	13	224	0	19	232	0	24	240	0	30	248	0
10 years																		
1	40	83	917	50	80	920	60	76	924	80	69	931	100	63	939	120	57	934
2	37	87	830	46	83	837	55	80	844	75	75	856	94	69	868	113	64	879
3	33	90	740	42	88	749	51	85	758	69	81	776	87	76	792	106	71	808
4	30	94	646	37	92	657	46	90	668	62	87	689	79	84	709	97	80	728
5	26	97	549	33	97	561	40	96	572	55	94	595	71	92	617	87	90	638
6	22	101	448	28	101	459	34	102	471	48	101	494	62	101	516	77	100	538
7	18	105	342	23	107	353	28	108	363	39	110	384	52	111	405	65	112	425
8	14	110	233	18	112	241	22	114	249	31	118	266	40	122	282	51	126	299
9	9	114	119	12	117	123	15	121	128	21	128	138	28	134	148	36	141	158
10	5	119	0	6	123	0	8	128	0	11	138	0	15	148	0	19	158	0

MORTGAGE REPAYMENT DATA (CONTINUED)

Loan of	4%			5%			6%			8%			10%			12%		
	I	P	L	I	P	L	I	P	L	I	P	L	I	P	L	I	P	L
20 years																		
1	40	34	966	50	30	970	60	27	973	80	22	978	100	17	983	120	14	986
5	34	39	818	43	37	833	53	34	847	72	30	872	92	26	893	112	22	912
10	26	48	597	33	47	620	41	46	642	58	44	683	76	41	722	95	38	756
15	15	58	328	20	60	347	26	61	367	38	64	407	51	66	445	66	68	483
20	3	71	0	4	76	0	5	82	0	8	94	0	11	107	0	14	120	0
25 years																		
1	40	24	976	50	21	979	60	18	982	80	14	986	100	10	990	120	7	993
5	36	28	870	45	25	884	55	23	897	75	19	920	95	15	938	116	12	952
10	30	34	712	38	33	736	47	31	760	66	27	802	86	24	838	107	21	868
15	22	42	519	29	41	548	37	41	576	54	40	629	72	39	677	91	37	720
20	13	51	285	18	53	307	23	55	330	35	59	374	48	62	418	63	65	460
25	2	62	0	3	68	0	4	74	0	7	87	0	10	100	0	14	114	0

MORTGAGE REPAYMENT DATA (CONTINUED)

Loan through	6%			8%			10%			12%			14%			16%		
	I	P	L	I	P	L	I	P	L	I	P	L	I	P	L	I	P	L
30 years																		
1	60	13	987	80	9	991	100	6	994	120	4	996	140	3	997	160	2	998
5	57	16	929	77	12	948	97	9	963	118	7	974	138	5	986	158	3	987
10	51	21	833	71	18	872	92	14	903	113	11	927	134	9	951	155	7	960
15	44	29	706	63	26	760	83	23	807	104	20	846	126	17	890	147	15	903
20	34	38	535	51	38	596	69	37	652	88	36	701	108	35	751	130	32	782
25	21	51	306	33	56	355	46	60	402	61	63	488	83	60	494	95	66	530
30	4	69	0	7	82	0	10	96	0	13	111	0	16	127	0	22	140	0
40 years																		
1	60	6	994	80	4	996	100	2	998	120	1	999	140	1	999	160	0	1000
5	58	8	964	79	5	977	99	3	986	119	2	992	139	2	995	160	1	997
10	56	11	915	76	8	944	97	5	964	118	4	977	138	3	989	159	2	991
15	52	15	850	73	11	895	94	9	928	115	6	951	136	5	973	157	3	978
20	47	20	762	67	17	823	88	14	871	110	11	906	130	11	942	153	7	951
25	40	26	645	59	24	718	80	22	778	102	20	826	123	18	874	145	15	894
30	31	35	489	48	36	563	66	36	628	86	35	685	109	32	742	129	31	775
35	20	47	280	31	53	335	45	58	388	60	61	437	85	56	487	95	66	525
40	4	63	0	6	78	0	9	93	0	13	108	0	18	123	0	22	138	0

Note—All figures rounded to nearest £.

6.   FARM RECORDS

The following records should be kept for management purposes:

Basic Whole Farm Financial Position

1.   Cash Analysis Book, fully detailed.

2.   Petty Cash Book.

3.   Annual Valuation, including physical quantities of

    i.   Harvested crops in store

    ii.   Livestock (breeding and fattening) at (near) market value, less any variable costs yet to be borne.

    iii.   Fertilisers, seeds, sprays, casual labour or contract work applied to growing crops should be recorded, but "cultivations" and manurial residues can be ignored for management purposes.

    iv.   Fertiliser, seed, sprays and other sundry direct items in store,

4.   Debtors and creditors at the end of the financial year.

Other Financial and Physical Records

5.   Output (quantities and value) of each crop and livestock enterprise for the "harvest year" (or production cycle). It may be possible to get information of sales from a fully detailed cash analysis book (although, for crops, the financial year figures will then have to be allocated between crops from the current harvest and those from the harvest in the previous financial year, in order to check on the accuracy of the opening valuation of crops in store; this is particularly a problem with Michaelmas ending accounts). The following records of internal transfers and consumption will also be required:

    (a)   Numbers and market value of livestock transferred from one livestock category to another, e.g. dairy calves to dairy followers or beef enterprise, or dairy heifers to dairy enterprise.

    (b)   Quantity and market value of cereals fed on farm and used for seed.

    (c)   Quantity and market value of milk and other produce consumed by the farmer or his employees, used on the farm (e.g. milk fed to calves), or sold direct.

6.   A monthly record of livestock numbers; preferably reconciled with the previous month according to births, purchases, deaths, sales and transfers.

7.   Costs and quantities of concentrate feed to each category of livestock, including home-grown cereals fed on the farm.

8.   Allocation of costs of seed, fertiliser, sprays, casual labour and contract work specific to an enterprise. This is in order to calculate gross margins, where required.

9.   Breeding record for cows, including bulling dates, date(s) served, type of bull used, pregnancy testing, estimated calving date, actual calving date, and date when dried off.

10. For each crop, total output and yield per hectare, in both quantity and value. Include each field where the crop has been grown and its approximate yield, where this can be satisfactorily obtained.

11. For each field, keep one page to cover a period of say, ten years. Record on this, each year, crop grown, variety sown, fertiliser used, sprays used, date sown, date(s) harvested, approximate yield (if obtainable), and any other special notes that you feel may have significance for the future.

12. A rotation record. On a single page, if possible, list each field down the side and say, ten years along the top. Colour each field-year space according to the crop grown, e.g. barley yellow, potatoes red, etc.

13. It is important to note that other farm records are required for legislative and cross compliance purposes including:

    i.   Livestock movements, identification, flock and herd records etc

    ii.   Nitrate Vulnerable Zone (NVZ) records and calculations including livestock loadings, manure storage, fertiliser plans and usage etc

    iii.   Pesticide application and storage records, risk assessments

    iv.   Farm waste storage and disposal records and necessary exemptions / permits / transfer certificates

    v.   Integrated Pollution and Prevention Controls (IPPC) records (for pig and poultry units)

    vi.   Soil Protection reviews and risk assessments

    vii.   Financial (HMRC) records including VAT, PAYE, NI etc

IX.   MISCELLANEOUS DATA

1.   CONSERVATION COSTS

Note: Costs can vary quite widely, depending on geographical location and the type and size of the job. Markets for such services can be highly localised, sparse in some areas, competitive in others.

Hedges

Hedge Cutting. From £300 per day at an average of 3 miles per day.

Hedge Laying (Making hedges stock proof and rejuvenated by selective cutting and positioning). Depends on hedge thickness (single or double). Mechanical Laying: up to 250m/day (2 people) £360 plus materials. Manual hedge laying approximately 20m/day at £7/metre.

Hedge Planting. Transplants av. £43/100; netlon guards 50p; canes 10p; fencing (labour and materials): stock proof £3.75/metre, rabbit proof (dug in) up to £5.75/metre. Overall, £2.50/metre unguarded and unfenced, £9.75/metre guarded and fenced. Contract labour: planting up to £2.35/metre, fencing up to £2.70/metre. Contractor 100-150 metres/day. Pref Oct./March. Above includes repair.

Hedge Coppicing. By hand: 2 men and a chain saw, £5-6/metre plus burning debris. Contractor: tractor mounted saw, driver and 2 men, 13 metres/ hour, £37.50/hour.

Dry Stone Walls

Dry Stone Walling. Cost of stone approximately £100/tonne, varying regionally and depending on local stone. Cost of building wall £70-£85 per square metre.

Trees

Amenity Tree Planting; (half acre block or less). Transplants av. 90p; shelter plus stake and tie £1.20; stake 50p; whip 75p. rabbit spiral guard 33p; netlon guard av. 50p; cane av. 12p. Trees per man day: farmer 200, contractor 400; (large-scale, 33 man days/ha). Optimal time November to April.

Shelter Belts. Per 100 metre length: 100 large species (oak, lime, etc.) £50; 66 medium species (cherry, birch, etc.) £43; 100 shrubs, £34; 166 tree stakes, shelters and ties, £265; (site preparation, weed control, labour and fencing extra). DEFRA standard costs £670/ha; windbreaks £36.00/ha.

Woodland Establishment. Conifers £200/1,000. To supply and plant oak or beech transplants (2-3ft tall) in tubes £3.50-£4.00 each, dependent on shelter size. Rabbit fencing £5.75/metre (dug in). Contract labour: conifers at 2m (inc. trees) £1,500/ha; broadleaves at 3m (inc. trees) £1,000/ha; forest transplants (not inc. trees) £280/1,050. 12.5 days/ha (contractor). Optimal timing November to April. (Above not including maintenance).

Forestry, General. Contract labour: chain sawing £20/hr., brush cutting £12.00/hr, extracting timber/pulp £4.50-£10.50/tonne, chemical spot weeding 7p-10p/tree, rhododendron control £640-£850/acre.

Pollarding and Tree Surgery. Pollard: £45-£67/stool; surgery: £165/ tree. Pollarding: 2 or 3 trees/day. Surgery: 2 days/tree. Winter. Pollard every 20-40 years.

Ponds and Ditches

Pond Construction. Butyl lining (0.75mm) £5.20/m^2; other linings up to £3.25/m^2. Contract labour: 150 Komatsu £28/hr.; bulldozer D6 LGP £44/hr, 13t 360° excavator £39/hr (excluding haulage), Flailmowers from £17.50/hr. Autumn (dry ground conditions).

Pond Maintenance. Hymac £39/hr.; Backhoe £22.50-25/hr. 100 m^2/day (contractor). Timing: probably winter; time depends on ground condition and species whose life cycles may be disturbed. Every 5 to 50 years.

Ditch Maintenance. Backhoe excavator £21.50/hr; 13 tonne 360° excavator £31.50/hr.; labour £11.00/hr. preferably in winter. Every 3 to 7 years on rotation.

Grassland

Permanent Grass Margins at Field Edges. To provide wildlife benefits and help control pernicious weeds, reducing herbicides at the field edge. (A sterile strip provides virtually no wildlife benefit and the initial establishment costs may be offset by savings in maintenance costs in future years.) Costs per 100 metres inc. seeds as follows.

- Establishment: 2m grass margins, £5.00-£6.00;
- 6m grass margins, £15-£20;
- beetle banks, £4.50-£6.00 (6m wide).
- Maintenance: 2m margins, 55p to 70p;
- 6m margins, £1.80-£2.10.

Establishment of Wildlife Grassland Meadow. £170-265/ha for ground preparation, depending on weed burden, more for heavy land or exceptional weed burden. Seed costs very variable, but as a guide:

- Native Perennial wild flowers and grasses, £11.50/kg, 25kg/ha = £285-320/ha
- Nectar mix for bumble bees and butterflies £12.00/kg, 25kg/ha = £300/ha
- Bird Seed sward £4.60/kg, 12kg/ha = £55/ha for single year crop, £3.30/kg, 50kg/ha = £165 for longer sward.
- Single species native grass seeds vary from £2.50/kg (e.g. Meadow Fescue) to £60/kg (Sweet Vernal).
- Single species native perennial wild flower seeds vary from £44/kg (Lady's Bedstraw) to over £450/kg (Cowslip)
- Buffer strip grass margin mix for cross compliance, ELS and HLS compliance, £3.30/kg drilled at 25kg/ha = £85/ha. Costs of ground preparation and drilling are usually higher than the seed.

Acknowledgement: Thanks to - Cotswold Seeds, 0800 252 211.

2. FERTILISER PRICES

Compounds	Analysis			Price Per Tonne
	N	P$_2$O$_5$	K$_2$O	£
	0	24	24	302
	0	18	36	326
	0	20	30	307
	0	30	15	294
	0	30	20	321
	5	24	24	333
	8	24	24	352
	10	26	26	(B) 389
	11	15	20	(B) 287
	13	13	20	286
	15	15	20	312
	16	16	16	(B) 303
	22	4	14	(B) 248
	20	10	10	(B) 255
	25	5	5	(B) 225
	26	0	15	251

Straights	Price per tonne £
Ammonium Nitrate: UK (34.5% N)	215
Ammonium Nitrate: Imported (34.5% N)	206
NS grade: UK (27% N, 30% SO$_3$)	193
Sulphate of Ammonia (21% N, 60% SO$_3$)	180
Urea (46% N.): granular/ prills	287
Liquid Nitrogen (26% N, 5% SO$_3$)	166
Triple Superphosphate (TSP) (46% P$_2$O$_5$)	315
DAP (18/46/0)	427
MAP (12/52/0)	431
Muriate of Potash (MOP) (60% K$_2$O)	325

Average price (p) per kg:	N :	62.3	(UK AN)
	P$_2$O$_5$:	68.5	(TSP)
	K$_2$O :	54.2	(MOP)

The prices above are for fertiliser delivered in 600kg bags; delivery in bulk averages £6.50/tonne less; collection of bags by farmers £8/tonne less. They are spot prices in August 2010; they vary according to area and bargaining power. (B) is blended; prices for granular (where available) average around £4/tonne more. They assume delivery in 25-27 tonne loads; add approximately £3/tonne for 10 tonne loads, £8 for 6-9 tonne loads, £15-20 for 4-5 tonne loads.

3.   MANURE VALUE OF SLURRY

Nutrient Values of Common Farm Yard Manure Types

		(kg N/t)		(kg P₂O₅/t)		(kg K₂O/t)	
	Dry Matter %	Total N	Available N	Total P	Available P	Total K	Available K
Cattle FYM *	25	6.0	0.6	3.2	1.9	8.0	7.2
Pig FYM	25	7.0	1.0	6.0	3.6	8.0	7.2
Sheep FYM	25	7.0	0.7	3.2	1.9	8.0	7.2
Duck FYM	25	6.5	1.0	5.5	3.3	7.5	6.8
Horse FYM	30	7.0	N/a	5.0	3.0	6.0	5.4

For manure stored for 3 months or more. FYM = Farmyard Manure

Note: these nutrient contents are for guidance only and will vary between different livestock systems and storage methods. Analysis should be performed to understand the specific values of manure.

Manure Output per Head during the Housing Period

	Undiluted Excreta t or m³	Total Kg		
		N	P₂O₅	K₂O
1 dairy cow ~ 6,000 to 9,000 litres milk yield	11.6	60	26	46
1 beef cow ~ >500 kg	8.2	41	15.5	33
1 finishing pig ~ per place ~ 86% occupancy	1.6	10.6	5.6	5.6
1,000 broiler hens ~ per hen place ~ 85% occupancy	19	330	220	340

Note: These figures should not be used for calculating NVZ compliance as they only allow for the time spent in the buildings and therefore exclude manure deposited in fields during grazing. Refer to the DEFRA NVZ guidance booklets for NVZ calculation methodology and annual manure output tables.

Lime

The cost of lime is divided between cost of the material, cost of hauling it to the field and the cost of application. The grade and quality varies greatly, with differing contaminants, and is milled more at differing grades, some through a maximum sieve of 4mm, others farm larger. As a guide, a reasonable grade of lime, delivered 12 miles and applied at 5 tonnes per hectare (2t/acre) would currently cost in the region of £15/tonne.

Biosolids (Sewage Sludge)

Biosolids act as good soil conditioner and fertiliser to farmers, whilst providing the most environmentally favourable method for water companies to dispose of the sludge. Biosolids vary in nutritional composition depending on processing and location, but RB209 describes its content as follows:

Biosolid Key Composition

	Digested Cake	Thermally Dried Pellets	Lime Stabilised
Dry Matter	25%	95%	40%
Total Nitrogen *kg/t*	*11*	*40*	*8.5*
Available N *kg/t*	1.6	2	0.9
Available P_2O_5 *kg/t*	9	35	13
Available K_2O *kg/t*	0.5	1.8	0.7
Available SO_3 *kg/t*	6	23	8.5
Guideline Price £/t applied	£2.50	£25	£2.50

Nutrient data taken from RB209(2010)

4.   AGROCHEMICAL COSTS

Only the names of the active ingredients are given below, with their principal use. These materials should only be applied in accordance with the manufacturers' recommendations.

Application rates vary and there are differences between the prices of various proprietary brands. The list is not intended to be exhaustive and there is no implied criticism of materials omitted.

The variation in costs per hectare is because of varying application rates rather than price variation between suppliers. It is priced on the purchase of chemical alone, i.e., not the agronomy service. The separate service can be priced in various ways, but for cereal farms roughly £8.50-£9.00/ha is normal when the two are separated or a percentage of agrochemical sales when combined.

Crop	Function		Material	Cost £/ha per application
Cereals	Herbicides	General	Mecoprop-P	5.50-12.70
			Ioxynil+Bromoxynil	4.60-9.20
			Dicamba +Mecoprop-P + MCPA	17.70-22.10
			Metsulfuron-methyl	16.30
			Mesosulphuron + Idosulphuron	30.00
			Difflufenican	4.65 – 7.75
			Clortoluron	13.80 – 23.00
		Cleavers	Fluroxypyr	11.60-15.50
			Amidosulfuron	8.00-12.00
			Florasalum + Fluroxypyr	13.90-20.90
		Wild Oats	Pinoxaden	16.40-42.50
		Wild Oats & Blackgrass	Clodinafop-propargyl	42.00
			Fenoxaprop-P-ethy	14.00-21.00
	Growth Regulator		Chlormequat	2.20
			Chlormequat + Choline Chloride	3.20
			As above + Imazaquin	10.00
			2-chlorethylphosphonic acid	5.20-10.35
			2-chloroethyl phosphonic acid + Mepiquat Chloride	7.20-15.00
			Trinexapac-ethyl	14.40-18.00
	Fungicides		Azoxystrobin	33.20
			Fenpropimorph	14.50-19.40
			Epoxiconazole	26.20
			Tebuconazole	16.80
			Prothioconazole	18.50-37.30
			Chlorothalonil	6.30
		Seed Dressing	Fuberidazole + Triadimenol	7.30-11.60

Crop	Function	Material	Cost £/ha per application
		Fuberidazole + Triadimenol + Imidacloprid	16.00-25.60
		Prythoconazole + Clothianidin	10.60-17.00
		Silthiofam	22.75-36.40
		Imidacloprid + tebuconazole + triazoxide	13.00-20.80
	Aphicide	Deltamethrin	3.30-4.10
		Pirimicarb	9.50
		Chlorpyriphos	6.30-12.60
	Slug Killer	Metaldehyde	11.85
		Methiocarb	24.23
Oilseed Rape	Herbicides	Propyzamide	35.25
		Metazachlor	24.00-40.00
		Metazachlor + Quinmerac	51.75
		Clomazone	23.20
	Insecticide	Deltamethrin	4.10
		Pirimicarb	9.50-14.20
		Alphacypermethrin	2.90-5.75
	Fungicide	Iprodione + thiophate-methyl	23.00-34.50
		Tebuconazole	8.40-16.80
		Flusilazole + Carbendazim	15.00-19.20
		Metconazole	20.00
	Dessicant	Glyphosate	5.50
Potatoes	Herbicides:	Metribuzin	14.50-29.00
		Linuron	18.00-34.50
		Diquat	9.20-18.40
		Clomazone	23.20
	Blight Control	Cymoxanil + Mancozeb	11.90
		Cymoxanil + Famoxadone	14.00-20.00
		Fluazinam	11.70
		Mancozeb+Metalaxyl	24.50
	Haulm Dessicant	Diquat	37.80

Sugar Beet

	Herbicides: Pre-emergence	Chloridazon:	
		overall	24.80-58.00
		band spray	8.25-19.40
	Post-emergence	Phenmedipham:	5.60-9.40
		Triflusulfron-methyl	20.00
	Insecticide	Oxamyl	36.40-54.50
		Pirimicarb	9.50

Crop	Function	Material	Cost £/ha per application
Beans	Herbicide	Bentazone	62.00
		Pendimethalin	16.40-19.70
		Clomazone	111 per l
	Fungicide	Chlorothalonil	18.80
		Tebuconazole	16.80
		Azoxystobin	33.20
Peas and Beans			
	Herbicide	Pendimethalin + Imazamox	38.20
	Insecticide	Pirimicarb	9.50
		Deltamethrin	4.10-5.00
Maize	Herbicide	Prosulfuron + Bromoxynil	34.20
		Nicosulfuron	21.80-32.70
		Bromoxynil	21.50
		Mesotrione	30.80
Brassicas	Herbicides	Metazachlor	32.30
		Pyridate	34.00
Broadleaved Grass weeds and volunteer Crops			
	Cereals	Fluazifop-P-butyl	21.20-31.80
		Propaquizafop	10.00-21.10
		Cycloxydim	23.00-38.25
Grassland	Herbicides	MCPA	7.80-13.00
General	Weed and Grass Killer		
	Couch Grass Control	Glyphosate	5.50-7.50
		clopyralid + fluroxypyr + fluroxypyr	25.70-51.50

The above prices are based on retail prices paid by farmers (2010) and reflect the discounts available where there are competing products from several manufacturers. The range in prices per hectare reflects the varying application rates. This is the price for the product, not including the agronomic advice that often comes with it.

Acknowledgement: thanks to Bartholemews 01243 784 171

5.   SEED ROYALTY RATES

Farm-saved seed payment rates for autumn 2010 and spring 2011

	£/ha	**£/tonne**
Wheat	5.88	36.10
Winter Barley	5.82	35.06
Spring Barley	7.24	40.20
Oats	4.80	32.42
Peas	7.91	34.99
Beans	9.64	47.71
Oilseed Rape	9.63	1,965.40
Linseed	6.97	118.11
Triticale	7.64	41.74
Potatoes	£18 to £258	(variety dependant)

Seed purchased from a merchant includes a component of royalty for the seed breeder. Those farmers who save seed from the previous season (farm saved seed) are legally obliged to pay the royalty. If the seed is cleaned and dressed, the royalty payment is taken at this point (per tonne), if not, the farmer is responsible for paying (per hectare). Many older varieties no longer have royalty payments payable. It is illegal to sell or buy seed unless under license. View eligible varieties at www.BSPB.co.uk .

6.   SEED DRILLING RATES

		Thousand Grain Weight (g/1000 grains)											
		35	**38**	**41**	**44**	**47**	**50**	**53**	**56**	**59**	**62**	**65**	**68**	**71**
	150	53	57	62	66	71	75	80	84	89	93	98	102	107
	175	61	67	72	77	82	88	93	98	103	109	114	119	124
	200	70	76	82	88	94	100	106	112	118	124	130	136	142
	225	79	86	92	99	106	113	119	126	133	140	146	153	160
	250	88	95	103	110	118	125	133	140	148	155	163	170	178
	275	96	105	113	121	129	138	146	154	162	171	179	187	195
	300	105	114	123	132	141	150	159	168	177	186	195	204	213
	325	114	124	133	143	153	163	172	182	192	202	211	221	231
	350	123	133	144	154	165	175	186	196	207	217	228	238	249
	375	131	143	154	165	176	188	199	210	221	233	244	255	266
	400	140	152	164	176	188	200	212	224	236	248	260	272	284
	425	149	162	174	187	200	213	225	238	251	264	276	289	302
	450	158	171	185	198	212	225	239	252	266	279	293	306	320

Seeds Planted per m^2 (row label)

Measured in Kg/Ha

7. FEED PRICES

			£ per tonne
Cattle	Dairy:	High Energy Parlour	170 - 180
		Medium Energy Blend	155 - 165
	Beef	Pellets (16% CP)	165 - 175
		Concentrate	165 - 185
	Calf	Milk Substitute (bags)	1,480 – 1,600
		High Fat (bags)	1,100
		Calf Weaner Pellets	210 - 225
		Calf Rearer Nuts	175 - 185
Sheep	High Energy Lamb Pellets.		175 - 185
	Medium energy sheep		160 - 170
	Sheep/lamb cake		160 - 170
	Ewe cake		170 - 180
Horses	Horse and Pony Pencils		250 - 350
Goats	Goat Nuts		205 - 220
Pigs	Piglet Weaner		280 - 295
	Sow Nuts		175 - 195
	Early Grower Pellets (20-24% protein)		230 - 250
	Grower/Finisher Pellets		190 - 210
	Sow Concentrate		285 - 295
	Grower Concentrate		295 - 305
Poultry	Chick and Rearer Feeds		175 - 215
	Layers Feeds		175 - 215
	Broiler Feeds		245 - 255
	Turkey Feeds		245 - 250
Straight Feeds	Fishmeal (66/70% CP)		960-1,100
	Soya Bean Meal (Hipro; 50% CP)		265 - 275
	Rapeseed Meal (34-36% CP)		190 - 205
	Palm Kernel Meal/Cake (17% CP)		120 - 130
	Sunflower Seed Pellets (30/33% CP)		160 - 170
	Citrus Pulp Nuts/Pellets		120 - 130
	Wheatfeed Meal (14-18% CP)		90 - 100
	Wheatfeed Pellets (14-18% CP)		95 - 105
	Maize Gluten		135 - 155
	Molasses (Cane) (5% CP)		165 - 175
	Sugar Beet Pulp (Molassed Nuts/Pellets)		130 - 140
	Brewers' Grains		20 - 40
	Distillers wheat grain		170 - 185
	Distillers Barley Grains		135 - 155

Compound feed prices are approximate ranges in July 2010; the range incorporates differences in the ingredients. They are delivered prices for hauls more than 10 miles in 25 tonne loads. The additional farm delivered cost for bags ranges from £18.00 to £27.50 a tonne.

8. FEEDSTUFF NUTRITIVE VALUES

Typical Energy and Protein Contents of Some Common Feeds

Type of Feed	Dry Matter Content g/kg	Metabolizable Energy MJ/kg DM	Crude Protein g/kg DM
Forages:			
Barley Straw	860	7.0	10
Grass Silage (typical clamp)	250	10.8	150
Hay (typical meadow)	850	8.8	100
Maize Silage	300	11.0	90
Pasture (rotational grazed)	180	11.5	160
Whole-crop Wheat (fermented)	400	10.5	95
Cereals:			
Barley	860	13.2	120
Oats	860	12.5	120
Wheat	860	13.6	130
Maize	880	13.8	90
Roots:			
Fodder Beet	180	12.0	60
Potatoes	200	13.3	100
Wet By-Products:			
Brewers Grains	260	11.5	250
Pressed Sugar Beet Pulp	260	12.5	100
Straights:			
Cane Molasses	750	12.7	40
Distillers Barley Grains	900	12.2	260
Distillers Maize Grains	900	14.0	310
Distillers Wheat Grains	900	13.5	340
Dried Citrus Pulp	900	12.6	70
Dried Molassed Sugar Beet Pulp	900	12.5	100
Extracted Rapeseed Meal	900	12.0	400
Extracted Soyabean Meal	900	13.4	530
Extracted Sunflower Meal	900	10.0	390
Field Beans	880	13.3	290
Lupin Seed Meal	900	14.2	350
Maize Gluten Feed	880	12.8	210
Palm Kernel Meal	900	11.4	200
Wheat-feed	880	11.3	190

For relative values of different feeds, see previous page.

9. AGRISTATS

These basic agricultural statistics relate to U.K. agriculture. All figures are for the UK in 2009 calendar year unless otherwise stated.

INDUSTRY STRUCTURE

Agriculture's Economic Contribution

Agriculture's contribution to total economy Gross	£7,168 million
Value Added (provisional):	0.61%

Agricultural Workforce

1. Agriculture's proportion of total workforce in employment: 1.59%
2. Numbers of Persons Engaged in Agriculture (June) (to nearest '00): 534,500

Employed:	Male	Female	Total
Regular Full-time..................................	54,500	11,700	66,300
Regular Part-time*..............................	29,000	17,900	46,900
Seasonal, Casual and Gang.................	43,600	18,100	61,700
Salaried Managers			12,200
Total Employees..			187,100

Farmers, Partners Directors and their Spouses

Full-time..	147,900
Part-time*..	199,500
Total Farmers, Partners Directors and their Spouses	347,400
Total Labour Force**	534,500

*   Part-time is 39 hours or less per week in England and Wales, less than 38 in Scotland and less than 30 in Northern Ireland.

**   Total labour force excludes schoolchildren but includes 'official' trainees.

Livestock Numbers (June '000 Head)	2004	2009
Total Cattle and Calves................................	10,588	10,025
of which: Dairy Cows	2,129	1,857
Beef Cows................................	1,736	1,626
Heifers in Calf...	690	-
Total Sheep and Lambs	35,817	32,038
of which Female Breeding Flock	17,630	14,912
Total Pigs	5,159	4,724
of which Female Breeding Herd	515	445
Poultry Broilers..	119,888	159,288
Laying Flock	29,655	26,757
Growing Pullets..	8,156	8,356
Farmed Deer..	33	35
Goats	92	101

Crop Areas (June)	Area ('000 ha) 2004	Area ('000 ha) 2009	% Total Area 2009	% Crops & Grass 2009*
Wheat	1,990	1,814	9.7	14.8
Barley (% winter in brackets)	1,007 (42)	1,160 (35)	6.2	9.4
Oats	108	131	0.7	1.1
Mixed Corn, Triticale and Rye ...	25	28	0.1	0.2
Total Cereals (excluding maize) .	3,130	3,133	16.7	25.5
Potatoes	148	149	0.8	1.2
Sugar Beet (England and Wales only)	154	117	0.6	1.0
Oilseed Rape..............................	498	582	3.1	4.7
Peas harvested dry (GB only)	30	43	0.2	0.3
Field Beans (GB only)................	118	190	1.0	1.5
Linseed	29	29	0.2	0.2
Vegetables & Salad grown in the open	125	124	0.7	1.0
Orchards, Small Fruit and Grapes	34	34	0.2	0.3
Other Horticulture......................	15	12	0.1	0.1
Maize..	118	166	0.9	1.4
Other Crops	124	125	0.7	1.0
Bare Fallow	29	244	1.3	1.9
Total Tillage	4,552	4,948	26.4	40.2
Temporary Grass (under 5 years old)	1,246	1,262	6.7	10.3
Total Arable...............................	5,864	6,212	33.1	50.5
Permanent Grass (5 years, and over)	5,620	6,085	32.5	49.5
Total Grass*	(6,866)	(7,347)	39.2	
Total Tillage & Grass*................	11,418	12,295	65.6	100
Rough Grazing**........................	5,563	5,413	28.9	
Set-aside (incl. any in non-food crops)	559	-	-	
Woodland	563	779	4.2	
Other Land on agricultural holdings	262	264	1.4	.
Total Agricultural Area***.........	18,365	18,751	100	

*   *Excluding Rough Grazing*

**   *Including 1,238,100 ha of common grazing in 2009; 1,237,000 ha of common grazing in 2004.*

***   *Urban land and forest each approximately 2.0 million ha; other non-agricultural land   approximately 1.5 million ha; total U.K. land area including inland waters: 24.1 million.*

Size Structure
Number and Size Distribution of UK Holdings, 2008 (latest data):

Size group (ha)	Total land area			Tillage and grass area		
	No. ('000)	%	% area	No. ('000)	%	% area
0.1 to 19.9..........	198.1	61.0	5.3	67.5	56.3	6.2
20.0 to 49.9	48.9	15.1	9.3	21.9	18.3	12.2
50.0 to 99.9........	36.0	11.1	14.7	14.8	12.3	17.9
100 and over......	41.5	12.8	70.7	15.8	13.1	63.7
Total	324.5	100.0	100.0	120	100.0	100.0

Average area (ha/[acres]) per holding: 53.8 (132); tillage and grass 50.6 (121).

Size of Holding (SLR)	'000 of Holdings	% of holdings	% of total SLRs
Under 1 SLR	255.8	78.3	17.4
1 to under 2 SLR	31.2	9.6	15.8
2 to under 3 SLR	15.5	4.7	13.5
3 to under 5 SLR	14.1	4.3	19.1
5 SLRs and over	10.0	3.1	34.2
Total	326.6	100.0	100.0

The Standard Labour Requirement (SLR) for a farm business represents the labour requirement (in full-time equivalents) for all the agricultural activities on the farm, based on standard coefficients for each commodity on the farm. The SLR is representative of labour requirement under typical conditions for enterprises of average size and performance. Average size of holdings is 0.9 SLR. For those holdings over 1 SLR (i.e. full-time) the figure is 3.2 SLRs.

Number and Size distribution of holdings in England and Wales, 2000 (latest data)

Size group (ha)	By total land area				By tillage and grass area			
	Holdings		Hectares		Holdings		Hectares	
	'000	%	'0,000	%	'000	%	'0,000	%
Under 10.....	62.8	36.0	212	2.0	53.2	33.6	195	2.3
10 to 30	35.2	20.2	646	6.2	33.9	21.4	628	7.3
30 to 50.......	19.6	11.2	771	7.4	19.9	12.6	779	9.1
50 to 100.....	27.0	15.5	1,937	18.6	26.6	16.8	1,900	22.2
100 to 200...	19.0	10.9	2,641	25.3	17.0	10.7	2,340	27.3
200 to 300...	5.5	3.2	1,342	12.9	4.4	2.8	1,056	12.3
300 to 500...	3.7	2.1	1,386	13.3	2.5	1.6	916	10.7
500 to 700...	1.0	0.6	592	5.7	0.6	0.4	344	4.0
700 and over	0.8	0.5	897	8.6	0.4	0.3	411	4.8
Total	174.6	100	10,425	100	158.5	100	8,570	100

Average Size of Enterprises

Hectares	2003	2008	No. ('000)	2003	2008
			Dairy Cows....................	67	71.1
Cereals (excl. maize)	52.1	60.2	Beef Cows................	26.9	25.3
Oilseed Rape..........	36.3	38.6	Breeding Sheep............	221.7	211.2
Potatoes	9.3	14.4	Breeding Pigs	95.1	78.1
Sugar Beet	21.8	24.3	Fattening Pigs...............	451.8	376.5
			Laying Fowls	1,658	1,230
			Broilers.........................	39,616	35,834

Tenure *(England and Wales, 2000 – latest data available)*

Tenure	No. of Holdings	Area owned (%)	Area rented (%)
Wholly owned	119,254 (68.2)	4,969 (47.2)	-
Mainly owned..........	19,850 (11.4)	1,805 (17.1)	456 (4.3)
Wholly rented	22,643 (13.0)	-	1,826 (17.3)
Mainly rented	13,010 (7.4)	345 (3.3)	1,137 (10.8)
Total	174,757 (100)	7,119 (67.6)	3,419 (32.4)*

Mixed tenure holdings: mainly owned = over 50% owned;
mainly rented = over 50% rented.

Wholly or mainly owned, 79.6% of holdings; wholly or mainly rented, 20.4%

* As the above figures for rented land include family arrangements (e.g. farmers, or family farming companies, renting from other members of the family, or family shareholders) the percentage of 'truly' rented land is almost certainly a few percentage points less than the figures given above.

FINANCE

Inputs and Outputs *(2009 Provisional)*

Inputs	£m	Outputs	£m	%
Animal Feed	3,476	Wheat	1,590	8.9
Seeds	784	Barley	687	3.8
Fertilisers	1,114	Oats and other cereals	77	0.4
Pesticides	674	Oilseed rape	475	2.6
Hired Labour	2,604	Potatoes	644	3.6
Depreciation: equipment	1,363	Sugar beet	241	1.3
Depreciation: buildings	725	Fresh vegetables	1,055	5.9
Maintenance: materials	779	Fruit	571	3.2
Maintenance: buildings	452	Plants and flowers	877	4.9
Fuels	682	Other Crops	566	2.8
Electricity	341	Cattle	2,256	12.5
Agricultural services	844	Sheep	895	5.4
Veterinary expenses	342	Pigs	1,016	5.7
Net rent	268	Poultry	1,586	8.7
Interest	444	Milk	3,114	17.2
Other goods and services	2,648	Eggs	526	2.9
		Other livestock	242	1.1
	____	Miscellaneous	1,652	9.2
Total inputs	17,540	Total gross output	18,072	100.0
Total Income From Farming	4,069	Single Payment & subsidies	3,540	
	21,609	Total output	21,609	
		Total crops	4,280	23.7
		Total horticulture	2,503	13.9
		Total livestock	5,753	31.8
		Total livestock products	3,882	21.5
		Other	1,652	9.1

The above layout differs substantially from that published by DEFRA.

Income from Farming

(a) *Index of UK Total Income from Farming* in Real Terms (av. 1974-76 = 100)*

Year	Index	Year	Index	Year	Index	Year	Index
1975	93	1984	80	1993	82	2002	39
1976	109	1985	42	1994	89	2003	48
1977	96	1986	48	1995	103	2004	42
1978	85	1987	55	1996	92	2005	35
1979	69	1988	51	1997	54	2006	36
1980	55	1989	52	1998	37	2007	38
1981	62	1990	43	1999	36	2008	62
1982	76	1991	44	2000	27	2009	58
1983	64	1992	58	2001	29		

* 'TIFF' = business profits plus income to farmers, partners and directors and others with an entrepreneurial interest in the business. It refers only to farming, i.e. diversification incomes and expenditures are excluded. There are no imputed charges (such as a rental value for owned land or value of the farmer's own labour).

(b) *Recent TIFF Values (£ million)*	Actual	At 2009 Prices
1995 (the 1992-1997 peak)...	5,041	7,273
2002..	2,235	2,710
2003..	2,855	3,363
2004..	2,550	2,918
2005	2,211	2,460
2006..	2,344	2,527
2007..	2,568	2,656
2008..	4,362	4,337
2009..	4,069	4,069

(c) *Index of UK Farming Income* in Real Terms (av. 1940-69 = 100)*

Year	Index	Year	Index	Year	Index	Year	Index
1940-49 ...	101	1978	89	1989........	45	2000.........	26
1950-59 ...	100	1979	73	1990........	43	2001.........	29
1960-69 ...	99	1980	56	1991........	41	2002.........	37
1970........	95	1981	66	1992........	56	2003.........	46
1971........	96	1982	77	1993........	79	2004.........	40
1972........	110	1983	57	1994........	86	2005.........	34
1973........	138	1984	86	1995........	99	2006.........	35
1974.......	103	1985	37	1996........	88	2007.........	36
1975........	98	1986	46	1997........	52	2008	59
1976........	113	1987	50	1998........	36	2009.........	56
1977........	98	1988	34	1999........	35		

* As this figure is no longer produced by DEFRA the figures from 1997 onwards are only approximate. Up to that year a figure for 'Labour: family, partners and director' was deducted from Total Income from Farming (TIFF) to give Farming Income.

Average Farm Business Income in Real Terms per Farming types in England

(whole data for UK not yet available) (£/farm, at 2009/10 prices)

Farm Type	2004/05	2005/06	2006/07	2007/08	2008/09	2009/10 (provisional)
Dairy.............................	33,100	33,600	30,800	55,100	69,400	61,500
Grazing Livestock (LFA)	16,200	15,800	10,500	10.400	17,100	24,500
Grazing L'stock (Lowland)	9,300	9,400	11,400	12,400	18,500	25,000
Cereals..........................	29,200	29,000	45,900	73,400	69,700	52,000
General Cropping	42,400	36,900	62,200	81,000	96,000	77,000
Specialist Pigs...............	25,900	30,300	24,500	6,300	59,100	146,000
Specialist Poultry..........	86,000	93,100	100,600	139,200	47,700	89,000
Mixed	23,900	25,800	27,200	37,300	29,300	41,000

Balance Sheet of UK Agriculture *(2008 Provisional)*

			£m	£m
Assets: Fixed:		Land and buildings....................	188,766	
		Plant, machinery and vehicles....	8,358	
		Breeding livestock	<u>6,646</u>	
	Total Fixed Assets:			*203,770*
	Current	Trading livestock	3,034	
		Crops and stores.........................	3,140	
		Debtors and cash deposits..........	5,403	
	Total Current Assets:...			*11,577*
	Total Assets:	....		**215,348**
Liabilities: Long &		Bank loans	3,546	
	Med-term:	AMC and SASC.........................	1,069	
		Other..	<u>57</u>	
	Total Long and Medium Term Liabilities			*5,983*
	Short-term	Bank overdrafts..........................	2,988	
		Trade credit................................	1,862	
		Hire purchase and leasing..........	1,064	
		Other..	<u>139</u>	
	Total Short-term Liabilities:			*6,052*
	Total Liabilities:...			**12,036**
Net Worth:				**203,312**
% Equity (Net worth as a % of Total Assets):				95.53%

Total Income from Farming (TIFF) 2009 as % of   a) Net Worth: 1.88%

   b) Total Assets: 2.00%

Note: no charge has been made for farmers' own labour or management

Bank Lending to Agriculture, Hunting and Forestry (2009 year average): £11,294m

MISCELLANEOUS

UK Crop Yields and Prices, 2005-2009 *(2009 Provisional)*

Average Yields (harvest years) (tonnes per hectare)

(tonnes per hectare)	2005	2006	2007	2008	2009	Average 2005-09
Wheat	8.0	8.0	7.2	8.3	7.9	7.9
Barley (all)	5.9	5.9	5.7	6.0	6.0	5.9
Winter Barley	6.5	6.7	6.1	6.7	6.5	6.5
Spring Barley	5.4	5.3	5.3	5.4	5.3	5.3
Oats	5.8	6.0	5.5	5.8	5.8	5.8
Oilseed Rape (excl. set-aside)	3.2	3.3	3.1	3.3	3.4	3.3
Linseed (excl. set-aside)	1.8	1.4	1.6	1.8	1.9	1.7
Field Beans (for stockfeed)	3.8	3.4	3.0	4.5	3.8	3.7
Dried Peas (for stockfeed)	3.8	3.3	3.1	4.0	5.0	3.8
Potatoes (all)	43.7	40.8	39.7	42.8	43.1	42.0
Early Potatoes	14.3	15.7	12.5	13.3	14.0	14.0
Maincrop Potatoes	46.6	43.0	43.	46.7	47.0	45.3
Sugar Beet (adj. to 16% sugar)	58.5	56.6	53.8	63.8	69.9	60.5

Average Prices (calendar years) (£ per tonne)

(£ per tonne)		2005	2006	2007	2008	2009	Average 2005-09
Wheat	milling	76	76	109	152	122	107
	feed	66	72	99	127	108	94
Barley	malting	78	80	124	153	123	112
	feed	66	70	106	118	87	89
Oats	milling	63	65	75	93.6	114	82
	feed	63	66	77	92.5	115	83
Oilseed Rape (excl. set-aside)		137	162	200	313	194	201
Field Beans (for stockfeed)		83	83	176	137	112	118
	Dried Peas (for stockfeed)	83	82	174	143	113	119
Potatoes (all, inc seed)		101	129	144	152	126	130
	Earlies	141	194	153	207	149	169
	Maincrop	96	125	141	144	118	125
Sugar Beet (per adjusted tonne)		32	24	24	27	29	27

Self-sufficiency 2009 provisional, (2003 in brackets)

(a) *Total Food*   all food types .... 59.0% *(60.7%)*

                          indigenous type food .... 72.5% *(73.6%)*

(b) *Individual Products (production as a % of total new supply for use in the UK):*

	2003	2009		2003	2009
Wheat	124	108	Beef and Veal	70	83
Barley	120	112	Mutton and Lamb	86	88
Oats	124	102	Pigmeat	49	52
Total Cereals	113	104	Poultrymeat	91	91
Oilseed Rape	108	88	Butter	63	67
Potatoes	82	84	Cheese	61	54
Sugar	76	64	Cream	144	102
Fresh Vegetables	63	59	Hen Eggs	84	79
Fresh Fruit	8	12			

3. Food Consumption and Expenditure, UK 2006-2008

(a) *Food and Drink Consumed Within the Household*

Average quantity consumed / expenditure per person per week:

(2006-08)	2006 kg per week	2007 kg per week	2008 kg per week
Milk and Cream (litres)	2,022	1.984	1.957
Cheese	0.116	0.119	0.111
Meat	1.042	1.030	0.998
Fish...	0.170	0.165	0.161
Eggs (number)	1.50	1.60	1.60
Fats...	0.184	0.181	0.184
Sugars and Preserves	0.126	0.125	0.127
Potatoes	0.810	0.781	0.776
Other Vegetables	1.142	1.140	1.118
Fruit..	1.313	1.281	1.199
Bread	0.692	0.667	0.659
All Other Cereals and Cereal Products	0.530	0.536	0.535
Beverages (litres).................................	0.055	0.056	0.055
Soft Drinks (litres)	1.807	1.686	1.682
Alcoholic Drinks (litres)......................	0.760	0.772	0.706
Confectionery	0.123	0.129	0.131

(b) *Food and Drink Consumed Outside the Household*	£ per week
Food and Drink excl. Alcohol..	8.16
Alcoholic Drinks	3.04
Total..	11.20

(c) *Total Food and Drink*	£ per week
Food and Drink excl. Alcohol..	31.17
Alcoholic Drinks	11.20
Total..	42.37

Sources: Agriculture in the UK: 2009 (DEFRA). All items except for the following:

A5, (part), A7: Other DEFRA Statistics.

B4, Bank Lending: Bank of England, Financial Statistics Division.

C3: Family Food Survey, DEFRA.

10. RATE OF INFLATION; PRICE AND COST INDICES

RETAIL PRICE INDEX (ALL ITEMS)

Year	% inc. on year earlier	Index (1970 = 100)	Index (1987 = 100)	Year	% increase on year earlier	Index (1970 = 100)	Index (1987 = 100)
1991	5.9	721	133.5	2001	1.8	935	173.3
1992	3.7	748	138.5	2002	1.7	951	176.2
1993	1.6	760	140.7	2003	2.9	979	181.3
1994	2.4	778	144.1	2004	3.0	1,008	186.7
1995	3.5	805	149.1	2005	2.8	1,036	192.0
1996	2.4	824	152.7	2006	3.2	1,070	198.1
1997	3.1	850	157.5	2007	4.3	1,116	206.6
1998	3.4	879	162.9	2008	4.5	1,166	214.8
1999	1.5	892	165.4	2009	-2.0	1,137	213.7
2000	3.0	919	170.3	2010 (f.cast)	5.0	1,194	224.4

Note; Index in 1965: 80; index in 1962: 70. 1970-1994 figures available in earlier editions.

UK ANNUAL PRICE AND COST INDICES 2005-2009 *(2005 = 100)*

Producer Prices	2005	2006	2007	2008	2009
Feed Wheat	100.0	114.3	158.2	216.2	159.8
Feed Barley	100.0	111.3	162.7	189.9	133.1
All Cereals	100.0	111.8	166.7	207.1	150.1
Oilseed Rape	100.0	119.8	143.9	232.9	183.4
Potatoes (main crop)	100.0	130.9	149.1	155.0	124.4
Sugar Beet	100.0	96.2	74.8	77.3	83.2
Desert Apples	100.0	105.7	121.5	130.9	131.4
All Fresh Vegetables	100.0	108.2	122.1	117.5	113.9
All Fresh Fruit	100.0	104.1	107.4	126.4	124.6
All Crop Products	100.0	109.4	133.6	153.7	131.1
Milk	100.0	97.2	112.2	140.4	128.4
Cattle	100.0	108.3	109.9	141.7	151.2
Sheep	100.0	102.0	90.6	116.0	143.8
Wool	100.0	36.4	77.7	78.9	71.4
Pigs	100.0	101.0	104.1	121.7	140.2
Poultry	100.0	98.6	107.1	134.6	134.6
Eggs	100.0	104.0	118.3	140.4	144.7
All Animal Products	*100.0*	*101.0*	*108.5*	*136.0*	*138.6*
All Products	100.0	104.5	118.8	143.3	135.5
Input Prices					
Seeds	100.0	89.5	100.1	111.2	109.1
Fertilisers	100.0	107.4	113.3	229.4	233.7
Plant Protection Products	100.0	99.6	101.6	103.7	99.9
Energy and Lubricants	100.0	112.2	117.9	158.2	132.9
Animal Feeding Stuffs	100.0	104.6	129.7	167.3	153.7
Maintenance and Repair of Plant	100.0	105.8	109.9	116.3	121.5
Machinery and Other Equipment	100.0	97.8	95.7	90.8	91.7
Buildings	100.0	105.9	113.0	120.3	120.6
General Expenses	100.0	105.9	113.0	120.3	120.6

11. METRIC CONVERSION FACTORS

Metric to Imperial   *Imperial to Metric*

Area

1 hectare (10,000m^2).... 2.471 acres	1 acre .... 0.405 ha
	1 square mile .... 259 ha
1 square km .... 0.386 sq. mile	1 square mile .... 2.590 sq. km
1 square m .... 1.196 sq. yard	1 square yard .... 0.836 sq. m
1 square m .... 10.764 sq. feet	1 square foot .... 0.093 sq. m

(m = metre, km = kilometre)

Length

1 mm............................. 0.039 inch	1 inch. .... 25.4 mm
1 cm.............................. 0.394 inch	1 inch .... 2.54 cm
1 m............................... 3.281 feet	1 foot...................................... 0.305 m
1 m............................... 1.094 yard	1 yard .... 0.914 m
1 km........................... 0.6214 mile	1 mile .... 1.609 km

(mm = millimetre, cm = centimetre)

Volume

1 millilitre .... 0.0352 fluid oz	1 fluid oz............................... 28.413 ml
1 litre .... 35.2 fluid oz	1 fluid oz............................. 0.028 litre
1 litre .... 1.76 pints	1 pint..................................... 0.568 litre
1 litre .... 0.22 gallon	1 gallon .... 4.546 litres
1 cubic m.................. 35.31 cu feet	1 cubic foot .... 0.028 cu m
1 cubic m .... 1.307 cu yard	1 cubic yard........................ 0.765 cu m
1 cubic m..................... 220 gallons	1 gallon .... 0.005 cu m
1 ha of 10mm water. 22,000 gallons	1 acre-inch .... 102.75m^3

Weight

1 gram............................. 0.0353 oz	1 oz .... 28.35 gm
1 kg................................. 35.274oz	
1 kg................................. 2.205 lb	1 lb... 0.454 kg
50 kg.............................. 0.984 cwt	
1 tonne (1,000 kg)........... 19.68 cwt	1 cwt. .... 50.80 kg
1 tonne........................... 0.984 ton	1 ton .... 1.016 tonne

Milk

1 litre 1.03kg	
1kg................................ 0.971 litre	
1 litre .... 1.709 pints	1 pint...................................... 0.585kg
1 tonne..................... 213.63 gallon	1 gallon 4.681kg

Yields and Rates of Use

1 tonne/ha.	0.398 ton/acre	1 ton/acre	2.511 tonnes/ha
1 tonne/ha.	7.95 cwt/acre	1 cwt/acre	0.125 tonne/ha
1 gram/ha	0.014 oz/acre	1 oz/acre	70.053 g/ha
1 kg/ha	0.892 lb/acre	1 lb/acre	1.121 g/ha
1 kg/ha	0.008 cwt/acre	1 cwt/acre	125.5 g/ha
1 kg/ha (fert.)	0.797 unit/acre	1 unit/acre	1.255 kg/ha
1 litre/ha	0.712 pint/acre	1 pint/acre	1.404 litre/ha
1 litre/ha	0.089 gal/acre	1 gal/acre	11.24 litres/ha

Power, Pressure, Temperature

1 kW	1.341 hp	1 hp	0.746 kW
1MW	1,000kW		
1 kilojoule	0.948 Btu	1 Btu	1.055 kilojoule
1 therm	10,000 Btu	1 Btu	0.0001 therm
1 lb f ft	1.356 Nm	1 Nm	0.738 lb f ft
1 bar	14.705 lb/sq.in.	1 lb/sq.in	0.068 bar
°C to °F	x1.8, + 32	°F to °C	-32, ÷ 1.8

12. USEFUL CONTACT DETAILS

GENERAL

Agricultural Engineers' Association
Samuelson House, Paxton Road, Orton Centre, Peterborough, Cambs. PE2 5LT
www.aea.uk.com   01733 371 381

Agriculture and Horticulture Development Board ~ AHDB
Stoneleigh Park, Kenilworth, Warwickshire, CV8 2TL   0247 669 2051
                                                                    www.ahdb.org.uk/
Includes:

Horticultural Development Company, HDC	www.hdc.org.uk
English Beef and Lamb Executive EBLEX	www.eblex.org.uk
English Pig Executive	www.bpex.org.uk
DairyCo	www.dairyco.org.uk
HGCA	www.hgca.com
Potato Council	www.potato.org.uk

Agricultural Law Association
6 St. Peters Close, Chislehurst, Kent BR7 6PD   020 8467 0722
www.ala.org.uk

Agricultural Industries Confederation (AIC)
Confederation House, East of England Showground, Peterborough,
PE2 6XE
www.agindustries.org.uk   01733 385 230

Agricultural Wages Board
Ergon House, Area 3A, Horseferry Road, London SW1P 2AL   020 7238 6523
http://www.defra.gov.uk/farm/working/agwages/awb/index.htm

Association of Independent Crop Consultants
Agriculture Place, Heath Farm, Heath Road East, Petersfield,
Hampshire, GU31 4HT
www.aicc.org.uk   01730 710 095

BBC Radio 4 Farming To-day
The Mail Box, Birmingham B1 1RF   0121 432 8888
http://www.bbc.co.uk/radio4/news/farmingtoday/

British Agricultural and Garden Machinery Association (BAGMA)
1st Floor, Entrance B, Salamander Quay West, Park Lane,
Harefield, Middlesex UB9 6NZ
www.bagma.com   0870 205 2834

British Association of Seed Producers
Manor House, Woodhall Spa, Lincolnshire, LN10 6PX.   01526 352 368

British Crop Protection Council (BCPC)
7 Omni Business Park, Omega Park, Alton, Hampshire GU34 2QD   01420 593 200
www.bcpc.org

British Deer Society
Burgate Manor, Fordingbridge, Hampshire SP6 1EF   01425 655 434
www.bds.org.uk

British Egg Industry Council (BEIC)
2nd Floor, 89 Charterhouse Street, London EC1M 6HR   020 7608 3760
www.britisheggindustrycouncil.com

British Grassland Society
PO Box 237, University of Reading, 1 Earley Gate, Berks. RG6 6AR 0118 931 8189
www.britishgrassland.com

British Institute of Agricultural Consultants (BIAC)
The Estate Office, Torry Hill, Milstead, Sittingbourne,
Kent ME9 0SP 01795 830 100
www.biac.co.uk

British Pig Association
Trumpington Mews, 40b High Street, Trumpington, Cambs. CB2 2LS 01223 845 100
www.britishpigs.org.uk

British Poultry Council
Europoint House, 5 Lavington Street, London SE1 0NZ 020 7202 4760
www.poultry.uk.com

British Sheep Dairying Association
The Sheep Centre, Malvern, Worcs. WR13 6PH 01684 892 661
www.sheepdairying.com

British Society of Plant Breeders
Woolpack Chambers, Market Street, Ely, Cambs. CB7 4ND 01353 653 200
www.bspb.co.uk

British Sugar
PP Box 26, Oundle Road, Peterborough, Cambs. PE2 9QU 01733 563 171
www.britishsugar.co.uk

British Veterinary Association
7 Mansfield Street, London W1G 9NQ 020 7636 6541
www.bva.co.uk

British Wool Marketing Board
Wool House, Roydsdale Way, Euroway Trading Estate,
Bradford, West Yorkshire BD4 6SE 01274 688 666
www.britishwool.org.uk

CAB International
Nosworthy Way, Wallingford, Oxon OX10 8DE 01491 832 111
www.cabi.org

Campaign to Protect Rural England (CPRE)
128 Southwark Street, London SE1 0SW 020 7981 2800
www.cpre.org.uk

Central Association of Agricultural Valuers (CAAV)

Market Chambers, 35 Market Place, Coleford, Gloucestershire
GL16 8AA
www.caav.org.uk 01594 832 979

Centre for Agricultural Strategy
University of Reading, P.O. Box 237, Whiteknights Road, Earley Gate, Reading,
Berks. RG6 6AR 01183 788 150
www.apd.reading.ac.uk

Country Land and Business Association (CLA)
16 Belgrave Square, London SW1X 8PQ 020 7235 0511
www.cla.org.uk

Crop Protection Association UK
4 Lincoln Court, Lincoln Road, Peterborough, Cambs PE1 2RP 01733 349 225
www.cropprotection.org.uk

Dairy Industry Association Ltd.
93 Baker Street, London W1U 6QQ   020 7486 7244
www.dairyuk.org

Department of Agriculture and Rural Development (DARDNI)
Dundonald House, Upper Newtownards Road, Belfast BT4 3SB   028 9052 0100
www.dardni.gov.uk

Department of Environment, Food and Rural Affairs (DEFRA)
Nobel House, 17 Smith Square, London SW1P 3JR   020 7270 3000
www.defra.gov.uk

English Heritage
23 Savile Row, London W1S 2ET   020 7973 3000
www.english-heritage.org.uk

English Hops and Herbs Ltd
Hop Pocket Lane, Paddock Wood, Tonbridge, Kent TN12 6DQ   01892 833 415
www.botanix.co.uk   intray@botanix.co.uk

Environment Agency
Rio House, Waterside Drive, Aztec West, Almonsbury, Bristol
BS32 4UD   0870 850 6506
www.environment-agency.gov.uk

European Commission (London Office)
Jean Monnet House, 8 Storey's Gate, London SW1P 3AT   020 7973 1992

FACE (Farming and Countryside Education)
National Agricultural Centre, Stoneleigh Park, Warks. CV8 2LZ   024 7685 8261
www.face-online.org.uk

Family Farmers' Association
Osborne Newton, Aveton Gifford, Kingsbridge, Devon TQ7 4PE   01548 852 794

Farmers Club
3 Whitehall Court, London SW1A 2EL   020 7930 3751
www.thefarmersclub.com

Farmers Union of Wales
Llys Amaeth, Plas Gogerddon, Aberystwyth, Ceredigion SY23 3BT   01970 820 820
www.fuw.org.uk

Farming and Wildlife Advisory Group (FWAG)
National Agricultural Centre, Stoneleigh Park, Warks. CV8 2RX   024 7669 6699
www.fwag.org.uk

Food and Drink Federation
Federation House, 6 Catherine Street, London WC2B 5JJ   020 7836 2460
www.fdf.org.uk

Food from Britain
4th Floor, Manning House, 22 Carlisle Place, London SW1P 1JA   020 7233 5111
www.foodfrombritain.com

Food Standards Agency
Aviation House, 125 Kingsway, London WC2B 6NH   020 7276 8000
www.foodstandards.gov.uk

Forestry Commission
231 Corstorphine Road, Edinburgh EH12 7AT   0131 334 0303
www.forestry.gov.uk   enquiries@forestry.gsi.gov.uk

Grain and Feed Trade Association (GAFTA)
GAFTA House, 6 Chapel Place, Rivington Street, London EC2A 3SH 020 7814 9666
www.gafta.com

Guild of Agricultural Journalists
Isfield Cottage, Church Road, Crowborough, East Sussex TN6 1BN 01892 611 618
www.gaj.org.uk

Health and Safety Executive (Agriculture Sector)
National Agricultural Centre, Stoneleigh Park, Warks. CV8 2LG 024 7669 8350
www.hse.gov.uk

Institution of Agricultural Engineers
West End Road, Silsoe, Bedford MK45 4DU 01525 861096

Institute of Agricultural Management
Farm Management Unit, University of Reading, PO Box 236,
Reading RG6 6AT 0118 931 6578

Institute of Agricultural Secretaries and Administrators
National Agricultural Centre, Stoneleigh Park, Warks. CV8 2LG 024 7669 6592
www.iagsa.co.uk

Institute of Chartered Foresters
7a St. Colme Street, Edinburgh EH3 6AA 0131 225 2705
www.charteredforesters.org icf@charteredforesters.org

International Grains Council
1 Canada Square, Canary Wharf, London E14 5AE 020 7513 1122
www.igc.org.uk igc@igc.org.uk

Land Drainage Contractors Association
National Agricultural Centre, Stoneleigh Park, Warks. CV8 2LG 01327 263 264
www.idca.org secretary@idca.org

Land Heritage
Summerhill Farm, Hittisleigh, Devon EX6 6LP 01647 24511
www.landheritage.org.uk enquiries@landheritage.org.uk

Lantra
Lantra House, National Agricultural Centre, Stoneleigh Park,
Warks. CV8 2LG 024 7669 6996
www.lantra.co.uk connect@lantra.co.uk

LEAF (Linking Environment and Farming)
National Agricultural Centre, Stoneleigh Park, Warks. CV8 2LZ 024 7641 3911
www.leafuk.org enquiries@leafuk.org

London Commodity Exchange (Euronext Liffe)
Cannon Bridge House, 1 Cousin Lane, London EC4R 3XX 020 7623 0444

National Agricultural Centre (NAC)
Stoneleigh Park, Warks. CV8 2LZ 024 7669 6969
www.stoneleigh-park.co.uk

National Association of Agricultural Contractors (NAAC)
Samuelson House, (62) Forder Way, Hampton, Peterborough PE7 8JB 08456 448 750
www.naac.org.uk

National Association of British & Irish Millers (NABIM)
21 Arlington Street, London SW1A 1RN 020 7493 2521
www.nabim.org.uk info@nabim.org.uk

National Beef Association
Mart Centre, Tyne Green, Hexham, NE46 3SG 01434 601 005

www.nationalbeefassociation.com   info@nationalbeefassociation.com

National Cattle Association (Dairy)
Brick House, Risbury, Leominster, Herefordshire HR6 0NQ   01568 760 632
www.nationalrural.org

National Dairy Council
164 Shaftesbury Avenue, London WC2H 8HL   020 7395 4030
www.nationaldairycouncil.org   ndc@dairyinformation.com

National Farmers' Retail and Markets Association (FARMA)
12 Southgate Street, Winchester, SO23 9EF   0845 458 8420
www.farma.org.uk

National Farmers' Union (NFU)
Agriculture House, Stoneleigh Park, Warks. CV8 2LZ   024 7685 8500
London Office, Kings Buildings, 16 Smith Square, London SW1P 3JJ 020 7808 6600
www.nfuonline.com

National Non-Food Crops Centre ~ NNFCC
Innovation Centre, York Science Park, Innovation Way, Heslington,
York YO10 5DG   01904 435 182
www.nnfcc.co.uk   enquiries@nnfcc.co.uk

NFU Scotland
Rural Centre, West Mains, Ingliston, Midlothian EH28 8LT   0131 472 4000
www.nfus.org.uk   webmaster@nfus.org.uk

National Federation of Young Farmers Clubs
YFC Centre, 10th street, National Agricultural Centre, Stoneleigh Park,
Warks. CV8 2LG   024 7685 7200
www.nfyfc.org.uk   post@nfyfc.org.uk

National Office of Animal Health (NOAH)
3 Crossfield Chambers, Gladbeck Way, Enfield, Middlesex EN2 7HF 020 8367 3131
www.noah.co.uk   noah@noah.co.uk

National Sheep Association
The Sheep Centre, Malvern, Worcs. WR13 6PH   01684 892 661
www.nationalsheep.org.uk

National Trust
32 Queen Anne's Gate, London SW1H 9AB   01793 817 400
www.nationaltrust.org.uk

Natural England
1 East Parade, Sheffield S1 2GA   01142 418 920
www.naturalengland.org.uk   web@naturalengland.org.uk

Processed Vegetable Growers' Association Limited (PGVA)
133 Eastgate, Louth, Lincolnshire LN11 9QG   01507 602427
www.pvga.co.uk   postbox@pvga.co.uk

Renewable Energy Association
17 Waterloo Place, London, SW1Y 4AR   020 7925 3570
www.r-e-a.net

Royal Agricultural Benevolent Institution (RABI)
Shaw House, 27 West Way, Oxford OX2 0QH   01865 724 931
www.rabi.org.uk   info@rabi.org.uk

Royal Agricultural Society of England (RASE)
National Agricultural Centre, Stoneleigh Park, Warks. CV8 2LZ   024 7669 6969
www.rase.org.uk   info@rase.org.uk

Royal Association of British Dairy Farmers
Unit 31, Stoneleigh Deer Park, Stareton, Kenilworth, Warks CV8 2LY   0845 458 2711
www.rabdf.co.uk   office@rabdf.org.uk

Royal Forestry Society of England, Wales and N.I.
102 High Street, Tring, Herts. HP23 4AF   01442 822 028
www.rfs.org.uk   rfshq@rfs.org.uk

Royal Highland and Agricultural Society of Scotland
Ingliston, Edinburgh EH28 8NF   0131 335 6200
www.rhass.org.uk   info@rhass.org.uk

Royal Horticultural Society
80 Vincent Square, London SW1P 2PE   08452 605 000
www.rhs.org.uk   info@rhs.org.uk

Royal Institution of Chartered Surveyors (RICS)
12 Great George Street, Parliament Square, London SW1P 3AD   020 7222 7000
www.rics.org   contactrics@rics.org

Royal Society for the Protection of Birds
The Lodge, Sandy, Bedfordshire SG19 2DL   01767 680 551
www.rspb.org.uk

Royal Welsh Agricultural Society
Llanelwedd, Builth Wells, Powys LD2 3SY   01982 553 683
www.rwas.co.uk

Rural, Agricultural and Allied Workers Trade Group (TGWU)
Transport House, 128 Theobalds Road, Holborn, London WC1X 8TN   020 7611 2500
www.tgwu.org.uk   tgwu@tgwu.org.uk

Rural Payments Agency
Kings House, 33 Kings Road, Reading RG1 3BU   0118 958 3626
www.rpa.gov.uk

Scottish Executive Environment and Rural Affairs Department (SEERAD)
Pentland House, 47 Robb's Loan, Edinburgh EH14 1TY   0131 556 8400
www.scotland.gov.uk   ceu@scotland.gsi.gov.uk

Tenant Farmers' Association
5 Brewery Court, Theale, Reading, Berks. RG7 5AJ   0118 930 6130
www.tfa.org.uk   tfa@tfa.org.uk

The Stationery Office
The Publications Centre, PO Box 276, London SW8 5DT   0870 600 5522
www.tso.co.uk

Ulster Farmers Union
475 Antrim Road, Belfast BT15 3DA   028 9037 0222
www.ufuni.org

Welsh Assembly Government, Agriculture and Rural Affairs Department
Crown Offices, Cathays Park, Cardiff, CF10 3NQ   029 2082 5111
www.countryside.wales.gov.uk   webmaster@wales.gsi.gov.uk

Women's Food and Farming Union
National Agricultural Centre, Stoneleigh Park, Warks. CV8 2LZ   024 7669 3171
www.wfu.org.uk

COMMERCIAL BANKS: AGRICULTURAL DEPARTMENTS

Agricultural Mortgage Corporation (AMC)
Charlton Place, Charlton Road, Andover, Hants. SP10 1RE   01264 334 747

Bank of Scotland
Agricultural Business, Chatterhall House, City Road, Chester CH88 3AN0845 3072 852
www.bankofscotland.co.uk/corporate

Barclays Bank
24th Floor, 1 Churchill Place, London, E14 5HP   020 7166 5515
www.barclays.com

Clydesdale Bank
AgriBusiness Banking Centre, 10 Fleet Place, London EC4M 7RB   020 7395 5662

Farming and Agricultural Finance Limited (FAF)
PO Box 234, Upminster, Essex RM14 2WS   0800 225 567

HSBC Bank
Agriculture Head Office, 51 De Montford Street, Leicester LE1 7BB   0116 281 8328

Lloyds TSB Group
Business Banking Agricultural, PO Box 112, Canons House,
Canons Way, Bristol BS99 7LB   0117 943 3114

National Westminster Bank

Agricultural Services, Gogaburn Business House C, PO Box 1000
Edinburgh EH12 1HQ   0131 626 0151

The Royal Bank of Scotland

Agricultural Services, Gogaburn Business House C, PO Box 1000
Edinburgh EH12 1HQ   0131 626 0151

RESEARCH ORGANISATIONS

Biotechnology and Biological Sciences Research Council (BBSRC)
Polaris House, North Star Avenue, Swindon, Wilts. SN2 1UH   01793 413200
www.bbsrc.ac.uk

Broom's Barn Research Station
Higham, Bury St. Edmunds, Suffolk IP28 6NP   01284 812200

Brooms.barn@bbsrc.ac.uk

CEDAR (Centre for Dairy Research)
Arborfield Hall Farm, Reading Road, Arborfield, Reading,
RG2 9HX   0118 976 0964

East Malling Research
New Road,East Malling, Kent ME19 6BJ   01732 843 833
www.emr.ac.uk   enquiries@emr.ac.uk

Elm Farm Organic Research Centre
Hamstead Marshall, Newbury, Berkshire RG20 0HR   01488 658 298
www.efrc.com

Hannah Research Institute
Ayr, Scotland KA6 5HL   01292 477 006
www.hannahresearch.org.uk

Institute for Animal Health
Compton, Newbury, Berks. RG20 7NN   01635 578 411
www.iah.ac.uk   iah@bbsrc.ac.uk

Institute of Food Research
Norwich Research Park, Colney, Norwich NR4 7UA
www.ifr.ac.uk
01603 255 000

Institute of Grassland and Environmental Research (IGER)
Aberystwyth Research Centre, Plas Gogerddan, Aberystwyth,
Ceredigion SY23 3EB
North Wyke Research Station, Okehampton, Devon EX20 2SB
01970 823 000
01837 883 500

Kingshay Farming Trust
Bridge Farm, West Bradley, Glastonbury, Somerset BA6 8LU
www.kingshay.com
01458 851 555
contact.us@kingshay.co.uk

Macauley Land Use Research Institute
Craigiebuckler, Aberdeen AB15 8QH
www.macaulay.ac.uk
01224 318 611
enquiries@macaulay.co.uk

Morley Research Centre
Morley St. Botolph, Wymondham, Norfolk NR18 9DB
01953 713 200

NIAB
Huntingdon Road, Cambridge CB3 0LE
www.niab.com
01223 342 200
info@niab.com

Processors and Growers Research Organisation (PGRO)
The Research Station, Great North Road, Thornhaugh,
Peterborough PE8 6HJ
www.pgro.org
01780 782 585
info@prgo.com

Roslin Institute
Roslin, Midlothian EH25 9PS
www.roslin.ac.uk
0131 527 4200

Rothamsted Research
Harpenden, Hertfordshire AL5 2JQ
www.rothamsted.ac.uk
01582 763 133

Rowett Research Institute
Greenburn Road, Bucksburn, Aberdeen AB21 9SB
www.rowett.ac.uk
01224 712 751

Scottish Crop Research Institute (SCRI)
Mylnefield, Invergowrie, Dundee DD2 5DA
www.scri.ac.uk
01382 562 731
info@scri.ac.uk

The Arable Group (TAG)
Manor Farm, Lower End, Doglingworth, Cirencester, Glos. GL7 7AH
www.thearablegroup.com
01285 652 184
tag@thearablegroup.com

UNIVERSITY AGRICULTURAL ECONOMICS

(Farm Business Survey work)

Northern: School of Agriculture, Food and Rural Development, University of Newcastle, Newcastle-upon-Tyne NE1 7RU 0191 222 6902

North Eastern: Rural Business Research Unit, Askham Bryan College, Askham Bryan, York YO23 3FR 01904 772 233

East Midlands: Rural Business Research Unit, University of Nottingham, Sutton Bonington Campus, Loughborough, Leics. LE12 5RD 0115 951 6070

Eastern: Rural Business Unit, Centre for Rural Economics Research,

	16-21 Silver Street, Cambridge CB3 9EP	01223 337 166
South Eastern:	Farm Survey Section, Imperial College London, Wye Campus, Ashford, Kent TN25 5AH	020 7594 2925
Southern:	Department of Agriculture and Food Economics The University of Reading, 4 Earley Gate, Whiteknights, PO Box 237, Reading RG6 6AR	01189 875 123
South Western:	Centre for Rural Research, The University of Exeter, Lafrowda House, St. German's Road,Exeter EX4 6TL	01392 263 836
Wales:	Institute of Rural Studies, University of Wales, Aberystwyth, Llanbadarn Campus, Aberystwyth, Ceredigion SY23 3AL	01970 622 253

Scottish Agricultural College
Regional Offices:

North:	SAC Aberdeen, Ferguson Building, Craibstone Estate, Bucksburn, Aberdeen AB21 9YA	01224 711 000
East:	SAC Edinburgh, Bush Estate, Penecuik, Midlothian, EH26 0PH	0131 535 3430
West:	SAC Auchincruive, Ayr KA6 5HW	01292 525 252

Northern Ireland (Advisory Services also)

Economics & Statistics Division, DARDNI, Dundonald House,
Upper Newtownards Road, Belfast BT4 3SB   028 9052 0100

NATIONAL AGRICULTURAL COLLEGES

Cranfield University, Silsoe Campus
Silsoe, Bedford MK45 4DT   01525 863 000
www.cranfield.ac.uk

Harper Adams University College
Edgmond, Newport, Shropshire TF10 8NB   01952 820 280
www.harper-adams.ac.uk

Institute of Rural Sciences
Llanbadarn Campus, Aberystwyth, Ceredigion SY23 3AL   01970 624 471
www.irs.aber.ac.uk   irs-enquiries@aber.ac.uk

Royal Agricultural College
Stroud Road, Cirencester, Glos. GL7 6JS   01285 652 531
www.royagcol.ac.uk

Scottish Agricultural College (student recruitment)
Auchincruive Campus, Ayr KA6 5HW   0800 269 453
www.sac.ac.uk

Shuttleworth College
Old Warden Park, Biggleswade, Beds. SG18 9EA   01767 626 222
www.shuttleworth.ac.uk   enquiries@shuttleworth.ac.uk

Writtle College
Lordship Road, Writtle, Chelmsford, Essex CM1 3RR   01245 424 200
www.writtle.ac.uk   info@writtle.ac.uk

INDEX